The United States

and the United Nations

The United States and the United Nations

EDITED BY FRANZ B. GROSS

Waldo Chamberlin · Harold Karan Jacobson

William F. Kintner · Hans Kohn

Norman D. Palmer · Robert Strausz-Hupé

Arthur P. Whitaker

WITH PUBLIC ADDRESSES BY

GEORGE H. BALL · WILLIAM Y. ELLIOTT

HENRY M. JACKSON · JOHN F. KENNEDY

DEAN RUSK

UNIVERSITY OF OKLAHOMA PRESS : NORMAN

This book is the product of research carried out
under the auspices of the
Foreign Policy Research Institute
University of Pennsylvania

Library of Congress Catalog Card Number: 64–20766

Editor's Preface

THE POLITICAL COLLABORATION of world society—an ideal for centuries—has become both technically possible and, in embryonic form, a structural reality in the twentieth century.

The purpose of this book is to examine the impact of the new world organization—the United Nations—on American policy. The transcendent objective of the United States is the creation of a stable world order based on Western concepts of man and legality. Can the United Nations, despite the rending confrontations within its ranks, help to promote such a world order?

The foreign policy of the United States encompasses more than its relations with the United Nations. Yet the interactions between United Nations decisions and United States policy are becoming increasingly important. Because of the changing role and composition of the United Nations, the United States needs to come to grips with the question of whether the United Nations, under all circumstances, will facilitate the evolution of a peaceful and just world order.

In its brief life the United Nations organization has undergone continuous change. Technological advance, rampant nationalism, and political crises complicate the task of surveying the future of the world body. Even during the period of preparation of this volume, the flood of changes forced reconsideration of premises that initially had appeared valid.

The contributors to this book have surveyed aspects of the United Nations performance and prospects from various points of view. The wide range of the book as well as the diverse perspectives of the authors prohibit a common approach to the problems. The fact that knowledgeable writers have looked at the United Nations structure and functions from divergent points of view is an asset rather than a liability.

v

It is hoped that this book will contribute toward an evaluation of the United Nations based on realistic appraisals of its capabilities and expectations. As a common framework, all contributors have accepted the United Nations as an existing factor in world politics, yet subject to critical analysis as any other phenomenon in world politics.

The present volume was planned by the Foreign Policy Research Institute of the University of Pennsylvania with the support of the Dolfinger-McMahon Foundation. Professor Waldo Chamberlin, dean of Dartmouth College, started the project on its way. To his editorship, the book owes its original conception. Unfortunately, for reasons of health, Professor Chamberlin was forced to withdraw from the task. The work would not have been completed without the support of the Director of the Foreign Policy Research Institute, Professor Robert Strausz-Hupé, and the Deputy Director, Professor William R. Kintner. In addition to their contributions to the book, they assisted me in my efforts. The manuscript was subjected to the extensive and critical discussion of the Associates of the Foreign Policy Research Institute; however, the views expressed in *The United States and the United Nations* are those of the authors.

Robert C. Herber, administrative officer of the Foreign Policy Research Institute, helped in many ways; Diane Kressler and Robert Pfaltzgraff, staff members of the Institute, contributed considerable research materials to the west European chapter; Anand Prabhakar, research assistant of the Institute, gave invaluable assistance during the whole period of editing; and Carole Nein, Marilyn Tolles, Kay Christiansen, Patricia Martin, Margaret Capotrio, and Elaine Eisemann, secretaries and editorial assistants of the Institute, performed a variety of important services, from typing the manuscripts to reading proofs. My greatest debt is owed to my wife Peggy, who gave me the benefit of her years of experience in the Secretariat of the United Nations, and to my son Christopher, who sacrificed the pleasures of many weekends to permit me to work on this volume. I am grateful for their contributions.

FRANZ B. GROSS

Pennsylvania Military College
May 15, 1964

Contents

Notes on the Contributors

Franz B. Gross, the editor of this volume, is professor of political science and chairman of the Liberal Arts Division (Humanities and Social Sciences), in Pennsylvania Military College. He has also been visiting professor of political science and a member of the International Relations Group Committee of the University of Pennsylvania.

Waldo Chamberlin, the dean of Dartmouth College, is also the current chairman of the New York Regents' Committee on International Understanding.

Harold Karan Jacobson is associate professor of political science in the University of Michigan.

William R. Kintner is the deputy director of the Foreign Policy Research Institute and professor of political science in the University of Pennsylvania.

Hans Kohn is professor emeritus of the City College of New York and visiting professor in the Center for Advanced Studies, Wesleyan University. He is also an associate of the Foreign Policy Research Institute.

Norman D. Palmer is professor of political science and chairman of the International Relations Group Committee of the University of Pennsylvania. He is also an associate of the Foreign Policy Research Institute.

Robert Strausz-Hupé, director of the Foreign Policy Research Institute, is also professor of political science and former chairman of the International Relations Group Committee of the University of Pennsylvania.

Arthur P. Whitaker is professor of history in the University of

Pennsylvania. He is also an associate of the Foreign Policy Research Institute.

George H. Ball is Undersecretary of State of the United States.

William Y. Elliott, professor emeritus of government of Harvard University, is presently University Professor in American University.

Henry M. Jackson is senator from Washington in the United States Senate.

The late John F. Kennedy was the thirty-fifth President of the United States.

Dean Rusk is Secretary of State of the United States.

The United States

and the United Nations

CHAPTER I

Introduction

BY ROBERT STRAUSZ-HUPÉ

MANKIND IS PASSING THROUGH the last phase of the evolution of community upon this earth—the phase of global "convergence," as Pierre Teilhard de Chardin calls this age of rapid population increase, of the universal spread of scientific method and the consequent rise of a new, universal culture. Mankind is converging—and converging dangerously. Mounting population pressures in Asia, Africa, and Latin America point toward fierce economic struggles and, if history repeats itself, to revolutions and wars. The spread of mass-destruction weapons, effective over ever-lengthening distances, has been creating a tightening international community of fear.

Today's problems, however, are but the latest phenomena of a process that has been unfolding for a long time. As early as the 1870's and 1880's, several intelligent and compassionate men—with commendable foresight—discerned the shape of things to come, the need to create instruments of interstate co-operation. Their insights and labors brought forth the first international conventions on the rules of war, communication and transportation, arbitration and adjudication. It is difficult to say whither these efforts might have led international society, had there been no World War I. Chances are that whatever international organization might have capped these diverse initiatives would have been a compromise between a variety of political systems and philosophies—between democratic republics, parliamentary monarchies, and absolutist autocracies. Czarist Russia, for example, one of the latter species, played a leading role in some of the early international conventions.

While the movement toward international co-operation was still in its beginnings, however, World War I intervened, bringing on its orgy of global lawlessness. When the Western democracies prevailed over the Central Powers and their allies, the League of Nations became the victors' incontestable creation. It reflected, as a matter of course, their political principles and preconceptions. Even had the defeated been accorded a share in the drafting of the Covenant, they could have added little of cogency and value. Losing a war is a more time- and energy-consuming business than winning it. Defeat severely narrows the losers' vision.

During the war, most of the thinking about the future world order had been expressed by statesmen and students of the Western democracies, especially those of the United States, the country least affected by the absorbing, day-to-day exactions of war. Woodrow Wilson played the leading role in this effort, albeit the President's views were undoubtedly influenced by other contemporary opinions, such as those expressed in the Phillimore report and Smuts's *Practical Suggestion*.[1] Not so surprisingly, the Western democracies envisaged the League of Nations as a parliament of man, an international approximation of the institutionalized democracy which they themselves practiced.

Wilson, whose Fourteen Points became the framework for the League's Covenant, wrote: "Only the free peoples of the world can join the League of Nations. No nation is admitted to the League of Nations that cannot show that it has the institutions which we call free. No autocratic government can come into this membership, no government which is not controlled by the will and vote of its people."[2]

But history had added another ingredient to the democratic recipe. Because of a series of accidents, the idea of national self-determination had, by the mid-nineteenth century, become closely associated with the idea of popular self-government. The fact that these two ideas were not necessarily germane or complementary did not weigh heavily upon those whose deliberations led to the founding of the League of Nations. Neither does it appear to have troubled the drafters of the United Nations Charter a generation later.

Profound changes in the world political climate and within the United Nations organization itself have occurred since the Charter was drawn in San Francisco. It is tempting to judge the Charter makers' achievement solely in the light of subsequent developments, but most of these were unanticipated. In order fully to evaluate the present state of the

[1] J. C. Smuts, *The League of Nations: A Practical Suggestion* (New York, 1919).

[2] Hamilton Foley, *Woodrow Wilson's Case for the League of Nations* (Princeton, Princeton University Press, 1923), 64.

United Nations, we must seek to reconstruct the thought processes that culminated in the creation of that organization in 1945.

To begin with, the unique conditions that favored the rise of the League of Nations and might have kept it going did not obtain at the end of World War II. The dominant members of the League were democracies and could have kept the League alive indefinitely—had they stuck together. Their combined power could have repulsed any and all challenges to the existing, *their* world order. At the close of World War II the power of American democracy was paramount. Yet the great democracies of Europe had been gravely weakened by the war. Totalitarian Communism had carved out its place in the circle of the major victors and had been admitted with remarkable solicitude and cordiality to the co-operative charting of the United Nations.

Once again the new international organization was the construction of the victors. More specifically, the drive and preparatory effort poured into its creation were supplied mainly by the strongest of the victors, the power that emerged from the war with the largest uncommitted resources and the least damage to its territory. President Franklin D. Roosevelt and Secretary of State Cordell Hull, keenly aware of America's predilection for isolationism, had sought to avoid mistakes which they believed had led the United States to shun the League. Early in the war, the Administration had begun planning future peace machinery. It had been felt that some system of organized international relations, firmly based upon the wartime coalition, was essential to ensure postwar security and a framework for promotion of the general welfare of all mankind.

It is no exaggeration to say that Americans, of all peoples, had wanted the United Nations most, had thought and debated about it most, and had contributed more in ideas, diplomacy, and money to the finished product than anyone else. Again the twin lodestars of the new world order were to be democratic process, the parliament of man, and national self-determination, an equal voice for all nations. True enough, the functions of the steering committee, the Security Council, could not be easily reconciled with either of these two key ideas. But the wording of the Charter's preamble, the role envisaged for the secretary-general, and the provisions for Charter revision leave no doubt that the draftsmen, mostly American, hoped somehow, once the tensions of war and the rivalries of peace settlements had abated, to bridge the gap between oligarchic upper house and democratic commons—between the Security Council and the General Assembly.

It must be remembered that the Charter was drawn while the war was still being waged. The Charter makers shared a common feeling at San Francisco that any proposals or improvements which might endanger Great Powers solidarity or the concerted military action would be not only imprudent but controversial. Few observers in that preatomic period foresaw a rapid end to the war in the Pacific.

Thus the founders sought to draw a charter that would provide a working organism capable of life and growth, realizing full well that "life and growth depend not only on the words of the Charter, but on the way Member States meet their responsibilities and exercise their rights and privileges under the Charter."[3] The founders clung to the hope that what they had created was a document that would be accepted not merely for its words but for its spirit as well—an instrument with a purpose higher than any national or ideological one.

This theme of the progressive perfectability of the United Nations— its continuous approximation to a *real* parliament of man—runs so clearly through a host of American official and unofficial utterances as to warrant its equation with the underlying purpose of American statecraft and with the aspirations nurtured within the collective breast of American leadership. One of the most telling arguments advanced by proponents of the United Nations in the United States, prior to the ratification of the Charter by the Senate, was the assertion that had the United States been a member of the League, World War II could have been averted. Almost as if to atone for the sin of remaining out of the League, the United States moved into the van of United Nations supporters.[4]

The American public—with an anxiety often bordering on neurosis—

[3] Benjamin V. Cohen, *The United Nations* (Cambridge, Harvard University Press, 1961), 30.

[4] "Public opinion, however fickle through alternating national crises of panic and overconfidence over a fifteen-year period, registers general approbation of the United Nations and faith in its prospects. Citizens' organizations through the country publicize the United Nations and its family of specialized agencies on a scale unparalleled elsewhere in the world. There can be no question that in terms of words, hopes, and promises, the United States, certainly of all the great powers, has been the prime supporter of the United Nations from the beginning to the present." Lincoln P. Bloomfield, *The United Nations and U.S. Foreign Policy* (Boston, Little, Brown and Company, 1960), 3.

clutched at the vision of the United Nations as the only or best means of achieving an international environment in which this nation could enjoy its prosperity without outside threat or interference. Despite abundant evidence that such a hope is, at least for the present and foreseeable future, no more than an illusion, large segments of the public apparently still cannot bear to relinquish it.

In the years since its founding the United Nations has moved continuously away from the Wilsonian vision of an association of governments, each responsive to the will of its people. Membership in the organization has more than doubled since 1945. The governmental structures of most of the 113 members of the United Nations are not "democratic," as Wilson and other founders of the League understood this term. Despite these differences, Americans have tended to transfer to the United Nations much of the loyalty which they feel they ought to have sworn to the League of Nations.

True enough, a close reading of the Charter, as well as of Congressional debate, reveals how well defined and clearly understood—by the initiated—were the many reservations in the Charter. These left United Nations authority about as limited as that possessed by the long-suffering League of Nations. But prudent as the American drafters and negotiators may have been when it came to grinding out the fine print of the Charter, their realism did not dim the popular image of the United Nations. From the outset that popular image was optimistic far beyond the warrant of the Charter's text. Official statements tended to abet popular beliefs. Governmental spokesmen did next to nothing to illuminate the discrepancies between original assumptions and actual developments, between illusions and reality.

That reality has certainly been plain enough for anyone willing to acknowledge it. The Soviet Union made it abundantly clear, in 1945–46, not only at conference tables in Potsdam, London, and Moscow but by its conduct in Iran and Greece, that it had no intention of continuing its wartime co-operation with the West. By 1947 the Soviets through their veto had rendered the Security Council impotent and forced an East-West impasse in nearly every organ of the United Nations, including its Atomic Energy Commission and Military Staff Committee.

Obviously, the evolution of the United Nations has not conformed to the anticipations entertained in this country at the time of its founding. The influx of new states, nearly all of them non-Western countries and few of them governed democratically, has altered profoundly the countenance of the organization. The General Assembly, at the bidding of the United States itself, has assumed a greater role in the United Nations as a result of the inability of the Security Council to function effectively. Thus, small states have acquired a power in the councils of the United Nations far greater than that which their national resources justify. The United States is no longer certain of a "safe" majority in the General Assembly. The issue of Chinese representation vividly demonstrates the diminishing likelihood that the United States can always secure a majority favorable to its views. In the fall of 1960 the General Assembly voted against considering the admission of the Peking regime, forty-two to thirty-four, with twenty-two abstentions. For the first time the abstaining members held the balance. In previous years the United States could have carried the day even had the abstaining members changed their minds and voted on the side of Red China. Nor was the disappearance of the West's clear-cut majority in the General Assembly the only troublesome matter to arise. The position of the secretary-general has also been gravely challenged. More important still, the great issues of war and peace appear further removed from the collective authority of the United Nations than ever before.

It seems clear that some of the assumptions woven into the fabric of the United Nations, explicitly or implicitly, were in error. Some massive changes in the world balance of power as well as in the configuration of the world body itself have made mandatory a reappraisal of the United Nations—its underlying assumptions and its actual operation, its likely future and its role in American policy. That this reappraisal has not been made or, in any case, has not been made publicly, is due in no small measure to the inertia of political reputations and vested interests.

The Communist camp does not view the United Nations in the same light as the Western democracies, i.e., as a world agency of co-operation, a conclave for the peaceful settlement of issues, and a mechanism for containing aggression and war. To the Communists, the United Nations is no more than an instrument of conflict, the same protracted conflict being waged by various stratagems of psycho-political attrition, "Byzantine" diplomacy, guerrilla and subversive warfare, nuclear blackmail, and, in the last resort, by any means of violence which promises to destroy the opponents' will to resist.

8

The Communists themselves insist categorically that their doctrine is a blueprint of conflict—conflict waged simultaneously on several levels: vertically, between classes; and horizontally, both among imperialist states in the "advanced stage of capitalism" and between imperialist states and colonial peoples, as well as between the world Communist party and world capitalism. This doctrine has been hammered out so firmly and so noisily that only he who is bereft of sight and hearing could be unaware of it.

To every Communist this doctrine is as valid and as convincing today as it has ever been: the new Soviet man, product as he is of an educational process more persuasive, sophisticated, and methodical than the cruder indoctrination of the earlier Socialist era, is as certain of the dialectic issue as he is of the sequence of night and day. He is serenely confident of the outcome of the protracted conflict because he has been conditioned to accept the complete validity of the doctrine that explains everything in its own terms: the internecine ("imperialist") conflicts of the Western ("capitalist") peoples; the "wars of liberation" in Asia and Africa; the perennial division of the foes of Communism ("capitalist competition"); and the military-technological triumphs of the Soviet Union ("fruits of socialist planning and teamwork"). To the Communist, the weight of evidence is stacked heavily on the side of his doctrine, notwithstanding some strategic retreats abroad and frustrations at home which he has learned to sublimate into the long-range view of the over-all expansion of Communist power. Doctrine, as well as the evidence sifted in the light of doctrine, compels him to reject the mixed universalism of the United Nations, a congeries of capitalist, socialist, and "uncommitted" nations. To him, this kind of coexistence can be no more than a transient makeshift, a contradiction that must yield to the dialectic of history. It is inconceivable to a Communist that either permanence or perfectability inheres in so divided an organization as the United Nations—divided on class lines, vertically, and along Leninist lines of battle among the "imperialists" and between the "imperialists" and the forces of "national liberation."

Clearly, if one set of premises predisposed the United States to identify the United Nations with its own interests, an entirely different set of premises led the Soviets to the same conclusion, even though the interests of the two nations are diametrically opposed. Premier Stalin was hardly renowned for his sensitivity to democratic parliamentary institutions; only the most naïve could equate his concern for national self-determination with the Western ideal of national self-government. The Communists have their own peculiar conceptions of society and man, and, being universalists, of world organization. In their view, a people cannot aspire to full national independence lest they determine themselves into a Communist state—or are led into it by a trained Communist elite. They consider "bourgeois" national emancipation—in other words, the kind of national self-government which satisfies the requirements of Western democracy—as a mere way station on the road to the Communist state.

To be sure, Stalin had no objection to national liberation—just so long as this process led the emergent state into the community of Communist nations, i.e., it must become another local unit in a world-wide and uniform Communist system. Stalin, in fact, wrote a treatise on this particular subject. Any student of Soviet federalism can easily understand what he (or any Communist) means when he speaks of national autonomy. Stalin was probably his own best student. Of course, he knew full well that the United Nations concept, so closely tailored to American preconceptions, did not jibe in the least with his understanding of democracy, i.e., Popular Democracy; or national self-rule, i.e., the Autonomous Socialist Republic; or a world order under law, i.e., International Communism. But this antinomy of outlook, so obvious in the light of the Communist record and so well hidden by the Western Allies' own diplomatic conduct and propaganda, did not deter Premier Stalin's quest for a say in the making of the Charter and a place, a strategic place, in the United Nations organization. Even though the ship could not be built to his specification, he grasped firmly one spoke of the vessel's helm.

For the Communist, every non-Communist is either a potential convert or simply an opponent who must be fought. Communists participating in any non-Communist organization seek to subvert it and thus bend it to their own purposes or, failing that, to destroy it. The United Nations has not been excepted from this rule of Communist conduct. From the first years of the United Nations existence, the Soviets attempted to bend the organization to their purpose, a purpose inherently at odds with the United Nations own.

The primary motivation for the Soviets' behavior has undoubtedly been provided by their doctrine. A secondary source stems from the

Soviet experience as a minority power: they have sought to frustrate the efforts of the hostile majority "in control" of the United Nations.[5] It has also been suggested that the United Nations has a positive value for the Soviets as both "a listening-post and . . . a meeting ground."[6]

During the conferences preceding the formation of the United Nations the Soviet representatives made a strong effort to limit the scope of the new organization to international security problems only, arguing that the League of Nations had been overburdened with "secondary" matters. Although yielding at Dumbarton Oaks to the inclusion of non-security functions in the future United Nations organization, the Soviets evinced no inclination to participate or co-operate in the many social, economic, and cultural activities of the organization during most of its first decade of existence. It is not surprising that the Communists—whose goal is the destruction of the capitalist structure of society—would seek to avoid such "reformist methods," which they regard as "both futile and fraudulent."[7] The apparent change of attitude on this point, which became evident about mid-1953, must be attributed to post-Stalinist developments in the Soviet Union. It represents only a change in tactics, not in objectives.

One major concession won by Stalin at the early conferences was the Security Council voting formula, which requires unanimity among all permanent members on non-procedural matters. This represented a compromise of sorts—the West had opposed the right of veto when it would make a Great Power a judge in its own case, while Stalin had at first demanded the veto even on procedural matters. The concession was sufficient, however, to enable the Soviets permanently to hamstring the Security Council from taking effective action whenever their own national interests were at stake.

Soviet United Nations strategy has aimed at exploiting conflicts among the Free World and deadlocking the United Nations whenever it has sought to halt or penalize Communist incursions into the non-Communist sphere. On the one hand, Soviet diplomacy in the United Nations has never failed to aggravate disputes that embroiled the West-

[5] Alexander Dallin, "The Soviet View of the United Nations," *International Organization* (Winter, 1962), 20.

[6] Rupert Emerson and Inis L. Claude, "The Soviet Union and the United Nations," *International Organization* (February, 1952), 2–3.

[7] *Ibid.*, 18–19.

ern nations with one another or with the new states of Asia and Africa; on the other hand, it has denied the Free World a say in—or even a view of—the tension-laden problems of the Communist empire.

Choice examples of Soviet spoiling operations in the United Nations are not hard to find. Consider, for example, the series of policy shifts designed to exacerbate the Israeli-Arab and Pakistani-Indian controversies; the unfailing Soviet support in the United Nations of any faction that could be relied upon to prolong the Algerian conflict; persistent Soviet sabotage of United Nations initiatives in the Congo, approved by the majority of United Nations members, including Soviet refusal to share in the expense of United Nations intervention; and beginning with 1961, Soviet vilification of the late Secretary-General Dag Hammarskjold. The second prong of Soviet strategy—that of interdiction aimed at blocking the United Nations whenever it sought to halt Soviet incursions in the Free World or extend its authority to the Communist bloc itself—is well illustrated by such instances as the Soviets' blunt refusal to recognize the competence of the United Nations in the case of Soviet aggression against Iran in 1946; the Berlin Blockade; the Korean War; the Hungarian uprising; and Soviet tactics stymieing the United Nations when it sought, prior to the outbreak of war in 1950, to unify Korea. The list is far from complete.

In carrying out its tactics, the Soviet Union has appeared as both a defender and a foe of the *status quo*, depending on which position matches its own self-interest. Where the Communists have stood to gain, they have supported change, as in Iran, Greece, or Berlin or, where change would mean a setback to the Western "imperialists," as in Indonesia, Syria, Lebanon, Palestine, the Italian colonies, Suez, and Algeria. Where an alteration of the *status quo* would mean a defeat to the Soviet Union or its allies, as in the Corfu Strait, Korea, Hungary, and Cuba, they have argued loudly that a change would be an infringement of the domestic jurisdiction clause of the Charter which protects national sovereign rights.

The pattern is plain: the United Nations lies in the great "war zone" of Soviet conflict management, a zone which embraces all countries not yet under Communist domination. In contrast, the Soviet Union and its satellites compose the "peace zone" which is closed to extraneous influences. The Soviet Union is a member of the United Nations; but Soviet membership is effective only when someone else's ox is being gored; whenever the United Nations seeks to extend its writ to the Communist bloc, the door of the Soviet veto slams shut. Thus the United Nations is not exempt from the peculiar effects of the Iron Curtain.

It is likely that Soviet diplomacy carefully assessed the risks of participation in the United Nations before its negotiators ever sat down at the conference table with the Western powers. The Soviets had acquired ample working experience in their career in the League of Nations. As long as the democracies maintained overwhelming military and economic superiority, and as long as the *status quo* powers formed the majority of the Assembly and supported the United States, the road of Soviet diplomacy in the United Nations was strewn with many pitfalls. But this risk was outweighed by Communist understanding of the revolution of our times and, specifically, of the dynamics of national revolution in the underdeveloped world.

The mounting crisis of colonialism—accelerated partially by the Japanese conquest of a large part of Asia and partially by the old colonial powers' surfeit with and renunciation of responsibilities—stood to bring ever so much nearer the distant vistas of Lenin's ruminations on capitalist imperialism and colonial revolt. A goodly number of peoples were about to throw off the colonial yoke or had, at any rate, been promised by their colonial masters that they would be free to do so in the near future. Given the Western democracies' own concepts of national self-determination and national sovereignty, it was a foregone conclusion that these "emergent" nations would each begin their sovereign lives with a seat in the United Nations, as the first and altogether pleasing token of sovereign identity and equality. The Communists relied heavily on *their* understanding of history: delight at United Nations status would not necessarily diminish the resentments of the newcomers against their former overlords—now sitting humbly on the same circular benches as their former wards—nor would it necessarily bring them closer in affection and interest to the United States, which had striven so hard to make the principle of universalism prevail in the United Nations procedure for admission.

On the face of it, Stalin's decision to grasp the nettle firmly and take the Soviet bloc into the United Nations was fraught with one other forbidding risk: how could the Soviet regime reconcile, in the eyes of its own subjects, its acceptance of the parliamentary formalism of the

United Nations with its absolute refusal to submit to majority rule at home? This danger, however, was only apparent. Public opinion in the Soviet Union is far less alert than in the Free World. Moreover, it is highly affected by the official doses of Marxist-Leninist interpretations of international events. The Soviet press, in reporting United Nations sessions, exercises severe selectivity. There never was a counterpart in the Soviet Union to the immense publicity given by government, press, educational organizations, and volunteer groups in the United States to every and all transactions in the United Nations. Nor can one discover in Soviet public attitudes anything comparable to the mystique of the United Nations which so strongly moves large segments of the American and other Western publics. The published materials available to the Soviet public are marked by their sobriety and terseness. Maximum space is reserved for the utterances of Soviet delegates. At best, statements of opposing views are given in the briefest of summaries; more often than not, they are omitted altogether. Whatever hopes or loyalties the average Soviet citizen might attach to the United Nations are very feeble, or are secrets so well kept as to render them unfathomable. The Soviet government has had not a few things to say about the United Nations since its inception. Most of these official statements have been highly critical; no Soviet foreign minister has ever identified the sum and substance of Soviet foreign policy with the United Nations, as did at least one American secretary of state.

When, during the Sixteenth Session of the United Nations, Premier Khrushchev staged his extraordinary performance as chief delegate of the Soviet Union, his monumental contempt of the living symbol of world order appears to have shocked no one less than the Soviet people. Most certainly, he gave spontaneous—perhaps all-too spontaneous—expression to every Communist's deepest belief, for a Communist cannot but view the United Nations as a fraud, a device for blurring the image of the true world order: the global Communist society without class conflict and international war. It would be a grave injustice to traduce Premier Khrushchev as a complete cynic; his contempt for the United Nations flows from settled conviction. The particular mode of his performance—his fists, then his boot striking rhythmically the chaste furniture of the United Nations in plenary meeting—might have been prompted by a fit of autocratic fury or, more likely, by a calculated attempt to stun the weak and wavering among his audience with brute violence. But his indifference to the decorum of the United Nations was not feigned; his contempt of the United Nations spirit was real.

In that halcyon epoch when the United States could count confidently on majority support in the United Nations, the Soviets had to content themselves with making the best of their limited opportunities: they started fires or fanned the flames which someone else had started; they paralyzed the will of the majority when that will threatened to interfere with Communist expansionism or intrude into the Communist "peace zone." The beginning of the 1960's, however, marked a momentous change. A large increase in United Nations membership coincided with a relative decrease in United States power, a consequence largely of a shift in the military-technological balance. A large number of the new members belong to the class of "emergent" nations; not a few are poor and internally unstable. Nearly all of them are weak militarily. These circumstances alone, even if it were not for certain psychological and ideological attitudes characteristic of the ruling elites in most of these new countries, would suffice to explain the attractions of neutralism— and of being neutralist, by a shade at least, *against* the Western powers and *for* the Communist bloc.[8] Although the novel ways of the "new neutralism" diverge considerably from the path of traditional neutrality, they have acquired legitimacy and respectability. The United States, reluctant at first, now accepts neutralism as the "natural" attitude of the former colonial peoples, who nevertheless call clamorously for United States economic assistance.

The Communists, although they insist that no one can be neutral in the struggle between capitalism and socialism, now center their diplomatic and propaganda efforts, as well as their foreign economic program, on the neutralist bloc. They seek to consolidate it. If this attempt succeeds, the lines of division in the United Nations will be threefold, namely, between the West, the Communist bloc, and the "uncommitted." More important still, the Free World will have been split down the middle. This struggle has taken on added significance in view of the shift in power within the United Nations, from the Security Council to the General Assembly.

[8] Of the total United Nations membership of 113 in 1964, the Afro-Asian group constitutes a total of 59, of which 35 states are African. With the exception of Iran, Pakistan, the Philippines, Japan, Thailand, and Turkey, which are aligned with the West in defensive pacts, the Afro-Asian states fall under the category of "neutralist" nations.

The neutralists' "strategy" in the United Nations is seriously concerned only with those matters of common interest to them, namely, national self-determination or the political development of the non-self-governing territories, and the economic development of the weak new states. The Afro-Asian group of neutralists "regard intervention in 'cold war' issues as taking sides in a power struggle from which they prefer to remain aloof. They are ready to prevent the cold war from spreading to new areas, but are not ready to step in and help solve existing cold war problems."[9] To be sure, the neutralists are not above exploiting East-West tensions to gain aid from all quarters. The competition for their votes in the General Assembly provides a handy leverage for extracting benefits from the Cold War.

The bloc of the uncommitted, standing alone, consists of an aggregate of military and economic impotence that mere addition cannot transform into power. It is incapable of concerted positive action. Hence, it does not pose any dangers for the Soviets. To the contrary, since the psychological and ideological formations of its leading elites favor the Communists or, at least, do not make for a determined opposition against Communism, the uncommitted bloc offers considerably more openings to Communist penetration than to Western influence. It is these circumstances, and not the fear of what an angry United Nations could do to an even more angry Soviet Union, which prompted Premier Khrushchev's celebrated "troika" proposal: three secretaries-general instead of one, each chosen by a bloc. From Khrushchev's point of view, the charm of this proposal lies in the three quite pleasing alternatives it would offer him should it ever be adopted: If it did not lead to the Communists' absolute control of the United Nations, Khrushchev could still cap the Soviets' divisive United Nations stategies by making permanent the split of the non-Communist peoples and sealing off the third bloc against Western initiatives and influences; or, he could simply wreck the United Nations itself whenever he pleased. This is a bold plan, but one that no longer can be discounted as a Communist phantasmagoria; the Communists have carried out plans even more ambitious. There is no doubt that if it were to be adopted, the United Nations would have seen the last of the sort of "preventive diplomacy" carried on, with some effectiveness, by the late Dag Hammarskjold.

[9] William R. Frye, "Afro-Asian Bloc: Center Stage at U.N.," *Foreign Policy Bulletin*, Vol. XL, No. 3 (October 15, 1960), 17.

Introduction

The meeting at Belgrade of the neutralists in September, 1961, appears to justify Premier Khrushchev's boldness. The neutralists achieved unity on virtually nothing but "anti-colonialism" and the hope that they might be kept safe from nuclear harm. For the United States, the conference dispensed but the coldest of comforts. Its muffled complaints at the resumption of nuclear testing by the Soviets were couched in language so ambiguous as to leave doubtful exactly who the drafters felt was at fault: the Soviets or the Americans? The meeting did provide an occasion for drumming up support among the "uncommitted" for Premier Khrushchev's proposed solutions for all world problems. Premier Nkrumah of Ghana declared himself in accord not only with Premier Khrushchev's ideas on disarmament and how to bring peace to Berlin, East Germany, and the rest of Europe but also with the "troika" solution. To the pained surprise of United States observers, Nkrumah's speech elicited congratulations from some delegates and but the mildest criticism from others. In the United States it had been taken for granted that Premier Khrushchev's antics in the United Nations—especially his open violation of United Nations decorum—had strengthened the new members' loyalties to the organization. Was it not their United Nations? Did not they, the weak and poor, have the greatest stake in keeping the United Nations united and strong against the divisive inroads of the Cold War? These illusions, as well as others, evaporated in Belgrade.

It would be unfair to blame the neutralists for their indifference toward the West's conceptions of what is right and meet in such matters as the Berlin crisis, nuclear testing, general disarmament—and the shape and solidarity of the United Nations. All countries, we ourselves included, take their cue from the prevailing balance of power. Most certainly, the weak "uncommitted" have no other choice. Their quick discernment of changes in power relationships—who is winning and who is losing—is their main defense. It is this preoccupation with survival, rather than residual resentments against their former Western masters, that provides the key to "neutralist" diplomacy in and outside of the United Nations. Among themselves, the neutralists are not united on any major world issue. They are divided by many internecine quarrels; many neutralist elites realize full well that their best hope for the economic improvement of their peoples lies in the well-filled coffers of the West, that Soviet economic assistance, at least for a long time, will be less ample and more capricious than Western trade and investment.

More important still, a goodly number of neutralist politicians, intellectuals, managers, and professionals would, all other things being even, be glad to adopt the West's political institutions, once their fellow countrymen were literate and prosperous enough to use them. But these considerations cannot be relied upon to attract the neutralists to the Western camp or even to ensure their even-handed support of the United Nations, as long as the West's power position continues to undergo progressive deterioration, thus increasing general insecurity and the danger of Communist aggression.

The neutralists' opinions about political power, mirrored in their votes at the United Nations, should certainly induce us to re-examine the validity of our preconceptions about national sovereignty and national self-determination, the outdated and counter-productive companion piece of the liberal prescription for a world order under freedom. A United Nations minus the ideals of Western humanism that inspired the Charter is a mere shell that, sooner or later, war or no war, will be filled and burst asunder by Communist power.

It is often said that Western humanism is losing out in non-Western lands, or is inaccessible to those other cultures who now, under the mantle of national liberations, are about to displace the Western intruder. This is only a half-truth: Western humanism has suffered at the hands of the West's own defectors. Not a few of the former colonial peoples delight in sweeping out Western values together with their former masters. More important still, the prestige of Western values is intimately connected with the West's power—the power to take care of its own and to restrain the would-be aggressor. But the West's own aberrations, the psychosis of national "emergence," and the present effulgence of Soviet military-technological prowess are, by themselves, not enough to halt the march of Western power, trade, science, and political institutions which began several centuries ago. What could well compound the embarrassment of Western institutions and values into final defeat and the destruction of the humanist heritage is the consistent misreading of Communist strategy and tactics and a deficiency of will in countering them with imaginative plans and efficient measures of the West's own.

Since the United Nations happens to be one battlefield of the universal struggle over a unitary world order and of the protracted conflict forced by Communism upon a free people, we must develop plans for preserving the United Nations as a first, albeit most imperfect, cast of world order—a likely model, so to speak, that may help us design a more unitary and elaborate structure. This, the first cast, is flawed by errors of preconception and inexperience. To attempt to remedy the flaws by eulogizing them as perfections—the United Nations as the "last best hope of man on earth"—is to delude ourselves and to condemn the United Nations to certain destruction. So absurd a behavior profits no one except the Communists, who have assiduously fostered a false United Nations mystique abroad while stifling, at home, whatever loyalties the United Nations may have aroused among its masses.

The United Nations has been designed as an instrument for fashioning a world order under law. To this extent, it is a worthy instrument of American statesmanship. It is a vehicle of the traditional Western concepts of the rule of law, the nonviolent settlements of disputes, and decision by majority after free debate in a representative assembly. Of course, the mechanism must be used in keeping with its capabilities and limitations. No stigma should attach to using *any* of its parts, including such constitutional safeguards as the veto in the Security Council. It is doubtful that the United States has much to gain in attempting to buy majority support in the General Assembly by watering down its stand on an important issue or evading the issues altogether. Majority support cannot be salted away like a hunk of pork. Such concessions should not be justified by concern for world opinion, for the United Nations— for statistical and epistemological reasons—cannot furnish a reliable gauge of world opinion. Let us hope that the rightness of United States policies will always command a majority in the General Assembly; if it does not, the United States has no other choice in the United Nations but to state its views vigorously in free debate and by every means of communications at its disposal—and to use every constitutional device, procedural and substantive, to block the dissenting majority. These procedures are legitimate ones under the United States Constitution, a constitution designed for a system far more expressive of popular majority opinion than is that of the United Nations.

The United Nations cannot be relied upon for a solution to all the problems which confront us in an era of protracted conflict. The United Nations, in a sense, is the open society writ large. The Soviets would derive lasting pleasure not from its successes but only from its ultimate subversion and failure.

For the United States, the United Nations is one of the important ideological and diplomatic battlegrounds of the protracted conflict. The organization can serve as a useful instrument of American policy in several ways:

1. The United Nations provides a channel of diplomatic communications with the Soviet Union. The principal task of American diplomacy in respect to the Soviet Union is to conduct an unofficial dialogue for the purpose of exploration and gradual persuasion. The "corridor diplomacy" in the United Nations not only lends itself to this objective, but occasionally yields some fruitful results. Thus, for example, the Soviets lifted their blockade of West Berlin in 1949 as a result of quiet conversations in the United Nations between the chief delegates of the United States and the Soviet Union.

2. The specialized agencies of the United Nations carry out broad humanitarian projects in the indigent areas of the globe, and other secondary activities involving dependent areas and technical assistance.

3. For the time being, the United Nations and its specialized agencies can serve as a multilateral funnel for American economic and technical assistance to nations whose economic health is vital to our objectives, but who, for various reasons, are reluctant to accept aid on a bilateral basis. The United States should keep a watchful eye on the effectiveness of United Nations aid programs. At some point in the future, there may be plausible arguments for increasingly assigning this function to appropriate institutions within the Atlantic Community.

4. The United Nations can provide some measure of peace enforcement in highly charged emotional issues in which neither side can risk a loss of face—or, indeed, in which one side may be unwilling officially to recognize the existence of the other. A good example of this function is the UNEF contingent stationed in Gaza and at Sharm el Sheikh after the Suez Canal crisis in 1956.

5. The United Nations can be useful in averting the total breakdown of order in strife-torn nations. United Nations intervention in the Congo in the summer of 1960 was the only feasible alternative to complete chaos. Of course, the tragic course of events in the Congo may well have been averted had the NATO allies concerted their policies in good time.

6. The United Nations can shine a useful spotlight on areas of Communist embarrassment and thus aid Western strategy in countering the

Communists should a future Hungary- or Tibet-like situation develop. It may on occasion be possible to use the United Nations to provide world-wide exposure to Communist subversion, and thus counteract it. Disclosure in the United Nations of Soviet clandestine activities in the Congo and in Cuba are prime examples.

The United Nations, in short, still offers a forum in which hope for the promotion of peace—and especially the peaceful evolution of the underdeveloped areas—can be kept alive. For the United States, the United Nations has many uses. Among these not the least important is that of mirror to all peoples' thoughts, especially their thoughts about political power. Reflections in that mirror can give valuable guidance to our policies. Indeed, they can help us to develop a healthful sobriety in judging the conditions needed to establish one day a true parliament of man. But as long as the Soviet Union continues to seek a dictated, universal peace by the ultimate destruction of nations opposed to Communism, the survival of Western society depends less upon the United Nations than upon American determination to match Soviet power by organizing within regional political frameworks the economic, military, and moral power of the Free World. Indeed, it is not a question of choosing the United Nations *or* regional groupings. Healthy development of regional groupings throughout the world can eventually provide the United Nations with the strong underpinnings it now lacks. For the United Nations, founded upon the legal artifact of national sovereignty, must keep pace with the federative movement which bids fair to gain further momentum during the latter half of the twentieth century.

CHAPTER II

The United States National Interest and the United Nations

BY FRANZ B. GROSS

THE RELATIONSHIP of the United States foreign policy and national interest to the purposes of the United Nations has been the subject of debate since the founding of the United Nations in San Francisco. In fact, ever since the earlier League of Nations became a reality, the proper United States attitude toward international institutions has been the subject of investigation both by those responsible for policy decisions and by the American public.

The "winds of change" which have blown hard upon the world during this last decade have had their effect on the United Nations. The organization is not the same institution envisaged in 1945; indeed, it would be an indication of sterility were this so. These changes make imperative frequent re-evaluations of the aims and purposes of United States foreign policy and its effect upon policies and trends influencing the United Nations and its organs.

The need to review United States policy toward the United Nations was emphasized in a speech by Senator Henry M. Jackson, which was notable for three salient points. The Senator stressed that we "need to take another look at our role in the United Nations, remembering that the UN is not a substitute for national policies wisely conceived to uphold our vital interests"; he questioned whether our "present relations with the United Nations assist the wise definition of our vital interests and the establishment of sound policies"; and he emphasized that the United Nations "is, and should continue to be, an important avenue of American foreign policy."[1]

A re-evaluation of United States policy toward the United Nations might well begin with an examination of recent changes within the United Nations and in the methods of multilateral diplomacy.

[1] See Appendix II in this volume.

When, on November 30, 1962, Acting Secretary-General U Thant was elected to a full term as secretary-general of the United Nations, he shared the platform with Mohammad Zafrulla Khan, a Pakistani, and C. V. Narasimhan, an Indian. Only a little more than a year before, the same key positions had been held by Dag Hammarskjold, a Swede, F. H. Boland of Ireland, and Andrew Cordier, an American. These changes seem symbolic of trends in the United Nations. It would be mistaken, however, to assume that the changes are more radical than indeed they are. For a Swedish civil servant has been replaced by a Burmese neutral, a former British schoolmaster—i.e., one neutral has been replaced by another; an American college professor has been replaced by an Indian civil servant of long service with the United Nations; and, in the normal process of geographic rotation, an Irish diplomat has been replaced by a Pakistani who was formerly a justice of the International Court of Justice.

Essentially, one group of officials of the English-speaking community has been replaced by another group which shares in large part similar ideas and attitudes.[2] Yet, since the latter group comes from former colonies in Asia, it reflects undeniably a change in emphasis in the world which is now mirrored in the United Nations. There seems little doubt that the former dominance of Europeans and Americans in the United Nations is gradually being replaced by the control of a group of Asians and Africans who, though educated to share many of the principles and aspirations of the former, bring to their tasks minds steeped in the struggle for independence.

If the United Nations has faced the problem of blending Asian and African aspirations into an organization founded on essentially European institutions, United States foreign policy concerning the United Nations has also faced its dilemmas, wavering between isolationism and internationalism, between idealism and realism.

In the United Nations a new dimension of diplomacy challenges United States policy. Formerly relations between states were, to a large degree, conducted through confidential negotiations between diplomats trained in the centuries-old art of reaching agreements by "playing the

[2] It was not without pride that Mohammad Zafrulla Khan said to U Thant after his election, "Asia has yielded up one of its best for the service of the United Nations but U Thant does not belong to Asia alone; he belongs to humanity."

game" according to mutually accepted rules and values. In many respects United States policy is still geared to bilateral diplomacy, reacting to the exigencies of each crisis and parleying with the parties concerned only as situations arise. The role of United States policy in the United Nations often appears to be that of a pained and anxious spectator rather than that of a leading actor.

The new dimension of diplomacy might well be called "international parliamentary diplomacy" since, although no body of the United Nations has true legislative functions, its resolutions have substantial influence on the outcome of important issues, even including some that touch on war and peace. Diplomats often engage in speechmaking for the purpose of wooing domestic support; yet the gap between what the negotiator can achieve and what domestic public opinion can accept is frequently widened by public exposure.

A further important aspect of United Nations multilateral diplomacy is the minute scrutiny to which United States policy is subjected in the international forum by all states opposed for one reason or another to the United States. Each United States statement provides an opportunity for attack by the Soviet bloc, which misses no chance to distort issues and to gain some measure of support from nations basically hostile to the United States or normally "neutral" in most conflicts, or even nations generally friendly to the United States.

Ideally, the United States should seek to engage the United Nations only in problems where substantial support for its position can be won, and to prevent lengthy debates or resolutions on other questions. Although this ideal objective cannot be reached under all circumstances, the United States, by careful planning, the development of good diplomatic relations with other delegations, and the seizure of the initiative on all possible occasions, can exercise a more consistent leadership and greater control over the United Nations agenda.

The search for an effective United States strategy in the United Nations should also include an examination of the traditional American attitudes toward world affairs, particularly the differing approaches of the realistic and the idealistic schools.

The roots of the realistic and idealistic views of United States policy toward the United Nations go back to America's outward development since the turn of the century. President Theodore Roosevelt, a strong proponent of the policy of realism and expansion, addressed Congress, in 1904, as follows:

> All that this country desires is to see the neighboring countries stable, orderly and prosperous. Any nation whose people conduct themselves well can count upon our hearty friendship. If a nation shows that it knows how to act with reasonable efficiency and decency in social and political matters, if it keeps order and pays its obligations, it need fear no interference from the United States. Chronic wrongdoing, or an impotence which results in a general lessening of the ties of civilized society, may in America, as elsewhere, ultimately require intervention by some civilized nation, and in the Western Hemisphere the adherence of the United States to the Monroe Doctrine may force the United States, however reluctantly, in flagrant cases of such wrongdoing or impotence, to the exercise of an international police power.

He further stated that intervention, at least in Latin America, though it should be based on American self-interest, was really a moral duty:

> We would interfere with them only in the last resort, and then only if it became evident that their inability or unwillingness to do justice at home and abroad had violated the rights of the United States or had invited foreign aggression to the detriment of the entire body of American nations.[3]

President Roosevelt advocated a policy of action based on national interest, yet tempered by the moral precepts of American traditions.

Under Woodrow Wilson, self-imposed limitations on United States power became the essence of United States foreign policy. President Wilson stressed American idealism without, however, losing sight of power realities. In an Independence Day speech delivered just before the outbreak of World War I, he stated:

> My dream is that as the years go by and the world knows more and more of America it . . . will turn to America for those moral inspirations which lie at the basis of all freedom . . . and that America will come into the full light of day when all shall know that she puts human rights above all other rights, and that her flag is the flag not only of America, but of humanity.[4]

[3] *House Doc. No. 1* (4780), 58 Cong., 3 sess., xli–xl.

[4] Ray S. Baker and William E. Dodd, *The Public Papers of Woodrow Wilson* (New York, 1927), III, 147.

Only three years later Wilson was forced to send a message to Congress asking for a declaration of war:

> We shall fight for the things which we have always carried nearest our hearts, for democracy, for the right of those who submit to authority to have a voice in their own governments, for the rights and liberties of small nations, for a universal dominion of right by such a concert of free peoples as shall bring peace and safety to all nations and make the world itself at last free.[5]

However, Woodrow Wilson's dream of a concert of all free peoples was only partially realized. The League of Nations was created; but the United States did not join it.

Nevertheless, the State Department developed a policy toward the international organization. Since the defeat of the Covenant in the Senate counseled prudence, the Department confined itself at first to limiting United States intercourse with the League to occasional liaison through Swiss, French, or Netherlands channels. From March 4 to August 19, 1921, the State Department did not reply to communications received from the Secretary-General of the League. In the summer of 1921 it even neglected to forward—until that failure was publicized—to the United States members of the Permanent Court of Arbitration invitations to nominate candidates for the Permanent Court of International Justice. This affront to a large body of American opinion was soon corrected, however, and a more courteous procedure of sending prompt but stereotyped and negative replies was adopted—to continue for many months after unofficial American organizations, such as the Rockefeller Foundation, and individual Americans had begun to co-operate wholeheartedly in the work of the League.

During the second stage, when matters of interest to the United States were discussed, a policy of official co-operation issued in the appointment of representatives to attend various permanent committees of the League. Still, the appointments were always carefully camouflaged, conveying the impression that such actions of the United States were not official. This formula served for some years as a bridge between Washington and Geneva, although the bridge was too frail for heavy traffic. The elections of 1924 paved the way to more confident United States action. In 1925 the United States government was fully repre-

[5] *Congressional Record*, 65 Cong., 1 sess., Vol. LV, Pt. I, 102.

sented at two important conferences held in Geneva—the Conference on Opium and the Conference on Arms Traffic. Regular representation at special conferences continued thereafter.

In 1932 a direct line of telephonic communication was installed between the League and the Department of State. The third stage of official co-operation had started, and in June, 1934, Congress formally approved United States membership in the International Labor Organization.

The steady growth of United States co-operation declined somewhat in the first term of Franklin D. Roosevelt, who displayed marked indifference toward the League. Although in the second Roosevelt term the State Department tried to co-operate fully with the League, the next test case, the Italo-Abyssinian war, found the United States bound by neutrality legislation. Despite general approval in the United States of League sanctions, even among supporters of the Neutrality Act, the Secretary of State could reply to the League committees only with expressions of good will, not with firm commitments.

The rising menace of Hitler and Mussolini and the weakness of the League without United States support finally induced President Roosevelt to attempt to educate public opinion on the necessity of a positive attitude toward international organization in order to curb potential aggressors. In his famous Quarantine Speech in Chicago, Roosevelt tried to turn the tide and to convince the American people that

> There is a solidarity and interdependence about the modern world, both technically and morally, which makes it impossible for any nation completely to isolate itself from economic and political upheavals in the rest of the world, especially when such upheavals appear to be spreading and not declining. There can be no stability or peace either within nations or between nations except under laws and moral standards adhered to by all. International anarchy destroys every foundation for peace. It jeopardizes either the immediate or the future security of every nation, large or small. It is, therefore, a matter of vital interest and concern to the people of the United States that the sanctity of international treaties and the maintenance of international morality be restored. . . . It seems to be unfortunately true that the epidemic of world lawlessness is spreading.[6]

[6] President Roosevelt's Quarantine Speech (October 5, 1937), *Peace and War; United States Foreign Policy, 1931–1941* (Washington, U.S. Government Printing Office, 1943), 383–87.

The exact intent of the President's speech was not clear, particularly since he was known to look with substantial reservations upon collective security arrangements. His words met with strong opposition which seems to have induced him to maintain a prolonged period of silence.

Roosevelt's warning was therefore not immediately heeded; it took the shock of World War II to arouse public opinion against "world lawlessness." Then, following the precedent of Wilson, and in the highest tradition of American idealism, Roosevelt proclaimed the Four Freedoms, cherished by Americans, to be applicable to everyone, everywhere in the world.

World War II wrought a decided change in American attitudes. It had become clear that support of an international organization was a necessity for a peaceful world as well as in the best national interest, and was not merely the fantasy of dreamers and idealists. As early as December, 1939, the State Department created a Committee on Peace and Reconstruction. Gradually the President veered to the conviction that a general security organization designed to replace the League of Nations would have to be planned and founded. This position, a blending of idealism and realism, was reflected by United States foreign policy at the Moscow and Teheran Conferences, and by the Dumbarton Oaks Conversations in the summer of 1944 during which the United Nations Charter was devised.

The plans for the United Nations incorporated Woodrow Wilson's idea of a parliament of nations; Theodore Roosevelt's concept of a (United States) police force used under international control and based on the moral duty of great powers to keep order; and finally, Franklin Roosevelt's emphasis on common action to preserve the international order as the best safeguard of the United States vital interest in peace and security.

The Charter of the United Nations was essentially a product of the wartime alliance between the United States and its Western allies and the Soviet Union. It was based on the experiences of the League, although both the United States as a nonmember of the League and the Soviet Union, expelled from the League after the attack on Finland, carefully refrained from any reference to the parent organization.

For the United States, the new international organization was a potential guarantor of permanent peace and the potential controller of an effective international police force. Voices of caution and warning were scarcely heard during the early postwar period. It seemed as though, after years of isolationism, internationalism was to be the bulwark of United States policy, and security was to be achieved through collaboration among the Great Powers, particularly the United States, the Soviet Union, and Britain. This spirit of collaboration preceding the first General Assembly, in January, 1946, led to the establishment of an Atomic Energy Commission by unanimous vote on January 24. But in that same month, with the introduction of the Iranian complaint into the Security Council, the atmosphere deteriorated, and in March and April of the following year, the Cold War came to the surface for the first time.

United States foreign policy, based on a commitment to the territorial integrity and political independence of all nations, large or small, had little choice but to insist upon the complete evacuation of Soviet troops from Iran. This move was deeply resented by the Soviet Union as unwarranted interference. The United States had previously warned the Soviets that, should the dispute remain unresolved, it would feel compelled to support the Iranian complaint.[7] The way the case was handled convinced the Kremlin that, two days after the inauguration of the Security Council, Iran had raised the complaint at the instigation of British Foreign Secretary Ernest Bevin. The Soviets were displeased at the breach in the "solidarity" of the Great Powers and felt that their apprehension concerning their minority position in the organization had been justified. Confronted by a hostile majority, they were forced to withdraw from Iran. When the Soviets came to realize that the United States had every intention of performing in the spirit of the Charter, the Cold War began.

Moreover, Stalin considered the concern of the Western powers over eastern Europe another case of interference in a mutually agreed sphere of Soviet influence. The Western governments were supposed to be tolerant of Soviet interests in this area. Later a precedent with unfavorable implications for the Soviet Union was established when the West secured action through the United Nations to defend the independence of Greece, where Communist influence eventually was eliminated by the British and Americans. The Soviets have always contended that the Yalta agreements had given them a free hand in eastern Europe; they

[7] See James F. Byrnes, *Speaking Frankly* (New York, Harper & Bros., 1947), 119–20.

claim that their extension westward was based on this assumption. Thus, they viewed with concern the encirclement of the Soviet Union by the "hostile capitalist world" which was considered to be interfering in their "legitimate" sphere of influence. In fact, because of this feeling, even before the San Francisco Conference the Soviets had, in comparison with their businesslike attitude at Dumbarton Oaks, lost interest in the forthcoming negotiations which would establish the United Nations.

This impasse forced United States policy in the United Nations to take a new turn. The assumption of Great Power collaboration had collapsed, and a new working basis for the future had to be found. However, at the time, the American public was still riding the first wave of enthusiasm for the new world body. It was therefore inopportune to inform them of the problems and tribulations ahead.

Up to this period the people of the United States were willing to agree that the principles of the Charter should be regarded in the same order of precedence as they were given at San Francisco. It was assumed that the first duty of the United Nations was to induce all nations to preserve peace (Preamble of the Charter) and that war was outlawed (Article 2, paragraph 4). Second priority was given to the establishment of human rights, and third priority to guaranteeing the territorial integrity and political independence of all states, by sanctions or military force (Chapter VII) if necessary. Fourth, steps for the attainment of higher standards of living, social progress, and cultural co-operation were to be promoted (Chapters IX and X). Finally, colonialism was to be eliminated gradually through the institution of self-government on the basis of the paramount interest of the inhabitants.

These five principles were (and are) in full accord with American aspirations and could be supported without reservation. The United States therefore could, with enthusiasm, assume leadership for the achievement of these ideals. However, with the breakdown of wartime collaboration the United States was forced to shift its position and withdraw its support in many areas. Social and political pressures and financial limitations caused a reduction of United States support on human rights programs and, later, on humanitarian and social problems as well as economic development plans. The International Bill of Rights, for instance, was still under discussion in 1963, and the proposed Court was no longer even under serious consideration.

Just as the highest hopes of the United Nations in the economic and social spheres were limited partially by lack of United States leadership and active support, so also agreements in the Military Staff Committee were prevented by Soviet obstruction. The International Police Force which, according to the Charter, was to have been created to enforce Security Council decisions and to preserve collective security was abandoned. Nonetheless, through a series of makeshift arrangements, the United Nations did succeed in keeping the peace by its action in preventing any major outbreak of hostilities in Iran, Indonesia, Kashmir, Greece, and Palestine. It was in Korea that the United Nations met its first decisive challenge.

At the time of the Korean attack, the major problem confronting the United States was to achieve approval for concerted action by the United Nations despite the lack of a standing military force. The act of aggression was confirmed by a United Nations commission already in existence. Since the Soviet Union had decided to leave the Security Council, the United States was able to secure the passage of a resolution declaring North Korea the aggressor. On the basis of that resolution, the Commander of the United States forces in Japan was made the Commander in Chief of the United Nations forces in Korea.

The United Nations action in Korea seemed to indicate that a world body could successfully engage in collective action. In the days of the League, the Abyssinian conflict had dealt a severe jolt to the concept of collective security; in the United Nations era, the first action against an aggressor nation was successful.

Once again there was a coalescence of realism and idealism in United States policy. The idealistic school condemned aggression anywhere in the world as an attack on the territorial integrity and political independence of a nation, while, from a realistic viewpoint, the United States was committed to the support of South Korea for reasons of its own national interest. The sanction of the international organization permitted the United States to fight for the purposes of a concert of nations instead of being unjustly branded as waging a "colonial" war.

As an aftermath to the conflict, two questions arose. First, would the Security Council be able to act in support of the United States foreign policy in other cases of aggression if the Soviet Union were present and capable of exercising its veto power? Second, how should "aggression" be defined?

The first issue was resolved with considerable dispatch when the General Assembly in 1950 passed the "Uniting for Peace Resolution," proposed by Secretary of State Dean Acheson and John Foster Dulles. This resolution provides that any seven members of the Security Council, by a procedural vote, can take any dispute off the agenda of the Council and move it to the General Assembly. The Assembly can then make recommendations to the countries involved. Like any other proposal, this one may not always operate as its originators intended it should; it may someday work against the interests of its proponents. The "Uniting for Peace Resolution" has been used since 1950 mainly by the Soviet Union against the Western powers, as in the case of Suez and Lebanon. Nevertheless, it still retains its basic justification: In the event of an act of aggression, the Western nations can move the issue to the General Assembly and appeal for military action without the threat of Soviet veto.

The second question—"What is aggression?"—is one of the key problems in the interpretation of the Charter. A great many discussions have been held without reaching any agreement on a clearly defined statement. Therefore, we might go back to the definition of aggression accepted by the League in a Committee of the Disarmament Conference, in July, 1933, which gave the following five criteria:

(1) Declaration of war upon another State;

(2) Invasion by its armed forces, with or without a declaration of war, of the territory of another State;

(3) Attack by its land, naval or air forces, with or without a declaration of war, on the territory, vessels or aircraft of another State;

(4) Naval blockade of the coast or ports of another State;

(5) Provision of support to armed bands formed in its territory which have invaded the territory of another State, or refusal notwithstanding the request of the invaded State, to take in its own territory all the measures in its power to deprive those bands of all assistance or protection.[8]

As a definition, it must be viewed in relation to the current international situation, particularly with respect to the establishment of missile bases

---

[8] These criteria were accepted in treaties by the Soviet Union with Afghanistan, Estonia, Finland, Iran, Latvia, Poland, Romania, and Turkey.

in a third country, but it is still our most authoritative definition of aggression.

It is of importance, after the events in Suez, Lebanon, the Congo, Cuba, and Yemen, that the United States should seek agreement with other nations on the establishment of one standard for all parties acting in aggressive ways against their neighbors. Unfortunately we have at present essentially three standards: one for the Western nations who cleave to the letter and spirit of the concept of aggression; a second for the Soviet Union and the east European satellites who sometimes follow its letter but rarely its spirit; and finally, a concept for former colonial territories who feel privileged to disregard established principles and attack their neighbors without fear of counteraction by the United Nations. Examples of the latter are India's action in Goa and Indonesia's absorption of West Irian, as well as Egyptian intervention in the civil strife in Yemen.

As the United Nations activities developed, other divergencies among its member-nations became apparent. While the United States continued to stress questions of peace and security and human rights, a great number of the United Nations members—particularly from Latin America and Asia—interested themselves primarily in economic development projects for which they hoped to receive support through the creation of new financial institutions (to be financed chiefly by the United States, Great Britain, and France).

At the same time the Asian nations, under the leadership of India, emphasized questions of racial conflict and colonialism. India, in particular, in every Assembly, brought to the agenda the issue of the treatment of Indians in the Union of South Africa—even though this question does not lie clearly within the jurisdiction of an international organization and might be considered as "essentially within the domestic jurisdiction" of South Africa. Previously the issue of independence for Indonesia, at first considered to be within the realm of United Nations action, was referred back for solution to the parties concerned; in order to act it would have been necessary for the United Nations to assume that peace and security in the rest of the Far East were threatened by the Dutch-Indonesian conflict. Nevertheless, the perennial "Indian" issue in the General Assembly led to other attempts to weaken the "domestic jurisdiction" clause. Gradually colonialism and the treatment of African

33

and Asian peoples by their colonial rulers or white settlers became a major concern of the United Nations. This emphasis was strengthened when, in 1960, seventeen African nations were admitted, to be followed by more in 1961 and 1962; by 1963 the African and Asian nations comprised 50 per cent of the membership of the United Nations.

In 1960 a resolution sponsored by forty-three African and Asian nations was adopted by the General Assembly. Called the "Declaration of the Granting of Independence to Colonial Countries and Peoples," it was adopted with eighty-nine in favor, none against, and nine abstentions (Australia, Belgium, Dominican Republic, France, Portugal, Spain, Union of South Africa, United Kingdom, and the United States). The resolution affirms the right of all peoples to self-determination. It reads in part as follows:

> Immediate steps shall be taken, in Trust and Non-Self-Governing Territories or all other territories which have not yet attained independence, to transfer all powers to the peoples of those territories, without any conditions or reservations, in accordance with their freely expressed will and desire, without any distinction as to race, creed or color, in order to enable them to enjoy complete independence and freedom.[9]

The abstention of the United States signified opposition to a resolution which supported immediate—and mostly premature—independence for all countries irrespective of the state of their economic or political development. Yet for lack of a well-planned strategy, the United States, despite a long tradition of supporting self-determination and freedom for colonial territories, found itself among a small minority in apparent opposition while the Soviet Union, with widespread dominion over Asia and control over eastern Europe, could align itself with the Afro-Asian countries, Latin America, and most of Western Europe in a loud affirmation. Effective United States leadership might have forestalled the situation by initiating wide support, including the more "liberal" governments among those which abstained, for a more concrete and less ill-advised expression of determination to see all men their own masters as rapidly as possible within the framework of international order and assistance.

[9] General Assembly Resolution 1514 (XV), *Official Journal* (December 14, 1960). See also General Assembly Resolution 1654 (XVI), *Official Journal* (November 23, 1961).

Since the passing of this resolution in 1960, efforts to focus each successive General Assembly on the issue of colonialism have been successful. The Sixteenth and Sevententh Sessions, in 1961 and 1962, passed resolutions calling for the implementation of the original declaration. The 1962 resolution

> Calls upon the Administering Powers concerned to cease forthwith all armed action and repressive measures directed against peoples who have not yet attained their independence, particularly against the political activities of their rightful leaders;
>
> Urges all Administering Powers to take immediate steps in order that all colonial territories and peoples may accede to independence without delay.[10]

The transition-of-power problems of Great Britain were hauled before the United Nations, even though they were essentially questions to be solved by Great Britain and the territorial leaders, and on the whole were solved by them with some success. However, the Soviets did not miss the opportunity to champion the Afro-Asian cause, particularly in the case of Southern Rhodesia. Speaking on this issue in 1962, Platon Morozov of the Soviet Union declared that that territory must receive independence during 1962, and stated that the 1961 Constitution was "from beginning to end a racist constitution" without provision for universal suffrage or representative administration and government.[11] Coming from a Soviet envoy, such a statement is not without irony.

The United States position on colonialism—wavering between idealistic support of independence for any people and realistic support of its NATO allies, and seeking proper administrative, economic, and military preparation of the former colonies so that they will not be subject to Communist influence—has created a situation where it has at times been opposed by Africa, Asia, Latin America, and part of western Europe.

The leaders of the United States delegation to the United Nations could not have prevented a debate on the colonial issue. There is at present no way to keep an item off the agenda of the General Assembly, except by securing a majority negative vote—an unlikely occurrence,

[10] General Assembly Resolution 1810 (XVII). See *United Nations Review* (January, 1963), 91.

[11] "Assembly Considers Proposals on Southern Rhodesia," *United Nations Review* (July, 1962), 11.

given the present membership of the world body. However, in the future, the United States should attempt to seek support for the establishment of a screening committee whose duty would be to ensure that each subject discussed conforms to the letter and spirit of the Charter, i.e., that each subject is primarily a matter of peace and security and international concern, and not intervention in a domestic affair.

The United States and Western position supporting a strict interpretation of the Charter received a near-fatal blow when India decided to occupy Goa, Damão, and Diu in December, 1961. Ambassador Adlai Stevenson of the United States solemnly declared that "at this fateful hour in the life of the United Nations" the Security Council should earnestly urge India "to withdraw its armed forces from the territory it has invaded." Mr. C. S. Jha of India countered that this was a colonial question, that India was eliminating the jurisdiction of colonialism, that Goa and other Portuguese enclaves were an integral part of India, and that there could be no question of aggression against one's own "frontiers, against one's own people."[12]

Only seven countries voted in favor of condemning this act of aggression—just enough to pass the resolution had there been no Soviet veto. But the Soviet Union voted against a cease-fire and restoration of normal conditions in Goa and resumption of negotiations between Portugal and India, as did Ceylon, Liberia, and the United Arab Republic.

The Indian delegate, Mr. Jha, defending his position, stated:

> We are criticized here by various delegations which say, "Why have you used force? The Charter absolutely prohibits force"; but the Charter itself does not completely eschew force, in the sense that force can be used in self-defense, for the protection of the people of a country—and the people of Goa are as much Indians as any other people. . . .
>
> I have been misquoted by the representatives of Turkey. I have not said that we do not accept international law—we are governed by the tenets of international law—but that we cannot in the twentieth century accept that part of international law which was laid down by European jurists—though great men, great jurists whose contribution to law has been really remarkable—specifying that colonies in Asia and Africa which were acquired by conquest conferred sovereignty on the colonial power. That is no longer acceptable. International law is not a static institution. . . . Just as the process of decolonization is irreversible and irresistible,

[12] Security Council Document S/PV 988 (December 18, 1961), 53.

the embodiment of the principles in resolution 1514, which has been accepted by virtually every member around this table, is irresistible. One cannot go behind that now. This is the new dictum of international law.[13]

Ambassador Stevenson gave expression to the feelings of the majority of the Security Council members in his concluding remarks:

I believe that I am the only representative at this table who was present at the birth of this Organization. Tonight we are witnessing the first act in a drama which could end with its death. The League of Nations died, I remind you, when its members no longer resisted the use of aggressive force. So it is with a most heavy heart that I must add a word of epilogue to this fateful discussion, by far the most important in which I have participated since this Organization was founded sixteen years ago.

The failure of the Security Council to call for a cease-fire tonight in these simple circumstances is a failure of the United Nations. The veto of the Soviet Union is consistent with its long role of obstruction. But I find the attitude of some other members of the Council profoundly disturbing and ominous because we have witnessed tonight an effort to rewrite the Charter, to sanction the use of force in international relations when it suits one's own purposes. This approach can only lead to chaos.[14]

A double standard had been established. Aggression in cases such as Suez and Hungary was to be treated differently from "liberation" of territories by a former colony. India proved willing, for the sake of a few square miles, to disregard precedents and any previously accepted definition of aggression. The United States was powerless to mobilize the necessary two-thirds majority in the General Assembly to ensure Assembly action after the Soviet veto. While it might be said that on issues concerning colonialism the majority of Afro-Asian nations are willing to adhere to a double standard, the situation demonstrates also the lack of leadership of the United States and other nations who have, in the past, supported the principles of international law and order.

The degree to which United States leadership has diminished is shown by a General Assembly resolution passed on November 9, 1962, against the policy of apartheid in South Africa. This resolution, despite opposition by the United States, Great Britain, France, and even Japan, was passed by sixty-seven votes in favor and sixteen against, with twenty-three abstentions.[15] The Charter in Article 41 specifies that it is the duty

[13] *Ibid.*, 52–55.   [14] *Ibid.*, 87.

[15] Besides the United States, Great Britain, and France, the following states voted

of the Security Council to "decide what measures not involving the use of armed force are to give effect to its decisions" after it has (under Article 39) determined "the existence of any threat to the peace, breach of the peace, or act of aggression." Nevertheless, despite the Charter's clear delegation of these responsibilities to the Security Council and despite the absence of any "threat to the peace" or "aggression," the General Assembly requested member states to take the following measures: to break off diplomatic relations with the government of South Africa; to close all ports to vessels flying the South African flag; to enact legislation prohibiting the ships of each state from entering South African ports; to boycott all South African goods and to refrain from exporting goods, including all arms and ammunition, to South Africa; and to refuse landing and passage facilities to all aircraft belonging to the government and companies registered under the laws of South Africa.[16]

Obviously the General Assembly has the power only to recommend action, but resolutions passed by the majority of Afro-Asian states with Soviet connivance seem to disregard any limitations on the Assembly's authority. However much any state would like to condemn the domestic policies of South Africa's government, this question is hardly a threat to international peace and security.

As it did in the time of Presidents Theodore Roosevelt and Woodrow Wilson, the United States must assert its active leadership as a world power, not the least in the United Nations. In accordance with American traditions and ideals, United States policy should support the newly independent countries in their struggle for full and real independence. But the United States has an even greater interest in seeing that change is effected without violence, i.e., within the provisions of the Charter concerning the use of force. Any sudden dislocation of local administration, such as the events following the abrupt granting of independence to the Congo, is likely to lead to bloodshed and provide an opening for Communist intervention. Similarly, in the Cuban missile crisis, the exist-

---

negatively on the resolution: Australia, Belgium, Canada, Greece, Ireland, Japan, Luxembourg, Netherlands, New Zealand, Portugal, South Africa, Spain, and Turkey. Abstentions were Argentina, Austria, Bolivia, Brazil, Chile, Colombia, Costa Rica, Denmark, Dominican Republic, El Salvador, Finland, Guatemala, Honduras, Iceland, Italy, Nicaragua, Norway, Panama, Peru, Sweden, Thailand, Uruguay, and Venezuela.

[16] *United Nations Review* (December, 1962), 68.

ing balance of power, which the Soviet Union sought suddenly and clandestinely to alter, had to be restored to the *status quo ante* to avoid a conflict. It is in the vital interest of the United States to exert all necessary efforts to uphold international order and provide for evolutionary, not revolutionary, change.

There is general agreement in the United States on the essential function which the United Nations fulfills and on the need to overcome certain weaknesses in the United Nations caused by the sudden influx of new nations. Therefore it is to be hoped that the United States will soon re-evaluate and define, in terms of the national interest, the long-term purposes and policies of the United States in the United Nations.

This policy must be a blending of the traditional concern for world peace, and for the enjoyment of freedom and human rights by all men, tempered with a realistic appreciation of the exigencies of the current international situation. Long-term policy aims should include a redefinition of aggression to include situations peculiar to the nuclear age, as well as acceptance of certain minimum standards to designate "aggressive intentions"; renewed interest in the importance of human rights for all persons irrespective of race or color, including the rights of minority groups; and a new emphasis on economic development. The United States might also support the creation and expansion of a stand-by military force, as established by the Scandinavian nations, ready to intervene in the face of aggression. While such a force cannot deter major powers bent on aggression, it can intervene to settle or even prevent local conflicts between smaller powers.

Action should be taken immediately to ensure that the United States and other responsible nations are not in the minority when resolutions contrary to the spirit and intent of the Charter come to a vote. The first step in this direction should be an effort by the United States, as the leader of a world-wide group of free nations, to consult regularly with various groups and blocs within the United Nations, and eventually to organize a large caucusing group under United States leadership. This group should include western Europe, Latin America, the British Commonwealth, and a number of countries in Asia and Africa such as Japan, Iran, the Philippines, Turkey, Lebanon, and the Monrovia group in Africa. There is little doubt that such a group would be able to agree on common aims and policies and to exert influence in most areas under consideration.

A second step, for the purpose of preventing the abuse of the voting procedures in the United Nations, would be the reorganization of the General Committee of the General Assembly. This Committee consisted until recently of the president of the General Assembly, the chairmen of the seven main committees, thirteen elected members (vice-presidents), and the five permanent members of the Security Council. In the Eighteenth Assembly in 1963 the General Committee was enlarged by increasing the number of vice-presidents from thirteen to seventeen. At the same time the geographical distribution was made mandatory. Ten members of the Committee are to be selected from Afro-Asian states, two from eastern Europe, four from Latin America, three from western Europe, and one alternately from Latin America and western Europe. This change gives more power to the new members of Africa and Asia. The Committee could be reorganized by General Assembly resolution to grant permanent membership to all countries contributing more than 1 per cent of the budget of the United Nations plus six (or more if it seemed necessary) elected members representing the smaller nations of western Europe, Latin America, Africa, Asia, eastern Europe, and the British Commonwealth. On the basis of the 1962 scale of contributions, the Committee would be increased from twenty-one to twenty-four and would include the five permanent members of the Security Council and thirteen others eligible for continuous membership: four from western Europe (Belgium, the Netherlands, Italy, and Sweden); two each from the British Commonwealth (Australia and Canada), Latin America (Argentina and Brazil), and Asia (India and Japan); and finally, three members of the Soviet bloc (Czechoslovakia, Poland, and the Ukraine). The president of the Assembly and the chairmen of the seven main committees would automatically be representatives of countries with permanent or elected membership on the Committee. A committee composed in this manner would most likely act to ensure peaceful and orderly change, and to prevent the cluttering of the agenda with items designed mainly to gain domestic support for some specific delegation.

It seems clear that in a rapidly shrinking world which contains an increasing number of national units and potential problem areas, the United Nations has become an instrument essential to the interests of the United States. These interests can be advanced through consistent efforts in bilateral and regional diplomacy, combined with global parliamentary diplomacy in the United Nations. United States aims and purposes should be regularly proclaimed, and every effort should be made to attract friendly and neutral nations to their support.

But however important the formulation of purpose, the execution of strategy, and the mustering of support, these are not the only dynamics of leadership. The essence of leadership goes beyond. The leader in world affairs today must have the self-confidence born of knowing that his own purposes and intentions are those which will attract support across the globe.

Consider the highlights of United States policy and strategy in the postwar era: the Marshall Plan, the Point Four program, the decision to fight in Korea, the Open Skies proposal, the offer to pool atomic resources for peaceful purposes. Not all these plans were entirely successful, but all are examples of inspirational leadership based on confidence of purpose. In spite of all Soviet counterefforts, these policies were widely hailed as the fulfillment of a peculiarly American mission. To find and to project this confidence and this purpose is the great challenge to United States leadership in the United Nations.

CHAPTER III

Nationalism in the United Nations

BY HANS KOHN

~~~~✿☆~~~~✿☆~~~~✿☆~~~~✿☆~~~~✿☆~~~~✿☆~~~~✿

NATIONAL SELF-DETERMINATION has always been an issue in the United Nations,[1] no matter whether it is inscribed in the agenda under that title or under some other, such as colonialism, information from non-self-governing territories, or trusteeship. The concept itself is Western. The Communists, however, sometimes appear to understand better than the West its uses in the protracted conflict within the United Nations. It is not easy for the United States to solve the dilemma of having positive sympathy with the forces caring for man's freedom and dignity, and at the same time to marshal forces against Communist threats and subversion. However, there is hardly any alternative for the United States but to associate American interests with the aspirations of the majority of mankind.

The twentieth century has so far been characterized by the world-wide spread of nationalism as a dominant force. It made itself felt after 1918 in the peace settlements in central eastern Europe, and consequently in the League of Nations. Since 1918 the impact of nationalism has widened geographically to an extent unforeseen even in 1918. Na-

[1] Article 1 makes a specific reference to the principle of "self-determination." It states that one of the principles of the United Nations is "to develop friendly relations among nations based on respect for the principle of equal rights and self-determination of peoples and to take other appropriate measures to strengthen peace." Article 55 reiterates that "conditions of stability and well-being . . . are necessary for peaceful and friendly relations among nations and based on respect for the principle of equal rights and self-determination of peoples."

The two Draft Covenants on Human Rights adopted by the Third Committee of the General Assembly in 1955 expanded the principle of "self-determination" by stating that "all peoples have the right of self-determination. By virtue of this right they freely determine their political status and freely pursue their economic, social, and cultural development." See General Assembly Resolution A/3077 (November 29, 1955), for the full text.

tional aspirations and demands for self-determination are playing an even more important role in the United Nations than in the League of Nations.[2]

Historical Aspects of the Concept of National Self-Determination and Its Development in Europe

The future historian may very likely regard as the greatest "revolution" of the twentieth century not Lenin's overthrow of the short-lived Kerensky regime in Russia in November, 1917, but the less conspicuous—in this case there were not ten days or even ten years that shook the world—and yet more far-reaching process which brought Europe's four-hundred-year-old dominion of the globe to an end, but at the same time spread the Western principle of self-determination and nationalism to the most distant corners of the earth.

It is easily understandable that such a tremendous change which progresses with bewildering rapidity produces many serious strains, and demands powerful reappraisals and readjustments. The shift of gravity takes place simultaneously at several levels. In the Western world the political and economic power center has been transferred from western Europe to North America. In the non-Communist world as a whole the influence of Asian and African nations, many of whom did not exist a few years ago, is growing. Even in the totalitarian world of Communism the Asian partner, China, has been asserting a growing role, first shown in Chou En-lai's visit in 1956 to Warsaw, Budapest, and Moscow to help settle conflicts among European Communists.

National self-determination is an inherent part of the modern Western tradition which started with the American and French revolutions in the late eighteenth century. From the beginning the Americans saw in the Declaration of Independence a model for all peoples. On June 24, 1826, half a century after the Declaration and ten days before his death, Jefferson wrote referring to the Declaration: "May it be to the World, what I believe it will be (to some parts sooner, to others later, but finally to all) the signal of arousing men to burst the chains under which monkish ignorance and superstition had pursuaded them to bind them-

[2] The total membership in the League of Nations reached the highest number of 60 in 1934. The United Nations was founded with its original membership of 51 states in 1945; its membership increased to 104 in 1962 and to 113 in 1963.

selves, and to assume the blessings and security of self-government." Some years later, by 1848, the time had come for the spread of the theory of national self-determination to central Europe.

Public opinion in the English-speaking countries supported this trend. It endorsed Mazzini, Garibaldi, and Kossuth; it favored Greeks and Poles. Pasquale Stanislao Mancini, one of the great Italian jurists of the nineteenth century and, later, minister of justice and then of foreign affairs of united Italy, delivered at Turin in 1851 his famous lecture *"Della nazionalità come fondamento del diritto delle gente"* ("On Nationality as the Foundation of International Laws"). There he declared with words clearly intended against Austria that a state in which several nationalities found themselves forced into a union was not a political body but a monster incapable of life. "The nationalities," he said, "which do not possess a government issuing from their inmost life (*governo uscito dalle proprie viscere*), and which are subject to laws which are imposed upon them from the outside—are used for the purposes of others and, therefore, mere objects." In those words, Mancini justified the ethos of national self-determination by linking it with the teaching of Locke, Rousseau, and Kant, with the Declaration of Independence and the Declaration of the Rights of Men.

As World War I dragged on and as its character changed after the Russian Revolution of March, 1917, and the entry of the United States into the war a month later, the rights of nationality and of national self-determination became one of the principles for which the Allies avowedly fought. Lloyd George declared on January 5, 1918, that "a territorial settlement—based on the right of self-determination or the consent of the governed" was one of the three fundamental conditions of a permanent peace. In the same month President Woodrow Wilson declared: "An evident principle runs through the whole program I have outlined. It is the principle of justice to all peoples and nationalities, and their right to live on equal terms of liberty and safety with one another, whether they be strong or weak. Unless this principle be made its foundation no part of the structure of international justice can stand." In that way the Allied war aims in the last stage of the war took up, and tried to fulfill, the goal of the European "Spring of the Peoples" of 1848. The United States under Woodrow Wilson led the effort to make national self-determination one of the fundamental principles of international law. From Woodrow Wilson down to the present, the United

States, more than any other great power in history, has believed in and tried to bring about self-determination for all peoples.

National Self-Determination and Colonialism

It was Edmund Burke who in the second half of the eighteenth century insisted that the government of dependent territories, especially of those inhabited by less developed populations, was a sacred trust in which the interests of the native population had to be primarily considered. From Burke on, this concept dominated much of British and American thought until it found its expression in the League of Nations and in the United Nations. The trusteeship idea, long before it was put down in legal terms, provided the rationale for British rule in India. Moritz Julius Bonn in his article on "Imperialism" in the *Encyclopedia of the Social Sciences* summed up the reasoning about the connection between modern Western civilization at home and self-government in territories, where the West penetrated:

> The natives were . . . taught to believe that penetration and permeation of the alien European civilization were essential to their well-being and might lead ultimately to self-government. The growth in England of liberal ideas of justice and economy and the development of democratic institutions made such alien rule appear irrational to rulers as well as ruled, and it was philosophically justified only as a sort of temporary control at the end of which stood independence and partnership.[3]

In this spirit Macaulay introduced the Government of India Bill in the House of Commons in 1833:

> We are told that the time can never come when the natives of India can be admitted to high civil and military office. We are told that we are bound to confer on our subjects every benefit—which we can confer on them without hazard to our own domination. Against this proposition I solemnly protest as inconsistent alike with sound policy and sound morality . . . . It may be that [the] public mind of India may expand under our system till it has outgrown that system—that, having become instructed in European knowledge, they may, in some future age, demand European institutions. Whether such a day will ever come, I know not. But never will I attempt to avert or retard it. Whenever it comes, it will be the proudest day in English history.

[3] Quoted from the *Encyclopedia of the Social Sciences* (New York, The Macmillan Co., 1932), 609.

The liberal British ideas of trusteeship and self-government applied to colonial territories determined also United States policy after 1898. The United States regarded itself as trustee for the people of under-developed areas temporarily under its control. In his first annual message to Congress at the end of 1913, Woodrow Wilson said of the Philippines: "We must hold steadily in view their ultimate independence, and we must move towards the time of that indepencence as steadily as the way can be cleared and the foundations thoughtfully and permanently laid." In the Jones Act of 1916, Congress asserted that "it is, as it has always been, the purpose of the people of the United States to withdraw their sovereignty over the Philippine Islands and to recognize their independence as soon as stable government can be established therein." Thus the two great democracies of the West laid the foundations for a conscious and evolutionary growth of self-determination and political liberty throughout the politically and economically dependent or under-developed parts of mankind.

At the beginning of the twentieth century Woodrow Wilson predicted the course of this policy of self-determination in the article "Democracy and Efficiency" in which he wrote: "The East is to be opened and transformed [and] whether we will or no; the standards of the West are to be imposed upon it; nations and peoples which have stood still the centuries through are to be quickened, and made part of the universal World of commerce and of ideas which has so steadily been a-making by the advance of European power from age to age. It is our peculiar duty, as it is also England's, to moderate the process in the interests of liberty," and to secure to the peoples thus driven out on the road of change, "the free intercourse and the natural development which will make them equal members of the family of nations."[4] The family of nations within which this transition could be achieved in an orderly way was organized under Wilsonian inspiration in the League of Nations first, and then in the United Nations.

The Spread of National
Self-Determination in Asia and Africa

What World War I, under American leadership, did for establishing the principle of national self-determination for central and east central

---

[4] *Selected Literary and Political Papers and Addresses of Woodrow Wilson* (New York, Grosset and Dunlap, 1926), I, 132–33.

Europe, World War II did for Asia and Africa. In east central Europe itself national socialist and later Communist action—originally in co-operation in 1939–41—destroyed the principle and reality of national self-determination, either by abolishing it entirely or by imposing upon the various nationalities forms of government and political ideology alien and often abhorrent to those nationalities. On the other hand, the principle of self-determination in Asia and Africa was helped by being proclaimed as one of the goals of Anglo-American policy in the Atlantic Charter, signed by Franklin D. Roosevelt and Winston Churchill in August, 1941.[5] The effect of the Charter remained great, even though its application was not clearly defined.

More influential in accelerating the movement for national self-determination in Asia and Africa than the policy statements of Western leaders were the quick and total collapse of French resistance to German aggression and the Japanese conquest and "liberation" of European colonial possessions in the Far East. These events profoundly changed the attitudes of the Asian and African masses. The war, started by European (German and Soviet) power ambitions and by Japanese imperialism, roused the peoples outside Europe out of lethargic acceptance of their status. Soviet propaganda had little to do with it. The transformation was the work of Western influence and of examples, good and bad, set by the West. After 1945 the European empires, although they did not always recognize it, lacked the power to enforce a resumption of the old status.

In this changed situation a return to pre-1939 "normalcy" was unthinkable. The United States understood it well. In spite of suggestions that the date of granting full independence to the Philippines should be reconsidered as a consequence of the ravages of war and the co-operation of prominent Filipinos with the Japanese, the United States kept its promise and the islands became independent on July 4, 1946. Nor did Britain, in her liberal and realistic wisdom, attempt to restore her valuable and renowned Asian empire, India. From 1947 on, she brought to fulfillment the work of true liberation which she had started throughout the empire before World War I. The former British India is one of the few new nations in which, thanks to British policy and in spite of great difficulties presented by differences of race, language, religion, and caste,

[5] For the text of the Atlantic Charter, see the *Year Book of the United Nations, 1946–47* (New York, United Nations, 1947), 2.

parliamentary democracy has worked on the whole well and the democratic spirit of moderation continues to prevail. The other leading western European power, France, however, smarting under her humiliation in World War II, sought to restore her old imperial glory. Britain was held responsible for France's "loss" of Syria and Lebanon, and American economic imperialism or naïve innocence, or perhaps a combination of both, were suspected of having abetted the national liberation movements in Indochina and North Africa. Yet France was able to fight her wars in Indochina and Algeria only with the help of American arms and money.[6] Africa south of the Sahara seemed not to present an immediate problem of national self-determination in the late 1940's or even in the early 1950's. Britain again took the lead in the Gold Coast, which became the independent nation of Ghana. The question of national self-determination has since loomed larger and larger in the United Nations.

The Ambiguities of National Self-Determination

The ambiguities of national self-determination arise out of the manner in which it is interpreted and applied in international relations. With the growth of national self-determination, as seen above, the problem has become more and more an issue in the Cold War. The Soviet conception of national self-determination may be traced back to Lenin.

In 1918 the United States was not alone in appealing to and for national self-determination. On the eve of the October 1917 revolution Lenin, understanding the trends of the time, embraced and proclaimed the principle of national self-determination, even though it glaringly contradicted all the doctrinal and organizational principles of Communism.[7] Lenin intended his appeal to the principle of national self-

[6] See the text of the Joint United States–French Communiqué dated September 30, 1953, in *U.S. Dept. of State Bulletin*, Vol. XXIX, No. 746 (October 12, 1953), 486.

[7] Writing the draft of the "Programme of the Russian Social-Democratic Labour Party" (Revised Draft) in May, 1917, Lenin proclaimed that "the constitution of the democratic republic of Russia must ensure . . . the right of all nationalities which are now part of the Russian State freely to separate and to form independent states." Earlier, announcing the platform of a proletariat party under the title "The Tasks of the Proletariat in Our Revolution," Lenin declared: "As regards the national question, the proletariat party must, first of all, insist on the promulgation and immediate realization of full freedom of separation from Russia for all nations and peoples who are oppressed by tsarism, who were forcibly included or forcibly retained within the boundaries of the state, i.e., annexed." V. I. Lenin, *Collected Works* (New York, 1929), XX, Bk. 1, 143–44, 337–38.

determination as a tactical move to win the co-operation first of the non-Russian nationalities in the Russian Empire which he restored on a new basis, and then of peoples outside the Empire.[8] From the beginning his attention was directed toward Asia. Even before 1914 he had noted and understood the importance of the new nationalist movements, over-looked by most Western statesmen.[9] For the Communists, the meaning of the term "national self-determination" had as little in common with Western usage as is the case with other terms like "peace," "democracy," or "liberty." Communist practice could not, nor did it ever, recognize self-determination, whether for individuals or for groups. To Communists, persons and nationalities alike were not ends in themselves but instruments to be used in various and opportunist ways for the ultimate goal, the realization of the Marxist-Leninist goals throughout world-wide society. In his "The Law of the Soviet State," Andrei Vyshinsky reiterated the "equality of rights of all nationalities," and the "inalienable right of nations to self-determination, including the right of withdrawal,"[10] a theoretical right guaranteed the nationalities of the Soviet Empire in the Constitution yet never realizable in a system clearly con-

[8] For example, in a speech on the "National Question," on May 12, 1917, Lenin clearly shows duplicity of approach to the question of "separation." Referring to the Polish Social-Democrats advocating "internationalism," Lenin spoke: "Why should we Great Russians, who have been oppressing a greater number of nations than other people, why should we repudiate the right of separation for Poland, the Ukraine, Finland? We are asked to become Chauvinists, because by doing that we would render the position of Social-Democrats in Poland less difficult. We make no pretense at seeking to liberate Poland, because the Polish people dwell between two states capable of fighting. But instead of teaching the Polish workers that chauvinists have no place in the Socialist Party and that only those Social-Democrats are real democrats who maintain that the Polish people ought to be free, the Polish Social-Democrats argue that just because they find the Union with Russian workers advantageous they are opposed to Poland's separation. They have a perfect right to do so. But these people fail to understand that to enhance internationalism it is not at all necessary to *reiterate the same words.* In Russia we must stress the right of separation for the subject nations, while in Poland we must stress the right of such nations to unite. The right to unite implies the right to separate. *We Russians must emphasize the right to separate, while the Poles must emphasize the right to unite.*" (Italics added.) *Ibid.,* 312–13.

[9] See Lenin's articles "Inflammable Material in World Politics" written in August (July), 1908; "Democracy and Narodism in China," written in July, 1912; and "Regenerated China" written in November, 1912. *Ibid.,* IV, 297–313.

[10] See Andrei Vyshinsky, *The Law of the Soviet States* (New York, The Macmillan Co., 1951), 213–19.

trolled from the center of world Communism and where all actions were to be judged from the point of view of world Communism alone.

The American version of national self-determination may be retraced to the Wilsonian dictum, when in his address before the League to Enforce Peace in May, 1916, President Wilson declared "that every people has a right to choose the sovereignty under which they shall live." Even though national self-determination was found, soon after, to be incapable of universal application, it nevertheless constituted "a magnificent gospel." When Wilson spoke of national self-determination, he had in mind primarily those territories in central and eastern Europe which had long been under the domination of the Austro-Hungarian and Russian empires.

The principle has gained wider emphasis and acceptance in the last half-century. While the Covenant of the League of Nations did not mention the phrase "national self-determination" at all, the Charter of the United Nations, based on drafts submitted by the United States, mentions it twice.[11] The Charter also develops the principle of self-determination in Chapter XI, which sets forth a very broad concept regarding non-self-governing territories and imposes upon member nations the duty "to develop self-government, to take due account of the political aspirations of the peoples, and to assist them in the progressive development of their free political institutions." In Article 76 the Charter proclaims the desirability of "independence" in accordance with "the freely expressed wishes of the peoples concerned."

Yet the United Nations does not insist on independence; it does insist on self-government. Independence of small or nonviable entities may defeat its purpose. The principle of true federation on the basis of real equality is in some cases more promising than that of national independence. National independence is not an essential element in the democratic tradition; self-government is.

Even with such a limited definition, the term "self-determination" is subject to much ambiguity. In 1955, when considering the recommendations of the Commission on Human Rights, the Economic and Social Council recommended that the Assembly establish an *ad hoc* commission on self-determination, consisting of five persons to be appointed by the secretary-general, to conduct a thorough study of the concept of self-

[11] See footnote 1 of this chapter.

determination.[12] The terms of reference of the commission were to include examination of the concept of peoples and nations; the essential attributes and the applicability of the principle of equal rights and of self-determination and other Charter principles; and finally, the economic, social, and cultural conditions under which the application of the principle is facilitated.

Consideration of the Economic and Social Council's recommendation was postponed at the Assembly's Tenth, Eleventh, and Twelfth Sessions, in 1955, 1956, and 1957, respectively. Finally, on November 28, 1958, the Third Committee, after much deliberation, rejected the proposal of the Economic and Social Council by a roll-call vote of forty-eight to sixteen, with eight abstentions.[13]

The principle of national self-determination, although not precisely defined, forms a large part of mid-twentieth century thought and politics. It is ambiguous in its meaning as well as in regard to its implementation. However, the principle of national self-determination has nothing to do with race, as some speakers often imply. It was first invoked by "white" peoples against "white" peoples in Europe and America— the Anglo-Americans and the Latin-Americans, the Irish and the Poles, the Italians and the Norwegians, the Baltic and the Balkan peoples, the Finns and the Ukrainians, and many others—and later on with changing historical circumstances by Germans and Hungarians. In the twentieth century "colored" peoples, following Western examples, appealed to the principle of self-determination against white domination in Asia and Africa. Today Ukrainians, Latvians, or Estonians might invoke it against the Soviet Union if they could voice freely their desires. In the last few years, demands for self-determination have been voiced by "colored" peoples finding themselves in a minority position in the newly created Asian states—by the Pathans in Pakistan, the Nagas in India, the Moluccans in Indonesia. As the territorial settlements of 1919, based on the principle of national self-determination, gave rise to new demands based on the same principle, so did the settlements after World War II. The United States is entirely sympathetic with the demands of self-determination by all peoples. It has not only championed the principle and insisted on its inscription in the Charter, but it also has always

[12] Economic and Social Council Resolution 586D (XX) (July 29, 1955).

[13] United Nations Document A/C3/L/703 (November 23, 1958).

wanted "to see it applied wherever feasible to well defined groups of people just as soon as they are capable of determining their own destiny and can do so without bringing undue injury to others."[14]

National Self-Determination in the United Nations

The United Nations and the United States, in view of their origins and acknowledged principles, have always favored national self-determination. But in a world situation of great tension and conflicting vital interests no principle can ever be fully applied. Here the Communists had an easier stand: they invoked the principle of self-determination to the fullest when it suited their tactical or strategic goals and as fully and simply denied it when it interfered with their goals, as in the case of Hungary or Tibet.[15] The United States, on the other hand, had to take into consideration not only what some of its allies, rightly or wrongly, regarded as their needs or rights but also the future of the dependent peoples themselves, whose own security and well-being might be endangered by too sudden a change in status. The United States had not only to meet the pressure of certain groups within itself—a situation unknown to countries less democratic or less heterogeneous than the United States—but occasionally had to make choices antagonizing some, though never the majority, of its NATO allies.[16]

Yet it would be a mistake to conclude from this situation that the

[14] Robert Murphy, "The Principle of Self-Determination in International Relations," *U.S. Dept. of State Bulletin*, Vol. XXXII, No. 857, (November 28, 1955), 891.

[15] Similarly, the Soviet Union has expressed a highly selective notion of "self-determination" when it comes to implementing the "right of self-determination" as laid down in Article 1 of the Draft Covenants on Human Rights. The Soviet delegate has always insisted "that the implementation of the provisions of the Covenant on Human Rights falls within the domestic jurisdiction of States." See General Assembly Official Records, Fifth Session, Doc. A/1576, Annexes, Agenda item 63 (December 1, 1950), 35.

[16] For example, the United States (and the Soviet Union's) affirmative vote on an Afro-Asian draft resolution in the Security Council on March 15, 1961, requesting the appointment of an investigating subcommittee on "The Situation in Angola," was cast against Portugal, a member of the NATO alliance. The draft resolution failed to be adopted in the Security Council, but in the General Assembly on April 20, 1961, the United States supported a similar resolution which was adopted by an overwhelming majority of seventy-three to 2, with nine abstentions. On June 30, 1961, Salazar accused the United States of siding with the Soviet Union for political purposes over Angola and said that it was, therefore, pursuing a policy that was not in accord with the objectives of the North Atlantic Treaty.

Soviet Union has been able to carry the assent of the peoples or governments of formerly dependent territories in the United Nations. The Soviet Union has failed to do so in all concrete issues—Greece, Korea, Palestine, Hungary, and the Congo. It was then recognized that the United States was the true champion of self-determination, whereas the Russians or Chinese tried to force people to accept Communism and thereby to be subject to their leadership. In all these issues the Soviet Union remained in a minority, except in the question of Palestine, including the Israeli-Franco-British aggression against Egypt in 1956. In that case the Soviet Union was not in a minority because it shared or accepted the position taken by the United States and by the overwhelming majority of the members of the United Nations.

Only in one case, when the General Assembly debated a general principle and the United States was too scrupulous to agree to generalities which could not be concretely applied in all cases, was the United States in a minority. In the discussion of a draft resolution on self-government, Mrs. Eleanor Roosevelt, representing the United States, declared on December 16, 1952, that "the United States government and the American people believe whole-heartedly in the principle of self-determination of peoples and nations, and they believe that the right of self-determination should be exercised by the peoples of all territories, according to the particular circumstances of each territory and the freely expressed wishes of the peoples concerned."[17] The United States delegation had, however, justified reservations concerning the practical applicability of the principle to sparsely populated or strategically important small areas, and to its new extension to economic national "rights." Accordingly, it voted against the draft resolution on self-government which was, nevertheless, adopted by the, at that time, predominantly "white" and Western Assembly by a vote of forty to fourteen.[18] Most of the Latin-American and Asian nations, including Nationalist China, voted for the resolution; six nations—Ecuador, Israel, Nicaragua, Paraguay, Thailand, and Turkey—abstained.

A concrete example which proved that the United States when championing self-determination received the co-operation of the majority of the United Nations—irrespective of "white" or "colored," of NATO membership or former dependent status—was supplied by

[17] *U.S. Dept. of State Bulletin*, Vol. XXVII, No. 705 (December 29, 1952), 1043.
[18] General Assembly Resolution 637A (VII) (December 16, 1952).

the discussion on Puerto Rico. Its status as a United States dependency had long been a cause of complaint in Latin America. Now this status was changed, and even though Puerto Rico was far from achieving independence, the autonomy granted was large enough to secure the consent of the governed. The new Puerto Rican constitution was worked out by a freely elected Puerto Rican legislature and adopted by a free Puerto Rican plebiscite. It represented, in the eyes of most Puerto Ricans, an adequate and acceptable solution according to the principle of national self-determination. The General Assembly of 1953 recognized that the people of Puerto Rico had attained a new constitutional status by democratic means, that the association between the Commonwealth of Puerto Rico and the United States had been established on the basis of mutual agreement, and that the Puerto Ricans had effectively exercised their right to self-determination. Thus the Assembly ruled that, "Due to these circumstances the declaration regarding non-self-governing territories and the provisions established under it in Chapter XI of the Charter can no longer be applied to the Commonwealth of Puerto Rico."[19] The United Nations Assembly was informed on November 27, 1953, by the United States representative, on the authority of President Eisenhower, that if at any time the Puerto Rican legislature adopted a resolution in favor of complete independence, the President would immediately recommend to Congress that such independence be granted and would welcome an independent Puerto Rico as a member of the Organization of American States and the United Nations.[20]

The vote which was taken on the same day revealed the fluidity of the blocs. The United States resolution was adopted by twenty-six votes to sixteen, with eighteen abstentions. Besides the United States most Latin-American countries voted in favor, as did several Asian states, among them Iran, Thailand, and Turkey. The Communist nations voted against the resolution. They were joined not only by India and Indonesia but also by the Union of South Africa, Australia, Belgium, Canada, and Mexico. Most of the European NATO nations did not vote for the United States but abstained. Among these were Great Britain, Denmark, other Scandinavian nations, and France. They were joined by Egypt, Lebanon, New Zealand, Pakistan, Saudi Arabia, and Syria. With a similar distribution of votes, the Fourth Committee, upon

[19] See General Assembly Resolution 748 (VIII) (November 27, 1953).

[20] See *U.S. Dept. of State Bulletin*, Vol. XXIX, No. 755 (December 14, 1953), 841.

American insistence, had rejected on September 30 and on October 26 requests for an oral hearing of the Puerto Rican Independence Party and the Nationalist Party of Puerto Rico.[21] Thus, though only with a small majority and without support of most NATO partners, the American point of view regarding the changed status of Puerto Rico prevailed.

Similar recognition was given by the Assembly in 1954 to the changed status of Greenland, which was accepted as a fully self-governing part of Denmark. Hermod Lannung, the Danish representative, stressed in the Fourth Committee on November 15, 1952, that "the fundamental factor should be the freely expressed will of the people. If the people of a territory and the administrating power both thought that the people had obtained a full measure of self-government as provided in Chapter XI of the Charter, the United Nations should obviously not place any obstacles in their way."[22] The General Assembly supported the Danish point of view, but the Chilean representative felt the need to warn his Danish colleague as follows: "This attitude of my delegation towards the Danish government and the people of Greenland is in no way a precedent for the future. On the contrary, we shall become increasingly cautious with regard to the rights of peoples still living under colonial system, which the inter-American system has outlawed for ever and which we in particular will combat within our hemisphere."

On December 20, 1952, the General Assembly passed a resolution approving the cessation of the transmission by the Netherlands of the information required for dependent areas in respect of Surinam and the Netherlands Antilles. The resolution was passed by fifty-five votes to none, with four abstentions. Even the Indonesian delegate voted in favor of it. In 1955 the Assembly recognized that, under the new constitutional status, Surinam and the Netherlands Antilles had become equal partners with the Netherlands as a result of a freely expressed approval by freely elected representative bodies. Thus, the United Nations, whether in the Western or Eastern Hemisphere, did not interpret national self-determination in a narrow sense as independence but as the attainment of a status of self-government and equality in conformity

[21] See *Year Book of the United Nations, 1953* (New York, United Nations, 1954), 535–36.

[22] General Assembly Official Records, Seventh Session, Fourth Committee (275th Meeting) (November 15, 1952), 173.

with the freely expressed wishes of the peoples involved. The United Nations generally followed the mediating lead of the United States. The Trusteeship Council not only achieved improvements in the conditions of the indigenous peoples; with active United States guidance, it slowly created an atmosphere in which the representatives of governments administering trust territories and of those not administering such territories learned to work together and to begin to appreciate each other's points of view and intentions.

Revolutionary Nationalism and the United Nations

The participation of the new Asian and African nations in the United Nations has certainly created difficulties for the Western nations; but, seen in a long-range perspective, it is working out to the West's advantage. The spirit and the procedures of the United Nations have been shaped by Western democratic traditions. Representatives of peoples to whom these traditions have been alien are becoming familiar with them in the discussions of the United Nations and its various agencies. Even the Communists have to adapt themselves in the United Nations, at least formally, to the ways of argumentation used in parliamentary bodies. The Fascist powers, Germany, Japan, and Italy, refused a similar adaptation before World War II and left the League of Nations with all signs of contempt and derision. The Communists, even though they are always in danger of finding themselves in a minority, frequently mustering only four or five additional votes to their own eleven, stay in the United Nations, if perhaps for no other reason than that they understand its value as an international forum. The United Nations is not a superstate nor an international legislative body. At the present stage of world development such a world state with legislative and executive functions would be unacceptable everywhere, and certainly to Congress and the people of the United States. And yet it would be a mistake to underestimate the educational value of the United Nations toward the formation of world opinion and a more civilized behavior on the part of those governments which have to present and defend their points of view before it.

The thinking of most Asians and Africans is obviously still swayed by psychological and emotional reactions to the recent past, by indiscriminate anti-colonial slogans, and by lack of historical perspective. But formerly "oppressed" European peoples show the same attitude of mind, and for many decades Americans, conscious of their own revolution, glorified the struggle for independence as a "liberation" from oppression. In view of this general human attitude in the age of nationalism it is rather remarkable that such men as Habib Bourguiba in Tunisia, Nehru in Asia, and the leaders of most of French-speaking Africa have shown a loyal understanding of the liberal Western tradition in which they were brought up during colonial rule, and of this tradition's contribution to the newly won freedom of their countries.

The tensions and misunderstandings between the United States and other nations are not confined to Asia and Africa. The Canadians, who have more in common with the United States in background and political, social, and economic attitudes than any other people, show similar and growing apprehensions. In 1958 a leading Canadian journalist wrote in *Foreign Affairs* that, even though the American threat to Canada's independence was not primarily military, "in the last century every weapon of diplomacy and commercial pressure was used by Washington against the infant Canadian nation; and it early became a deep-rooted instinct in Canadians to avoid close commercial dependence on the United States for fear of its leading to political dominance."[23]

Revolutionary nationalism, suffused with socio-economic appeals to downtrodden masses, came into power first not in Asia but in Mexico in 1910. Bitter anticapitalist and anti-imperialist resentments, directed especially against the United States, led to great unrest and to the rule of the generals from 1913 to 1946, then to the seizure of large agricultural holdings and foreign oil property and to antireligious legislation, and finally to open sympathy with Germany in World War I. In 1934, General Lazaro Cardenas radicalized the revolution. Under the slogan "Mexico for the Mexicans" economic independence was to be achieved. The masses were swayed by the slogans of Marxist class struggle. Vincente Lombardo Toledano formed his Confederation of Mexican Workers, extreme leftist in complexion. Communism gained hold of Mexican intellectuals and artists. Yet a wise and conciliatory policy on the part of the United States changed the picture. During World War II, Mexico collaborated with the "colossus of the north." Revolution was turned into reform, although many of its outward trappings remained, down to the name of the Party of the Institutionalized Revolu-

[23] Michael Barkway, "Canada Rediscovers Its History," *Foreign Affairs* (April, 1958), 414.

tion. Mexico is a one-party state, but the party is broadly based. A strong middle class is emerging in the country. An originally violent anti-imperialist and anti–United States nationalism has proved a safeguard against Communism.

Such was not the case in China. There the leader of the Nationalist revolution, Sun Yat-sen, turned to Moscow for support after he failed to receive such aid from the United States. Before his death in 1925 he publicly expressed, in what may be regarded as his testament to Nationalist China, his hope that the Chinese would fully co-operate with Leninist Russia in a common struggle for the liberation of mankind from imperialism. The understanding shown by the Hoover and Roosevelt administrations for the Mexican revolution was not always given to similar movements in Asia and Africa.

In the Cold War atmosphere which developed in the 1950's, the United States seemed too often to regard other lands as strategic real estate instead of considering the people living there, their problems and their needs. This may not be a true interpretation of American intentions, but peoples in the underdeveloped countries who have been accustomed for decades to being told what to do and to being used for the ends of foreigners are suspicious and hypersensitive.

This is especially the case with the Arab peoples, in view of their experiences from 1918 on. The Arabs regard, rightly or wrongly, Gamal Abdul Nasser as the first man to hold out a promise of a life of greater human dignity and free from foreign interference. Arab nationalism, which is only part of a general movement sweeping Asia, Africa, and Latin America—a movement fundamentally for national self-determination—long predated Nassar, who is its present symbol. In February, 1955, Israeli armed forces, with superior equipment, attacked Egyptian positions in the Gaza Strip and caused many casualties. The United Nations Security Council unanimously condemned Israel as it has done on previous occasions. But when Egypt wished to re-equip her army, she turned in vain to the United States and Great Britain. Rebuffed by the West, Egypt acquired arms from Communist lands. The growing strength of Arab nationalism induced Israel, France, and Britain to attack Egypt in the fall of 1956 to overthrow Nasser.

The overwhelming majority of the United Nations, including most European and American nations, opposed this aggression in November, 1956. The United States sided with the majority, though not out of sympathy for Egypt, which was even refused help to deal with the war damages. American action was motivated by considerations for the Western position in Asia and Africa and by a realistic estimate of the consequences of the invasion. Desmond Stewart, an English expert on the Middle East, wrote from Beirut in the March, 1958, *Encounter*, the British organ of the anti-Communist Congress for Cultural Freedom:

> There are those who now argue that the Egyptian collapse was imminent, and that Eden's greatest error was not to go on. . . . One can only have an opinion, and mine is that if the Canal Zone had been successfully occupied, Egypt would have continued to fight; if the Delta had been occupied, and the Nile Valley, then the arms already issued to the "army of liberation" would have been in an underground war far more bloody and far better organized than the war in Algeria, in which the Egyptians would have been actively supported by help from outside, and inspired by the sympathy of all Asia and Africa. . . . A Suez venture continued would have been ten times more a disaster than Suez abandoned.

Militarily, Nasser's armed forces had been defeated. Yet in Arab eyes his resistance was a major victory. The masses might overrate Egypt's strength and believe the boastful nonsense spread by the Egyptian radio. The educated Arabs knew that Egypt was a poor country, unable to stand up in open battle to trained and highly skilled Western armies. "But at Port Said a weak country refused to be weak; a people with no modern tradition of military glory fought on, and refused to surrender; a people whose government had been frequently changed on the orders of foreigners did not obey the implicit order to overthrow Nasser." The Egyptians were determined to continue to fight; so at least it appeared to public opinion in Asian and African lands. A new pride in being Arab was born. The aggression of Israel and of the colonial powers did more for Nasser's prestige than anything he did on his own.

The Blocs and National Self-Determination

It would be contrary to the principles of a democratic order to assume that any one state or group of states—so-called blocs—participating in an international organization are entitled to control it. Like every democratic institution, developed under the modern Western tradition, the United Nations constitutes a parliamentary body in which various members, blocs, and pressure groups try to exercise their influence to win their point or to arrive at some acceptable compromise. As Asian and African nations received a better representation in the United Nations, some Western spokesmen expressed concern over the influence of an Afro-Asian bloc. Naturally the Western powers did not complain about a Western bloc nor the Communist countries about a Soviet bloc. Groupings of common interest are a democratic phenomenon. With the exception of the Communist bloc, the blocs in the United Nations do not exist as rigid formations. The Soviet bloc is in a permanent and, for it, painful minority position. The Western bloc, the Latin-American bloc, and the Afro-Asian bloc are fluid groups. In various matters they co-operate. Their members vote freely (in spite of frequent pressures from within and without the bloc) according to their interests and convictions. The United States can be well satisfied with the influence which it exercises in the United Nations. It does not always succeed in getting everything it wants, but that is impossible in any democratic organization. No one should always "win."

The important votes on issues on which the United States and the Soviet Union disagreed during the four sessions of the Assembly of the United Nations from 1957 to 1960, when the number of Afro-Asian members was steadily growing, showed the strength of the United States position and at the same time the extreme fluidity of the non-Communist blocs. In 1957 the Assembly voted in favor of the United States demand to postpone a debate on the admission of Communist China by forty-seven to twenty-seven votes, with seven abstentions. The nine Communist votes were naturally cast against postponement. But Denmark, Ireland, Norway, and Sweden voted also against postponement. Among the seven abstentions were Israel and Portugal. Iraq, Jordan, Lebanon, Libya, and Malaya voted with the United States.[24] Two years later, in 1959, the same issue was put before the Assembly, and again a number of Asian and African nations joined with the United States to assure a majority of forty-four votes. Other Asian and African nations voted for considering the admission of Communist China and were joined by several European nations, including the Scandinavians and Ireland. A number of nations abstained—not only Saudi Arabia, Tunisia, and Libya but also Portugal and Israel.[25]

The extreme fluidity of the non-Communist blocs was also shown in

[24] General Assembly Resolution A/1135 (XII) (September 24, 1957).
[25] General Assembly Resolution A/1351 (XIV) (September 22, 1959).

the 1957 Assembly by two key votes on the increase of the membership of the Disarmament Conference and on the continuing support for the Middle Eastern United Nations Emergency Force. In both votes the Communist bloc remained practically alone. In the first vote the United States was joined by many Asian nations, among them Burma and India.[26] Among the eleven abstentions were Ireland, Israel, and Liberia. On the second vote the nine Communist nays were joined by Chile and Ecuador. Burma, Ghana, India, Indonesia, Jordan, Pakistan, and Yugoslavia voted with the United States. Several Latin-American nations and Nationalist China abstained.

Questions of national self-determination which were of crucial importance were those of Hungary and Tibet. All the votes showed the isolation of the Communists. In the 1956 vote of censure against the Soviet Union concerning Hungary, fifteen Afro-Asian nations voted for censure and eleven abstained.[27] In 1957 the number of those who again censured the Soviet Union had grown to eighteen, while the abstentions diminished to nine.[28] Among the members of the commission which drew up the indictment against the Soviet Union, Tunisia played a leading role. On the other hand, no effort was made by Tunisia or other Afro-Asian nations in 1957 to press for a strong censure of French violent suppression of the Algerian demand for freedom.[29] The influence of the United States prevailed to allow France more time to carry out a program of self-determination in the spirit of the United Nations Charter.

Yet the Afro-Asian nations were conscious of the fact that it took the Soviet Union only a few weeks to crush the Hungarian fight for independence, whereas the large French army in Algeria was unable for more than six years to break down the resistance of the Algerian fighters for freedom. While the Communists claimed that the Hungarian revolt was inspired by Western "imperialism" and led by "fascist" elements, the French ascribed the tenacious Algerian struggle for independence to the influence of Communism, of Nasser, or of Bourguiba. In both cases, of course, such influences, as far as they existed, played only a minor role in what were indigenous and genuine demands for national self-

[26] General Assembly Resolution A/1150 (XII) (November 19, 1957).

[27] See General Assembly Resolution A/1004 (ES–11) (November 4, 1956).

[28] See General Assembly Resolution A/1133 (XI) (September 14, 1957).

[29] General Assembly Resolution A/1184 (XII) (December 10, 1957).

determination. There was, however, one great difference—and this difference was not lost on public opinion in Asia and Africa: In the Communist orbit no voice of protest or criticism was raised against Soviet action in Hungary, whereas in France, Catholics, Liberals, and even individual officers of the armed forces spoke up against terror and repression, on behalf of what they regarded as the true values of France and the West. Throughout the Western world sympathy for the Algerian aspirations for independence and dismay at French methods of action were voiced. The final success of the Algerian struggle was to no small degree accelerated by the action and support given to Algeria in the United Nations.

Afro-Asian nations continued to support the United States in the votes against the Communist powers on Hungary and Tibet in 1959. In both votes only the Communists voted against the resolutions. All the Asian and African nations either voted with the United States or abstained in the case of Hungary. Among the seventeen abstentions were Israel and Finland.[30] On the resolution expressing concern at the denial of human rights in Tibet twenty-six nations abstained, but the several Afro-Asian nations were joined by Belgium, Britain, the Dominican Republic, France, and Portugal. Not one non-Communist nation voted in either case with the Communists.[31] On October 8, 1960, some Asian and Arab nations voted with the United States not to consider Chinese Communist admission to the United Nations. Among those who voted for consideration and who remained in the minority were the Communists, the Scandinavian nations and Ireland, and some Afro-Asian nations. Other Afro-Asian nations abstained, together with Israel and Portugal.[32]

The fluidity of the blocs has rather grown in the last years with the accession of more Asian and African members to the United Nations. Questions directly concerning national self-determination and the trusteeship principle involved the Union of South Africa and its position in South-West Africa, a formerly German territory put under South African mandate by the League of Nations, and Portugal. On November 17, 1959, the General Assembly denounced the apartheid policy of the Union of South Africa and its administration of South-West Africa.

---

[30] See General Assembly Resolution A/1454 (XIV) (December 9, 1959).

[31] See General Assembly Resolution A/1353 (XIV) (October 21, 1959).

[32] See General Assembly Resolution A/1493 (XV) (October 8, 1960).

The texts of the resolutions were drafted by the Trusteeship Committee. The United States and most other nations voted for the resolution; Britain, France, and Portugal voted against it; and eleven nations abstained.[33] On November 12, 1960, the Trusteeship Committee, by forty-five votes in favor, six against, and twenty-four abstentions, called upon Portugal to supply information on her overseas territories. A Communist amendment to strengthen the text of the resolution was defeated. The Asian and African delegations that sponsored the motion were subjected to ridicule and pressure by the Communist bloc, which regarded the resolution as too weak. They responded with open criticism of the Soviet Union. In a roll call on the resolution asking Portugal to report on her overseas territories, twenty-eight Afro-Asian, nine Latin-American, and eight western European nations voted for it. Both the Communist bloc and the United States abstained.[34]

The Soviet Union suffered defeat when, on December 14, 1960, the General Assembly called for immediate steps toward complete independence for non-self-governing territories. Several Soviet moves for strengthening the resolution in an anti-Western sense were defeated, among them the call for a one-year deadline for complete independence and the request to place the subject of colonialism on next year's agenda. By this action the United Nations, with an overwhelming majority, endorsed the principle of national self-determination. The vote was eighty-nine to none. Five European nations, the colonial powers—Great Britain, France, Belgium, Portugal, and Spain—and two American nations—the United States and the Dominican Republic—abstained, as did Australia and the Union of South Africa.[35] James J. Wadsworth, United States delegate, declared that the United States abstained with deep regret.

United States Policy in the United Nations

Not all difficulties faced by the United States today can be ascribed to the existence of totalitarian Communism. Many of them spring from the slow and painful ascent of underprivileged groups and peoples everywhere toward equality and a better life, and from their hope and deter-

---

[33] See General Assembly Resolution A/1360 (XIV) (November 17, 1959).

[34] See United Nations Document A/C4/L.6497 Rev. 1 and Corr. 1 and Add. 1—meeting 1048 (November 11, 1960).

[35] See General Assembly Resolution A/1514 (XV) (December 14, 1960).

mination to attain these goals. The process of emancipation started in nineteenth-century Europe; since then, it has been spreading, thanks to the expansion of the liberal nations, all over the globe. It is part of the Westernization of the world, which is seen too often only in its technological and material aspects.

To direct the new aspirations into constructive channels and to prevent the inevitable tensions, anxieties, and "provocations" from degenerating into bitter class and race conflicts and wars—this is the task of the United Nations. There, for the first time in history, all human races and civilizations—great and small, advanced and backward—can meet on a footing of legal equality and try to solve the difficult problems of world-wide accommodation to revolutionary changes by the democratic means of discussion and moral pressure.

These efforts can be facilitated by wise and generous guidance. Such an attempt at guidance underlies—not always consciously—the often poorly verbalized and imperfectly carried through policy of the United States in and through the United Nations. Sometimes the United States creates the impression that it abandons moral principles—its own principles—for considerations of strategy and that it is being too much swayed in its course by Soviet threats and by the pressure of its Allies rather than by consideration of justice and humanity. But only a policy of positive sympathy with the forces caring for man's freedom and dignity—a policy in agreement with the message which the United States and modern Western civilization have carried everywhere—can, in the long run, defeat the threat of Communist or Fascist totalitarianism. The United States will be on sound ground if it will consistently favor self-determination in the true sense of the word. The United Nations should safeguard the free expression of the will of the populations involved by supervising the vote and by helping formulate the questions submitted for the vote so as to allow a true choice between various alternatives. This will not be an easy policy for the United States and the United Nations in a world threatened by Communist aspirations. But such a policy is the only one which will prevail in the long run without war and which combines the enlightened self-interest of the West with the aspirations of the majority of mankind, aroused by the West itself to seek a new and better way of life.

CHAPTER IV

Arms Control and Limitation

BY WALDO CHAMBERLIN

THE CONCEPT OF PROTRACTED CONFLICT between the United States and the Soviet Union in the United Nations has nowhere been better illustrated than in the extended negotiations on arms control and limitation. On no other subject of serious United Nations concern have the positions taken by the United States been as strongly supported by the overwhelming majority of the members of the United Nations. Despite a seeming narrowing of the gap, from 1945 on, between the positions of the two great powers, there has been no fundamental agreement because of entirely different attitudes toward employment of the threat to use military force.

The Soviet Union has sought to prevent the establishment of any system of regulation of armaments that would deprive it of the possible advantages to be obtained from threatening to use force. The United States has sought to create a system in which the possiblity of a threat to use force would first be reduced and then eliminated. The threat or the use of force by the Soviet Union in situations brought to the attention of the United Nations is not the subject matter of this chapter. The issue before the United Nations has been, and remains, one of trying to eliminate the fears of any member state that military force will be used against it. Whatever system of disarmament may be devised must set this fear at rest.

The Era of Seeming Agreement, 1944–46

The years of negotiations began at Dumbarton Oaks in August, 1944, when it was agreed that a system for control and regulation of armaments by the United Nations was to come into being simultaneously with the evolution of a procedure for pacific settlement of disputes. It was anticipated that national armed forces would become less and less important, because of their being available at the call of the Security Council, and because of pledges by members never to use force, or the threat of force.[1] The acceptance of the Dumbarton Oaks proposal was taken by some to mean that the Soviet Union wanted to get on with the rest of the world, at least to the point where it could co-operate in developing the United Nations as an agency for pacific settlement of disputes and control and regulation of armaments. Most individuals who were following such matters closely saw ground for optimism in the basic agreement at Dumbarton Oaks and in the negotiations at San Francisco, in the spring of 1945, that ended in the adoption of the Charter of the United Nations. It was difficult to believe that the Russians would have fought so hard at San Francisco unless they believed that the United Nations could become a system for peaceful settlement of disputes and control of armaments that could be to their advantage, even though simultaneously offering advantages to other powers.[2] It is argued sometimes that the fact that the Charter was "pre-atomic" (the explosion of the atomic bomb over Hiroshima took place shortly after the Charter was signed in June, 1945) materially affected the Soviet Union and consequently the pattern of international relations and planning as reflected in the Charter. The fact is that the Charter could hardly have been improved in the circumstances then prevailing, that is, before the defeat of Japan. Even if it were possible to make the Charter "atomic," how would it have altered the postwar international situation or the pattern of negotiations on arms control and disarmament that followed? The crux of the matter is that even though there was the appearance of agreement on a procedure for achieving world order wherein armaments would be substantially reduced, as manifest in the provisions of the Charter, it is open to question whether any such agreement was really reached. As seems more likely, there is reason to believe that before the Russian delegation went to

[1] See Ruth B. Russell and Jeannette E. Muther, *A History of the United Nations Charter* (Washington, The Brookings Institution, 1958), 237–40, 264–71, 476–77, 685–87.

[2] The United Nations Charter mentions "disarmament" and "the regulation of armaments" only twice, in Articles 11 and 47. In contrast, the League of Nations regarded disarmament as a primary requirement for the maintenance of peace. Article VIII, part 1, of the Covenant states that the maintenance of peace requires the reduction of national armaments to the lowest point consistent with national safety and the enforcement by common action of international obligations.

Dumbarton Oaks, "A crucial decision was reached in Moscow in the summer of 1944. The decision was, in substance, to force Stalinist Communism on every country in the world, by every means within the power of the Soviet Union, this even before the German power was finally broken."[3]

If that is what happened, there were few Americans who were aware of it. In the light of experience with Russian negotiators since 1944, it can be argued that suspicions would have been aroused when the Russians brought to Dumbarton Oaks a proposal for an international police force but immediately withdrew it when they saw the United States draft of what was to become the Charter of the United Nations—a draft that suggested national contingents to be available to the Security Council but did not include the concept of international force.

After the war ended in August, 1945, the United States, believing that the United Nations system for pacific settlement of disputes and control and regulation of armaments was workable, and that it would be to the self-interest of both the United States and the Soviet Union to see that it came into existence as soon as possible, moved rapidly to demobilize and "get the boys home by Christmas." The United States had the bomb, but events were in motion that would soon lead to proposals to give it to the United Nations. Few Americans paid any attention to the fact that the Soviet Union was demobilizing very slowly, and no one, apparently, knew that Soviet agents were transmitting information on the bomb to Moscow, and had been doing so for some time. As 1945 came to an end, the Russians were in a very powerful position. They were retaining conventional military forces that were more than equal to all those of the United States and its allies. Simultaneously, they were moving rapidly to develop atomic weapons, using the skills of captured German scientists and the information being passed to them by Klaus Fuchs and other intelligence sources. In a position of such strength, the Soviet Union had nothing to fear from any step-by-step form of arms reduction. It had nothing to fear, that is, if reduction of armaments in contrast to armed forces was what was desired. Thus there was a confrontation between the United States and the Soviet Union, but only the Russians knew it.

[3] Adolph A. Berle, Jr., *Natural Selection of Political Forces* (Lawrence, University of Kansas Press, 1950).

The Atomic Energy Commission

Being alone in possession of the nuclear weapon in 1945, and conscious of the responsibility of this position, the United States initiated extensive studies of the problems involved in preventing the spread of nuclear weapons to other nations and in devising a system under which nuclear power would be used exclusively for peaceful purposes. The heads of the three nations which had co-operated in developing the atomic bomb during the war—the United States, the United Kingdom, and Canada—met in November, 1945, and proclaimed the necessity to establish a system of international controls which would prevent the development of nuclear weapons and ensure the peaceful use of nuclear energy.[4]

This was followed by the Moscow Conference of Foreign Ministers in December, 1945, when the United States and the United Kingdom obtained agreement from the Soviet Union to co-sponsor a United Nations resolution establishing an Atomic Energy Commission.[5] It seemed, therefore, that there was agreement among all three powers that the potential of atomic weapons was so terrifying that it had to be controlled internationally. On January 24, 1946, the United Nations Atomic Energy Commission was created to "inquire into all aspects of the problems presented by the discovery of atomic energy and by other weapons of mass destruction."[6] As far as the United States was concerned, this step in itself was a reason for optimism about Soviet co-operation in the postwar world, although the clouds of disagreement with the Soviets had already appeared in the matter of the peace treaties.

Encouraged by the creation of the United Nations Atomic Energy Commission, the United States took it for granted that members of the United Nations had agreed that the new power of nuclear fission was potentially so destructive that all of them would be willing to join in devising means for its control. Having had the greatest amount of experience with the new weapons, the United States made the first proposal. Careful study by a distinguished group of civil servants, scientists, soldiers, and businessmen culminated on March 28, 1946, in what is commonly known as the Acheson-Lilienthal Report. The Report stated:

[4] For the text of the joint declaration made on November 15, 1945, see U.S. Dept. of State, *The International Control of Atomic Energy: Growth of a Policy*, Publication 2702, 118–20.

[5] *Ibid.*, 125–27.   [6] General Assembly Resolution 1 (I) (January 24, 1946).

We have concluded unanimously that there is no prospect of security against atomic warfare in a system of international agreement to outlaw such weapons controlled *only* by a system which relies on inspection and similar police-like methods. . . . So long as intrinsically dangerous activities may be carried on by nations, rivalries are inevitable and fears are engendered that place so great a pressure upon a system of international enforcement by police methods that no degree of ingenuity or technical competence could possibly hope to cope with them. . . . every stage in the activity leading from raw materials to weapons, needs some sort of control, and . . . this must be exercised on all of the various paths that lead from one to the other; . . . at no single point can *external* control of any operations be sufficiently reliable to be an adequate sole safeguard; . . . for effective control, the controlling organization must be as well and as thoroughly informed about the operations as are the operators themselves.[7]

No more comprehensive statement on armaments control and regulation has ever been made. The statement departed from all previous discussions of the problem of disarmament in its recognition of the fact that national security was impossible without complete international control.

On June 14, 1946, Bernard Baruch offered to the United Nations Atomic Energy Commission, on behalf of the United States government, a comprehensive plan for the international control and regulation of atomic energy. He proposed the establishment of an International Atomic Development Authority that would be entrusted with all phases of the development and use of atomic energy, starting with the raw materials and including 1) managerial control or ownership of all atomic energy activities potentially dangerous to world security; 2) power to control, inspect, and license all other atomic activities; 3) the duty to foster the beneficial uses of atomic energy; and 4) research and development responsibilities of an affirmative character intended to put the Authority in the forefront of atomic knowledge and thus to enable it to comprehend and detect misuse of atomic energy. Once an adequate system for control was agreed upon and put into effective operation, Baruch proposed that manufacture of atomic bombs should stop, that existing bombs should be disposed of pursuant to the terms of the treaty, and that the proposed Authority should be given possession of full informa-

[7] U. S. Dept. of State, *The International Control of Atomic Energy*, 35–36.

tion concerning the production of atomic energy.[8] The American position was clear: there was no way to secure adequate control of atomic energy except by United Nations monopoly, and adequate control was absolutely necessary for the safety of the people of the world. The United States was willing to give up all its knowledge and facilities to the United Nations in order to enable the world to enter the nuclear age in a joint and peaceful endeavor.

There are some people who believe that June 14, 1946, marks the United States "finest hour" because, while it was rapidly dismantling its conventional armed forces, it offered to give to the United Nations the only real military power it had, in the form of the bomb. The entire course of negotiations on arms control during 1946 and 1947 is meaningless unless the extent of the American demobilization is understood. The United States had reached the point where it was unable to threaten the Soviet Union by conventional arms, even if it had wished to, and it was in the process of offering to the world organization, of which the Soviet Union was a member, the only remaining effective American weapon. The American position was that if there were effective control of atomic weapons, it would be relatively easy to achieve control of conventional weapons. The United States believed that its offer of real reduction and regulation of armaments starting with atomic weapons, as made by Baruch, would be accepted by all the Great Powers.

The first Russian reaction to the Baruch plan came within five days. On June 19 the Soviets made their counterproposals, calling for the conclusion of an international convention prohibiting the production and employment of weapons based on the use of atomic energy for the purpose of mass destruction, and suggesting the study of measures for an exchange of scientific information. The Soviet delegate made it quite plain that "the situation existing at the present time, which has been brought about by the discovery of the means of applying atomic energy and using them for the production of atomic weapons, precludes the possibility of normal scientific cooperation between States of the world."[9] In other words, the Soviet Union would not co-operate until it reached the status of parity in atomic weapons and know-how with the United States, which then held superiority. The Soviet proposals thus called for an exchange of information and outlawing of the bomb before any system of control should be established. Although the Baruch plan was not

[8] *Ibid.*, 50.   [9] *Ibid.*, 211.

rejected at this point, presumably for fear of giving the United States advantages of propaganda, the fundamental difference between the two powers was clear: the Russians wanted disarmament (through outlawing of atomic weapons) before controls were established, and the Americans insisted upon effective controls before there could be disarmament. This was the basic point of difference in 1946 and has essentially remained so ever since. How far apart the two powers really were was not recognized for some time, because on October 2, 1946, the Scientific and Technical Committee of the Atomic Energy Commission reported that it "did not find any basis in the available scientific facts for supposing that effective control is not technologically feasible." Russian concurrence in this statement kept alive the hopes of those who still believed that agreement was possible.[10]

Recognition of Basic Conflict, 1947–48

It is not possible to say just when the United States became convinced that its objectives and those of the Russians, where regulation of armaments was concerned, were fundamentally different. Some responsible United States statesmen became aware of this fact in the course of the many negotiations with the Russians that were taking place in Korea, Berlin, Lake Success, and elsewhere. For others, there still seemed to be reason for hope when it was agreed by the United Nations Security Council in February, 1947, to set up the Commission for Conventional Armaments, even though the Russians had made it clear that they were opposed to separating the negotiations on conventional arms and atomic weapons. It is difficult to see how any American official, by the end of 1947, could have remained naïve enough to believe that the Soviet Union and the United States had similar objectives in the area of arms control. Two events in 1947 made the existence of conflict quite clear: the report of the Military Staff Committee in June, and the Cadogan-Gromyko questions and answers in September.

The Report of the Military Staff Committee, June 23, 1947

The representatives of the Chiefs of Staff of the five permanent members of the Security Council constituted the Military Staff Com-

[10] For the Committee report see United Nations Atomic Energy Commission Official Records (AECOR), First Year, Special Supplement, "Report to the Security Council" (1946), 20–37.

mittee.[11] On February 16, 1946, the Council asked the Committee to consider the kind of military forces that should be provided by the permanent members of the Security Council. The discussions in the Military Staff Committee went on for fifteen months. The Committee records were never published; however, on June 23, 1947, the Committee published a report that showed almost complete disagreement on the major issues of the size of military units to be submitted, composition of the units, command, air contingents, bases, and withdrawal of forces after completion of mission.[12]

The United States wanted forces about twice the size of those favored by the other four members of the Military Staff Committee. What use the United Nations could have had for forces on the scale proposed is difficult to imagine, when it is remembered that, because of the veto, they could never be used against any of the permanent members of the Security Council. No other nation could have stood against the "big five" when they were in agreement. The refusal of the United States to accept the Russian estimates presented to the Military Staff Committee raised a question of negotiating tactics that has never been answered. The question is, why did the United States not accept the Russian figures as a basis for negotiaton and place the burden of proof on the Soviet Union to produce detailed plans for the next phase of negotiation. Some observers believe that the United States has missed several opportunities to strengthen its position in the eyes of the world when American delegates have not been permitted to accept various proposals of the Soviet Union, at least as a basis for further negotiation. This thesis is based on the assumption that if the Soviet Union had been forced to specify how its usually highly generalized proposals would be implemented, it would have to come up with a workable plan for arms control, or "welch" on its proposals. In any event, the United States did not use this tactic in the Military Staff Committee, and the Soviet Union was not forced into a corner in the disarmament negotiations.

The Military Staff Committee negotiations, while not strictly a part of the arms control problem, were important because upon them depended the establishment of any future United Nations force—a force that would, it was hoped, make the national military establishments less

[11] Charter, Article 47.

[12] See Report of the Military Staff Committee in United Nations Security Council Official Records (SCOR), Second Year (1947), Special Supplement No. 1.

and less important. It might be said that in these negotiations the United States was sometimes overly technical and inflexible, and exasperated even its friends. But the Soviet Union disagreed with all the other members of the Committee on so many fundamental issues that it appeared to stand alone in opposition to the creation of the forces envisaged in Article 43 of the Charter. The argument against infringement of national sovereignty appeared as it did in all the negotiations on the various phases of disarmament. In the Military Staff Committee the Russians argued that national sovereignty would be jeopardized if military units of one member, that were available on the call of the Security Council, were stationed on bases in the territory of another member. This was, in its essence, the same argument that has been used against adequate international inspection. This argument, when taken with the extent of Russian disagreement on other issues before the Committee, tended to reinforce doubts concerning whether the Soviet Union really wanted any effective system of arms control.

The Anglo-Russian Questions and Answers, September, 1947

The September, 1947, meetings of the Atomic Energy Commission were held after the failure of the Military Staff Committee. From the beginning of the Commission's meetings in June, 1946, the delegates were never quite sure whether the Russians did or did not want an international system for the control of atomic energy. On June 11, 1947, the Soviet Union presented its first detailed proposals for the international control of atomic energy, but repeated questioning by other members failed to produce clarification of whether the proposal envisaged an effective control system. The Soviet proposals, in contrast to the Baruch plan which envisaged the international ownership and management of atomic materials and facilities for their production, suggested that atomic materials be left in national hands but made subject to inspection. The inspection was to be reasonably extensive but periodic, and there was provision for special inspections in the event of any suspicion of violation. Finally, the inspections (controls) were to begin only after the United States had destroyed its atomic weapons.

The representative of the United Kingdom, Sir Alexander Cadogan, on August 11, 1947, handed his Russian colleague, Andrei Gromyko, a carefully phrased list of questions relating to the Russian proposals of June 11. Apparently these questions were considered carefully by the

Russians because they did not reply until September 5. The Soviet Union still insisted that atomic weapons must be prohibited before a control system could be established, and left no doubts that the Soviets were not advocating an effective control system. When the Soviets were asked what was meant by "periodic inspection," they replied: ". . . periodical inspection of all facilities subject to inspection—and that there must be advance warning of any other inspection, through the device of requiring that the control commission itself authorize such additional inspections." In other words, international inspectors were not to have free access to any place in any country, at any time and without advance notice—the fundamental requirement for any effective system of inspection.

These answers were given during the Atomic Energy Commission's debate on its second report to the Security Council, dated September 11, 1947.[13] There was to be a third and final report in 1948, but it was the second report that clarified how far apart were the views of the Soviet Union and the United States. The arms negotiations did not, of course, take place all by themselves. In 1947 the United States was also facing Soviet intransigence in the Council of Foreign Ministers, in the Balkans, in Korea, and in the Security Council over the admission of new members to the United Nations. All these things working together were responsible for the change in the American attitude toward the good faith of the Russians.

Reply and Response, 1947–48

During 1947 and 1948 there appeared to be a pattern of reply and response in the confrontation between the Soviet Union and the United States. There can be little doubt that the Baruch and other American proposals of 1946 and early 1947 placed the Soviet Union in an unpleasant position while the rest of the world was wondering about its motives and intentions. In order to improve this situation, the Soviet Union may have decided to introduce its proposals of June 11, 1947, merely as a propaganda countermove designed to give it respectability in the eyes of a world that wanted real disarmament. When this move failed, under the hammering questions of the other members of the

[13] See United Nations Atomic Energy Commission Official Records, Second Year, Special Supplement, "Second Report to the Security Council" (September 11, 1947). For a discussion of Soviet proposals of June 11, 1947, and the answers to the United Kingdom questionnaire, see United Nations Document AEC/c.1/76 (April 5, 1948).

Atomic Energy Commission, and as the United States continued to argue for an effective system of arms control, the Russians tried another approach. In the autumn of 1948, in the General Assembly of the United Nations, the Soviet Union proposed that all the Great Powers reduce their conventional armaments by one-third.[14] There was no suggestion of international verification of such a reduction, but the Soviet Union again tried to portray itself as an advocate of partial disarmament.

As each Soviet proposal during 1947 and 1948 failed to provide any measures for effective control, and as Russian delegates in international meetings became more and more difficult to deal with, the United States was finally forced to conclude that the Soviet Union did not want an effective international control of armaments that would be part of a broader system of peaceful settlement of disputes. If a date can be put on the final acceptance by the United States of this conclusion—a conclusion that had been avoided as long as possible—it would be June 11, 1948, when the Vandenberg Resolution was adopted by the United States Senate. This resolution, in addition to calling for control and regulation of armaments, proposed that the United States develop regional and other collective self-defense arrangements, in accordance with the United Nations Charter. This was tacit recognition that United Nations plans for a world in which it would be impossible for a state to threaten to employ military force were not feasible under present circumstances. With Russian insistence on retaining the means of using the threat of force, the Vandenberg Resolution said, in effect, that it was time for the United States to develop means for its own defense against any possible future Soviet threat to use force. The result was the North Atlantic Treaty signed on April 4, 1949.

The Balance Sheet of Confrontation, 1944–49

If we accept Adolph Berle's thesis that the Soviet Union decided in 1944 not to work with the rest of the world, the Russian actions and words from 1944 through 1948 present a thoroughly consistent picture. On the other hand, the Soviet Union was playing for time in order to develop its own bomb. The United States, not being aware that the Soviet Union was following any such policy, sought to develop a system in which no nation, itself included, would have sufficient military power seriously to threaten any other. If Berle's thesis is not accepted, it is clear,

[14] See United Nations Document A/658 (September 25, 1948).

at least, that the Soviet Union was determined not to permit the rest of the world to learn the status of Russian military forces. Whether or not there was any intent, at this time, to use such forces or to threaten to use them can be argued. What cannot be argued, however, is the Russian determination to block any effective international verification or inspection within the confines of the Soviet Union. As this gradually became clear, the rest of the world quite naturally wondered what the Russians had to conceal.

The men at the Kremlin must have been aware that the rest of the world was asking itself this question. They reacted to unfavorable world opinion with new proposals that gave the appearance of being sincere and attempted to find a solution to the disarmament problem. Superficially, it was possible for those who were looking for evidence of Soviet good will to conclude that these proposals constituted a real effort to arrive at some agreement on reduction and control of armaments. But in each case the Russian proposals called upon the members of the United Nations to trust the Soviet Union to reduce its armaments without giving the rest of the world means of verifying that such reduction had taken place.[15] The United States and the rest of the non-Communist world refused to accept such assurances without the right of verification.

Meanwhile, debate in the General Assembly and the resolutions adopted did not resolve the differences between the Soviet Union and the Western powers. They could not come to basic agreements on the approach to disarmament. In November, 1948, the Assembly approved the recommendations of the Atomic Energy Commission for establishing an effective system of international control of atomic energy. The Soviet Union voted against the resolution on the ground that it failed to prohibit the use of atomic weapons and infringed national sovereignty.[16] A similar resolution in 1949 was also opposed by the Soviet Union on the same grounds.[17]

All during the disarmament debates of 1946 and 1948 there was

[15] For example, in reply to the question how does the Soviet proposal of June 11, 1947, deal with the matter of secret activities in general, the Soviet representative said: "Governments responsible under the convention for the implementation of measures on their territories take the obligation to implement the convention, and from this it follows that secret activities would be excluded" (p. 71). See United Nations Document AEC/CI/PV 34.

[16] General Assembly Resolution 191 (III) (November 4, 1948).

[17] General Assembly Resolution 299 (IV) (November 23, 1949).

discussion of such matters as how and what sanctions were to be applied against any state that was found to have violated any possible disarmament agreement. That is, should decisions be made within the framework of the Security Council veto, or outside in some veto-free organ or committee. In themselves, the questions were unimportant until there was mutual acceptance of an adequate system of inspection that could determine whether or not there had been violations of any agreement. The Russians would not accept any system that would assure the world of knowledge of possible clandestine military activity. The United States insisted that such assurance was absolutely necessary, and it was upon this note of fundamental disagreement that the 1944 to 1948 effort to work out a plan for control and regulation of armaments ended. There were individuals who argued in 1948 that there was no point in continuing to negotiate as long as the Soviet Union refused to consider any effective method of inspection. There was a much larger group of individuals, both within and outside the government of the United States, who believed that negotiations should proceed, in the hope that some area of agreement with the Soviet Union could be found. It was the latter point of view which dominated the discussions that took place from 1949 through April, 1955.

The Search for Limited Areas of Agreement, 1949–55

The negotiations on disarmament languished for three years, with both sides making minor concessions. The situation had radically changed after the Soviet atomic explosion in September, 1949. By early 1950 the United States began to realize that once nuclear stockpiles had accumulated, there was no method known by which secret stock piles could be detected and controlled. With the Soviet Union in the atomic club, it was necessary to seek ways of establishing sufficient confidence between the two sides so that a limited area of agreement could be found and negotiated. Effort in this direction had begun in the Commission for Conventional Armaments which the Security Council established in February, 1947,[18] but apart from the approval of a French plan calling for census and verification of armed forces and armaments, the Commission for Conventional Armaments was almost stillborn.

In the spring of 1950 the Soviet Union walked out of both the Atomic Energy Commission and the Commission for Conventional

[18] See United Nations Document S/PV 105 (February 13, 1947).

77

Armaments in protest over the question of Chinese representation in the United Nations. It was not until the General Assembly session in 1951 that any development of significance in the field of disarmament took place. The General Assembly, in an effort to reconstruct the negotiations in the light of new developments,[19] created on January 11, 1952, a single Disarmament Commission to replace the Atomic Energy Commission and the Commission for Conventional Armaments.[20] The new Commission held its first meeting in March, 1952, and for the next five years there were more or less constant negotiations, in one form or another. Much of the work of these years concerned the stages or phases that would be necessary in order to arrive at a desired goal of arms regulation and control. During these years the United States conceded that international ownership and management of atomic facilities (the Baruch plan) was no longer necessary. The United States also accepted the idea that a considerable degree of disarmament should coincide with the first stages of an inspection system. The Soviet Union, on the other hand, conceded that disarmament need not precede control and that the two should proceed simultaneously.

There was still no agreement on what constituted effective control, and the Soviet Union persisted in its contention that the type of control desired by the United States would constitute undesirable interference in the domestic affairs of states. The United States held to its basic position that the key issue was international inspection at any place, at any time, and without prior notice because there was no other way to give nations even reasonable assurance that a state was not engaged in clandestine military preparations.

The Soviet Union's Proposals of May, 1955

In the fall of 1953 representatives of some of the smaller powers, hoping that recent international events would create a more propitious atmosphere for reconsideration of the disarmament question, urged in a General Assembly resolution that "the Disarmament Commission

[19] The Fifth Session of the General Assembly on December 13, 1950, established a committee consisting of the representatives of the Security Council and Canada to consider the desirability of consolidating the two disarmament agencies into one body. (See General Assembly Resolution 496 [V] [December 13, 1950].) The Committee met during 1951 and on October 23, 1951, it recommended that the General Assembly establish a new commission to replace the existing two.

[20] General Assembly Resolution 715 (VIII) (November 28, 1953).

study the desirability of establishing a sub-committee consisting of representatives of the Powers principally involved, which should seek in private an acceptable solution and report to the Disarmament Commission."[21] The death of Stalin on March 3, 1953, and the Korean armistice on June 27, 1953, had given cause for optimism to the smaller powers. Accordingly, the Disarmament Commission established in April, 1954, a subcommittee consisting of representatives of Canada, France, the Soviet Union, the United Kingdom, and the United States to discuss privately the question of disarmament.[22] The work of the subcommittee continued through September, 1957.

Its first meeting was held in New York on April 23, 1954, to discuss procedure. The subcommittee met in London in June, and it was at this meeting that the Anglo-French plan was introduced.[23] This proposal provided for a three-stage disarmament scheme. The first phase provided for a "freeze" on military man power and budgets to levels of December 31, 1953. The second phase called for one-half of the agreed reductions of conventional armaments and armed forces, and following the completion of these reductions, the cessation of the manufacture of all nuclear and other prohibited weapons. In the final phase, the other half of the reduction in conventional armaments and armed forces would take effect, on completion of which total prohibition and elimination of nuclear and other weapons and the conversion of existing stocks of nuclear materials for peaceful purposes would be carried out. The whole scheme was to be subject to inspection and effective control by an international control organ which would certify the completion of each phase before the next phase was to begin.

The Soviet Union rejected the Anglo-French plan, saying that the prohibition of nuclear weapons, instead of being immediate, was indefinitely relegated to the final stage.

In September, 1954, when the Ninth General Assembly met, the Soviet Union had second thoughts about the Anglo-French plan and agreed to discuss a disarmament treaty on that basis. But in February, 1955, the Soviet Union reversed its position again. On March 29, 1955, the United Kingdom and France jointly submitted to the subcommittee a memorandum calling for reduction of armed forces to a ceiling of

---

[21] General Assembly Resolution 715 (VIII) (November 28, 1953).

[22] United Nations Document DC/4919 (April, 1954).

[23] United Nations Document DC/SC 1/10 (June 11, 1954).

1,500,000 persons for the United States, the Soviet Union, and China, and 650,000 persons for the United Kingdom and France.[24] The Soviet Union rejected these figures on the ground that such reduction would be less than the Soviet proposal of a one-third cut all around. On April 19, 1955, in another attempt to meet all Soviet objections halfway, the Western powers offered to prohibit the use of nuclear weapons and to eliminate all nuclear stocks during the final quarter of reductions in armed forces and conventional armaments, i.e., after 75 per cent of those reductions had been completed.[25] This proposal also was rejected by the Soviets on the question of the control mechanism, which they contended was designed to set up espionage centers.

On May 10, 1955, the Russians submitted a counterproposal and accepted the force ceilings of the Anglo-French plan and the 75 per cent formula for prohibition of nuclear weapons.[26] Most significant of all was the fact that for the first time there was acceptance of the idea of some effective inspection during the first stage of disarmament and that disarmament was linked with international confidence through political settlement of outstanding issues. A proposed international control agency was to set up control posts in big ports, railway junctions, motor roads, and airports in the Soviet Union and other countries in order to watch for dangerous concentrations of military forces. There were, however, no specific provisions regarding the facilities for checking the reduction of armed forces and weapons. Actually what the Russians were proposing was a system of what later became known as "warning against surprise attack." We shall never know whether the Russians would have backed down when it came to negotiating the details.

The United States response came on September 6, 1955, when Harold Stassen, sitting for the first time as the United States representative, placed "a reservation upon all of its pre-Geneva substantive positions taken in this sub-committee or in the Disarmament commission or in the United Nations . . . pending the outcome of our study jointly or separately of inspection methods and control arrangements and of review of this important problem."[27] The United States stated its position as requiring a new and comprehensive study of the entire

---

[24] United Nations Document DC/SC 1/20 (March 29, 1955).

[25] United Nations Document DC/SC 1/24 (April 19, 1955).

[26] United Nations Document DC/SC 1/26, Rev. 2 (May 10, 1955).

[27] United Nations Document DC/SC 1/PV 55 (September 6, 1955).

inspection system in the light of significant changes, particularly since the Soviet Union had exploded its first hydrogen bomb the previous May. The United States representative suggested that the subcommittee concentrate on the factor of surprise attack, on the delivery system question, and on openness concerning military posture and potential.

We do not know why, in the spring of 1955, the United States did not accept the Russian proposals for ground inspection as a first step toward a broader system of inspection. Instead, the discussion of the Soviet draft was postponed, and when on October 11, 1955, President Eisenhower finally agreed to accept the Russian proposal for ground inspection teams at important points if the Russians would accept his plan for an exchange of military blueprints coupled with a system of aerial reconnaissance—the "open skies" offer made by Eisenhower at the July, 1955, Summit Meeting in Geneva—the Soviet Union rejected not only "open skies" but all other Western proposals.

Negotiations in the Subcommittee, 1956–58

Throughout the years 1956–58, negotiations continued and a wide variety of proposals were made, including suggestions by the United Kingdom and Poland that selected areas in Europe be used as test grounds for limited forms of arms control, and by the United States that the Arctic be similarly used. On March 19, 1956, in a renewed effort, the United Kingdom and France submitted a joint plan somewhat revised from the old Anglo-French plan of June, 1954, and incorporating the realizable aspects of previous Western and Soviet proposals.[28]

The new plan made certain concessions to the Soviet Union with regard to reduction in conventional armaments and forces as well as in the timing of the prohibition of nuclear weapons manufacture. In a Soviet counterproposal of April 3, 1956,[29] the question of nuclear disarmament was omitted, and a draft international agreement based on the reduction of conventional armaments and armed forces as a prelude to prohibition of atomic and hydrogen weapons and their elimination was suggested.[30]

In March, 1957, the Soviet Union advanced certain proposals for

[28] See United Nations Document DC/SC 1/39 (March 19, 1956).
[29] United Nations Document DC/SC 1/42 (April 1956).
[30] United Nations Document DC/SC 1/41 (March 27, 1956).

disengagement in Europe, including the territory of both parts of Germany (800 kilometers of inspection zone from the East-West line of division in Europe).[31]

Harold Stassen, the United States representative, in turn introduced in the subcommittee the proposals for "partial" disarmament as put forward in the General Assembly on January 14, 1957.[32] These proposals called for international inspection of testing of intercontinental missiles and other objects entering outer space. The Soviets refused to negotiate on objects entering outer space; less than three months later Sputnik I was successfully launched.

On August 29, 1957, the Western powers put forward in the subcommittee the most comprehensive proposals so far for partial measures of disarmament.[33] With Soviet rejection of the compromise formula for a nuclear test ban on August 27, two days before the Western proposals for "partial" disarmament, the chances for working out any agreement seemed remote. Nonetheless, the Western proposals, submitted in the Twelfth Session of the General Assembly, were passed by a vote of fifty-six to nine, with nine abstentions (the Soviet bloc opposing).[34]

During 1958 the only problems under consideration were the elimination of the testing of nuclear weapons and the development of a system of warning against surprise attack. The Soviets had unilaterally stopped nuclear testing, beginning March 31, 1958, after having conducted an intensive series of tests. The Soviet Union, therefore, demanded as the price for their participation in scientific investigations a three-power nuclear test cessation. Negotiations were resumed on October 31, 1958, to explore the possibility of setting up a control system. Both the United States and the United Kingdom announced suspension of nuclear testing for a year, contingent upon Soviet suspension of testing. This moratorium was continued until it was broken by the Soviet Union in September, 1961.

As the scope of negotiation narrowed, the problem of inspection

[31] See "Declaration of the Soviet Government Concerning the Question of Disarmament and Reduction of International Tensions," on November 17, 1956, in *U.S. Dept. of State Bulletin* (January 21, 1957), 90–93.

[32] See United Nations Document DC/SC 1/PV 88 (March 18, 1957), 12–20, and DC/SC 1/PV 89 (March 20, 1957), 2–14.

[33] United Nations Document DC/SC 1/66 (August 29, 1957).

[34] General Assembly Resolution 1148 (XII) (November 14, 1957).

remained the stumbling block. Negotiations in the Geneva Conference on the Discontinuance of Nuclear Weapon Tests became more and more technical as the realization grew that an adequate system of inspection for the detection of small nuclear explosions was a very complex problem.

The whole character of the negotiations changed when, shortly before the resumption of Soviet tests in 1961, the Soviet delegate proposed that the idea of a test-ban treaty should be absorbed into the scheme for comprehensive disarmament. In their new plan the Soviets reversed their earlier position altogether by proposing a permanent ban on all the tests in the atmosphere, underground, underwater, and outer space but with no controls whatsoever. The Soviet Union charged that inspection was tantamount to "espionage." The West rejected the Soviet proposals and insisted on an international control and inspection system. In February, 1962, the talks almost came to the point of collapsing, only to be revived by the eighteen-nation disarmament conferences which began on March 14.

Total Disarmament, 1959–62

The character of debate in the disarmament conference underwent a complete change when Premier Khrushchev, from the floor of the United Nations General Assembly, proposed a "Program of General and Complete Disarmament" in September, 1959.[35] This plan provided for three stages of disarmament which were to be carried out within a period of four years following the conclusion of a disarmament settlement. The proposal did not outline any specific measures which would make possible the first essential requirement of disarmament: a halt in the arms race and creation of a generally stable military situation. The West presented a counter set of proposals which emphasized the need for verification and compliance at each stage.

On June 7, 1960, the Soviet Union put forward the most far-reaching plan for international inspection that it had ever advanced. The Soviet proposal read in part: "Each party to the treaty shall insure timely and unrestricted access to inspection teams within its territory *to any point*

---

[35] For the text of Premier Khrushchev's address, see General Assembly Official Records, Fourteenth Session, 799th Plenary Meeting (September 18, 1959), 34–38. For the Soviet plan on general and complete disarmament, see United Nations Document A/4219 (September 19, 1959).

where disarmament measures to be verified will be effected." The United States proposal countered: "These shall provide for *all necessary means* required for effective verification of compliance with each step of each measure."

The revised Soviet disarmament plan contained certain other provisions unacceptable to the Western powers. For example, in the first stage the Communists demanded the withdrawal of all foreign troops from the territories of other states and the elimination of all foreign military bases and stores. This approach was not agreeable to the West without the replacement of their troops and bases with the balancing measures necessary to maintain stability of the military environment in the interest of peace.

In 1961, as a result of the informal contacts between Gromyko and Stevenson, the McCloy-Zorin meeting and exchange of notes led to the issuance, in September, of a joint statement of agreed principles and guidelines for the conduct of disarmament negotiations. Encouraged by the progress made, the two powers agreed to initiate a new set of general disarmament negotiations on March 14, 1962. This eighteen-nation meeting was to be guided by the principles stated in the McCloy-Zorin agreement: that disarmament should be general and complete and that such disarmament should be accompanied by the establishment of reliable procedures for the peaceful settlement of disputes and by effective arrangements for the maintenance of peace in accordance with the principles of the United Nations Charter, that nations would be allowed to maintain armed forces only large enough to ensure internal security, and that the disarmament agreement would be implemented in stages, in a balanced form under strict and effective international control.[36]

While the behind-the-scenes diplomatic activity which produced the McCloy-Zorin agreement was proceeding, the Soviet Union broke unilaterally its three-and-one-half-year moratorium on nuclear testing by exploding the first of a series of thermonuclear devices on September 1, 1961. This Societ action caused immediate concern in the General Assembly. Resolutions followed, ranging from exhortations to the Soviet Union not to detonate its planned fifty-megaton atmospheric weapon[37] to applauding the agreement reached between the United

[36] See United Nations Document A/4879 (September 20, 1961).

[37] General Assembly Resolution 1632 (XVI) (October 27, 1961).

States and the Soviet Union with regard to the composition of the body designated to negotiate the terms for general and complete disarmament and the principles outlined in the McCloy-Zorin agreement.[38] On March 2, 1962, President Kennedy ordered resumption of nuclear tests. Atmospheric tests were carried out in the Pacific on April 25, 1962.

The New Setting: Eighteen-Nation Geneva Conference

The Eighteen-Nation Disarmament Conference, minus France, has been engaged in consideration of the Draft Treaty on General and Complete Disarmament submitted by the Soviet Union on March 15, 1962,[39] the United States Program for General and Complete Disarmament presented on September 25, 1961,[40] the United States Outline of Basic Provision of a Treaty on General and Complete Disarmament in a Peaceful World proposed on April 18, 1962,[41] and other proposals brought to light by the McCloy-Zorin agreement of September 20, 1961, and the General Assembly Resolution 1772 (*XVI) of December 20, 1961.

The American proposals for disarmament of April 18, 1962, were presented in the form of an outline, designed to provide in specific terms a substantial basis for the negotiations of arms control and disarmament treaty obligations. They call for "balanced" disarmament in three stages. Although the Soviet Draft Treaty also proposed a three-stage disarmament plan, the essential disagreements centered on the question of the control and inspection system and the disarmament measures in the first stage. In comparing the measures proposed by both sides, it became evident that the Soviet Union wanted to retain its superior conventional military strength by breaking the collective self-defense system of the West and by grounding the Western nuclear deterrent.

On the issue of the test-ban agreement, the United States and the United Kingdom went to great length to come to task with the Soviet obsession with secrecy.[42] Yet despite concessions, the Soviets charged

[38] General Assembly Resolution 1722 (XVI) (December 13, 1961).

[39] United Nations Document ENDC/2 (March 15, 1962).

[40] United Nations Document ENDC/6 (September 25, 1961).

[41] United Nations Document ENDC/30 (April 18, 1962).

[42] See the United States–United Kingdom draft treaty of April 18, 1961 (GEN/-DNT/110), as subsequently amended in United Nations Document ENDC/q, to accommodate Soviet objections to limited on-the-site inspections.

that on-site inspections were a cloak for espionage, since there was no real need either to suspect or to inspect. The Soviet draft agreement of November 28, 1961, on the other hand, did not provide for any international authority, since compliance with commitments was to be verified by each party, using its own national system of detection of nuclear and thermonuclear explosions.[43]

The United States expressed a willingness to cut back the number of detection posts and on-site inspections it would require each year in the Soviet Union, and to allow the detection posts to be staffed by the nationals of a state in whose territory they were situated, as long as they were "internationally supervised." Zorin, the Soviet chief negotiator, stated categorically that he saw "no change in substance" from previous United States positions.

Negotiations between the Soviet Union, the United States, and Great Britain were resumed in July, 1963. On July 20 a tentative agreement was reached on a draft treaty to ban tests in the atmosphere, in outer space, and underwater. The treaty also provided for the continuance of negotiations over underground tests, and contained an escape clause should any power feel its "extreme interests" jeopardized. The powers agreed not to encourage tests by other nations, and all countries were invited to subscribe to the treaty.

On August 5, 1963, the treaty was signed by Andrei Gromyko, Dean Rusk, and Lord Home at a Kremlin ceremony also attended by U Thant. The United States Senate ratified the treaty by eighty votes to nineteen on September 24, by which date ninety-nine countries, in addition to the Big Three, had subscribed to the treaty.

It was hoped that the signing of the Nuclear Test Ban Treaty was but a prelude to the conclusion of other more far-reaching disarmament accords between the Western nations and the Soviet Union. Yet such expectations have proved unwarranted. In the light of the evidence presented in this chapter, this fact should not prove surprising. The Soviet and United States positions on such divisive issues as the timing, control, and inspection of disarmament systems have not converged significantly between 1946 and the present. Thus, neither side appears likely to sign an accord which, in its viewpoint, would endanger its national survival.

[43] See United Nations Document ENDC/11 (November 28, 1961).

CHAPTER V

The United Nations Record of Handling Major Disputes

BY WILLIAM R. KINTNER

HAS THE UNITED STATES profited more than the Soviet Union from its handling of disputes considered by the United Nations? In order to determine which side has benefited the most from the solutions obtained in the United Nations, the divergent goals of the two super-powers must be taken into account. It can be plausibly contended that the Soviets regard the United Nations as but one operational sector in their global campaign of attrition against the power and influence of the West, and of the United States in particular. The Soviet Union seeks at least to neutralize the United Nations or to utilize it for the furtherance of its own objectives.

Kremlin leaders, however, have adjusted their tactics toward the United Nations to conform to the relative strength of Soviet power vis-à-vis the United States. Consequently, the rapid growth of Soviet power has been reflected in an increasingly bold and belligerent attitude on the part of the Soviets in United Nations councils. The Soviet rise to a position of power nearly equal to that of the United States convinces Soviet leaders that increased opportunities will open for them in which they can turn the tide of history to their advantage. Their advocacy of the "troika" plan for the office of the secretary-general and their threats to take unilateral action during the Suez and Congo crises are indicative of increased Soviet power and belligerency.

As early as 1946 the Soviet Foreign Minister, V. M. Molotov, stated: "In this international organization created after the war, we must strive to set up a united front of peace-loving states which will not permit the ignoring of any power, and which will be aimed against any attempts to resurrect aggressors."[1]

[1] Speech delivered on September 14, 1946, at the session of the Committee on Political and Territorial Questions of the Peace Treaty with Italy of the Paris Peace Conference.

A primary source of United States difficulties in the United Nations can be traced to the contrasting United States and Soviet aims at the inception of the world organization. The record of wartime discussion among the Big Three leaders reveals divergent attitudes toward the United Nations. The United States, as World War II progressed, regarded the creation of a universal security system as the major, if not the main, political objective of the conflict. The Soviet Union analyzed the emerging world situation in terms of ideological conflict and power politics. Secretary of State Cordell Hull, in contrast, reported to Congress on November 18, 1943, after a trip to Moscow, that in the new world that would follow the war there would no longer be need for "spheres of influence, for alliances, for balance of power."

The United States, haunted by the specter of a weak League of Nations in the interwar period, was determined to make a conclusive break with its long-lingering policy of isolationism. However, the United States, in backing the United Nations concept, initially ignored the persistent realities of power politics. In helping to organize the United Nations, the United States revived Wilsonian idealism. Wilson had placed the ability of the League to enforce its decisions upon the concurrence of the "Principal Allied and Associated Powers."[2] Nearly thirty years later the United States, with comparable naïveté, placed the credibility of United Nations enforcement powers upon the assumption that the five major powers on the Security Council would share a somewhat identical world outlook.

While the discussions leading to the United Nations Charter contain substantial evidence of agreement between the powers on the use of the United Nations for peaceful settlement of disputes, the Soviet Union and the United States, with diametrically opposed images of the postwar world, read loosely worded agreements from differing viewpoints. The Soviet Union at the Tripartite Anglo-Soviet-American Conference in Moscow in October, 1943, obtained United States–United Kingdom agreement to the principle that the United Nations would function under a "controlling nucleus" composed of the Big Three operating in unanimity. Negotiations from Dumbarton Oaks to San Francisco clarified the positions of the United States and the Soviet Union on this issue. The United States supported limitation of the veto, the right of small countries to bring complaints against the powers to the Security

[2] The text of the League Covenant, Article 4, Section 1, and Article 5, Section 1.

Council, and recognition of regional organizations. The Soviet Union sought an unrestricted veto and wanted the small powers in the United Nations solely for window-dressing. In order to maintain the appearance of Great Power unanimity and to obtain the minimum procedural agreement without which it feared the United Nations would founder, the United States acquiesced in Soviet territorial ambitions and—more fatally—in the loose wording of the agreements which gave some credence to Soviet definitions of peace, democracy, and basic human rights.[3] Initially, the Soviet Union could neither lead nor compel the United Nations to assist in achieving Communist objectives abroad, but could only neutralize United Nations operations by exercise of the "controlling nucleus unanimity" principle. This principle of a "controlling nucleus" has been tested in many disputes within the United Nations. None of the Great Powers intended to be coerced into military action against its will, but interpretations regarding the extent of the use of the veto power agreed upon in 1943 were substantially different. A United Kingdom proposal for obligatory abstention by Security Council members from voting on pacific settlement of disputes to which they were parties, supported by the United States at Dumbarton Oaks, was greeted with Gromyko's comment to Stettinius: "The Russian position on voting in the council will never be departed from."[4] The Soviet Union finally agreed to procedural changes which would at least permit small countries to raise complaints against a big power in the Security Council. Basically at issue was the Soviet objection against smaller countries' having any real voice in the establishment of the postwar order.

At San Francisco, under Western prodding, the Soviets agreed to a further limitation of the veto power, but only to the extent that there need not be unanimity on the question of whether a problem should be merely placed on the agenda or discussed, thus implicitly defining such a question as a procedural one. At San Francisco and later the Soviets laid great emphasis on the importance of the powers of the Security

[3] In the dealings of all United States administrations with the Soviet Union, the Communist representatives have been given credit for far less rationality, a lower boiling point, and less willingness to concede in the face of a firm stand than has actually been the case. Aided by Soviet dramatics, this attitude, coupled with the illusion that Communist-bloc participation is indispensable in the United Nations, has led many nations to accept a dangerous double standard regarding United States and Soviet actions.

[4] Robert E. Sherwood, *Roosevelt and Hopkins* (New York, Harper & Brothers, 1948), 854.

Council as contrasted with the much lower order of those of the General Assembly in which the smaller nations had equal status. At San Francisco the Soviets revealed great curiosity about the matter of regional arrangements and alliances. The Soviet Union reserved for itself the veto power in the Security Council over the calling of such groups into forceful action (Article 53) except in self-defense, and the right to take action against the enemies it had fought in World War II (Article 107).

Various more or less unsuccessful methods were developed up to 1950 in efforts to circumvent the Soviet veto, such as the Interim Committee and the practice of removing matters from the Council agenda by a procedural vote, as well as increasing reliance on the regional arrangements offered by the Charter. These measures culminated in the "Uniting for Peace Resolution" proposed by the United States and approved in November, 1950, partly as a result of the frustration of Security Council efforts in Korea after the hasty Soviet return to the United Nations.[5]

When the framers of the United Nations Charter sat down to decide what force, if any, should be available to the new peace organization, efforts were focused on giving the United Nations the kind of power and authority which France had sought so persistently and so fruitlessly for the League of Nations. Lacking such authority, the League had been unable to meet any of the major challenges that it had faced—Manchuria in 1931, Ethopia in 1935–36, Spain in 1936–37, and Finland in 1939.

Article 39 of the Charter, with which Chapter VII began, invested in the eleven-nation United Nations Security Council the duty to "determine the existence of any threat to the peace, breach of the peace, or act of aggression," and in such a case, to take action to "maintain or restore international peace and security." It could take "provisional measures" of an unspecified character (Article 40); it could order economic and political sanctions (Article 41); and if these were insufficient, it could "take such action by air, sea, or land forces as may be necessary" (Article 42). In order that the latter provision for military sanctions should be

[5] Although these measures, designed to enhance the role of the General Assembly, were usually initiated by the United States, they were often questioned by those who saw the United States foisting on the Assembly a role it was incapable of performing, who were concerned that the United States was attempting to avoid its call to leadership by leaving decision-making to a volatile Assembly, or who foresaw the changing composition and interests of the Assembly.

meaningful, a key article, Article 43, required all member states to earmark elements of their armed forces and other "assistance and facilities"
for use when the Council called for them. Article 43 provided, on paper,
a world police force, consisting of military quotas contributed by states.

The United Nations Military Staff Committee met for the first time
on February 4, 1946, and plunged into the task of planning the force.
Its many sessions were long, difficult, and frustrating. They ended in
August, 1948, in total failure. The assumption upon which Chapter VII
of the Charter was based—namely, postwar co-operation among the
Big Five—proved false; plans for a police force were swept up in the
Cold War. Great Power differences proved insurmountable.

Once again, as between the two world wars, efforts at world-wide
collective security broke down, although the Free World set up regional
collective security organizations such as NATO and the OAS superficially within the United Nations framework.

Even had the United Nations been successful in setting up forces
under Article 43, their use would have been subject to the veto of the
five permanent members of the Security Council and therefore probably
would not have been wholly effective.

A method of avoiding the veto was in fact devised in 1950, in the
midst of the Korean War. At its Fifth Session the General Assembly,
under the title "United Action for Peace," considered proposals advanced by the United States to enable the Assembly to perform more
effectively the functions entrusted to it by the Charter in the field of
international peace and security. After revision and amendment during
an extended debate, three resolutions were adopted on November 3,
1950, under the title "Uniting for Peace."

The principle resolution (Resolution A) included provision for:
emergency special sessions of the General Assembly on twenty-four
hours' notice on the vote of any seven members of the Security Council
or a majority of the members of the United Nations if the Security
Council, because of a lack of unanimity among the permanent members,
failed to act in any case where there appeared to be a threat to the peace,
breach of the peace, or act of aggression; establishment of a Peace Observation Commission composed of representatives of fourteen members, including the five permanent members of the Security Council,
to be utilized by the General Assembly, the Interim Committee, or the
Security Council to observe and report on the situation in any area where

international tension threatened international peace and security; maintenance by member states of elements of their national armed forces for prompt availability as United Nations units, and the appointment by the secretary-general of a panel of military experts to give technical advice to member states on request; and establishment of a Collective Measures Committee composed of representatives of fourteen members to study and report on methods which might be used collectively to maintain and strengthen international peace and security.[6]

The "Uniting for Peace Resolution" was passed under the unique conditions of the Korean War when the United States was easily able to rally a majority of the then member nations to support its proposals.

The Range of Disputes

The United Nations capability to settle international disputes has been put to crucial tests, within the United Nations, in a series of major East-West confrontations.

In the early years of United Nations operations, United States aims in specific disputes were achieved several times. In some cases, such as Iran in 1946, the United States was in a position to restrain the Soviets by supporting the processes set forth in the Charter. It should be noted that at that time Soviet efforts were concentrated on the consolidation of their hold on eastern Europe, the restoration of their war-ravaged country, and the task of neutralizing United States atomic power. The Iranian charge of Soviet interference in her internal affairs was brought before the Security Council in January, 1946. In response to United States pressure Soviet troops were evacuated from Azerbaijan on May 9, 1946.

While they were not directly matters of United Nations concern, the termination of the Berlin Blockade and the formation of NATO constituted two more major reversals to the Soviets. By May, 1950, the Soviet Union had ceased to participate in almost all United Nations activities, and Stalin's conversation with Secretary-General Trygve Lie suggested that the Communist bloc might be contemplating a permanent walkout from the United Nations on the ground that the United States was planning to emasculate the United Nations in favor of NATO.[7]

---

[6] *Everyman's United Nations* (New York, 1959), 75-76.

[7] Trygve Lie, *In the Cause of Peace* (New York, Macmillan, 1954), 267. See Alexander Dallin, *The Soviet View of the U.N.* (Cambridge, Center for International

The years from 1953 to 1955 were critical for the Soviet Union and its United Nations policy in the protracted conflict. Following the death of Stalin in March, 1953, certain schisms became apparent within the Kremlin. It might be said that the divisions over policy within the Kremlin were more a matter of style than of substance. Malenkov argued for real, if minor, concessions to break up the Western alliance while Khrushchev maintained, successfully, the position that apparent concessions outside the bloc need only be temporary and tactical.[8] Both appeared to agree that alternate application and relaxation of pressures from area to area would be profitable and that more ambiguous instruments of penetration should be used. Internal Soviet dissensions were compensated for by growing Soviet strength and masked by a seemingly united and more moderate policy toward the Free World. Some success in refurbishing the Soviet image under the new management and recognition of the changing complexion of the United Nations resulted in the cultivation of new approaches for participation in United Nations bodies and a long-range program aimed at broader use of the United Nations in projecting Communist objectives into regions otherwise beyond the reach of Soviet power.

In the 1954 Guatemala situation, the United States obtained in the face of Soviet protest what it considered to be acceptance by the Security Council majority of the principle of regional settlement of disputes. However, the victory scored by the United States in this encounter and the series of the United States post-Korea alliances and military-aid programs gave the Communist states an opportunity to assume a new role in the United Nations—the defenders of "peace" and anti-colonial nationalism against aggressive American imperialism. The success of this

Studies, M.I.T., 1959), 31–37, for a comprehensive review of the evidence of Soviet intentions to withdraw from the United Nations. Dallin concludes that Communist attacks on and temporary withdrawal from the United Nations were designed to wreck NATO and that the Soviet absence from the Security Council at the time of the Korean invasion was the result of Stalin's view of the United Nations as an insignificant force coupled with poor co-ordination among top-level Soviet planners. While this is plausible—and it does appear that the Soviet Union was caught napping by United States and Security Council actions in July—it seems more likely that Communist representatives delayed their return with the intention of supporting the Korean campaign as a *fait accompli*.

[8] H.S. Dinerstine, *War and the Soviet Union* (New York, 1959), 94–126.

Communist stand was reflected in the reception accorded Communist China at Bandung, and, more obviously, in the 1954 Geneva Conference. This Conference, which was held on United Nations premises but not under United Nations auspices, temporarily closed off aggressive action in the Far East after the Communist take-over of the northern half of Vietnam had been conceded.

Communist participation in United Nations activities was consequently expanded. Soviet spokesmen increasingly used the broader issues—disarmament, anti-colonialism, economic policies—to lend to the Soviet image in emergent areas an impression of dynamism, strength, and peaceful progress.

The Soviets seized many opportunities to identify themselves with the aspirations growing in the Afro-Asian bloc within the United Nations. The cry of the few remaining colonial areas for immediate independence coupled with the growing assertiveness of the newly independent states of Africa and Asia supported the Soviet advocacy of a sustained revolution against the established order. The United States, because of its close ties with its west European allies and its belief that viable democracies in Asia and Africa must develop gradually, necessarily favored a more orderly path toward responsible nationhood.

"Peaceful Communist coexistence" was momentarily unmasked by events in Tibet and Hungary. Soviet leadership nevertheless sought to use United Nations pressure groups to aid in frustrating or weakening Western responses to Communist aggression.

The Algerian rebellion and the Soviet penetration of the Middle East following the Suez crisis were used both inside and outside the United Nations by the Soviet Union to exploit the anti-colonial syndrome. Proposals and counterproposals for disarmament, cessation of nuclear testing, and the like have been myriad inside and outside the United Nations, with the Soviet Union reaping the propaganda benefit of a cynical approach. The Soviets have long realized that in psycho-political operations it is the projected image which counts, and they have conditioned the world to expect and accept the fact that the "revolutionary" states could legitimately adopt a different standard of conduct than the United States and its Western allies.

With this background in mind, the character of the West's reaction to the Soviet maneuvers in the United Nations will be explored in the five following key crisis situations: Greece in 1947, Palestine in 1948–50, the

94

Korean War, Suez-Hungary in 1956, and the Congo in 1960–63. Brief mention will be made of the United Nations involvement in the 1962 Cuban missile crisis.

1. *Greece*

The Communist-supported revolution to gain control of Greece after the German 1944 withdrawal failed because of prompt British counteraction. Later the Communist effort was renewed as the Soviet satellites of Bulgaria, Yugoslavia, and Albania along the borders of Greece aided, with Soviet backing, the Communist guerrilla campaign to take over the country.

On January 21, 1946, the Soviet delegation, under Article 35 of the Charter, requested the Security Council to discuss the situation in Greece on the grounds that "the presence of British troops in Greece after the termination of the war meant interference in the internal affairs of Greece and caused extraordinary tension fraught with grave consequences both for the Greek people and for the maintenance of peace and security."[9] The Greek question was considered by the Security Council on February 1, 1946. The United Kingdom stated that British troops were in Greece by agreement with the Greek government, and Greece denied interference.[10] On February 6, 1946, the Security Council accepted its President's suggestion to take note of the declarations and consider the matter closed.

But on August 24, 1946, the Ukrainian Socialist Soviet Republic took up the Communist cudgel and complained to the Security Council that the policies of the Greek government constituted a threat to peace.[11] Greece denied the charges and referred to frontier incidents allegedly provoked by Albania. On September 11, 1946, Albania itself asked the Council to consider the situation on the Greco-Albanian frontier allegedly resulting from continued violations by Greek soldiers.[12] Four draft resolutions were proposed, but all were rejected, and the Council regarded the case as closed.

On December 3, 1946, Greece sent a letter to the United Nations stating that its Balkan neighbors were giving their support to violent

[9] *Yearbook of the United Nations, 1946–47,* 336.   [10] *Ibid.,* 337.

[11] Text of the telegram dated August 24, 1946, addressed to the Secretary-General from the Minister of Foreign Affairs of the Ukrainian Socialist Soviet Republic, *Yearbook of the United Nations, 1946–47,* 351.

[12] *Ibid.,* 355.

warfare waged by guerrillas in northern Greece against public order, threatening the territorial integrity of Greece. The Greek government asked the Security Council for an on-the-spot investigation, in order that the causes of the situation might be ascertained.

In the Security Council, Greece charged that acts of aggression against Greece were being committed on the basis of a systematic plan, worked out in minutest detail. The Yugoslav representative denied these allegations. Instead he proposed an investigation of conditions inside Greece.[13] Bulgaria and Albania also denied the Greek charges.

A United States proposal that the Security Council establish a commission to ascertain the facts relating to claimed border violations, with authority to conduct on-the-spot investigations in such areas of Albania, Bulgaria, Yugoslavia, and Greece as the commission might consider necessary, and to report the results to the Council, was adopted unanimously (that is, with Soviet approval) on December 19, 1946.[14] The Committee of Investigation submitted a report which contained recommendations accepted by nine members of the commission, the Soviet Union and Poland disagreeing.

In the meantime, in March, 1947, the United States announced the Truman Doctrine for giving military and economic assistance to Greece and Turkey. The Soviet Union branded this policy a unilateral action and stated that any such aid should be given through the United Nations. A Soviet proposal to establish a special commission, composed of representatives of the members of the Council, to ascertain whether aid received by Greece from outside was used only in the interests of the Greek people was rejected by the Council on April 18.[15]

The General Assembly in 1947, in its Second Session, established an eleven-member United Nations Special Committee on the Balkans (UNSCOB) to assist Albania, Bulgaria, Yugoslavia, and Greece in settling their disputes and in complying with its recommendations. Poland and the Soviet Union—two of UNSCOB's members—declared

[13] *Ibid.*, 360.

[14] The commission assembled in Athens on January 29, 1947, where it held thirty-two meetings between January 30, and February 18, 1947. Its second main base of operations in Greece was established at Solonika, where it held twenty-eight meetings from February 25 to March 22. It also held meetings in Belgrade, Athens, and Sofia.

[15] *Everyman's United Nations*, 164.

that they would not take part in the work of the Committee as they considered that its functions violated the sovereignty of Albania, Bulgaria, and Yugoslavia.[16]

UNSCOB, in its report to the Fourth (1949) Session of the General Assembly, stated that Albania and Bulgaria had assisted the Greek guerrilla movement, and had also encouraged the guerrillas in their efforts to overthrow the Greek government. Yugoslavia had aided the guerrillas, but this aid had diminished (following Tito's break with Stalin) and might even have ceased.[17] On November 18, 1949, the General Assembly again adopted a resolution stating that outside assistance was being given to the Greek guerrillas; it called on the countries concerned to cease this aid.

The General Assembly on December 7, 1951, discontinued UNSCOB and then provided for the establishment of a Balkan Subcommission by the Peace Observation Commission. The subcommission was empowered to dispatch observers with the visited country's consent and to consider the data thereby received. The Subcommission presented reports of conditions and incidents in the frontier areas of Greece. The Soviet satellites involved refused to permit the Subcommission to visit their territories. On August 1, 1954, the observer group was discontinued at the suggestion of Greece.

The work of the investigating committees, even within their limited areas of access, established strong support for the United States position in the Greek dispute. The persistence of satellite efforts to support the guerrillas pointed up the Communist "war zone–peace zone" concept—namely, that for the Communists a dispute is settled only when the territory involved is permanently pulled behind the Iron or Bamboo Curtain. Again, while their spirited attacks on Greece and UNSCOB in the Security Council showed a real concern for United Nations opinion, the Communists' blatant disregard of United Nations resolutions made it apparent that this concern was secondary when substantive positions supported by the Soviet bloc were involved. Despite Communist persistence, the United States, aided by the Yugoslav defection, came out ahead in this dispute by use of the investigative authority of the United Nations coupled with United States power projected in consonance with the Truman Doctrine.

[16] *Ibid.*, 164.   [17] *Ibid.*, 165.

2. *Palestine*

The Palestinian imbroglio had its roots in World War I, when Britain secured Arab co-operation against the Turks in return for certain British guarantees of eventual Arab independence. The Arabs claimed that the agreement included Palestine. The subsequent Balfour declaration of November 2, 1917, committed Great Britain to the support of a "National Home for the Jewish people." The terms of the declaration, while not committing the British government to the establishment of a Jewish state, did not preclude that possibility.[18]

The British Mandate for Palestine was finally approved by the League of Nations Council on September 29, 1923. The Mandate made provision for the establishment of the Jewish National Home and for facilitation of Jewish immigration into Palestine.[19] The Jews considered the Mandate the legal basis of their claim to Palestine. The Arabs, on the other hand, pointed to the qualifications calling for the protection of the rights and position of the inhabitants of Palestine which they claimed were endangered by Jewish settlement in their country.

The period before World War II brought a sharp increase in Jewish immigration into Palestine, with a corresponding augmentation of Arab opposition. The British White Paper of 1939 envisaged limited Jewish immigration for five years, at the end of which further Jewish immigration would depend upon Arab consent. Jews throughout the world vehemently denounced the White Paper. After a temporary truce on the question during World War II, a campaign of violence was initiated at the end of the war against the British by Jewish terrorists, who were opposed to the British policy—the so-called White Paper barriers, preventing further immigration.

The Labor government in Great Britain reneged on its strong stand favoring Jewish immigration after coming to power in 1945. Arab support was considered essential in safeguarding Britain's vital oil interests in the Middle East. Furthermore, a new danger to the British loomed in the Middle East—the Soviet Union. Soviet designs in the Mediterranean and Middle East had already been made apparent by the demand at Potsdam for trusteeship of an Italian colony along the Mediterranean, by the pressing of traditional claims for control of the Dardanelles, and by Communist agitation in northern Persia. Under the cir-

[18] Joseph J. Zasloff, *Great Britain and Palestine* (München, 1952), 5.
[19] *Ibid.*, 7.

cumstances "The White Paper remained the keystone of British Middle Eastern policy. In 1939 the Middle East experts had argued that it was essential for achieving Arab neutrality in the event of war with Germany and Italy. Now in 1946 they argued that it could not be rescinded without throwing the Arabs into the arms of Russia."[20]

On May 1, 1946, a joint Anglo-American Commission of Inquiry advanced ten proposals for settlement of the dispute, one of which recommended the immediate authorization of 100,000 Jews to immigrate to Palestine.[21] Neither the Arabs nor the Jews were satisfied by the Commission's compromise proposals. The British were caught in a vise between the Jews and the Arabs. The British were prevented from carrying to completion the campaign to crush Jewish resistance because of United States opposition.[22] Facing what appeared to be an irreconcilable conflict of principle and interest between Jew and Arab, the British on April 2, 1947, requested that a special session of the General Assembly be called to examine the question of Palestine.

On April 28, 1947, the First Special Session of the United Nations General Assembly opened at Lake Success to deal with the Palestine issue. The session established a United Nations Special Committee on Palestine, known as UNSCOP, and instructed it to present a report on the question.

Soviet tactics at this First Special Session illustrate Soviet conflict strategy. Despite the fact that Soviet Russia had been traditionally anti-Zionist, the Soviet representative stated that "the aspirations of an important part of the Jewish people are bound up with the question of Palestine, and with the future structure of that country."[23] The Soviets gave their support to the Zionist appeal for a link between the Jewish displaced-persons problem and the future of Palestine. At the same time, the Soviet representative supported the Arab proposal that the General Assembly specify independence for Palestine, on the grounds that neither the Arabs nor the Jews wanted a continuation of British rule. It was evident that the Soviet Union sought to weaken the British position in the Middle East; thus she could support the claims of both Jews and Arabs so long as they contributed to that aim.

A united Anglo-American policy for Palestine would have been de-

---

[20] Richard Crossman, *Palestine Mission* (London, 1946), 122.

[21] Zasloff, *Great Britain and Palestine*, 34.

[22] *Ibid.*, 38.   [23] *Ibid.*, 53.

sirable. Although Great Britain publicly adopted a policy of neutrality between Jew and Arab in the United Nations—the same as that of the initial United States policy—it could not put this policy into practice.[24] The necessity of fighting Jewish resistance inside Palestine, the attempts to check illegal Jewish immigration, and the efforts to counteract Zionist propaganda in the United States, in addition to an awareness of its Arab interests, oriented British activity against the Zionists.

In August, 1947, UNSCOP presented to the General Assembly its report containing a majority plan and a minority plan. The majority plan called for the partition of Palestine into an Arab state, a Jewish state, and an international regime for Jerusalem, the three to be linked to an economic union. The minority plan proposed an independent federal state comprising an Arab state and a Jewish state with Jerusalem as its capital.

On November 29, 1947, the Assembly adopted the majority plan.[25] The plan was accepted by the Jewish Agency and was bitterly opposed by the Arab Higher Committee, which advocated the establishment of an Arab state that would protect the rights of a Jewish minority. The resolution also provided for the ending of the British Mandate in Palestine and withdrawal of British forces not later than August 1, 1948. A United Nations Palestine Commission was set up to implement these recommendations, and the Security Council was requested to take the necessary measures to put the plan into effect. The Security Council, after considering proposals of its permanent members to resolve the dispute, called for a new special session of the Assembly.

The General Assembly was in a race against time. The security situation continued to deteriorate steadily as more British troops were withdrawn in line with the British decision to terminate its Mandate by May 14, 1948. And it was readily apparent from the statements and actions of the Arab states that they intended to invade Palestine at the termination of the Mandate. Meanwhile, Arab strategy was aimed at preventing the formation of a Jewish state. The fighting became fiercer. On May 14, the day the British Mandate expired, a Jewish state was proclaimed under the name of Israel. On the following day the Arab states initiated a military attack upon Palestine.

[24] *Ibid.*, 54.

[25] This was adopted under substantial pressure from the United States. See *ibid.*, Chap. IV.

Heavy fighting continued until May 29, 1948, when both sides accepted a truce resolution of the Security Council.[26] Count Folke Bernadotte, who had been appointed United Nations mediator by a committee of the General Assembly on May 20, decided to attempt a political settlement between the Arabs and Jews. However, both sides continued to hold to their well-established positions and were confident that renewed fighting would lead to acceptance of their demands. Upon failure to renew the four-week truce, fighting again broke out on July 9.

A second truce was arranged in the middle of July. Again a political settlement was attempted by Bernadotte, but both sides were more adamant than ever. On September 17, 1948, Bernadotte was shot and killed while leaving the Israeli-held sector of Jerusalem. He was replaced by Ralph J. Bunche of the United Nations Secretariat. The day before his death, Count Bernadotte had presented his recommendations for a peaceful settlement before the General Assembly. One of the provisions called for assigning of the Negeb to the Arabs. However, bitter opposition to this arose from Israel, whose leaders did not want to lose the Negeb or the fruits of military conquest; from the Arabs, who did not even wish to discuss any plan which involved acceptance of a Jewish state; from the Soviet Union, who recognized that from these proposals the British strategic position would be fortified through her alliance with Transjordan; and from the United States, which was in favor of the original United Nations partition plan which would include the Negeb in Israel.

Fighting again broke out on December 22, 1948, and the Israeli success in seizing control of southern Palestine presented Great Britain with a *fait accompli*. Great Britain, although alarmed over the upsetting of the balance of power by the Israelis in the Middle East, now had no choice but to acquiesce.[27] On February 6, 1949, the British extended *de facto* recognition to Israel. Great Britain now used her influence to seek to restore stability in the Middle East based on Israel's permanent establishment. Egypt and Israel, in compliance with the Security Council's resolution of November 16, entered into armistice negotiations. The other Arab states soon followed suit. On April 3, 1949, an armistice agreement which for the most part recognized the military *status quo* was signed. The United Nations Truce Supervision Organization

[26] United Nations Document S/801 (May 29, 1948).
[27] Zasloff, *Great Britain and Palestine*, Chapter IX.

(UNTSO), since 1949, has assisted the Security Council in its consideration of complaints relating to the Palestine question.

Unfortunately, UNTSO has had neither the numbers nor the authority to do an effective job in the absence of full co-operation from both sides. Neither side has been willing to cease crossing each other's borders for the purpose of looting and killing. Incidents have continued, varying in frequency and seriousness. Whenever one of the parties has found a reason to issue a complaint in the United Nations, it has done so. The result is a censure, but it has not been followed up by any sanction or by the strengthening of the United Nations machinery so that it could prevent further incidents.[28] The result has been that the offending power merely shrugs off the reprimand and goes on resorting to the same measures. Both sides flout the United Nations whenever they desire to do so. However, UNTSO has adjusted many minor disputes, which in the absence of regulation might have expanded into full-blown war.

Palestine was a severe test for the United Nations. The United Nations partition plan provided the framework for the existing settlement; however, the United Nations was unable to prevent a full-scale Arab-Israeli war. The existing boundaries between Israel and Arab states were the result of military action rather than United Nations resolutions.

The Soviets gave their support to the United Nations partition proposal until the existence of Israel was fairly well assured in 1951. Then Soviet policy was reversed. The result was that tensions were raised as the Soviet Union increasingly championed the anti-Israel sentiment in the Middle East. The United States cannot match Soviet wooing of the Arabs because it is committed to a solution which guarantees the continuance of the Jewish state. The Soviet Union has gained from the partition of Palestine and ensuing Arab-Israeli conflicts the position as a powerful force in the Mediterranean with strong influence among the Arabs in North Africa and in the vital Middle East.

3. The Korean War

On June 25, 1950, North Korean tank columns and infantry crossed the thirty-eighth parallel in force, in an attempt to place all of Korea under Communist control. Within several days the Communists were

---

[28] Israel's raid on Qibliya and Egyptian interference with shipping through the Suez Canal destined for Israel are two examples of censured actions not followed up by sanctions.

at the gates of Seoul. The United Nations Commission on Korea was on hand to confirm that this act of naked aggression was executed as part of a carefully prepared plan. Within hours the United States requested an emergency session of the Security Council.

The absence of the Soviet Union from the Security Council (because of an earlier walkout in protest against the United Nations refusal to seat the Communist government of China) permitted that body to act quickly in declaring the attack "a breach of the peace," calling for an immediate cessation of hostilities and the withdrawal of North Korean forces to the thirty-eighth parallel, asking the United Nations Commission on Korea to observe the withdrawal and keep the Security Council informed, and asking United Nations members to give the United Nations assistance in the execution of this resolution.[29]

In accordance with this resolution, President Truman authorized the United States Far East Commander, General Douglas MacArthur, to furnish the Republic of Korea with military supplies and to employ air and sea forces. United States Army units were soon ordered into action. President Truman also ordered the American Seventh Fleet to prevent belligerent actions between Formosa and the Chinese mainland.

On June 27, 1950, the Security Council adopted another resolution requesting member states to assist the Republic of Korea. Fifty-three states approved the United States–sponsored resolution and thus gave their moral support. Sixteen states eventually offered armed forces. Other states gave supplies and services.

Another Security Council resolution of July 7, 1950, sponsored jointly by France and the United Kingdom, provided for the establishment of a unified command under the flag of the United Nations. The United States was asked to designate a commander and to make periodic reports on the course of action taken by the command. General Mac-Arthur was named as the Supreme United Nations Commander. The United Nations Command became the official title of the United Nations forces.

After the successful defense of Pusan, a brilliantly conceived amphibious landing at Inchon on September 15, 1950, caught the North Korean army by surprise. The United Nations Command now had the initiative, and it moved north toward the thirty-eighth parallel in con-

[29] Leland M. Goodrich, *Korea: A Study of U.S. Policy in the United Nations* (New York, Council on Foreign Relations, 1956), 105.

sonance with a General Assembly resolution of October 7. The resolution declared as its objective the unification of the country and the holding of elections in Korea in order to set up a "unified, independent, and democratic government." The resolution pledged that the "United Nations forces should not remain in any part of Korea otherwise than so far as necessary for achieving the objectives specified."[30]

The United Nations Command crossed the thirty-eighth parallel and drove north to capture the North Korean capital of Pyongyang, and reached the Yalu River by October 26, 1950. On November 26, 1950, the Chinese Communist "volunteers" entered the war, and their attack compelled the United Nations Command to retreat to a position well below the thirty-eighth parallel. General MacArthur claimed that the Chinese entry had changed the character of the war. He unsuccessfully urged President Truman to authorize the following: imposition of a naval blockade against Communist China, initiation of air reconnaissance of Chinese coastal areas and Manchuria, and removal of restrictions on offensive action from Formosa.

At United Nations headquarters in New York a representative of the Peoples' Republic of China was invited to appear before the Security Council. The Chinese Communist representative, Mr. Wu Hsin-chuan, delivered tirades against United States participation in the Korean War. Such tirades notwithstanding, the General Assembly on February 1, 1951, adopted a modified form of an American resolution branding the Chinese Communists as aggressors: "By giving aid and assistance to those who were already committing aggression in Korea, and by engaging in hostilities with the United Nations forces there, (the People's Republic of China) has itself engaged in aggression."[31] Sanctions against Communist China were not approved, but the resolution was welcomed by the United States. Communist China, like North Korea, was now labeled an "aggressor." Subsequently sanctions against Communist China in the form of an embargo were called for in the General Assembly resolution of May 18, 1951.

Meanwhile, the Chinese offensive had been brought to a halt and the Communists were slowly driven back. The question was again brought up concerning the desirability of recrossing the thirty-eighth parallel. President Truman declared that the October 7, 1950, resolution of the

[30] *Ibid.*, 126.   [31] *Ibid.*, 226.

General Assembly still was valid and that it was up to the Supreme United Nations Commander to decide whether the thirty-eighth parallel should be crossed again. Yet the feeling was beginning to permeate official Washington that a truce line at the thirty-eighth parallel might be practical. Such a consideration was extremely repugnant to MacArthur, whose strong advocacy of his differing views led to his dismissal on April 11, 1951.

The excitement caused by MacArthur's removal did not stop the fighting in Korea. On May 17, 1951, Senator Edwin C. Johnston introduced a resolution asking the United Nations to urge the belligerents in Korea to declare an armistice by June 25, the first anniversary of the war, along the thirty-eighth parallel, and to agree to the exchange of all war prisoners and to the withdrawal of all foreign troops by the end of the year.

On May 26, 1951, Canada's Lester Pearson, president of the General Assembly, declared that complete surrender of the aggressors might not be necessary. On June 1, 1951, United Nations Secretary-General Trygve Lie expressed the belief that the time was right to attempt to stop the fighting in Korea. United States Secretary of State Dean Acheson expounded similar views on June 2, 1951.

Because the Chinese Communists had been repulsed and were falling back with heavy losses, they accepted Yakov Malik's plea for a negotiated settlement on June 25, 1951. Armistice negotiations began on July 10, 1951. The Communists merely shifted the scene of conflict from the military field to the conference table. Yet military action continued and erupted into a series of bloody local battles in 1953. After two years of protracted negotiating, an armistice agreement was signed at Panmunjom in July, 1953. The agreement stipulated that no reinforcing personnel or combat equipment could be introduced except as a replacement. The Communists violated this from the start. Vetoes by Czechoslovakia and Poland immobilized the Neutral Nations Supervisory Commission in its attempts to conduct inspections in North Korea. The Communists again used disruptive and stalling tactics to prevent the 1954 Geneva political conference from resolving the Korean question as was provided for in the armistice agreement and a United Nations Assembly resolution of August 28, 1953.

Soviet diplomacy within and outside the United Nations during the period of Korean hostilities played on widespread fear of general war by using Communist "peace" offensives and confused neutralist sentiment with charges of United States atrocities and "germ" warfare. With calculated flexibility the Communist bloc was able to compensate for the military defeat of North Korea in September, 1950, and to prevent a military disaster from overtaking the Chinese Communist "volunteers" in June, 1951. After redressing an unfavorable military equation by political action, the Soviet Union used the two years of armistice negotiations to wipe off a large part of the tarnish which the Korean aggression had deposited on its badge of peace and to gain new adherents for the Communist cause among the new nations of Asia and Africa.

United Nations action in Korea did delay the Communist timetable for Asia. It also seems quite probable that from this experience the Soviets moved more adroitly in their subsequent ventures. Furthermore, the United Nations Command was given a definitive lesson in Communist negotiating techniques. Concessions that were granted (thirty-day truce and limitation of the number of North Korean harbors to be inspected) in order to facilitate the progress of the negotiations only made the Communists more intransigent and less accountable for fulfillment of any agreements reached.

The Korean War on the United Nations side was an international war waged for specifically limited objectives. The limitations came about because the collective security action involved directly or indirectly the two chief protagonists in the protracted conflict. It is doubtful that such a United Nations action will be undertaken again. Although the aggression was repulsed, the devastation wrought in South Korea and the loss of prestige suffered by the United States in Asia had dealt a nearly fatal blow to the concept of collective security. Disunity, timidity, and ambiguity have since increasingly hampered the efficiency of the United Nations efforts to preserve the peace.

The United States scored in Korea through its willingness to use power in the face of aggression, the fortuitous presence of United Nations observers in Korea and the absence of the Soviet Union from the Security Council, and mobilization of psychological support in the United Nations. However, the Soviets, by skillful political manipulation inside and outside the United Nations, prevented imminent military disaster from overtaking Communist forces and managed to extract much political gain from a military stalemate.

4. *Suez-Hungary*

United Nations response to the events of October–November, 1956, in Hungary and Suez clearly brought into focus the double standard which simultaneously decreased the influence of the United Nations as an organ for settlement of Cold War disputes but made it increasingly important as a psychological forum in the protracted conflict. In these disputes it was evident that the Soviet Union and important neutrals might be subject to criticism in the United Nations but that such criticism would not be backed by any collective United Nations power. On the other hand, states protected neither by firm United States support nor by an important voting bloc were likely to be subject to pressure both inside and outside the United Nations.

Tension in the Middle East resulting from Communist arms shipments to Egypt under cover of the "Geneva spirit" was heightened when Nasser proclaimed on July 26, 1956, the nationalization of the Suez Canal Company, placing the management of the Canal in the hands of an Egyptian operating authority. It should be noted that the decree provided for remuneration to stockholders in the Canal Company on the basis of the market value of the shares on the day preceding the seizure.

Lengthy negotiations then took place concerning methods of settling the control of the operation of the Canal. During August and September two conferences were held in London. At the first conference eighteen of the twenty-two nations attending agreed on certain proposals which were presented to Egypt in September by Australian Prime Minister Menzies. Nasser rejected outright the eighteen nations' plan for a Users Association as "collective colonialism."

France and the United Kingdom stated in a letter to the Security Council on September 12 that the action of Egypt in attempting to end the international operation of the Suez Canal might endanger the free and open passage of shipping, and that if the situation were allowed to continue it would constitute a danger to peace and security.[32]

The problem was given to the Security Council on September 23, at the request of France and the United Kingdom. The discussion which ensued focused on whether Egypt's legitimate right of nationalization meant the absence of international rights. While Egypt was quite willing

[32] United Nations Document S/3545. Letter of France and the United Kingdom to the Security Council on September 12, 1956.

to negotiate, she would not accept any system of international control as the basis of settlement. Egypt had taken over the Canal as a political gesture, an assertion of sovereignty. Nasser himself had announced it as a "declaration of independence" from imperialism. "How could he be expected to jeopardize all he had won by accepting a system of international control, which would have been more restrictive of Egypt's sovereignty than the concession to a foreign-owned but still legally Egyptian company which he had just annulled?"[33]

At the meeting of the Security Council on October 13 a resolution was unanimously adopted by which it was agreed that any settlement of the Suez question should meet certain requirements: free and open transit through the Canal without discrimination, respect of the sovereignty of Egypt, and settlement of disputes through arbitration.[34] Egypt accepted the requirements, and between October 13 and 19 the Secretary-General held private talks with the Minister of Foreign Affairs of Egypt on possible implementation arrangements. Negotiations, however, were interrupted by the military action in Egypt of Israeli and Anglo-French forces accompanied by the blocking of the Canal by Egypt. Israel attacked in the Gaza Strip on October 29, asserting its right to protect itself from raids by fellahin units from Egypt. The French and British attacked Egypt on October 31, after Egyptian refusal to comply with a twelve-hour ultimatum which demanded removal of Egyptian armed forces as well as advancing Israeli forces to a distance ten miles from the Canal. The Anglo-French attack was immediately considered by the Security Council. The United States presented a resolution calling for the cessation of the use of force, but use of the veto by Great Britain and France prevented the resolution from being adopted.[35] Therefore Yugoslavia submitted a resolution calling for an emergency special session of the General Assembly, as provided in the Assembly's "Uniting for Peace Resolution."[36] The resolution was adopted, thereby transferring the problem to the General Assembly meeting in emergency session.

In all probability, the British and French expected a quick military

[33] John C. Campbell, *Defense of the Middle East* (New York, Council on Foreign Relations, 1960), 101.

[34] United Nations Document S/3675 (October 13, 1956).

[35] United Nations Document S/3710. United States draft resolution of October 29, 1956.

[36] United Nations Document S/3719. Yugoslav resolution of October 31, 1956.

success, whereby they would seize the canal and oust Nasser before any-body else could take any preventive action.[37] However, they planned and conducted their military operations ineptly; they underestimated the capacity of the United Nations for speedy action (particularly when the United States and the Soviet Union were unexpectedly acting in concert); they underestimated the reaction of the Soviet Union, which took the form of threats of rocket warfare against western Europe; and they overestimated the reluctance of the United States on the eve of an election to take any action at all, particularly against Israel. The result was that the General Assembly, with the United States in a leading role, passed quickly and overwhelmingly a series of resolutions calling for a cessation of fighting and the withdrawal of foreign forces from Egypt.[38]

On November 2, 1956, the General Assembly requested the Secretary-General to submit a plan for setting up an emergency international United Nations force.[39] After the report had been submitted, on November 5, the Assembly adopted a resolution establishing a United Nations Command to secure and supervise the cessation of hostilities. The Assembly named General E. L. M. Burns of Canada as commander. Troops would not be drawn from the Great Powers; the force would be under the control of the Secretary-General; it would be a neutral, buffer force, not a fighting army, and would first have to obtain the consent of Egypt before entering upon Egyptian territory.[40]

The combined pressure of the United States, the Soviet Union, United Nations resolutions, world opinion, lack of the united support of the Commonwealth, and the strong opposition of the Labour party sufficed to bring Great Britain by November 6 to the point of agreeing to a gradual withdrawal from the only Egyptian territory captured, Port Said. The French had no choice but to follow suit, and Israel, its military actions having been successful, also stated its readiness to stop fighting. Anglo-French forces completed their withdrawal on December 22, 1956. Israel, on March 7, 1957, initiated withdrawal, with United Nations contingents being deployed in Gaza in order to maintain quiet

[37] Campbell, *Defense of the Middle East*, 109.

[38] Resolutions of November 2, 4, 5, 7, 13, and 24, 1956.

[39] United Nations Document A/3276. Canadian Draft resolution of November 2, 1956.

[40] Reports of November 5 and 7, 1956, by the Secretary-General to the General Assembly.

during and after the Israeli pullback. By early February, 1957, the United Nations had six thousand officers and men in the area.

The speedy formation of the United Nations force was a change from the usually cumbersome process of international peacemaking. Some countries, of course, considered it a great distinction to contribute troops to a United Nations peace force designed to check "imperialism" as witnessed by the flood of offers in the Suez crisis. Others, like the Scandinavians, based their offer to provide troops on their support as traditional neutrals of international law enforcement.

The Suez crisis was a monument to Western disunity. The crucial point when both the British and French governments should have asserted themselves arrived when Nasser openly defied their once dominant authority in the Middle East. Their positions as world powers seemed to be at the mercy of the upstart Nasser. They felt that at some point a solution would have to be imposed upon Egypt.[41] The United States, while agreeing with the principle of international regulation of the Canal, was opposed to the use of force. The British and French felt themselves left with a choice between force and surrender. The United States, aware for months that force might be used, apparently never told the British and French how it would react if they did employ force.[42] The subsequent attack opened wide fissures within the Western alliance. The wounds to Allied unity have never completely healed.

The Soviet Union played a strong hand during the crisis. Moscow had long determined to exploit Arab nationalism against the West. The 1956 crisis gave Moscow an opportunity for redoubled efforts, which fortuitously diverted attention from the Communist suppression of the revolt in Hungary. The Western powers seemed intent on digging themselves a grave in the Middle East. To help them do so, and to bury American interests along with those of Great Britain and France, Moscow made every possible appeal to Arab and Asian nationalism, to anticolonialism, to the principles of sovereignty and the rights of small nations, victims of aggression. America was pictured not as aiding Egypt but as scheming to replace European with American imperialism.

The Kremlin also wanted to convince the Arabs that the Soviet Union would fight if necessary in their behalf while the United States would not fight against them. The Soviets, however, took no step which would spread the war in the Middle East. But they did intervene diplo-

[41] Campbell, *Defense of the Middle East*, 109.   [42] *Ibid.*, 113.

matically in a dramatic fashion by proposing joint Soviet-American military action, threatening Great Britain and France with missile warfare, and talking of sending "volunteers."

Both the United States and the Soviet Union were competing for the role of defenders of the victim of aggression and were doing their best to capitalize on that role in the Middle East and to forestall each other's moves there. In this competition the Soviets had many tangible advantages: their earlier record of support for Arab nationalism; their insistence on the immediate and unconditional withdrawal of all foreign troops from Egypt and the Gaza Strip; and their hard talk to Israel, even calling into question its future existence as a state. The United States could not match the calculated irresponsibility of Soviet threats, promises, and propaganda.

The Suez crisis provided a most effective smoke screen to Communist suppression of the Hungarian revolt in November, 1956. An explosive and successful revolution of workers, soldiers, and intellectuals brought the more moderate Nagy regime to power while displacing the Gero government and forcing the temporary withdrawal of Soviet troops.

At this critical juncture the Israeli attack and the desultory ill-co-ordinated Anglo-French intervention against Egypt occurred. The United States had abandoned her traditional allies, sponsoring a series of Security Council and Assembly resolutions which would bring an end to the Suez adventure. The Soviet Union quickly and brutally crushed the Hungarian revolution while a Nagy request for United Nations aid resulted in a resolution calling for cessation of Soviet aggression but no concrete action. The resolution, adopted on November 4, 1956, called upon the Soviet Union to withdraw all its forces from Hungary without delay. It further affirmed the right of the Hungarian people to a government responsive to their national aspirations and requested the Secretary-General to investigate the situation caused by foreign intervention in Hungary, to observe the situation directly through representatives named by him and to report to the General Assembly, and to suggest methods of bringing to an end foreign intervention in Hungary in accordance with the Charter. The Assembly then called upon the governments of Hungary and the Soviet Union to permit United Nations observers to enter Hungary. On November 9 three similar resolutions were adopted, again calling upon the Soviet Union to withdraw its forces from Hungary. The Secretary-General was rebuffed in his attempts to send United Nations observers into Hungary by the Soviet-imposed Comumnist government in Hungary.[43] With the then-existing balance of forces in Europe the United States appeared unwilling to support any policy that would risk military action. On the other hand, imaginative measures, such as flying a significant portion of the Secretariat to Budapest in the two days during which the Nagy government threw itself on the protection of the United Nations, might have salvaged a great deal from the Hungarian tragedy.

United States policy shortcomings in dealing with the Suez and Hungarian crises were manifest. There was failure in the intelligent use of power and its projection, in communication with governments and peoples, in exploitation of the psychological advantages to be gained from our position. Confusion and lack of perceptive leadership masqueraded as moderation and economy in policies. Given more trust, a common purpose in the protracted conflict, and clearer communications among the Western allies, United States pressure inside and outside the United Nations could have prevented arms shipments to the Middle East and forced a reasonable settlement, heading off the Suez debacle. With this source of division removed, and stronger forces available in Europe, threats of Western "volunteers" for Hungary and a stiffer United Nations stand could have induced Soviet acquiescence in a neutralist or Titoist Hungarian regime.

The United States failed to exploit its transient gains in Suez while the Soviet Union used the crisis to muffle its repression of Hungary and later to increase its capital in the underdeveloped countries. Lack of willingness to use power to support a single standard of international morality cost the United States an unparalleled opportunity in Hungary. In December, 1962, the United States took the initiative in removing the Hungarian question from the United Nations agenda, presumably in the interest of easing East-West tensions.

5. The Congo

The Communist bloc, since the Peoples' Solidarity Conference held in Cairo in 1957, has played with increasing skill on racial prejudices, anticolonialism, and imperial ambitions of *ad hoc* proxies among the leaders of newly emergent nations in Africa. Their initial successes in Africa

---

[43] Note the parallel with the refusal of Castro to permit United Nations observers to check withdrawal of Soviet missiles from Cuba.

were strikingly illustrated in the Congo in July, 1960. When Belgian security troops in the newly independent Congo were sent to protect their nationals against race riots incited by Lumumba demagoguery, a Congo appeal for military aid to the Security Council resulted in resolutions for Belgian withdrawal.[44] In the meantime Moise Tshombe, premier of Katanga Province, proclaimed Katanga's secession from the Congo on July 11. In a reply to the threat of Tshombe to use force to prevent movement of United Nations troops in Katanga, United Nations Secretary-General Hammarskjold stated to the Ministerial Commission of the Congolese Cabinet on August 2: "The Security Council's appeal to the Government of Belgium to withdraw its troops, as well as the request of the Secretary-General for sending an emergency force under that resolution, applies without ambiguity to all the territory of the Congo, including Katanga."[45]

In reply to a message from Tshombe, in which Hammarskjold sought to reassure him, the following remarks are significant in relation to later events:

1. The (UN) troops are under the sole command and sole control of the United Nations.

2. The troops *are not permitted to interfere in the internal affairs* of the country in which they are deployed. They cannot be used in order to impose any particular political solution of pending problems, or to exert any influence on a balance of political forces which may be decisive for such a solution.

3. United Nations military units are not entitled to act except in self-defense. This rule categorically prohibits the troops participating in the operation from taking the initiative or resorting to armed force, but permits them to reply by force to an armed attack, in particular to any attempts to resort to force which might be made with the object of compelling them to evacuate positions which they occupy on the orders of their commander.

Hammarskjold further stated:

Nor is the problem one of a wish of the authorities of the province to secede from the Republic of the Congo. The question is a constitutional one with strong undercurrents of individual and collective political aims. The problems for those resisting the United Nations force in the Katanga may

[44] United Nations Document S/4387 (July 14, 1960).

[45] Taken from text of Hammarskjold's statement, *New York Times* (August 3, 1960), 10.

be stated in these terms: Will United Nations participation in control of security in the Katanga submit the province to immediate control and authority of the Central Government against its wishes? They consider this seriously to jeopardize their possibility to work for other constitutional solutions than a strictly unitarian one, e.g., some kind of federal structure providing for a higher degree of provincial self-government than now foreseen. The spokesmen for this attitude reject the unitarian formula as incompatible with the interests of the whole Congo people and as imposed from the outside.

This is an internal political problem to which the United Nations as an organization obviously cannot be a party. Nor would the entry of the United Nations force in Katanga mean any taking of sides in the conflict to which I have just referred. *Nor should it be permitted to shift the weights between personalities or groups or schools of thought in a way which would prejudice the solution of the internal political problem.*[46]

The foregoing principles were completely and deliberately violated by the United Nations in its operations against Katanga in December, 1962.

During the Belgian re-entry into the Congo to restore order, Patrice Lumumba, the Congolese premier, received assurances and an indeterminate amount of aid from Nikita Khrushchev in response to a request to the Soviet Union.

The Congo presented the Soviets with a number of propaganda opportunities, and the latter did not neglect them. Moscow's repeated threats to intervene in the Congo were designed to further its role as a champion of Congolese freedom and unity and to convince the other Africans that the Soviet Union was the one nation to which they could turn for support against the imperialists.

Also included in the Kremlin's arsenal of tactics were threats of unilateral action against the Belgians in the Congo. A Soviet government statement issued on July 31, 1960, read:

> In case the aggression against the Congo is continued and considering the dangerous consequences for the cause of universal peace, the Soviet government will not hesitate to take resolute measures to rebuff the aggressors who, as it has now become perfectly clear, are actually acting with the encouragement of all the colonialist powers of NATO.[47]

[46] *New York Times* (August 7, 1960), 28. (Italics added.)
[47] *New York Times* (August 1, 1960), 1.

The West was in a difficult position, for Belgium was a NATO ally. Hammarskjold called Belgian troops "a source of internal and international friction." Belgium maintained that the troops were in the Congo for the protection of her citizens. Belgium's stand aroused bitter resentment from the Afro-Asians, some of whom attacked the United States because of its association with Belgium.

Persuaded by Hammarskjold's assurances, Tshombe allowed United Nations contingents to enter Katanga. Throughout this period Tshombe declared his support for Congo unity, provided a federal system was instituted. In November, 1960, he met with central government leaders, and general agreement concerning a federal system was reached.

United Nations forces had restored some degree of order by August, 1960, and had facilitated Belgian withdrawal. But Hammarskjold, following Security Council instructions, refused to intervene in the internal affairs of the Congo despite strong pressures from the Soviet Union, supported by Nkrumah, Touré, Nasser, Sukarno, and Nehru.

Meanwhile, in late August, Lumumba had begun to act erratically and to perpetrate a number of outrages. He instigated and supported wanton attacks against whites, including United Nations personnel, and the murder of actual, potential, and fancied opponents.[48] Joseph Kasavubu, fearful of the strong-arm tactics used by Lumumba in his attempt to centralize power in the Congo, dismissed him on September 5.[49] Lumumba did not accept his dismissal. When placed under United Nations protection, he attempted to continue as premier, dismissed Kasavubu, and assembled some members of Parliament. Illegally convoked, and without a quorum, the lower house invalidated both dismissals. For a time, the Congo appeared to have two governments: the Ileo government which Kasavubu named to succeed Lumumba, but which had not been tested in Parliament, and thus was not legally established; and the Lumumba government, legally instituted but dismissed by the President. Anarchy prevailed until an army colonel, Joseph Mobutu, seized control and thereafter, with Kasavubu's assent, named a committee to run the Congo.

Seeing power slip from him, Lumumba secretly left his United

[48] United Nations Document A/4711. Documents presented to the United Nations by President Kasavubu.

[49] As early as August 6, Kasavubu's party supported Tshombe's stand for a federalized Congo. *New York Times* (August 7, 1960), 3.

Nations protected residence and attempted to join his supporters who had seized power in Stanleyville, where Antoine Gizenga, a vice-premier in Lumumba's dismissed cabinet, declared himself premier of the Congo on December 13, 1960. Deprived of United Nations protection, Lumumba was intercepted by Mobutu's forces and arrested on the basis of warrants signed by Kasavubu (the United Nations had previously prevented the serving of these warrants).[50] On January 18, 1961, Lumumba was transferred to prison in Katanga; he attempted a second escape there and was killed.[51]

On February 21, 1961, the Security Council authorized United Nations troops to use force to prevent civil war. Insisting that civil war threatened in and about Katanga, on April 1, the United Nations sent Gurkha troops to Katanga, citing the United Nations resolution of February 21. These United Nations forces were deployed in Katanga, although the province was far more peaceful that the other regions of the Congo.

On April 24 a second conference of Congo leaders took place in Coquilhatville to implement the Tananarive (March, 1961) decisions. Although the Tananarive accords were vague enough to permit a wide latitude of interpretation in good faith, each claimed that the other had refused to honor its word.

Reasoning that negotiations were impossible under the circumstances, Tshombe attempted to leave the conference. He was forcibly detained on April 25, arrested without warrant, and kept under harsh conditions. He was released on June 22, after having been compelled to promise to cease his opposition to a centralized government. Back in Elizabethville, Tshombe refused to consider himself obligated by a promise made under duress.

On September 13, 1961, United Nations troops initiated a military attack on Elizabethville; they failed to take the city despite considerable fighting. On October 13 a formal cease-fire was established; it was ratified on October 24 by the United Nations Secretariat. The United Nations recognized Katanga's right to protect itself from Central government attacks. Prisoners were exchanged, and the United Nations did

[50] Ernest van der Hoag, *The War in Katanga: Report of a Mission* (New York, American Committee for Aid to Katanga Freedom Fighters, 1962), 14.

[51] A United Nations commission which attempted to enquire into his death was not allowed to enter Katanga. It concluded that Lumumba was murdered.

not attempt to impose conditions on Tshombe's employment of mercenaries.

However, on November 24, 1961, the Security Council once more approved use of force to deport mercenaries from Katanga. After a considerable build-up, the fighting again broke out on December 5. This time the United Nations troops succeeded in taking Elizabethville. Under the protection of the consular corps of Elizabethville, Tshombe went to Kitona, where he met with Premier Adoula under the auspices of the United Nations. An agreement was signed and ratified by both parties. A *de facto* armistice prevailed in Elizabethville throughout most of 1962.

Before the year was out, however, the United Nations embarked on an all-out campaign to end the Katanga secession. On August 1, United Nations Secretary-General U Thant appealed to all United Nations members to use economic pressures to persuade Katanga authorities that "Katanga is not a sovereign state." In a letter to President Tshombe, United Nations Congo Chief Robert Gardiner, a citizen of Ghana, outlined steps necessary to end Katanga's secession. Shortly thereafter, on November 27, 1962, President Kennedy and Belgian foreign minister Spaak reaffirmed their support of U Thant's Congo reunification plan. In a joint statement they warned Katanga of "severe economic measures" if significant progress was not made toward reunification "in a very short time." On December 10, Gardiner warned Tshombe that the United Nations was ready to use all means short of war to end the Katanga secession.

On December 18, Washington announced that it was sending an eight-man military mission, headed by Lieutenant General Louis Truman, to the Congo to survey the needs of United Nations forces there. Almost concurrently fighting broke out between United Nations troops and Tshombe's *gendarmerie*. It quickly became evident that United Nations forces were determined to crush all opposition. On December 30, Secretary-General Thant announced that United Nations forces had successfully completed their operations against Katanga troops. On the same date United Nations Congo Chief Gardiner asserted in Leopoldville that the United Nations was "not going to make the mistake of stopping short this time." On January 17, 1963, President Tshombe surrendered his last stronghold at Kolwezi.

That same day United States Assistant Secretary of State for International Organization Affairs Harlan Cleveland endorsed United States support of the United Nations use of force. While admitting that the United Nations operation in the Congo was opposed in varying degrees by several major United States allies, he said:

> The secessionist bubbles [in the Congo] have burst. There are no uninvited foreign troops, no communist enclaves, no "army of liberation," no reason for a single American soldier to die there, no excuse for a Soviet soldier to live there. . . . our object in supporting the United Nations in the Congo is to advance United States policy for Africa. That policy is to help African leadership develop truly independent, cooperating, and progressive states going about the prime business of Africa, which is its own modernization. Our policy is to help legitimate governments which ask for help to maintain their territorial integrity and political independence and to defend themselves against chaos and subversion from any quarter. . . . The Congo crisis was not all a local affair from which we could abstain—because we could not depend on others to abstain. It was, and is, just about the most international affair one can imagine, from which we could abstain only at the ultimate peril of our own national security.[52]

Three days later United Nations Undersecretary for Special Political Affairs Ralph J. Bunche declared that once the military action was over, the Congo would need "the most massive technical assistance effort in human history."

It will take considerable time to determine whether the United Nations operations in the Congo can be regarded as a success from the American point of view. There is no question that the United Nations drifted far from its original purpose and agreement not to side with any faction. For example, with respect to Katanga, the United Nations had stated in August, 1960: "This is an internal political problem to which the United Nations as an organization obviously cannot be a party."[53]

United States support of the United Nations operations in the Congo will be justified only if Communist endeavors to gain influence in that crucial region in central Africa have been frustrated. The United States has claimed that support of Adoula (whose government includes many supporters of pro-Communist Gizenga) and suppression of Tshombe's secession would have this effect. Opponents of the United Nations operation among our allies in Europe as well as in the United States

[52] *Washington Post* (January 18, 1963).
[53] United Nations Document S/4417 (August 6, 1960), 11.

(Senator Thomas J. Dodd, for example) hold the opposite view. United States officials rejected a federal solution for the Congo on the grounds that only a centralized Congo state could be made economically viable. Throughout the entire United Nations operation in the Congo, United States and United Nations policy were indistinguishable. This fact makes the outcome of future developments in the Congo so important. Ironically, Moise Tshombe, the bête noire of both United States and United Nations policy-makers, became premier of the Congo a few days after the last United Nations forces withdrew on June 30, 1964. If, despite Tshombe's presence, the pessimists turn out to be right and anarchy and Communist influence spread from the Congo to Angola and Rhodesia, United States prestige in Africa will suffer and United States domestic support for the United Nations will decline correspondingly.

The United Nations can derive a clear lesson from the role which it has played in the Congo. It must cease to play favorites and assume an impartial role in internal domestic disputes and international conflicts as well. The United Nations assumption of an active role as director of operations instead of guide and mediator can have disastrous repercussions in the future for an organization which is as yet ill equipped to employ force to deal with deep-rooted international disputes.

6. *Cuba*

The Cuban missile crisis of October, 1962, was primarily a direct confrontation of United States and Soviet power personally directed by President Kennedy and Premier Khrushchev. The United States did, however, ask the United Nations to consider the problem and to inspect the departure of Soviet missiles from Cuba.

The United States, on October 22, 1962, asked for an emergency meeting of the United Nations Security Council "to take action against the latest Soviet threat to world peace." The United States resolution called for "the prompt dismantling and withdrawal of all offensive weapons in Cuba, under the supervision of United Nations' observers, before the quarantine can be lifted." On October 23, Fidel Castro asserted that Cuba would never accept the United States plan for a United Nations investigating committee to check on Soviet missile bases in Cuba. On October 23, 1962, United Nations Secretary-General U Thant declared: "Time should be given to . . . normalize the situation in the Caribbean. This involves on the one hand the voluntary suspension of all arms shipments to Cuba, and also the voluntary suspension of the quarantine measures involving the searching of ships bound for Cuba . . . for a period of two or three weeks."[54]

Soviet Premier Khrushchev accepted U Thant's proposal for a suspension of the United States blockade and Soviet shipment of arms. President Kennedy replied to U Thant by stating that "the existing threat was created by the secret introduction of offensive weapons into Cuba, and the answer lies in the removal of these weapons."

On October 26 a message from Premier Khrushchev reached President Kennedy. The *New York Times* had this to say about the message: "Not explicitly stated, but embedded in the letter was an offer to withdraw the offensive weapons under United Nations supervision in return for a guarantee that the United States would not invade Cuba."[55]

On October 30, 1962, United Nations Secretary-General U Thant visited Premier Castro in Cuba with regard to United Nations supervision and verification of the dismantling and removal of Soviet missiles from the island. Upon his return "it was the general belief at the United Nations that he (U Thant) had been unable to persuade Cuba to agree to his plan to have United Nations' inspectors check the removal of missiles."[56]

By early November the inspection issue was permitted to slip away. The *New York Herald Tribune* stated that "it was learned on reliable authority that in the last few days United States Ambassador Adlai E. Stevenson had been told by Soviet representatives in no uncertain terms that 'the United States is pushing this question too far.' "

On November 20, President Kennedy stated in a televised press conference that the "Cuban Government has not yet permitted the United Nations to verify whether all offensive weapons have been removed." Nevertheless, after the United States terminated its naval blockade of Cuba, there was no chance that any form of United Nations inspection of Soviet military installations in Cuba would ever take place. Of great significance is Castro's defiance (with Soviet support) of the United Nations authority. The long record of Communist refusal to permit the United Nations to operate, investigate, or inspect on territory controlled by Communist power remains unbroken.

[54] *United Nations Review*, Vol. IX, No. 11 (November, 1962), 7.

[55] (November 3, 1962).

[56] *New York Times* (November 1, 1962).

Conclusion

Both the United States and the Soviet Union have enjoyed diplomatic and phychological success in the handling of disputes referred to the United Nations.

Soviet successes in United Nations disputes can be chalked up to skillful exploitation of the long-range aspirations and fears of others coupled with growing Soviet power outside the United Nations. Successes can also be attributed to the Soviet Union's recognition of the United Nations psychological importance. The changing complexion of its membership has tempted the Soviet Union to try to convert this body into a potential social fission weapon to employ against the West in its most vulnerable spot—its relations with the emergent nations.

American power has often been neutralized in United Nations disputes, whereas Soviet power has been rendered effective beyond its normal reach. For most of the delegations in the United Nations, Soviet power is a fact. Changing it is beyond the means of most member nations. All they can do is accommodate themselves to this reality. In contrast, American power has frequently been something that can be talked out of existence. It can be rendered ineffective by the diplomatic action of a few small countries, not to speak of a majority resolution. The Congo crisis illustrated this situation. Geographically and physically the United States and its Western allies were the only countries capable of acting effectively in this region. Their financial and technical means made the United Nations military operation possible in the Congo. However, the direction of the United Nations effort in the Congo was influenced primarily by countries which were organically incapable of acting effectively in this region or pursued policies inconsistent with Western interests.

The Hungarian revolt in 1956 illustrated how the United Nations can provide United States policy-makers with a comfortable instrument of evasion. The United States appeared to be taking forthright action by dropping this matter into the lap of an organization which was incapable either of making any effective decisions or of making them stick without strong United States support. The United Nations thus became a substitute for action instead of a source of moral and political support for, or endorsement of, a power capable of action.

In the Stalin era, the Soviet Union sporadically used the United Nations to attempt to identify itself with progressive causes and to overcome diplomatically the political power of the United States atomic monopoly. Soviet propaganda in the United Nations was generally geared to specific positions taken by the Soviet Union in United Nations disputes. Now with growing power and more flexible and sophisticated tactics the Soviets are more and more on the offensive in the United Nations. The Soviet Union seeks to capture the United Nations through the cowing of the small nations or by "peaceful coexistence" tactics. An example of their increased confidence in their ability either to disrupt the United Nations or to twist it to their end was the 1961 "troika" proposal to render impotent the office of secretary-general.

Throughout the history of the United Nations existence relations between the Soviet Union and her non-self-governing satellites, and now Cuba, have remained essentially internal matters. Similar problems in the "war zone," such as the Congo, the Algerian revolt, and South African racial policy, are legitimate game for United Nations discussion. The Soviet Union remains the greatest exponent of power outside and high principles (unapplied) inside the United Nations. The minimum aim of Soviet United Nations policy is to identify the Soviet Union with the "wave of the future" and the hopes of underdeveloped countries and to paralyze action in the United Nations unless it furthers Soviet objectives. A further aim is to manipulate proxies in the United Nations to extend the arm of the Communist bloc to areas which it could not otherwise reach without unacceptable risk.

On many occasions the United Nations has been used by the United States to avoid making the hard decisions necessary for real leadership of the Free World. At times we have tried to force collective United Nations action when bilateral or local action would have been more effective. The United States, unlike the Soviet Union, attaches an exaggerated importance to majority votes. The fear of not getting a majority is often the excuse for not undertaking important actions. On the other hand, concrete and vital interests are often sacrificed for the sake of securing ephemeral majorities and popularity.

The Soviets have managed to prevent United Nations action inside the Communist bloc, as, for example, in the cases of Hungary and Tibet. Their handling of many world issues, their penchant for summit meetings, and their association with neutralist leaders have developed in many emergent nations mixed emotions of fear and admiration. Thus, Khrushchev used the U–2 incident not only to smash a summit meeting but, paradoxically, to identify himself in some quarters of the September, 1960, General Assembly session with peace, disarmament, and anti-colonialism.

The United States record is far harder to assess since it is a summation of intangibles and potentialities. The gradual dwindling of United States majorities in the General Assembly on key measures is not a disease but a symptom. Unless we can rally the opinion of a majority of mankind to our banner in the future, we may well suffer severe, if not fatal, political penalties. The picture which many new members of the General Assembly hold of the protagonists in the protracted conflict is distorted. The Soviet Union is perhaps regarded as ruthless and intransigent, but progressive and representing the "wave of the future." The United States is expected to be compromising and reasonable, but is tarnished as a vacillating defender of capitalism, economic imperialism, and the *status quo*.

Thus far the United States has prevented take-over of the United Nations as a popular front at a high price in reduced freedom of action. American delegates have achieved verbal support or avoidance of condemnation in key disputes such as Guatemala and Lebanon. In the "Uniting for Peace Resolution" and other measures, they breathed life into the General Assembly. A task for future American leaders may be to prevent the United Nations from developing into a Frankenstein monster, controlled by the emotional biases of the leaders of the emergent states, who even now seek to transfer to others blame for their failure to satisfy their peoples' expectations.

Even though—perhaps, because—the political and diplomatic atmosphere in the United Nations is becoming gradually less favorable to the United States, we must accept the Communist challenge in the United Nations forum, demonstrating that our views and programs are the truly revolutionary ones offering the best hope for mankind. Withdrawal, as an alternative, would leave the Soviet Union with a powerful ready-made "front." Consistent identification of Soviet violations of principles with those most galling to the emergent nations—colonialism, racism, and national discrimination—would pay great dividends. As the vestiges of Western colonialism are rapidly disappearing, the British have, with increasing force, conditioned the Assembly to references to satellites and Soviet republics as "non-self-governing territories." Hopefully, the United Nations agenda could one day be stacked with disputes concerning the Kazakh Soviet Socialist Republic and Bulgaria rather than South-West Africa and Angola. We should press key issues in the Cold War with persistence. We should work overtime at using the forum to teach new nations that ours is a revolutionary program which has built-in flexibility for progress in freedom and democracy and which has (unlike the Soviet Union's program) achieved demonstrable progress in this regard as well as economically.

One point of caution is necessary. Since the image to be fostered is one of strength and progress, as well as respect for human dignity, responsible liberty, and tolerance, the new approach must not lapse into one which makes substantive concessions to gain transient popularity. The psychological support for American policies that might be generated in the United Nations can be a useful auxiliary weapon in the protracted conflict. It is equally important that everything possible be done to dispel the images commonly held in the United States—that the United Nations is "our last, best hope" or the true center of international affairs. While theoretically and legally the United States is most reluctant to subscribe to anything that suggests a super-government, the United States often acts in the United Nations as if that body were some sort of higher international authority endowed with a will of its own and with independent means of action. The result of such confusion is to give artificial power to otherwise powerless member states or United Nations organs. Power thus conceded is unavailing against the Soviet Union, but it is effectively turned against the United States. The best hope of the United Nations lies in the simultaneous United States organization of the economic, military, and moral power of the Free World within a framework more immune to Communist wrecking techniques.[57]

[57] The author of this chapter wishes to acknowledge the assistance given him in the preparation of several sections of it by James F. McGarry, a former research assistant of the Foreign Policy Research Institute in the University of Pennsylvania.

CHAPTER VI

The Afro-Asians in the United Nations

BY NORMAN D. PALMER

As WITH MOST OTHER NATIONS, the neutralist nations use the United Nations primarily as a diplomatic instrument to advance their national and, wherever possible, their common interests. This they do by the weight of their votes, which when combined with the Communist votes form the majority in the United Nations General Assembly.[1] With the shift in power from the Security Council to the General Assembly, and the great increase in membership in the world organization, the United Nations naturally reflects more and more the attitudes and biases of the neutralist nations, most of which are in Asia and Africa.

The attitudes of the Afro-Asian states toward protracted conflict are, to put it mildly, ambivalent ones. Most of them, including even some who are associated with Western powers in security arrangements, seem to regard the situation of protracted conflict as one which has arisen from the division of the world into "two camps" or "two blocs," which in turn is an unhappy consequence of the propensity of the Western powers to play "power politics." The Afro-Asians insist that they do not want to be involved in the bitter rivalries of the big, bad powers of the West, and that they have other and more important priorities. They want to remain as aloof as possible from the arena of protracted conflict, and they seem to think that this is possible, if they constantly resist the pressures of the Western powers to involve them in a direct

---

[1] Of the total United Nations membership of 113 in January, 1964, the Afro-Asian group constituted over one-half, with 31 African and 24 Asian members. Excepting Iran, Pakistan, the Philippines, Thailand, and Turkey, which are aligned with the West in collective security arrangements (SEATO and CENTO), and Mongolia, which must be included in the Communist bloc, all the members of the Afro-Asian group fall under the category of neutralist nations.

way. "The Afro-Asians," observed William R. Frye, "still regard intervention in 'cold war' issues as taking sides in a power struggle from which they prefer to remain aloof. They are ready to help prevent the cold war from spreading to new areas, but are not yet ready to step in and help solve existing cold war problems."[2]

This *ohne uns* approach to any contamination with Cold War problems is widespread in the Asian-African area. The spokesmen of neutralism constantly and publicly deplore the association of most of the major world problems with Cold War issues. They insist that the United Nations, in particular, should be immunized from such issues, and should be used for entirely different purposes in an entirely different atmosphere; yet at the same time they want the United Nations to be truly representative of all the states of the world. It is hard to see how Cold War issues can in fact be kept out of the world's greatest association of the members of the world society, although one can sympathize with the desires to keep these issues in their place and to work for ways and means of improving the relations among nations, rather than of exacerbating existing tensions. Certainly, after the antics of Premier Khrushchev and his associates in the Fifteenth Session of the United Nations General Assembly in the fall of 1960, it would be hard to overlook the fact that the United Nations is inevitably a forum for the airing of Cold War issues as well as for the consideration of questions of world import which transcend the Cold War. Yet the Afro-Asian nations, and particularly the neutralist states, will continue to emphasize their desire to remain outside the Cold War arena even while they recognize in varying degrees that this desire may in fact be an unrealistic one. Speaking in the Lok Sabha on December 8, 1958, Prime Minister Jawaharlal Nehru of India expressed the aspirations of most of the Afro-Asian states in this respect:

> This question of cold war covers every question in the world today—whether it is in the Near East, whether it's in the Middle East, whether it is in the Far East or whether it is these military pacts or groups—everything is to form part of the cold war, and it becomes difficult even to consider a question in the United Nations which can be separated from this approach to the cold war. I suppose it is inherent in the situation today

2 "Afro-Asian Bloc: Center Stage at UN," *Foreign Policy Bulletin*, Vol. XL (October 15, 1960), 17.

in the world. We have endeavored with some success to keep out of it; when we talk about the policy of non-alignment it obviously means non-alignment in this cold war conflict.

In their attitudes the neutralists show real concern only for matters of common interest to them, i.e., national self-determination or political development or "liberation" of the non-self-governing territories and the economic development of the less developed countries. It follows, therefore—and quite logically—that the techniques which the neutralists employ in fulfillment of their strategy vary between "action" or "inaction," depending on their reading of any given situation. Herein, "inaction" constitutes an action in itself. The fact that no one criterion is used in the reading of any given situation by the neutralists explains why they do not always vote as a bloc on all the matters considered by the United Nations.

"Action" as a neutralist technique amounts to no more than casting an affirmative vote in favor of a resolution sponsored by the West, by the Communists, or by the neutralists themselves. In those situations where the United Nations has directly intervened, as in Suez and the Congo, "action" goes beyond mere voting. Here the neutralists play a positive role in peace-keeping by supplying units of their armed forces for the use of the United Nations in its peace mission. On the other hand, "inaction" as the alternative neutralist technique has meant either casting a negative vote on any resolution sponsored by any of the three groups named above or merely abstaining.

To understand properly the strategy of the neutralists in the United Nations and the reasons why they vote in a certain manner, it is necessary to analyze some of the motivational aspects of their voting behavior. The following explanations are suggested:

1) The neutralists are quite aware of their military and economic impotency to force any solution of an issue involving a direct East-West confrontation. This does not, however, keep them from initiating resolutions in the United Nations, which, in the name of peace and other Charter principles, they shower on the Great Powers, often without making any reference to or taking account of the real issues involved. To many Western observers it often appears that the neutralists act in such instances as if they occupy a seat of judgment in the United Nations and, therefore, possess the right to pronounce everyone except-

ing themselves "naughty boys." Perhaps the best examples on this point are the neutralist resolutions and proposals on disarmament.[3]

2) The neutralists jealously guard their newly won independence and are extremely averse to any Western or, for that matter, Communist moves which they suspect would hamper the free exercise of their sovereign national rights or are a cloak for "neo-colonialism" or an excuse for "collective foreign interference."[4]

3) Soviet intransigence and Communist differences in approach and ideology are accepted by the neutralists as being so much a part of international life that they are either "innocently" dismissed or "innocently" ignored. Where, however, an attempt is made to weaken the effectiveness of the United Nations, as with the Soviet "troika" proposals, the neutralists rally to the defense of the organization, realizing that there is much to be gained in the present setup within the United Nations.

4) Domestic considerations in a number of countries impel certain stands in the United Nations. The position of many members of the United Nations on the issue of Chinese representation is an excellent illustration of this point. As Harlan Cleveland has pointed out, "like yearning for disarmament, the cumulative frustration over China policy is a factor in the domestic power struggle in every major nation. The recognition of Peking, and its admission to the United Nations, serve as an inexpensive blunt instrument with which leftist opposition in a dozen countries beat the sitting governments over the head. By the same token, to favor the seating of Communist China in the United Nations is an easy way for Presidents and Prime Ministers to throw a bone to quiet the growling on their left. (The bone costs nothing as long as the United States can be counted on to prevent delivery.)"[5]

5) Finally, their "uncommittedness" gives the neutralist nations a leverage on both Communist and major non-Communist powers, and enables them to exploit Cold War tensions to their own advantage. Moreover, it elevates their political stature and insures them against

[3] See John J. McCloy, "Balance Sheet on Disarmament," *Foreign Affairs*, Vol. XL (April, 1962), 341.

[4] See Geoffrey Goodwin, "The Expanding United Nations," *International Affairs*, Vol. XXVII (April, 1961), 170–80.

[5] Harlan Cleveland, "The Road Around Stalemate," *Foreign Affairs*, Vol. XL (October, 1961), 29–30.

being disregarded or ignored. Thus they benefit from following an "independent" course in world affairs; although often they have been accused, sometimes with justice, of being neutralist *against* the Western powers and *for* the Communist bloc. The Belgrade Conference of September, 1961, was a lesson for the West in this technique of "unneutral neutralism."[6]

When issues involving major conflicts and divergencies of view between the Western powers and the Soviet Union and the other members of the Communist bloc come before the United Nations, the natural inclination of the Afro-Asian states is to take no position on such issues, to urge the competing groups to seek to resolve their differences without involving other states, and to abstain or to absent themselves when votes on such issues are actually taken in United Nations bodies. Very rarely do the Afro-Asian members of the United Nations seek to use their individual or collective influence to restrain one of the major powers, except on matters in which they are immediately concerned. Yet at the same time the Afro-Asian states within the United Nations, numbering now approximately one-half of the total membership, are in an extraordinarily strategic position to bring leverage on the larger powers. When they stand together, they can block any resolution of which they disapprove, and their support is essential to produce the two-thirds vote necessary for the approval of substantive resolutions.[7] The first part of the Fifteenth Session of the United Nations, in Mr. Hamilton's view, demonstrated that "the Africa-Asian group is now so strong that its attitude this year will probably determine whether the United States or the Soviet Union is to be the dominant force in the United Nations."[8] This may be an overstatement, but the growing leverage of the smaller members of the United Nations, now spearheaded by the members of the Afro-Asian groups, upon the numerically fewer but vastly more powerful major states of the world is a significant fact of contemporary world politics. This leverage gives the small states

[6] For the proceedings of the Belgrade Conference and excerpts from all speeches, see *Review of International Affairs* (Belgrade), Vol. XII, No. 274 (September 5–20, 1961). For a commentary on the deliberations at the Conference, see H. F. Armstrong, "Close View of the Non-Aligned," *New York Times Magazine* (October 1, 1961).

[7] See "A New U.N.: New Members—and New Problems," *U.S. News & World Report* (October 3, 1960).

[8] "U.N. and Kennedy," *New York Times* (January 1, 1961).

generally an influence far out of proportion to their actual power, an influence more marked within the United Nations than outside.

To an amazing degree the small powers now determine the character and functioning of the world organization. This is reflected in the items which appear on the agenda of the General Assembly sessions; in the relative emphasis given to the purposes of the United Nations as stated in Article 1 of the Charter; in the staffing of the secretariats of the United Nations and the specialized agencies, as well as of special commissions and the two emergency forces organized under United Nations auspices, along the Arab-Israeli frontiers and in the Congo; and in the flattering amount of attention which representatives of the major powers pay to their colleagues from the less powerful states in the lobbies and corridors and missions of the United Nations.

The magnitude of the revolution that has taken place in the United Nations, without significant changes in machinery and with no changes whatever in the language of the Charter, is suggested in the following observations of William Clark:

> The automatic majority for the Western powers which could formerly be assumed in the General Assembly is no longer certain. . . . The ex-colonial states are prepared to use the United Nations to get the things they want—political emancipation for those countries still dependent and economic aid for themselves—and it is conceivable that the small Powers [could succeed in passing resolutions], with France, Britain, the United States and Russia all on one side and the small powers ranged against them.[9]

While the major powers may be outvoted in theory, in practice their influence guarantees them sufficient votes to command a majority if they should join together to make any proposals.

The Afro-Asians, or most of them, and the United States have a wide mutuality of interest, and in the protracted conflict within the United Nations they have usually stood with the United States, rather than with the Soviet Union. The problem for the United States is to find new means of working with the Afro-Asian members of the United Nations, rather than merely trying to get them to support United States positions.

[9] "New Forces in the United Nations," *International Affairs*, Vol. XXVI (July, 1960), 329.

The Nature of Asian and African "Neutralism"

Because of the Cold War and the present ideological struggle the neutral states are able to "play both ends against the middle" and to exploit the present divisions of the Great Powers for their own purposes. Thus they exert an influence in world affairs far out of proportion to their actual power. It is hardly surprising that they take advantage of such a unique opportunity.

For purposes of this discussion the "neutral" nations will be taken to include those nations of Asia and Africa which have not entered into formal military alliances or pacts with one or more of the major powers, or which are not under Communist domination. Admittedly this definition is a rather arbitrary and comprehensive one; but it has the merits of precision and simplicity, and it does in fact provide a formula for identifying those states which in contemporary parlance are labeled as "neutralist" in their policies. So defined, most of the nations of Asia and Africa are "neutral" nations. They include fifty-one of the fifty-seven members of the so-called Afro-Asian group in the United Nations. They embrace most of the Moslem world, all of the Hindu world, and much of the Buddhist world. They include the major country of south Asia—India—and the major country of southeast Asia—Indonesia. Over 70 per cent of the population of the neutral nations live in these two countries.[10] All of the Arab and African countries are "neutral" nations, according to this definition.

Most of these neutral nations have achieved their independence only since the end of World War II—some very recently indeed.[11] All are underdeveloped nations. All are strongly nationalistic, and are very sensitive on colonial issues. All have at least nominally chosen the democratic way, but they are handicapped by authoritarian traditions, political instability, economic weakness, social tensions, and outside pressures in their efforts to move in a democratic direction. For reasons which may be compelling but which are nevertheless disturbing, many of their so-called democratic leaders seem to harbor strange concepts of democracy. They speak of "guided" or "controlled" democracy, of the need to develop "a new system to save democracy." Most of them seem to be

[10] Yet India and Indonesia pay only 2.93 per cent of the regular budget for the United Nations.

[11] Thirty new members were admitted to the United Nations between January, 1960, and January, 1964.

committed to "the socialist pattern of society," to use a term which Nehru and the Congress party in India have popularized.

Great changes are under way in these countries. They form a major part of the area where "the revolution of rising expectations"—surely one of the major developments of the present era—is under way. They are moving rapidly along uncharted paths in uncertain directions. They are faced with grave problems of human and national survival. It is hardly surprising that in foreign affairs most of them tend toward neutralist views.

Western commentators on the policies and orientation of the majority of the states of Asia and Africa are inclined to describe these policies as neutral or neutralist, whereas spokesmen of these countries prefer to regard their policies as those of independence or nonalignment. The use of the term "neutral" is particularly unfortunate and misleading—unfortunate because it is resented by most of the countries to which it is applied, and misleading because the term is conventionally applied to the policies of states which attempt to avoid involvement in hostilities during wartime and because the policies of the Afro-Asian states are neutral only in certain respects. The term is used here chiefly because it is so widely used and generally understood in the Western world. Possibly the term "uncommitted" or "nonaligned" or "independent" would be preferable.[12]

Among the fifty-one nations of Asia and Africa which may be characterized as neutral according to our definition there are many shades and varieties of neutralism, both within the various countries and between countries. In India, for example, the major stronghold of neutralism, despite the opposition of an influential minority, most people who have any view at all on such matters seem to approve of the foreign policies of their government,[13] at least prior to the

[12] Some exponents of the policies of the neutral states object even to the use of such terms as "uncommitted" or "nonaligned," and insist that the only proper and acceptable characterization is "independent." See, for example, M. S. Rajan, "Indian Foreign Policy in Action, 1954–56," *India Quarterly*, Vol. XVI (July–September, 1960), 229.

[13] Even in India opposition to the policies and orientation of the government in foreign affairs is often voiced in Parliament, in the press, and at public meetings. On November 8, 1957, at the conclusion of an official visit to India by President Ngo Dinh Diem of the Republic of Vietnam, the *Eastern Economist*, a leading Indian journal of opinion as well as of economic affairs, stated editorially that "it would be political wisdom to

Chinese attack of late October, 1962; but their concepts of the nature of neutralism differ greatly. Some brands of Indian neutralism are vague and naïve, with a strong out-of-this-world flavor; others are well thought out and politically realistic. Some Indians lean as far toward Communism and the Soviet Union as their so-called neutralism permits, whereas others seem definitely to be neutral on the side of democracy and to have a strong pro-Western orientation. Each country exhibits its own peculiar patterns of neutralism. The neutralism of Burma did not prevent its delegates in the United Nations from denouncing Soviet brutality in Hungary while Nehru was still softpedaling the whole issue. The neutralism of Ceylon did not prevent its chief delegate to the United Nations from signing a report by a special United Nations committee on Soviet actions in Hungary which was a particularly damning indictment of Soviet policy and behavior. In this case, to be sure, the Ceylonese representative was widely criticized in his own country. During the Twelfth Session of the General Assembly twelve of the neutral nations of Asia and Africa voted in favor of a resolution condemning the Soviet Union for its intervention in Hungary, while nine of these nations abstained.[14] During the Fourteenth Session of the General Assembly, Malaya, an Asian

remain as friendly with peoples this side of the above delineated frontier [the seventeenth parallel in Vietnam], as it is in our power to be, specifically as a warning to a potential aggressor that he will have to face united opposition." Reflecting on the wisdom of India's orientation in foreign affairs, the *Eastern Economist* warned: "Nonalignment is, of course, an excellent thing, academically speaking; but let us not forget that, in time of crisis, it is the enemy who will decide whether we remain neutral. And in the present case, the enemy has left nobody in doubt about what is being aimed at: he is committed to aid and abet insurrectionary and subversive activity in a country not to his liking." Since the ruthless suppression of the Tibetan uprising by the Chinese Communists in 1959, and the incidents along the Sino-Indian frontiers, and more markedly since the major Chinese offensive against India on and after October 20, 1962, criticisms of the course and assumptions of the foreign policy of the government of India have been particularly frequent and vehement, in Parliament and in the country generally. Such evidences of critical thinking on the proper course of India's foreign policy, however, do not affect the validity of the conclusion stated above.

[14] Those who voted in favor were Burma, Cambodia, Ethiopia, Ghana, Iraq, Laos, Lebanon, Liberia, Libya, Morocco, Sudan, and Tunisia. Those who abstained were Afghanistan, Ceylon, Egypt, India, Indonesia, Nepal, Saudi Arabia, Syria, and Yemen. (General Assembly Resolution 1133 [XI] [September 14, 1957].)

neutral nation, joined with Ireland in sponsoring a resolution strongly condemning Communist China for its actions in Tibet in 1959.

An interesting commentary on the nature of his country's neutralism and on the reasons for it was given in an article by Prince Norodom Sihanouk of Cambodia in the American journal *Foreign Affairs*:

> In our foreign relations we have favored neutrality, which in the United States is all too often confused with "neutralism," although it is fundamentally different. We are neutral in the same way Switzerland and Sweden are neutral—not neutralist like Egypt or Indonesia. Let anyone examine our votes in the United Nations; they are not often "aligned" with those of the bloc of "neutralist" nations. Our neutrality has been imposed upon us by necessity. . . . Our neutrality is neither complaisance nor surrender to anyone. . . . By practising a genuine neutrality which eliminates any pretext for aggression we have a chance of not bringing down a storm on our heads; and a storm can be dangerous where there is no lightning conductor. . . . If, in spite of our manifest good intentions and our utter propriety in respect to the blocs, one of these should attack us, then I would be the first to advocate reconsidering our policy and invoking aid from the opponents of our aggressors.[15]

In these remarks, made by the leading statesman of a small Asian country which in his judgment is neutral but not neutralist, we find the common arguments that neutrality is a policy that is dictated by national interest and by necessity, that by adhering to it a weak country located between the two blocs has the best chance of avoiding aggression, that it is not the same as the neutrality practiced by certain other nations, that it is not a policy of "complaisance" or "surrender," and that it is a policy of genuine neutrality and not one which favors the Communist bloc.

At least one of the outstanding leaders of a neutral state has publicly voiced criticisms of neutralism. In March, 1956, Habib Bourguiba, president of the Republic of Tunisia, declared: "I am against neutralism and I think it is in our interest to join the North Atlantic Treaty Organization. We are an integral part of the Occident and the free world."[16] In an article in *Foreign Affairs*, Mr. Bourguiba wrote:

[15] "Cambodia Neutral: The Dictate of Necessity," *Foreign Affairs*, Vol. XXXVI (July, 1958), 582–83, 584, 586. The key issue of neutrality and national security is that the neutral nations expect outside, that is, United States, help if attacked but are unwilling to prepare collectively for this eventuality.

[16] *New York Times* (March 24, 1956).

"As for Tunisia, it has chosen unequivocally to follow the free world of the West.... Inasmuch as the free world and the Communist world are two opposite camps, Tunisia belongs to the former. Thus far it has seen no need to join any defensive alliance against Communist aggression, but if it felt threatened it would not hesitate to do so." Why, then, is Tunisia neutral? One reason was inadvertently suggested by Mr. Bourguiba when he stated that Tunisia did not feel threatened. Other reasons mentioned in his article in *Foreign Affairs* are the feeling that France has not yet abandoned her "colonial occupation" of his country; Tunisia's "allegiance to the Arab and Moslem world," which, however, he insisted, is "in no way inconsistent with her ties to the West"; and, above all, the prevailing attitudes of the Tunisian people. This latter point Mr. Bourguiba explained as follows:

> ... it should be appreciated that for a newly emancipated country without major resources neutralism appears to offer certain advantages. In the present state of latent conflict between the great world Powers, neutralism may keep smaller nations out of quarrels in which they have no direct concern and give them an illusory feeling of security. At the same time they may lay claim to moral superiority and seek to arbitrate the differences among the great Powers. And of course they are in an excellent bargaining position, because each rival group may try to outbid the other for their support.
>
> As the people of Tunisia are idealistic and peace-loving, they are instinctively attracted to neutralism. They do not wish to be drawn into armed conflict nor to find their country once more a battle-ground over issues which chiefly concern the Great Powers. ... Tunisians are therefore inclined to believe that neutrality might be a bar to invasion and save them from the terrible weapons which promise to characterize the next war.

Having demonstrated, consciously and unconsciously, that neutralism is strongly entrenched in Tunisia, Mr. Bourguiba nevertheless reverted to his criticism of a neutral policy:

> But Tunisian political leaders are realists. They know that the neutrality of a weak nation cannot save it from invasion if it stands in a belligerent's way. ... History proves that unilateral declarations of neutrality and even non-aggression pacts fail to stand up in the face of large-scale conflict. Neutralism in the cold war and neutrality in a "hot" one are equally precarious.[17]

[17] "Nationalism: Antidote to Communism," *Foreign Affairs*, Vol. XXXV (July, 1957), 646-53.

Therefore in its broadest aspects "neutralism" is almost incapable of definition. It has many shades of meaning and finds expression in many different ways. It is both an attitude and a policy. It is the natural policy for newly independent states to follow, especially since nearly all of them are weak, harbor deep-seated suspicions of great powers and of "power politics," tend to concentrate almost exclusively on internal problems and pressures, are anxious to play an active role in the United Nations without getting involved in "power politics," and are ultrasensitive to any efforts, real or imagined, of outside powers to threaten their newly won independence or to force them to commit themselves in world affairs. As an attitude, neutralism is the prevalent popular approach to world affairs in almost all of the newly independent countries, regardless of the orientation of their leaders, and is much in evidence in almost every country of the non-Communist world, including the United States.

Whatever the extent of neutralist feeling in the West, it is certainly widespread in Asia and Africa. It would, in fact, be difficult to determine whether it is more strongly manifest in committed or uncommitted countries of the area, nearly all of whom have had similar unhappy experiences with foreign rule in the recent past and are faced with similar problems of overwhelming magnitude today. Newly independent states are haunted by an unresolvable dilemma: they want to be left alone, and yet to have a voice in world affairs, and they must have outside help. And this help must come from the great powers of the West, including their former rulers, unless it comes from the Soviet Union and other Communist states. In any event, whatever the inescapable realities of their situation, the peoples of the newly independent states want to feel that they are the masters of their own destinies and can make their own decisions in their own way. To peoples with such an orientation neutralism comes very easy indeed.

The Afro-Asian Group in the United Nations

The neutral nations of Asia and Africa do not form a separate group in the United Nations, but they dominate the so-called Afro-Asian group, in which they form the decided majority. This remarkable grouping includes all but three of the Afro-Asian members of the United Nations. For varied and obvious reasons, Nationalist China,

Israel, and the Republic of South Africa do not participate in the deliberations of this group.

According to Mrs. Vijaya Lakshmi Pandit, the Afro-Asian group, which originally was called the Arab-Asian group, originated at the Asian Relations Conference in 1947.[18] Perhaps its first active role in the United Nations was played during the debates in the Third (1948–49) and Fourth (1949) Sessions of the United Nations General Assembly on the disposition of the former Italian colonies. Delegates of the Arab League states, supported by India, Pakistan, Afghanistan, Burma, and the Communist bloc, succeeded in mustering enough voting strength in the General Assembly to defeat a recommendation of the First Committee regarding the former Italian colonies which embodied an Anglo-French package deal, prepared with the support of the United States. This successful venture in opposition to the Western powers seemed to lay a basis for a substantial measure of Arab-Asian co-operation.

The group first came into general prominence in late 1950 and early 1951, when, at a crucial period in the Korean War, the leader of the Indian delegation in the Fifth Session of the General Assembly, Sir Benegal Rau, organized eleven Arab-Asian members of the United Nations into an effective pressure group in support of India's attempts to bring about a cease-fire in Korea.[19] Largely as a result of Sir Benegal's initiative the General Assembly, in December, 1950, set up a Cease-Fire Committee composed of Sir Benegal, Lester Pearson of Canada, and Nasrollah Entezam of Iran, then president of the Assembly. On January 13 the Committee transmitted to the Chinese Communist government its program for achieving a cease-fire in Korea by stages. Sir Benegal insisted that the Chinese reply, while it rejected the Committee's proposal, was sufficiently encouraging to warrant further negotiations; but the majority of the Assembly, under the strong prompting of the United

[18] Address in New Delhi, February 3, 1953, under the auspices of the Indian Council of World Affairs. The topic of Mrs. Pandit's address was "The Role of the Arab-Asian Group in the United Nations." The presiding officer was Sir Benegal Narsing Rau, who played a major role in bringing the Arab-Asian group into existence as an active and effective group.

[19] The eleven countries were Afghanistan, Burma, Egypt, India, Indonesia, Iran, Iraq, Lebanon, Saudi Arabia, Syria, and Yemen.

States, adopted, on February 1, a resolution condemning Communist China for aggression in Korea and calling on it to withdraw all its nationals and forces from the Korean Peninsula. The vote on this much-discussed resolution was forty-four to seven, with nine abstentions.[20] Even though the Afro-Asian group had steadfastly supported the efforts of the Cease-Fire Committee and had responded to India's leadership on this vote the group split in several ways. India was strongly opposed to the resolution and, along with Burma and the Communist bloc, voted against it. The rest of the members of the Afro-Asian group, however, did not follow India's lead. Three members, in fact, voted for the resolution; one did not participate; and the rest abstained.

In later consideration of the Korean question the Afro-Asian group did not take a conspicuous part. India, at least, seemed to feel that the group could not be depended upon to present a united front on Korean issues. Apparently India did not consult the group in the fall of 1952, when it attempted to find a formula for solving the prisoners of war issue.

Since 1950–51, the Afro-Asian group has met frequently to consider issues of mutual interest, and has functioned as a loosely organized body. It was given greater prominence and strength in 1955, with the convening of the historic Afro-Asian conference at Bandung, Indonesia, in April, and the admission of six more states of Asia and Africa to the United Nations in the "package deal" in December. Thereafter it was almost universally referred to as the Afro-Asian group, instead of Arab-Asian group. Before Bandung the group functioned on an *ad hoc* basis; after Bandung, with an enlarged membership, it was more formally organized on a regular basis.[21]

In the Eleventh and Twelfth Sessions of the General Assembly the Afro-Asian group, having gained new confidence from the Bandung Conference and new strength by the "package deal" of December, 1955, was particularly active. It acquired five additional members—Morocco, Tunisia, the Sudan, Ghana, and Japan—at the opening of the Eleventh Session, and another—Malaya—at the opening of the Twelfth Session. In the Eleventh Session the divisions within the Afro-Asian group were often reflected in split voting. The members of the group were

[20] General Assembly Resolution 498 (V) (February 1, 1951).

[21] See Thomas Hovet, Jr., *Bloc Politics in the United Nations* (Cambridge, Harvard University Press, 1960), 78–82.

united in their condemnation of the military action of Israel, Great Britain, and France against Egypt in 1956, but they were divided on the Hungarian question and on many other important issues.[22]

During the Twelfth Session of the Assembly the group met frequently, and was particularly active in the discussions on increased membership of various United Nations bodies, on Algeria, and on proposals for expanded programs of assistance to underdeveloped countries. Almost unanimous support was given by members of the group for placing the perennial questions of apartheid and the treatment of Indians in South Africa on the agenda of the Twelfth Session of the General Assembly. The question of West Irian (West New Guinea) was placed on the agenda by a roll-call vote of forty-nine in favor and twenty-one against, with eleven abstentions; four of the members of the Afro-Asian group abstained, but the rest solidly supported the Indonesian position on this hotly debated issue. On another controversial resolution, that of Hungary, which again condemned the Soviet Union for its intervention and approved the damning report of the Special Committee on the Problem of Hungary, the Afro-Asian group split wide open. The vote in the Assembly was sixty in favor and ten against, with ten abstentions.[23] The majority of the members of the Afro-Asian group, including twelve of the neutral members, voted in favor of the resolution; but nine of the ten abstentions on the resolution were provided by members of the group. All of these nine were neutral nations. Ironically enough, one of them was Ceylon, whose representative to the United Nations had joined with other members of the Special Committee on the Problem of Hungary in approving a strongly worded report, one of the most devastating and most highly publicized indictments of the Soviet Union that has ever been issued.

"The Assembly," declared the *New York Times* on March 3, 1957,

[22] For an analysis of the votes of the member states of the Afro-Asian group on five major issues which were considered by the Eleventh Session of the General Assembly, see "The Bandung 'Block,'" *The Economist* (January 26, 1957). This article presented the following interesting analysis of the "nuclei" and of the "floating" vote in the "Bandung 'Block'": "A. The Baghdad and SEATO allies—Iran, Iraq, Pakistan, Philippines, Siam, Turkey—plus Ethiopia and Liberia. (8 votes). B. The groups headed by Egypt and India, normally embracing Afghanistan, Indonesia, Saudi Arabia, Sudan, Syria and Yemen. (8 votes.) The 'floating' vote comprises Burma, Cambodia, Ceylon, Japan, Jordan, Laos, Lebanon, Libya, Morocco, Nepal, and Tunisia."

[23] General Assembly Resolution 1132 (XI) (January 10, 1957).

in a significant editorial entitled "The Assembly Grows Up," "is still a thing of blocs and groups." Apparently the *Times* regretted this development but it is a very logical one, and may be one of the most encouraging signs that the Assembly is in fact growing up. In a letter to the *Times,* commenting on this excellent editorial, Hans Kohn observed: "May I point out that outside the closed group of the Soviet Union, which is in a permanent and for it painful minority position, the other groups—the Western bloc, the Asian-African bloc, the South American bloc—are not always united; their members vote in complete freedom according to their interests and moral convictions. Such groups and blocs are, after all, characteristic of all parliaments and of all democratic procedure."

In the United Nations there is only one real bloc, in the sense of a group of member states which almost always vote as a unit. This is, of course, the Communist bloc, consisting of all of the ten Communist members of the United Nations with the exception of Yugoslavia. All other groupings are much looser, and their members often divide on votes and policies.[24] They are more properly called groups than blocs. In this sense the Afro-Asian nations, fifty-five in number as of January, 1964, is definitely a group rather than a bloc. It consists of a number of subgroups, sometimes with overlapping membership, which are often at odds on policy matters. Among these subgroups are the twelve Arab states which constitute the Arab League; the Brazzaville group (the African Malagasay Union), consisting of twelve of the thirteen states which were formerly associated in the French community; the Casablanca group (Algeria, the United Arab Republic, Ghana, Guinea, Mali, and Morocco); the Asian and African members of the Commonwealth (India, Pakistan, Ceylon, Malaya, Ghana, Nigeria, Sierra Leone, Tanganyika, and Uganda); the five so-called Colombo Powers (India, Pakistan, Ceylon, Burma, and Indonesia); the three Asian members of SEATO (Pakistan, Thailand, and the Philippines); and the three Asian members of CENTO (Turkey, Iran, and Pakistan). Within these various subgroups strong differences often exist, as between some of the Arab states. The African member states are so different in their outlook and policies that they can hardly be con-

[24] For a chart showing "Membership of Caucusing Blocs and Groups in the United Nations, December, 1962," see Thomas Hovet, Jr., "United Nations Diplomacy," *Journal of International Affairs,* Vol. XVII (November 1, 1963), 36.

sidered as a single subgroup at all, except in a geographical sense. The divisions among the African members of the United Nations were a decisive factor in one of the most important votes to be taken at the fall 1960 sessions of the Fifteenth General Assembly, on the question of great interest and particular concern to Africans of the seating of President Kasavubu and the delegation which he had appointed to represent the Congo. Nine African members, all formerly under French rule, voted in favor of seating Kasavubu and his delegation, five voted against, and seven others abstained.[25]

In the crucial vote on the controversial question of transferring China's membership in the United Nations from the Nationalist to the Communist government, during the Sixteenth Session of the General Assembly in December, 1961, seventeen members of the Afro-Asian group voted against granting the China seat to the Chinese Communist regime, twenty-one voted in favor, and fourteen abstained. Even within some of the subgroups, the voting pattern was varied. Two members of the Arab League—Libya and Jordan—voted against Communist China; six voted in favor; and two—Lebanon and Saudi Arabia—abstained. Eight of the members of the former French community abstained; five voted against; and only one—Guinea—voted in favor of seating the Chinese Communist government.

When the Afro-Asian group—then properly called the Arab-Asian group—began to function on an *ad hoc* basis in late 1950 and early 1951, in the Fifth General Assembly Session, it consisted of twelve members, half of whom were Arab states. By 1957 it had expanded to twenty-nine members, including ten Arab states and only eight African states. In 1963 its fifty-five members included thirty-one African states. As its membership has expanded the relative role of the members has often changed. India took the initiative in the organization of the Arab-Asian group, and for some years it was generally recognized—except perhaps by Mr. Nasser—as the leading member of the group. It is still a leading member, but other member states and several subgroups have emerged to challenge its former position. Japan, which occupies a peculiar place in the group, is clearly an aspirant for a leading role in the inner councils of the association. Nasser's Egypt, as has been indicated, has aspirations of its own, not only in the circles of the Arab League, all of whose members are in the Afro-Asian group,

[25] General Assembly Resolution 1498 (XX) (November 22, 1960).

but elsewhere in Africa and perhaps in Asia as well. Pakistan certainly does not recognize Indian leadership, in the United Nations or outside. Ghana under Nkrumah obviously has aspirations for African leadership—aspirations which are hardly appreciated by Nigeria, the Arab states of Africa, or some of the states of the former French community. Turkey is another rather isolated member of the group, since its relations with the Arab states are rather cool and since it is somewhat suspect because of its membership in NATO.

During sessions of the General Assembly the Afro-Asian group usually meets at least once a week, upon call of the chairman, and sometimes more frequently. The chairmanship rotates every month. The proceedings are usually quite informal, and votes are seldom taken. Within the group the neutral nations, who comprise the vast majority, do not function as a subgroup; but the practice has developed for representatives of some of these neutral nations to consult with each other more closely and more frequently than with other members. Thus, during the Twelfth Session of the General Assembly the representatives of India, Burma, Indonesia, Syria, and Egypt met quite often in what might be described as pre-caucus meetings. India, as usual, was an important spokesman for the neutralist position. Indonesia played a greater role than usual, perhaps because of the attention given to the West Irian issue, but perhaps more because its chief delegate, Dr. Sastro-amidjojo, was a former prime minister and a respected Asian leader. Syria and Egypt were more active than usual, chiefly because they had been very much in the world spotlight during this period. Both of these countries were represented by strong delegations. As an interesting sidelight, it may be noted that delegates of Ghana occasionally met with these five most vocal neutral nations. This may have been due to an understandable desire of this new nation to make its presence felt and to cultivate close relations with leading Asian-African states.

Thus, the so-called Afro-Asian group is in no sense a bloc; it consists of many subgroups which often are split within and between themselves and of many member states which are at odds with other members. It is hardly surprising that it has seldom functioned effectively as a unified group, and has not realized its full potential as the largest single group in the United Nations constellation. But it is a functioning and organized group, and its members have achieved a higher degree of unity on issues that have come before the United Nations than they showed prior to its existence. On issues on which they can unite, such as colonial issues, the group can have a decisive influence in the United Nations. Its members are quite aware of this fact.

> The Asian African group as now constituted, when it is united and identical, or nearly identical, in voting, can prevent the Assembly from passing issues with an overwhelming majority, if not actually defeat the majority. It is therefore already in a strong position to urge other groups to consider the desirability of making concessions and any concessions made for the sake of achieving overwhelming majorities may well serve to strengthen the cohesion and effectiveness of those receiving them.[26]

The Afro-Asian group often works closely with the Latin-American group, from which it usually obtains powerful support on issues involving colonialism, Great Power domination, and economic development. As far back as 1952 a keen observer of United Nations affairs called attention to this fact, and suggested that it symbolized "the growing independence of countries usually included in the 'Anglo-American majority'" and might in time lead to "a new power alignment":

> The Asian-Arab and Latin American nations more and more frequently find themselves taking the same position. The Bolivian delegate indicated one of the most obvious points of agreement when he said: "The march of colonial and semi-colonial peoples cannot be stopped." It is premature to talk of a formal alliance between the two blocs, or even of two integrated blocs, since certain Latin American countries are still safely attached to the inter-American policy. But there is an undeniable tendency for each group to follow its "own" line in the United Nations, and to take all possible advantage of the strength each gains from the support of the other. All this can lead, and is leading, to a new power alignment which is worth watching very closely as the Assembly passes from general debate to the handling of each issue on the agenda.[27]

The members of the Afro-Asian and Latin-American groups form almost three-fourths of the total membership of the United Nations, and when they work together either to promote certain lines of action or to block others, they can exert very great influence; but on many issues

---

[26] Hovet, *Bloc Politics in the United Nations*, 91.

[27] J. Alvarez del Vayo, "New Alignments in the U.N.," *The Nation* (November 1, 1952), 401.

there are differences both within and between these groupings, and they have not yet concerted their efforts sufficiently to form "a new power alignment."

On some controversial issues the Afro-Asian group is more likely to line up with the Communist bloc than with the NATO members of the United Nations. Even many of the "committed" members of the group, which outside of the United Nations are associated with Western powers in security arrangements and in many other ways, often find themselves voting against their Western allies and with the Soviet Union and other Communist members in the United Nations. This does not mean that these states are anti-Communist outside the United Nations and pro-Communist inside. For reasons of history, strategy, and propaganda, the Soviet Union is more inclined than the Western nations to line up with the Afro-Asian states on some issues of deep concern to them. It poses as a leading champion of anti-colonialism and of assistance to underdeveloped areas, whereas the United States, which has an anti-colonial tradition and which gives far more assistance to the underdeveloped areas than the Soviet Union, often takes positions displeasing to the Afro-Asian nations in the United Nations, either because of its desire not to offend unduly its NATO allies or because of its somewhat embarrassing position as major contributor to programs of economic assistance which potential recipients support with enthusiastic vigor. The Soviet Union has taken a more sympathetic view toward the Afro-Asian penchant for high-sounding principles of peace, as illustrated by the *Panch Shila* (or *Panchsheel*), so dear to Mr. Nehru's heart, and toward the prevailing opposition to continuance of atomic- and hydrogen-bomb tests. On all of these issues the Russian position appeals most particularly to the neutral nations, but, as has been pointed out, it also results in associating virtually all the members of the Afro-Asian group with the Communist bloc in voting in the United Nations.

The Role of the Afro-Asian
Neutral Nations in the United Nations

While the neutral nations of the Afro-Asian group are interested in all phases of the work of the United Nations, they tend to emphasize the nonpolitical aspects of this work and to shy away from any efforts to give meaning to the provisions of the Charter for the maintenance of peace and security. They wish to emphasize the role of the

United Nations in reflecting all points of view and in acting as a bridge between nations; conversely, they profess to a strong desire to avoid any actions which increase international tensions or cause divisions among members of the world organization. Actually, however great their efforts and their sincerity, this position is a difficult one to adhere to; for, as the neutral nations often point out, the United Nations represents the world as it is, and the world is full of tensions and divisions. Moreover, in their zeal to mitigate the effects of Great Power politics and to bring the two great power blocs closer together, they sometimes end by supporting Soviet moves which may have other motives than the professed intention to promote "peaceful coexistence."

It is also a noteworthy fact that whereas the neutral nations seem eager to bridge the gulf between the Communist and the non-Communist worlds, they do not show the same eagerness with respect to issues in dispute between newly independent states and former colonial powers; instead, they almost invariably side with the former against the latter, whatever the merits of the particular issues involved. Because of their own experiences and situation, they hold strong views on most issues of colonialism—and they can find colonialism in an amazing variety of issues—and they take a special interest in the promotion of human rights and fundamental freedoms, in the self-determination of peoples, in the struggle against racial discrimination, and in the economic development of underdeveloped areas. They feel strongly on questions of race and color, and these feelings condition their views on most other questions. Indeed, as an American observer has written, the United Nations has become "one of the principal mechanisms by which race relations are transformed into international relations."[28]

It is obviously impossible in this brief discussion to present any detailed case studies of the position which the neutral nations of the Afro-Asian group have taken on any of the many issues which have come before the United Nations. Here we shall attempt only to make a few more specific comments on two areas of the United Nations work in which the neutral nations have taken a very special interest and on which they have pronounced views. These areas, which have a direct bearing on protracted conflict in the United Nations, are those of coloni-

[28] Cora Bell, "The United Nations and the West," *International Affairs*, Vol. XXIX (October, 1953), 466. See also Harry N. Howard, "The Arab-Asian States in the United Nations," *The Middle East Journal*, Vol. VII (Summer, 1953), 279–92.

alism and self-determination, and the peaceful and conciliatory role of the United Nations.

COLONIAL ISSUES

Since the "package deal" of December, 1955, when the Afro-Asian group gained six new members, representatives of the colonial powers have frequently charged that the United Nations is being turned into a mere instrument for the anti-colonial campaign, and that this trend of events has greatly weakened the world organization and has limited its scope and usefulness in dealing with the realities of world politics. The neutral nations, most of whom were dependent areas until quite recently, admit that they are quite sensitive on colonial issues and wish to do everything they can to wipe colonialism from the face of the earth. In the language of the final communiqué of the Bandung Conference, the neutral nations hold that "colonialism in all its manifestations" is "an evil which should speedily be brought to an end." Quite clearly they regard the United Nations as a particularly suitable forum in which to promote their anti-colonial crusade; but they point out that the issue of colonialism is a deep-seated and pervasive one, which does not arise within the halls of the United Nations. "The United Nations," as Thomas J. Hamilton has observed, "is a forum for the anti-colonial issue, and a thermometer to measure its intensity, rather than an independent force."[29]

From the very beginning, anti-colonial issues have almost constantly been on the agenda of the Security Council and other organs and agencies of the United Nations, and the neutral nations have been most active in pressing them. Some are of long standing, while others have only recently been placed before the United Nations. In the birth of several of the new nations, such as Indonesia and Libya, the United Nations has played a truly significant role, functioning almost in the capacity of midwife.

In dealing with most colonial issues the United States has played only a peripheral and hortatory role. On such issues it is confronted with what has been aptly termed the "colonial dilemma," for it wishes to support genuine freedom movements throughout the world and at the same time it wishes to avoid major differences with its great allies

[29] "Anti-Colonialism Campaign a Hard Problem for West," *New York Times* (December 21, 1952).

of the Western world. An analysis of the consideration of the Moroccan, Tunisian, and Algerian issues in the United Nations will reveal the differences in approach to colonial problems on the part of the United States, for whom such problems are vexing and complicated, and the neutral states, which seem to view these problems in terms of black and white. On the other hand, the Soviet Union has not been confronted with the "colonial dilemma." It has enthusiastically encouraged and supported the Afro-Asian states in their attacks on colonialism, thereby gaining the good will of the Afro-Asians and at the same time embarrassing the colonial or former colonial powers of the West and their ally, the United States. For the Soviet Union this has been a "heads I win, tails you lose" situation, which it has always been quick to exploit.

1. *Moroccan and Tunisian Questions.* Over the strong opposition of France, and against the wishes of the United States and other Western powers, the United Nations General Assembly considered the Moroccan and Tunisian questions at several of its annual sessions. Attempts to place these questions on the agenda of the Security Council were not successful.[30] Six of the neutral nations tried to get the General Assembly to consider the Moroccan questions at the Sixth Session in 1951, but the Assembly postponed consideration "for the time being." During each of the next four sessions the question was debated, always over the objection and without the participation of France. In December, 1952, when a draft resolution introduced by thirteen Asian and African states requesting France and the Sultan of Morocco to enter into negotiations for a peaceful settlement in accord with the sovereignty of Morocco was rejected, these Afro-Asian states supported a less positive resolution sponsored by eleven Latin-American states. Before the Eighth Session of the General Assembly convened, the French government had deposed the Sultan and out-

---

[30] In 1962 a former member of the Indian mission at the United Nations wrote: "Eleven years ago, the case of Tunisia was excluded from the agenda of the Security Council. . . . Today Tunisia is a valued member of the United Nations and a Tunisian holds the highest post which this organization can offer—the office of President of the General Assembly. History is not lacking in its ironies; but this particular irony helps to underline the spectacular extent to which the United Nations has altered." B. Rajan, "Evolution on the East River," *Seminar*, No. 31 (March, 1962), 17. This entire issue of *Seminar*, a monthly journal published in New Delhi, is devoted to the United Nations.

lawed the Istiqlal party. The First Committee rejected a strong draft resolution submitted by several members of the Afro-Asian group, but it did adopt another draft resolution introduced by Bolivia and amended by India, Indonesia, and Burma. This resolution, however, did not receive the necessary two-thirds majority in the General Assembly. The Moroccan question was debated again at the Ninth Session of the Assembly. This time the Assembly, on December 17, 1954, adopted a rather innocuous resolution, originating with twelve Afro-Asian states, postponing consideration of the question and expressing confidence that promised negotiations between France and Morocco would lead to a satisfactory settlement. When the General Assembly, on September 30, 1955, voted to place the question on its agenda again, French representatives ceased to attend all meetings of the Assembly and its standing committee until November 25, when the Assembly decided that it was no longer seized of the question. On December 3 the Assembly voted to postpone any further consideration of the Moroccan issue. Three months later France recognized the independence of Morocco, with "interdependent links" with France.

Consideration of the Tunisian question followed a parallel course. On June 20, 1952, after the Security Council had rejected a request of eleven Asian and African members of the United Nations to consider "the present grave situation in Tunisia," the same eleven states, plus Lebanon and Syria, asked that a special session of the General Assembly be convened. When this request failed to receive majority support, the thirteen Afro-Asian states asked that the question be included on the agenda of the Seventh Session of the Assembly. After extensive debate in the First Committee and the General Assembly, in which France refused to participate on the ground that its relations with Tunisia, as with Morocco, were essentially a matter of domestic jurisdiction, the Committee rejected a draft resolution submitted by the thirteen Afro-Asian states. On December 17, 1952, the Assembly adopted a weaker resolution, sponsored by eleven Latin-American states, expressing the hope that France and Tunisia would enter into negotiations leading to self-government for the Tunisians. At the Assembly's Eighth Session a draft resolution on Tunisia, submitted by the thirteen Afro-Asian states and adopted in modified form by the First Committee, failed to receive a two-thirds majority in the Assembly. A year later, during the Ninth Session, the General Assembly adopted a resolution proposed by fourteen Afro-Asian states which noted with satisfaction that French and Tunisian representatives had entered into negotiations and which postponed further consideration of the Tunisian question by the General Assembly. On March 20, 1956, representatives of France and Tunisia signed an agreement for the independence of Tunisia, subject to certain reservations of uncertain meaning.

The most active role in the discussions in the General Assembly of the Moroccan and Tunisian questions was taken by the Afro-Asian states, particularly by the neutral nations. They took the initiative in proposing resolutions and in debating the issues, and they took advantage of the opportunity afforded by consideration of these questions to press their general anti-colonial views. The immediate results of their efforts were not impressive: a few watered-down resolutions, and eventual postponement of further consideration of the questions, while negotiations between France and Morocco and Tunisia were proceeding directly. The cost of such limited results was considerable, in that the debates exacerbated the tensions between the colonial or former colonial powers and their former dependencies and placed France in a most embarrassing predicament. In actual fact, the representatives of the Afro-Asian states were willing to settle for much more moderate steps than their own statements during the debates might suggest; and some of them were instrumental in finding compromise formulas at particularly tense periods of the discussions. Particularly noteworthy was the role of the Latin-American group in proposing compromise resolutions which were accepted, sometimes in amended form, by the Afro-Asian group, after the more strongly worded resolutions sponsored by the latter had been rejected. Anti-colonial resolutions supported by Latin America as well as by the Afro-Asian bloc commanded the two-thirds majority needed for passage.

2. *The Algerian Question.* Another colonial issue before the General Assembly was the Algerian question. For France this was an even more delicate issue than the questions of Morocco and Tunisia, for Algeria had never been a dependent territory; instead it had been a part of metropolitan France for more than a century, and all Algerians over twenty-one were French citizens. Nevertheless, the Afro-Asian states insisted on bringing the question of Algeria before the General Assembly, on the ground that, whatever the legal status of Algeria in French law, Algerians did not in fact enjoy the same rights as French-

men and were now demanding actual equality and independence. More-over, the situation in Algeria was a matter which was properly of concern to the United Nations, and involved questions of human rights, especially the right of self-determination.

The question was first brought officially before the United Nations in 1955. On January 5, 1955, Saudi Arabia, whose own record in the promotion of certain human rights was not spotless, brought to the attention of the Security Council the "grave situation in Algeria." On July 29 of the same year fourteen Asian and African states requested that the Algerian question be included on the agenda of the Tenth Session of the General Assembly. The General Committee recommended against this, after lengthy debate in which the United States, the United Kingdom, and New Zealand were the chief proponents of the French position and Egypt, Iraq, Pakistan, Thailand, India, and the Soviet Union led the campaign to place the item on the agenda of the Assembly. (Note the combination of two neutral nations with three committed members of the Afro-Asian group and the Soviet Union.) In a virtually unprecedented revolt against a recommendation of the powerful General Committee, the General Assembly, on September 30, 1955, voted to include the Algerian question on its agenda. The necessary votes were obtained largely from the Afro-Asian group, supported by the Soviet bloc and some of the Latin-American group. After the vote French delegates refused to participate in any meetings of the General Assembly or its standing committees.

This development led to sober second thoughts on the part of those states which had taken the lead in forcing a consideration of the Algerian issue, and steps were soon inaugurated to find a way out of the impasse. On November 23 the Chairman of the First Committee called attention to a proposal submitted by four Latin-American states—presumably with the knowledge of the Afro-Asian group—for removing the Algerian question from the agenda of the General Assembly. Two days later the First Committee adopted a procedural motion submitted by India, recommending that the General Assembly decide not to give any further consideration to the question at its Tenth Session, and the Assembly adopted this proposal without debate or objection. Thus the way was paved for France to return to the Assembly without loss of face.

The representatives of the Afro-Asian group seemed to be as relieved as any other delegates with this denouement. In the corridors of the United Nations and in the discussions in the First Committee, V. K. Krishna Menon of India was particularly assiduous in seeking a face-saving formula which would bring France back to the Assembly. The same cautious moderation prevailed during the Eleventh Session of the Assembly. Although the Afro-Asian group was successful in getting the Algerian question back on the agenda, the Assembly limited itself to passing a resolution expressing the hope that "in a spirit of cooperation, a peaceful, democratic and just resolution will be found."

At the opening of the Twelfth Session of the General Assembly the Afro-Asian group demanded acceptance of a stronger resolution, containing a specific endorsement of negotiations between France and the Algerian National Liberation Front in accordance with the principle of self-determination. In the First Committee supporters of France, including the United States, succeeded in amending the resolution in a way which led its Asian-African sponsors to vote against it. The result was a tie vote in the First Committee and hence no recommendation to the General Assembly. This cleared the way for a compromise resolution which was approved without debate by a vote of eighty to none (France did not participate and South Africa was absent) on December 10, 1957.[31] The resolution, introduced by Argentina, Brazil, Canada, Cuba, the Dominican Republic, India, Iran, Ireland, Italy, Japan, Mexico, Norway, Peru, Spain, and Thailand (note the strong representation of the Afro-Asian group, including both committed and uncommitted members, and the Latin-American group, with representatives of the NATO group, not including the major members, and the absence of any Communist bloc sponsors), took note of the offer of good offices by the King of Morocco and the President of Tunisia and expressed "the wish that in a spirit of effective co-operation *pourparlers* will be entered into, and other appropriate means utilized."

When General Charles de Gaulle assumed control of the government—and perhaps also of the destinies—of France in 1958, it was widely believed that a new era in the Algerian story had begun. "The General's vague promise of a 'preferred place' for Algeria alienated neither the European settlers, who wanted political integration of Algeria with France, nor the Front of National Liberation (FLN), which had by then been fighting for almost four years in the name of

[31] General Assembly Resolution 1184 (XII) (December 10, 1957).

Algerian independence. Because it left some hope for both sides, it had the virtue of giving the General a flexible framework within which to operate."[32] De Gaulle's position was greatly strengthened by elections at home and by a referendum in the French territories, in which every territory except Guinea voted overwhelmingly to maintain close links with France. In Algeria, which voted as a *département* of France, 96.7 per cent of those who voted (including about two-thirds of the eligible Moslems) supported the Constitution and De Gaulle. Shortly before the September referendum the FLN announced its transformation into the Provisional government of the Algerian Republic (GPRA).

In spite of this turn of events the Afro-Asian members of the United Nations insisted that the Algerian question should be considered by the Thirteenth Session of the General Assembly. For the first time since the Tenth Assembly, France refused to participate in any of the deliberations on Algeria. In December, 1958, a modified version of a strong resolution sponsored by seventeen Asian and African states fell short of the required two-thirds majority by one vote (thirty-five–eighteen–twenty-eight).[33] The United States voted against the resolution in the committee stage, but abstained in the final vote in the Assembly. Terming the continuance of the "war" in Algeria a threat to international peace and security, the resolution called for "negotiations between the two parties concerned" (thus giving virtually formal recognition to the FLN) and recognized "the right of the Algerian people to independence."

On the eve of the opening of the Fourteenth Assembly, De Gaulle in a radio speech pledged that after four years of peace Algerians would be given a choice of three alternatives: independence, "out-and-out identification with France," or "government of Algerians by Algerians, backed by French help and in close relationship with her." Perhaps because of this offer a very mild resolution, representing a considerable watering down of an originally mild Afro-Asian draft, failed to gain a two-thirds vote in the Assembly. France again refused to participate in the debate.

In the Fifteenth Session of the General Assembly in 1960, with the

[32] "Issues before the Fourteenth General Assembly," *International Conciliation*, No. 524 (September, 1959), 39.

[33] United Nations Document A/4075 (December 13, 1958).

addition of sixteen new member states from Africa, all of whom affili-
ated themselves with the Afro-Asian group, and another state, Cyprus,
which was invited to associate with the group, a resolution sponsored
by Asian and African states, calling for a referendum in Algeria under
United Nations auspices, fell short of a two-thirds vote because of a
split in the Afro-Asian group. Most of the former members of the
French community which had just been admitted to the United Nations refused to support the resolution.

Most of the members of the United Nations seemed to agree with
the request of twenty-five Asian and African states that the Algerian
question be placed on the agenda of the Fifteenth Session of the General Assembly, which contended that "the situation in Algeria is such
that it must continue to engage the attention of the United Nations
as long as a peaceful solution in conformity with the Charter is not
reached. Indeed, it is the responsibility of the United Nations to contribute in every possible way to the attainment of a solution."

The United Nations "responsibility to contribute" was invoked in
a General Assembly Resolution in December, 1960, but the exact
nature of the contribution which the United Nations was expected to
make was not specified.[34]

In January, 1961, President de Gaulle asked for and received, in a
popular referendum held throughout the French Republic, support for
his policy of self-determination for Algeria. Following this, talks were
resumed between the Algerian nationalists and French representatives
on the future of Algeria at Évian-les-Bains and Lugrin. Despite substantive differences on many issues which emerged during the Évian-Lugrin
talks, the desire to reach an accord resulted finally in the conclusion of
a cease-fire on March 19, 1962. This was followed by a popular referendum held throughout Algeria on July 1, 1962. The Algerian people
voted almost unanimously for independence but with continued ties
with France.

In the United Nations, during the Sixteenth Session, the First Committee held substantive discussions on the question of Algeria after
thirty-three Afro-Asian nations had requested that the Algerian question be inscribed on the agenda.[35] A draft resolution sponsored by the
same thirty-three nations was adopted in the First Committee calling

[34] See General Assembly Resolution 1573 (XV) (December 19, 1960).
[35] See United Nations Document A/4842 and Add. I. (August 11, 1961).

upon the two parties to the dispute to resume negotiations "with a view to implementing the right of the Algerian people to self-determination and independence respecting the unity and territorial integrity of Algeria." The draft resolution recommended in the report of the First Committee to the General Assembly was subsequently adopted in a plenary meeting of the General Assembly by a vote of sixty-two in favor, none against, and thirty-eight abstentions.[36]

On October 8, 1962, Algeria became the 109th member of the United Nations. The draft resolution for Algerian membership was sponsored by thirty-four states in the General Assembly; the vote was by acclamation.[37] Four days earlier, the Security Council had adopted unanimously (with China abstaining) a draft resolution sponsored by ten members of the Council recommending that the Assembly admit Algeria to membership. France supported Algeria's membership in both the Council and the Assembly.

It will be seen, therefore, that, as in the cases of Morocco and Tunisia, the Algerian question was once again resolved outside the United Nations with the latter acting as an overt pressure group seeking to persuade both sides to resolve the issues in the dispute peaceably and expeditiously.

3. *Colonialism and Self-Determination.* As James Frederick Green has stated, "The steadily mounting tension over colonial problems has affected the deliberations of the United Nations organs on many other aspects of human rights."[38] Of special concern to the neutral nations of Asia and Africa, with their recent memories of dependent status and their sensitivity on racial issues, are questions involving racial discrimination and the right of self-determination.

> On few aspects of human rights do delegations in United Nations meetings feel more deeply than on racial discrimination. Race, the first of the four grounds of discrimination enumerated throughout the Charter, has become for many the crucial issue. This preoccupation with racial discrimination underlies much of the emotionalism in the debates on human rights, self-determination, the trusteeship system and non-self-governing territories. It is in large part responsible for the debate on Indians in

[36] See General Assembly Resolution 1724 (XVI) (December 20, 1961).

[37] General Assembly Resolution 1454 (XVII) (October 8, 1962).

[38] "The United Nations and Human Rights," in Robert E. Asher, Walter M. Kotschnig, William Adams Brown, Jr., James Frederick Green, Emil J. Sady, and Associates, *The United Nations and Promotion of the General Welfare* (Washington, D.C., The Brookings Institution, 1957), 754.

South Africa, on race relations in South Africa, and on Tunisia and Morocco, and for the importance that the whole "colonial" issue has attained in the United Nations. It has contributed to the "neutralism" of the Near Eastern and Asian delegations toward the conflict between democracy and communism, and has been used to advantage by spokesmen of the Soviet bloc for attacking the United States. It has caused the Subcommission on Prevention of Discrimination and Protection of Minorities to become an almost sacrosanct organ in the eyes of the underdeveloped countries.[39]

Increasing concern over "the right of self-determination of peoples and nations" has been shown in discussions in many of the organs and agencies of the United Nations, notably in the General Assembly, the Economic and Social Council, the Commission on Human Rights, the Trusteeship Council, and the Committee on Information from Non-Self-Governing Territories. In 1950 the General Assembly called on the Economic and Social Council to request the Commission on Human Rights "to study ways and means which would ensure the right of peoples and nations to self-determination." Debates on questions of self-determination have featured almost every session of these United Nations agencies, and the consequences of these debates have not been altogether reassuring:

> These annual debates on self-determination clearly reveal the ever widening split between the administering powers and the non-administering powers in the United Nations. Both sides are taking increasingly extreme and recalcitrant positions. Thus far, the efforts of the United States, the Scandinavian delegations, and a few others to find compromise formulas have not succeeded. In particular, their efforts to broaden the concept of self-determination to cover all territories, not just the non-self-governing and trust territories, have been resented by the Asian-African Group. The resulting strain on the Organization is severe, and the threat to the unity of its Members is serious. Self-determination is one of the many issues before the United Nations that needs a greater degree of good will, patience and understanding than has been evident in recent years.[40]

Representatives of neutral nations of Asia and Africa have been exceedingly active in the work of the Committee on Information from Non-Self-Governing Territories and the Trusteeship Council, and they

[39] *Ibid.*, 728.   [40] *Ibid.*, 757-58.

have contributed in many ways to making this work meaningful. They have been assiduous in the examinations of reports from administering states and of reports of visiting missions to trust territories, and they have led the demands for more detailed and comprehensive information from non-self-governing territories and for more concrete evidence of the determination of the administering states to prepare these territories, wherever possible, for eventual self-government. They have insisted that the United Nations has general responsibility, as a guardian of the interests of the international community, for the welfare of the inhabitants of non-self-governing territories, where most of the still-dependent peoples of the world live, as well as of trust territories. On the whole, their concern for the interests of the still-dependent peoples has had a wholesome effect; but too often this genuine concern has become overlarded with preconceptions about colonialism and other major issues of world politics. As a result:

> There is something unreal about much that has happened in the United Nations on matters relating to dependent territories. There is little resemblance, for example, between enlightened colonial policy being carried out by the United Kingdom in most of its territories and the rigid, defensive position of that government on questions in the United Nations relating to dependent territories. Nor does there appear to be much relationship between many of the measures proposed by the anti-colonial nations in the United Nations and the conditions and needs of the territorial populations.
>
> This is not to say that genuine regard for the welfare of dependent peoples is not a motivating factor in the approach of most Members to colonial issues. But it is not the only factor, and in some cases, it is not the dominating one. It is also not possible to say that the colonial powers would have accelerated reforms in dependent territories as rapidly as they have without pressure from the United Nations. In discussions of colonial questions, in the United Nations, however, the national interests of non-administering as well as administering Members often obscure whatever recognition might be given, or should be given, to the principle enshrined in the Charter that "the interests of the inhabitants of these territories are paramount."[41]

PEACEFUL AND CONCILIATORY ROLE
OF THE UNITED NATIONS: INDIA AS AN EXAMPLE

The preoccupation of the neutral nations with anti-colonial issues,

[41] Emil J. Sady, "The United Nations and Dependent Peoples," in *ibid.*, 999.

questions of human rights and self-determination, and economic development of underdeveloped areas are illustrative of their general orientation to problems of world affairs and to the proper role of the United Nations. They seem to be primarily interested in the non-political aspects of the United Nations work. They are uneasy, and often obstructive, when political issues are at stake, especially political issues of the gravest moment which arise from the strained relations between the Communist and non-Communist world and which clearly involve questions of war and peace. They prefer to avoid such issues, or if they have to face them, they conceive their role to be a peaceful and mediatory one. They have different views from those entertained generally in the United States regarding the nature of present dangers, the priorities that should be assigned to the dangers that they recognize, and the steps that should be taken to deal with recognized dangers. They have very different assessments of the objectives of the Soviet Union and other Communist states, and are inclined to be much "softer" in their approach to the Communist states than is the United States.

Again, however, we must remember that there are many degrees of neutralism. Most of the neutral nations fear the consequences for themselves of Great Power rivalries, and they entertain rather naïve views regarding the role of power and force in international relations. The standards which they are accustomed to use in approaching international problems were effectively summarized by G. L. Mehta, former Indian ambassador to the United States:

> In Asia and Africa, the principal criterion for judging international policies is whether they help towards liberation of peoples and towards the stability of their countries. . . . The primary interest of the countries in Asia is their own peaceful development and "not a game of choose-up sides for an atomic war which would in any case destroy them." It is the growth of nuclear power, above all, that has compelled nations, large and small, to realize that it is risky for them to align themselves in a military sense and make themselves increasingly dependent on big powers. But these nations are prepared to align themselves and have done so in the cause of peace. They are frequently called "uncommitted" nations, and yet these so-called "uncommitted" nations are active members of the United Nations and its specialized agencies and participants in various schemes of international economic cooperation such as the Colombo Plan; they

have also endeavoured to make their contribution to the cause of international understanding and harmony. These countries are "uncommitted" only in the sense that they do not believe in bi-polarization of the world and alignment with power blocs.[42]

In the light of this kind of orientation to world affairs, it was inevitable that the increase in the number of neutral nations in the United Nations would, as Thomas J. Hamilton has noted, greatly diminish "the effectiveness of the United Nations as an organ of collective security."[43] The United Nations was from its inception, and from its very nature, a very limited instrument for the maintenance of peace and security, even though this was stated to be the first purpose of the organization in Article I of the Charter. The changing balance of power in the United Nations is only one of several developments which have further restricted its usefulness in this respect.

> The net result is that the United Nations is no longer an effective instrument for collective security, and would not be even if it had strong military forces at its disposal. There would still remain the necessity of obtaining authorization to use the force. The Soviet vote in the Security Council and the Asian-Africa-Soviet veto in the General Assembly are both symptoms of the two basic facts about the United Nations today: the continued disunity among the great powers, and the dilution of the collective strength of the United Nations, which started out as a continuation of the wartime alliance against the Axis but has been transformed as a result of the membership deal.[44]

The strongest opposition to the use of the United Nations in the interests of collective security has come from India. "India wants the world organization, at present, to concern itself with functions other than enforcement measures, for example, conciliation, negotiation, and mediation."[45] In view of its interest in social change and greater participation in world affairs by previously underprivileged peoples and nations, it may seem paradoxical that India has shown little desire to make any drastic revisions in the United Nations Charter or to

[42] Commencement address at Simpson College, Indianola, Iowa, June 3, 1956.

[43] "U.N.'s Role Changing as Members Increase," *New York Times* (1956), E3. This is a theme which Mr. Hamilton has stressed in many of his columns in the *Times*.

[44] "The United Nations," *The Atlantic*, Vol. CXCIX (April, 1957), 14.

[45] *India and the United Nations* (New York, Manhattan Publishing Company, 1957), 33.

qualify in any major way the so-called veto provision. It favors reten-
tion of the veto on the ground that its abolition would tend to "convert the United Nations into an executive agent of the anti-Communist alliance,[46] and would destroy the representative and universal
character of the world organization. "It is fully realized that the veto
very often makes the United Nations ineffective; but India prefers
an ineffective organization, representing all the major political elements in the international community, to an effective organization
which may grow into an instrument of one power bloc."[47]

India's position on the "Uniting for Peace Resolution" of 1950 and
the work of the Collective Measures Committee was more negative
than that of any other member of the Afro-Asian group. It was, in
fact, the only member of the United Nations to abstain in the voting
on the Resolution (there were no negative votes). It flatly announced
that it proposed to take no steps to implement the provision of the
Resolution, which called for the maintenance within the national armed
forces of the member states of units which could be made available
to the United Nations. It did not support the resolution of March 17,
1957, asking the Collective Measures Committee, established under
the "Uniting for Peace Resolution," to continue its work. "In explaining the Indian position, Mrs. Pandit recalled India's opposition to
the establishment of the Committee and suggested that 'the United
Nations should devote itself to a study of measures for peaceful settlement and conciliation of disputes.' This, she stated, 'was more urgent
and more constructive than the study of coercive measures.' "[48]

Officially the government of India has been a staunch supporter of
the United Nations, and a great deal of publicity has been given in
India to United Nations activities. India clearly regards the United
Nations as a useful forum for the airing of crucial world problems,
including those in which it is especially interested; for the reconcilia-
tion of differences among nations, especially between the "power blocs";
and for the elevation of the standards of international life. India has
been vocally disappointed with the record of the United Nations in
dealing with colonial and racial issues, such as treatment of Indians in
the Union of South Africa, the Moroccan, Tunisian, and Algerian issues, and the status of non-self-governing peoples. It has been especially vexed at certain resolutions of the Security Council on the Kash-

[46] *Ibid.*, 33.   [47] *Ibid.*, 209.   [48] *Ibid.*, 146.

mir question. Here we seem to have a clear case in which India has been out of step with majority opinion within the United Nations, and has indeed even appeared to flout certain United Nations resolutions; but India justifies its position on the ground that the resolutions of the Security Council which it disliked were pushed through by the United States and Great Britain and were dictated by considerations of "power politics." Like other members of the United Nations, including the other neutral states, India is interested in promoting the work of the United Nations which it regards as consistent with its own national interest, and in blocking any actions or resolutions which it regards as detrimental to its national interest. Fortunately India feels, as do the other neutral states, that the area of mutual interest is a very wide one.

The neutral states have taken an active interest in all efforts, in the United Nations and through other channels, to achieve agreement on the international control of atomic energy and on effective measures of disarmament. They have sometimes been criticized for giving more weight to professions than to performance, especially as far as the Soviet Union is concerned. India seems to be particularly vulnerable to this kind of criticism. It applauded the Soviet proposals for the prohibition of nuclear warfare and the cessation of the testing of atomic weapons; but in the Atomic Energy Commission, the Commission for Conventional Armaments, and the Disarmament Commission of the United Nations it generally voted in support of Western proposals. Indeed, India is charged with equivocating between a policy which holds that the United Nations is the proper organ for the advancement of disarmament and the international control of atomic energy and one necessitating secret, bipolar sessions—based on the premise that "the solution of problems in this field depends essentially on agreement between the United States and the Soviet Union."[49] India opposed a plan of the Western powers for the international ownership of atomic raw materials and productive processes, on the ground that the underdeveloped countries looked to atomic energy as "of enormous importance in raising the living standards and bringing them to some reasonable parity with those existing in the United States and Western European countries." Therefore India would not allow "any international organization, dominated by industrially advanced countries,

49 *Ibid.*, 141.

to control their activities in regard to the development of atomic energy."[50]

Policy Patterns and Voting Behavior of the Afro-Asians

This discussion of the position of the neutral states on certain issues which have come before the United Nations suggests that the policies of these states in the United Nations can profitably be analyzed under five main headings: policies that support the separate national interests of the neutral states, policies that support the collective national interests of these states, policies of neutral states that support and buttress Soviet national interests and objectives, policies of neutral states that support and buttress Western national interests and objectives generally, and policies of neutral states that support and buttress American national interests and objectives.

It is, of course, a necessary assumption that the policies of each neutral member of the United Nations are regarded by the policy-makers of that state as in the national interest, as they conceive it. It does not follow that their assumption is a correct one, but one can hardly challenge the right of the recognized leaders of a state to determine national policies. We have noted that the neutral members of the United Nations often, but not invariably, present a united front in United Nations debates and resolutions. Therefore, many of their individual policies are regarded as supporting their collective national interests. We have also seen that in votes on such issues as colonial questions and methods of peaceful settlement the neutral states have frequently voted with the Soviet Union and in opposition to the positions taken by the United States. In such instances, therefore, their policies have served to buttress and support Soviet national interests and objectives and to have a detrimental effect on United States national interests and objectives. It does not follow, however, that the policies of the neutral states are dictated by any pro-Soviet or anti-American biases. The neutral states, as do other members of the United Nations, vote in accordance with their conceptions of their own national interests. Fortunately, in most instances the mutuality of interests between the neutral states and the Western world is reflected in the similarity of voting records on most issues to come before the United Nations; but there can be no blinking the fact that on many of the issues which have been discussed in

[50] *Ibid.*, 141.

this chapter the positions of the United States and of the neutral states have frequently diverged, whereas the Soviet Union has, for its own reasons, generally supported the neutralist position.

The United States and the Afro-Asians

An analysis of votes in the General Assembly will demonstrate that the oft-encountered claims that the United States and the neutral nations take opposite sides on most issues which come before the United Nations whereas the neutral nations and the Soviet Union are usually to be found on the same side is a misleading myth.

The record shows that the majority of the neutral nations often vote differently from both the United States and the Soviet Union. On 482 roll-call votes in the General Assembly from 1946 to September, 1957, for example, India voted with the Soviet Union only 49.3 per cent of the time, and with the United States only 39 per cent of the time.[51]

On some questions of great importance to the Afro-Asian states, especially those relating to colonial questions and to methods of peaceful settlement of international disputes, the Soviet Union almost invariably supports the Afro-Asian position, whereas all too frequently the United States is found on the opposite side. As long as the resolutions are couched in rather vague and general terms the Afro-Asian states, regardless of their differences in orientation or point of view, are generally in virtually unanimous agreement on such issues. A particularly embarrassing example of the way in which an American position can cause bitter disappointment or worse in the Afro-Asian area occurred in the Fifteenth Session of the General Assembly of the United Nations, when the United States abstained on a resolution endorsing "the necessity of bringing to a speedy and unconditional end colonialism in all its forms and manifestations"—a resolution reminiscent of the one on colonialism passed at the Bandung Conference in 1955—which was drafted by some of the Afro-Asian states and approved by all forty-five members of the Afro-Asian group, as well as by the Communist bloc and most of the other members of the Assembly. In this case, the United States abstention was ordered from Washington and was known to be contrary to the desires of members of the United States delegation to the Assembly; in fact, the only Negro member of the

[51] Gertrude C. Boland, "India and the United Nations: India's Role in the General Assembly, 1946–57" (unpublished doctoral dissertation, Claremont Graduate School, 1957).

United States delegation stood up and applauded when the results of the voting on the resolution—eighty-nine for, none against, and nine abstentions—were announced.[52] However, this was merely a particularly flagrant example of the dilemmas which have haunted the United States, in the United Nations and outside, on most colonial issues. No formula has yet been found whereby the United States can take a more clear-cut stand in favor of self-determination and against colonialism without alienating its allies of the Atlantic Community. What is certain is that, as Thomas J. Hamilton points out, "if the United States continues to stand with the colonial powers in the United Nations it will find itself on the losing side many times in years to come."[53]

A most serious qualification to the past record of substantial concert in votes in the United Nations General Assembly between the United States and the Afro-Asian members of the organization is the growing evidence that the United States and the Afro-Asian states are voting together much less frequently than they used to. This trend has been manifest for some time, but it became strikingly evident during the first part of the Fifteenth Session of the General Assembly, in the closing months of 1960. The United States and the Soviet Union voted on opposite sides seventy-three times, excluding roll calls on which one of them abstained. With the exception of Turkey, Pakistan, Iran, seven states of the French community, and the Congo (Leopoldville), all of the Afro-Asian member states in the Middle East, South Asia, and Africa voted more often with the Soviet Union than with the United States; and only Turkey voted with the United States on more than half of the roll calls (most others abstained or were absent well over half of the time). These votes do not necessarily suggest any marked anti-American or pro-Soviet biases on the part of the Afro-Asian states; but they do suggest that for some reason the position of the United States on most of the issues which were brought to a vote in the Fifteenth Session of the General Assembly did not win favor with the majority of the Afro-Asian states, even those states which are generally considered to be pro-West, whereas the Soviet Union in one way or another managed to align itself with the majority of the states of Asia and Africa.

In view of the growing numbers and importance of the Afro-Asian

[52] General Assembly Resolution 1514 (XV) (December 14, 1960).
[53] *New York Times* (December 18, 1960), IV, 9.

members in the United Nations, and the growing success of the Soviet Union in identifying itself with the aspirations of these states, any signs of increasing alienation of the United States from the major group in the United Nations, representing the newly emergent and newly emerging states of Afro-Asia, are matters of profound concern. In the past one could say rather cynically that everyone seemed out of step except the Soviet Union. At present there seems to be a danger that the United States is veering toward this direction, although to a lesser degree. This is a trend which calls for a sober reappraisal of the positions taken by the United States in the United Nations and of the causes for the growing divergence between the United States and the emerging nations of Asia and Africa at the time when these nations are becoming more and more important in the United Nations and in world affairs generally. The Kennedy administration had undertaken such a reappraisal and tended to support positions in the United Nations which were in keeping with those of the Afro-Asian states, even at the risk of parting company with its NATO allies.

An even more profound question suggests itself at this juncture: Is the United States in fact cutting itself off from the hopes and aspirations of the majority of the nations and the peoples of the world, and is the Soviet Union succeeding in identifying itself with these hopes and aspirations?

The danger signals which the United States should heed are now clear for all to see. They have been well described by Thomas Hovet, who has made the most thorough analysis of bloc voting in the United Nations:

> One is forced to consider with some misgivings the future role of the United States in the United Nations. Virtually all the members of the many delegations who express their concern mention what they call the "failures" of the United States with reluctance. Most of them are basically sympathetic to the United States. And yet the sense of distrust, or at least doubt, appears to be increasing as the various delegations develop increasing degrees of rapport and intimate contacts with other delegations, the members of which recognize the alteration of diplomatic negotiation techniques which are demanded in the bloc and group structure of the United Nations.[54]

Shortly after the admission of sixteen new members to the United

[54] *Bloc Politics in the United Nations,* 119.

164

Nations in December, 1955, Francis O. Wilcox, then assistant secretary of state for international organization affairs, declared: "The United States must now assess the implications for its foreign policy of a United Nations in which European representation has been increased, the voice of Asia and the Middle East has become strengthened, the number of so-called uncommitted countries has been enlarged, and the proportionate numerical strength of the Latin American group reduced."[55] A few months later Wilcox stated: "The collision in the United Nations between these two currents, one running between the free world and international communism, the other between Europe and its old imperial holdings, has served to mold the United Nations to the shape of the world it represents. It may have set discouraging limits to the organization."[56]

The problems which have been created for the United States as a result of the changing balance within the United Nations are suggested by the general tenor of Wilcox's comments, and they are delineated sharply throughout this chapter and elsewhere in this volume. In many respects the changing balance presents the United States with a variety of embarrassing dilemmas which it would prefer to avoid. Nevertheless, as Wilcox suggests, the United Nations is now more nearly molded "to the shape of the world it represents and the United States has to learn how to live in the world as it is." Moreover, as Wilcox has also pointed out, the changing balance in the United Nations "has opened new possibilities for utilizing the United Nations to keep within peaceful bounds these sweeping tides and currents. . . . The enlarged United Nations will speak with wider authority. It will more accurately mirror underlying conditions as they are in the world and confront all of us in a more decisive manner with the crucial problems of the atomic age. A greater sense of responsibility will be required of all members if the organization is to develop in a sound and practical way and if problems are to be solved and not aggravated."

The United States has reason to be apprehensive of the consequences of the changing membership picture in the United Nations; but unless it can develop policies within the United Nations as well as outside which will commend themselves to the majority of the non-Com-

[55] Address before the National Press Club, Washington, D.C., January 13, 1956.
[56] Address before the American Society of International Law, Washington, D.C., April 27, 1956.

munist states of the world, including most of the neutral nations, it will jeopardize its basic national interests, whatever the composition of the United Nations. A measure of its success or failure will be the degree of support which it will be able to command in the General Assembly and other agencies of the United Nations. Indeed, as Wilcox has observed, "If the time should ever come when we found ourselves consistently outvoted on important issues in the United Nations, that would surely be a sign that we ought to re-examine in a hardheaded way our basic policies." Such an "agonizing reappraisal" would involve considerations of far greater import than voting habits in the agencies of the United Nations.

Undoubtedly the changing composition of the United Nations has added to the embarrassments and dilemmas of American foreign policy in dealing with certain sensitive issues; but these issues could hardly have been avoided, for they arise out of trends and pressures in the international community, and the United Nations may be able to exert an increasingly useful influence in dealing with them. If the United Nations is to play this role, it has formidable obstacles to overcome, including its own limitations; the vexing and complicated nature of the problems; the difficulties which the United States and other Western powers are experiencing in reconciling themselves to the new order of affairs in the world; the inexperience, naïveté, and resentments of the underdeveloped and newly independent nations; and the obstructionism and worse of the Soviet Union. There is a danger, as Reinhold Niebuhr has pointed out, that "Our devout expressions of loyalty to it [the United Nations] therefore become but a screen for our irresponsibility."[57] Certainly the United States cannot look to the United Nations to relieve it of basic responsibilities in world affairs; but it can look to the world organization as a vehicle, however imperfect, for promoting American national interests in a variety of ways. As long as these national interests coincide in broad outlines and ultimate objectives with the interests of the majority of the states of the world society, the United States should find scope for extensive operations in the United Nations. If this mutuality of interest ever ceases to exist, the United States would do well to re-examine its policies and its basic approaches.

[57] Reinhold Niebuhr, "Seven Great Errors of U.S. Foreign Policy," *The New Leader* (December 24–31, 1956).

In spite of some highly publicized exceptions, an analysis of the voting records will confirm the impression which one gets by observing the United Nations in operation, that the United States is by no means out of step with the majority of the non-Communist nations on most of the issues that come before the world organization. Even on questions on which it has felt obliged to take an equivocal or tentative position, the United States has often found it possible to work out acceptable compromises with the majority of the members of the United Nations, including most of the neutral states. There seem to be almost no limits to what the United States can do by patience and persistence, coupled with a genuine desire to consider other countries' points of view and to reconsider its own policies in the light of these other viewpoints. Obviously this does not mean that the United States must defer to other views on all issues on which there are divergences of opinion. Its record is in fact remarkably impressive in persuading representatives of other states to support American proposals. It can work with a United Nations in which the neutral states have a kind of veto in the General Assembly and other organs and agencies, just as the neutral states can work in a United Nations in which the United States still has a commanding influence. In this sense the United Nations may properly be regarded as an important instrument of American national policy, in areas where its interests coincide with those of the majority of the states of the world; but the United Nations can never be more than an adjunct in the pursuit of certain policies which require closer collaboration than the United Nations can possibly provide.

In the new United Nations, reflecting increasingly the interests and pressures of the numerically many but economically and politically weak new nations, the United States, if it is to continue to work with the majority of the members, must develop new methods and techniques for mobilizing majorities in support of its position on major issues, and it must show a greater understanding of the nature and role of the blocs and groups in the United Nations. But it is also faced with a much more important dimension of its activity in the United Nations, which is to reassess the place of the United Nations in the total complex of its foreign policy, to reconsider the ways in which the United Nations can be used as an instrument of national policy, to review the differences in policy and in orientation that are developing or that have always existed with relation to the other member states, and to reappraise past and present policies in the light of basic interests. If the American policies cannot commend themselves to the majority of the members of the United Nations, something must be radically wrong with those policies. Thus far the United States has not had to face the prospect of being out of tune with the majority of the members, and if it follows policies which are truly in the national interest there is no reason to believe that it will ever be too far separated from the interests of most of the other nations of the world.

There can be no doubt that the changing and growing membership in the United Nations has made the world organization far less manageable as far as the United States is concerned, and has created many new problems for American policy-makers and representatives. But as Adlai Stevenson, an old United Nations hand who is now the permanent representative of the United States to the United Nations, stated when he appeared before the Senate Foreign Relations Committee on January 18, 1961, when the Committee was considering his appointment to the United Nations, the increase in membership in the United Nations "has also greatly increased the opportunity to advance the ideas and the interests of the United States." This is a view which was also expressed by the Eisenhower administration, and which is not necessarily reflective of the real attitude, combining apprehension with hope, of the United States toward the changing composition of the world organization. But most Americans would surely agree with the view expressed by Ambassador Stevenson when he said: "It is a mistake, in my judgment, for us to see in the United Nations merely a desperate survival operation, without also exploiting its potential as a cooperative search for better answers to the overhanging question, 'After survival, what then?'" Thus the United States is at once faced not only with growing problems in its associations with the United Nations but also with new opportunties.

In the introduction to his annual report for 1955 the Secretary-General of the United Nations, the late Dag Hammarskjold, called attention to "the great upheaval in the relationship of nations and peoples that is under way," and emphasized that one major consequence of this upheaval was that "the peoples of Asia today, and of Africa tomorrow, are moving toward a new relationship with what history calls the West." He did not minimize the problems which such a massive development created for the United Nations or for the world society as a whole, but he insisted that "the world organization is the place where this emerging new relationship in world affairs can most creatively be forged." Recurring to this theme in his annual report for 1957, the Secretary-General declared: "The United Nations reflects, but is in no sense a cause of, the renaissance of Asia. The awakening of Africa, and the other great changes that are under way in the balance of power and relationships of the peoples are likewise part of the dynamic of history itself. As always, they bring with them many grave problems of adjustment."

For the United States the rise in numbers and influence of the new states of Asia and Africa, of which the neutral nations are in the vast majority, is a massive fact of contemporary international relations which can be neither minimized nor ignored. Inevitably this development creates all kinds of complications and dilemmas for the United States. It is only natural that in this difficult age the United States should be apprehensive of the consequences of a development of such disturbing and far-reaching import. It is finding the problem of adjusting itself to the Afro-Asian upsurge almost as difficult as that of dealing with the Communist world. Certainly it would be a colossal tragedy if it could not work out a satisfactory relationship, in the United Nations and outside, with newly emerging states which are seeking to follow the democratic way and which are dedicated to principles for which the United States has stood since its inception.

CHAPTER VII

The Latin-American Bloc

BY ARTHUR P. WHITAKER

THE TWENTY-NATION Latin-American bloc has been the most successful of all the blocs in the United Nations, if the criterion of success is being on the winning side. The majority of its members have been far ahead of any other group in voting with the majority of the General Assembly. In the early years its success was attributed mainly to its size, for it was much the largest bloc and accounted for two-fifths of the total United Nations membership. Yet, for reasons that will appear below, it is still on the winning side, despite the fact that it is now outnumbered by the Afro-Asian bloc and accounts for only one-fifth of the total membership in the United Nations.

Moreover, while parting company with the United States on some questions, the Latin Americans have given it invaluable support on the main issues of the Cold War as these have arisen in the United Nations. The role of this bloc is therefore a subject of special interest in a volume dealing with the United Nations from the point of view of United States foreign policy. The recent defection of Cuba to the Soviet bloc, together with the danger that the Cuban contagion and neutralism may spread, only adds poignancy to North American interest in this theme.

An inquiry into the past may suggest what is to be expected of the Latin Americans, and what we should do about them in the future. The compass of the inquiry in the following pages is necessarily so brief that only the most salient points can be touched on. The discussion deals mainly with the conclusions reached in two relevant studies of recent date. One treats the Latin-American bloc along with all the other blocs in the United Nations.[1] The other is devoted wholly to Latin America but stops with 1954.[2]

[1] Hovet, *Bloc Politics in the United Nations*.

The Nature of the Latin-American Bloc

While it is one of the oldest and best organized groups of its kind in the United Nations, the Latin-American bloc, unlike the Soviet bloc, is not monolithic. It has a permanent chairman, caucases regularly twice a month, and makes decisions.[3] But its decisions are not binding on the members, and in fact an analysis of General Assembly votes in the period from 1946 to 1958 shows that the Latin-American states have all voted the same way only a little more than one-third of the time. Another third of the time, however, they have missed unanimity only through the abstention of at most a few members, and anything approaching a clear-cut division among them has occurred on only three occasions out of every ten.[4] This degree of solidarity is remarkable in view of their great diversity in size, stage of economic development, type of political regime, literacy, ethnic composition, and other aspects.[5]

Many common ties tend to unite these highly variegated peoples. Their cultural heritage is largely of western European origin; if there is such a thing as an Atlantic Community, they are part of it. For the rest, their culture is rooted in the American past—in many cases the pre-Columbian past. In religion, the vast majority of their people are Roman Catholic. They are conscious of the common historical bond forged in their nineteenth-century struggle for political independence. This bond is being reinforced in the present generation by their struggle for economic independence—a struggle that is being carried on by the half-dozen countries that have achieved an intermediate stage of economic development as well as by the remainder, which are still economically underdeveloped. All of them have been caught up in the revolution of rising expectations, and yet all of them have been in some measure frustrated by a rate of population increase (1.3 to 4.4 per cent a year) which is one of the highest in the world. Moreover, in the scale of world power, even the strongest of their nations are weak.

[2] John A. Houston, *Latin America in the United Nations* (New York, Carnegie Endowment for International Peace, 1956).

[3] The Latin-American vice-president of the General Assembly automatically becomes the chairman of the bloc. In that capacity he can call meetings at any time. See Hovet, *Bloc Politics in the United Nations*, 65.

[4] *Ibid.*, p. 67 and Chart 19.

[5] The function of the caucus seems more to come to a common policy if possible, or otherwise to abstain.

In short, the Latin Americans are vulnerable from many points of view, and their vulnerability tends to make them seek strength in union. They are aided in the quest by their long tradition of solidarity, which stretches back to their most famous liberator, Simón Bolívar, and which is very much alive today. It was recently voiced by one of their best-known spokesmen, Víctor Raúl Haya de la Torre, in words that many Latin Americans would make their own: "For me, Latin America is 'the great fatherland' [*patria grande*], of which each of its states is an inseparable and interdependent part."[6]

These factors not only explain the cohesiveness of the Latin-American bloc in the United Nations, but they also help to explain why that bloc has almost always formed a part of the Western alliance when Cold War issues were involved, and yet has often lined up with neutrals and even Communist-bloc powers on other questions, particularly those which the Latin Americans regard as involving the political and economic emancipation of colonial or underdeveloped countries.

To this ambivalence is due in large measure the success that the Latin Americans have had in riding with—or, to be more accurate, in helping to form—the majority in the General Assembly most of the time since 1945. Fortunately for them, whichever category of problem was involved at a given time, the line preferred by them generally found enough support in other delegations to enable them to prevail. In short, the nature of their preferences, and their flexibility in promoting them, have been no less essential to their success in United Nations voting than have their large numbers and high degree of solidarity.

Whether the Latin Americans' special relationship to the United States strengthens or weakens their solidarity with one another is a question on which opinions differ. But there can be no question that, on balance, this special relationship has been a valuable asset to the United States—and, through it, to the West—in United Nations affairs. Its basis is the Western Hemisphere idea, which took shape early in the nineteenth century. The core of the idea is the belief that the peoples of this hemisphere form a distinct, coherent group, united by geography, interest, and political ideals. As I have shown elsewhere,[7] the influence

[6] Víctor Raúl Haya de la Torre, "Problemas de la América Latina," *Cuadernos* (Paris), No. 37 (July–August, 1959), 14.

[7] Arthur P. Whitaker, *The Western Hemisphere Idea* (Ithaca, Cornell University Press, 1954).

of this idea has declined in recent years, but it is by no means dead. While it has not led to the formation of a Pan-American bloc in the United Nations, it has been useful to the United States in obtaining Latin-American co-operation there. Also, it has been a main inspiration of Latin-American resistance to Soviet intrusion into Western Hemisphere affairs.

In 1960, Fidel Castro's Cuba not only picked a quarrel with the United States but also flouted the Western Hemisphere idea and welcomed the proffer of Soviet protection with rockets. In a sense this put a new face on the situation, for there was no direct precedent for it except the Communist-infected regime of Jacobo Arbenz in Guatemala in the early 1950's, which had sought and obtained Soviet backing in the United Nations, and that regime had soon been liquidated. Indirectly, however, there had been many advance warnings of the widespread Latin-American social ferment of which Castro's regime was only an extreme expression, and some of these signs were provided by the positions taken by Latin Americans in the United Nations, mainly on economic and social questions, though at times even on political questions. But the heed paid to these warnings by the United States was too little and perhaps too late.

As a result, the United States now faces the twin danger of the spread of Castro's contagion to other Latin-American countries and of further Latin-American defections from the Western alliance, either to the Communist camp or at best to that of the neutralists. The danger is serious because of the importance both of the Latin-American votes in the United Nations and of the United Nations role in the foreign policy of the United States as defined by President John F. Kennedy in his inaugural address of January 21, 1961.

That the relative strength of the Latin-American bloc has been cut in half since 1946 by the growth of the United Nations membership, and that its absolute numbers have been cut to nineteen by Cuba's defection, only enhances the value of that bloc's support. Most of the new members of the United Nations belong either to the Communist or to the neutral camp, so that the United States now has more need than ever before of every vote that it can get.

Ethics and Law

Latin America shares the Judaeo-Christian ethic with the rest of the Western world, and the record of success and failure in its application is much the same there as elsewhere. The same is true of international law. Yet there are significant differences. Chief among these is the tenacity with which Latin Americans have clung to the view that the two things are inseparable, that ethics must be the basis of international law and hence of international organization. Another difference is their special proclivity for taking a legalistic approach to public affairs, whether domestic or international. Two other important differences, of a more concrete kind, both of them deeply rooted in Latin-American tradition, are their insistence upon the validity of the concept of "American international law"—which seems to jurists in other parts of the Western world a contradiction in terms—and their firm attachment to the related principles of absolute nonintervention and the juridical equality of states.

That some of these positions are mutually contradictory need not detain us here, though we shall have occasion to note below an illustration of the fact. We shall also note signs that the traditional views sketched above are beginning to give way to an approach to public affairs that is less idealistic and more positive and pragmatic—or which is, if one prefers, unprincipled. Its most extreme but clearest exemplar is the Castro regime.

The traditional Latin-American attitude found strong expression in many ways during the formative stage of the United Nations. Three examples must suffice here. The first comes from the recommendations regarding a projected general international organization made in 1943 by the Inter-American Juridical Committee, all of whose members but one were Latin Americans.[8] Deploring the displacement of moral principles by the actual conduct of states as the basis of international law, the committee gave first place to its recommendation that the new international organization should be based on the priority of moral law and of the fundamental principles of international law derived from it.

The second illustration relates to the United Nations Charter Conference at San Francisco in 1945. Here the Latin-American bloc struggled valiantly but with little success to prevent the Charter from concentrating on the maintenance of peace and security, as contemplated by the Great Powers' Dumbarton Oaks proposals, and to make it "give

[8] Houston, *Latin America in the United Nations*, 8.

equal emphasis to supporting the principles of justice and international law."[9]

Third and finally, the Latin Americans labored hard at San Francisco in favor of their positions on the concrete questions mentioned above. They met with only partial success as regards nonintervention and with none at all as regards the juridical equality of states. But they were much better rewarded in their espousal of the regionalism reflected in their concept of American international law. In fact, they were mainly responsible for writing into the Charter Article 51, which might be called the Magna Charta of regionalism. But for it, there could have been no effective regional security systems, no Rio Defense Treaty, and no NATO; and by the exercise of its veto in the Security Council, any one of the Great Powers could have blocked enforcement action anywhere at any time. Fear that the Soviet Union would make such use of its veto in order to give free rein to conflicts in the Western Hemisphere, and thus create a favorable climate for Communist penetration, was one of the chief reasons why the Latin-American bloc insisted upon writing Article 51 into the charter.[10]

The Latin Americans' attachment to regionalism is one source of contradiction in their traditional views on ethics and international law. Another source is their attachment to the absolute rule of nonintervention. As we have noted, they sought to make the support of the principles of justice a major purpose of the United Nations. And yet, when these principles conflict with their doctrines of regionalism or nonintervention, the latter prevail. These contradictions suggest that their views reflect not only their conception of the eternal verities of ethics but also their condition as relatively small, vulnerable states.

The different view of these matters taken by the Castro regime in Cuba may likewise be a function of the social ferment that produced the deviation and that is now at work in many other parts of Latin

[9] *Ibid.*, 21.

[10] Article 51 states: "Nothing in the present Charter shall impair the inherent right of individual or collective self-defense if an armed attack occurs against a Member of the United Nations, until the Security Council has taken the measures necessary to maintain international peace and security. Measures taken by Members in the exercise of this right of self-defense shall be immediately reported to the Security Council and shall not in any way affect the authority and responsibility of the Security Council under the present Charter to take at any time such action as it deems necessary in order to maintain or restore international peace and security."

America. On the other hand, Castro's deviation may prove to be a unique product of the particular circumstances of his struggle for power, and hence have no sequel in the rest of Latin America. It is too early to be sure about this, but it is already clear that Castro represents a radical break with traditional Latin-American ideas of ethics, justice, and law. He has, among other things, seceded from the Western Hemisphere. At the moment, he stands alone, but it is his declared purpose to take the rest of Latin America along with him and make it over in his own image. To the extent that he succeeds, the position of the United States in the United Nations will, of course, be undermined.

National Self-Determination

The Latin-American bloc has had less success in riding with the majority on questions of national self-determination than on any other type of question that has come before the United Nations. On this type the Latin-American majority has voted with the General Assembly majority 75 per cent of the time, as compared with 90 per cent or better on all other questions.[11] The Latin Americans have, however, had about as much success in this respect as the United States, and have frequently voted with it. A rare exception to the latter rule was the support given in 1952 by all but three Latin-American delegates to a resolution on self-government which the United States opposed on the ground that its terms were so sweeping as to include cases in which its application would be impractical or undesirable.[12]

Insofar as generalization about the complex problem of national self-determination is possible, the explanation of the Latin-American record on it falls into two parts.

First, while the position of most Latin Americans on the dominant issue of colonialism is somewhat left of center, it is as distinct from the position of other anti-colonialists as from that of the colonial group. Latin Americans have never gone down the line with the extreme anti-colonialists. On the contrary, because of their European ties they have often shown a good deal of sympathy with the colonial powers. Italy did so in the case of Libya, as did France in the case of Morocco and Tunisia.[13]

[11] Hovet, *Bloc Politics in the United Nations*, p. 68 and Chart 23.

[12] General Assembly Resolution 637A (VII) (December 16, 1952). The three Latin-American states that abstained were Ecuador, Nicaragua, and Paraguay.

Likewise, the Latin Americans took the middle ground in the angry debates of the early years over the Trusteeship territories. Though second to none in their insistence that progress be made toward independence for these territories, they generally advocated gradual progress and careful preparation of the territorial peoples for self-government, especially through education and training in public affairs. In a typical instance involving the latter, they joined with the United States in supporting a compromise between the extreme anti-colonialists, who wanted to prescribe indigenous participation in detail, and the administering authorities, who wanted no prescription at all. The compromise resolution affirmed the principle of participation and invited the administering authorities to implement it.[14]

The anti-colonialism of the Latin Americans is generally most intense as regards dependencies in the Western Hemisphere.[15] Yet even in such cases they moderate it when circumstances seem to justify their doing so. The leading case involved Puerto Rico. The question was whether to approve the action of the United States in ceasing to transmit information on that dependency to the United Nations, and approval by a vote of twenty-six to sixteen was made possible by fifteen Latin-American votes. The latter did not signify either a modification of the Latin Americans' basic views, as Houston asserts,[16] or subservience to the United States, as extreme anti-colonialists charged at the time. Rather, Latin-American approval was forthcoming because Puerto Rico had in fact just achieved virtually complete local autonomy as a commonwealth (*Estado Libre Asociado*) and because, under the leadership of a Puerto Rican widely respected in Latin America, Governor Luis Muñoz Marín, the Puerto Rican people had voted overwhelmingly in favor of their new status in a free election.

In the second place, the Latin-American bloc has often been weakened by internecine disagreements over questions of self-determination. In a heated dispute in 1950 over Morocco, for instance, only thirteen Latin Americans constituted the bloc majority, while three voted against, three abstained, and one was absent. There were similar divisions over

[13] Hovet, *Bloc Politics in the United Nations*, 198–209.

[14] *Ibid.*, 164–68.

[15] For a discussion of this subject, see Arthur P. Whitaker, "Anticolonialism in Latin America," in *Idea of Colonialism* (New York, 1958).

[16] Houston, *Latin America in the United Nations*, 88.

the criteria of self-government, the question whether these were to be determined by the United Nations or the administering members, and a proposal to establish a United Nations supervisory commission for South-West Africa.[17] As a result of these family disputes, the margin of the majority in the Latin-American group is often not large enough to give it much bargaining power as regards other groups.

Political Disputes, Situations, and Collective Security

The three types of questions that will be considered under this rubric are those relating to intervention, the respective jurisdictions of regional organizations and the United Nations, and the Cold War. When these have involved collective measures, the Latin-American majority has usually voted with the United States, and both have been exceptionally successful in riding with the majority in the General Assembly.[18]

Devotion to absolute nonintervention has, as noted, been almost an obsession with the Latin Americans. Since the founding of the United Nations they have wavered on this issue in only one case, that of Franco's Spain at the close of World War II, and they soon returned to their original stand. The story of their relaxation and recovery is worth recounting in some detail since it illustrates the way in which Latin-American positions in the United Nations change in response to alterations in the international climate and in their own domestic situations. Moreover, as Houston has said, the Spanish question was "one of the most dramatic to come before the United Nations" in its first decade, and no question was "closer to the hearts of the Latin Americans."[19] As related elsewhere:

> After Spain had been denied membership by the San Francisco conference, the Spanish question next came up in the meetings of the Security Council and General Assembly in 1946, in the form of proposals to take some kind of positive action against the Franco regime. The solid front of Latin America against Franco broke down over this issue. A majority of the Latin American governments again took the anti-Franco side. For many in Latin America, as elsewhere, it was still urgent to eradicate the

[17] *Ibid.*, 187–89, 199, 218.

[18] Hovet, *Bloc Politics in the United Nations*, 106–10. The respective percentages of voting with the Assembly majority have been: Latin Americans, 98.1; United States, 96.0.

[19] Houston, *Latin America in the United Nations*, 88.

last vestiges of Nazi-Fascism, of which Franco Spain, they believed, was one. Some of the Latin American spokesmen went so far as to reject the very principle of non-intervention. In a curious alignment within the Security Council, Mexico and France sided with Poland and the Soviet Union in favor of a Polish resolution branding the Franco regime a threat to international peace and security and calling for a complete severance of diplomatic relations with it. The resolution was defeated. The United States, though still definitely anti-Franco, threw its weight in the General Assembly to a Belgian compromise resolution that recommended the recall of chiefs of mission from Madrid, not a severance of diplomatic relations. Even this proved too strong for nearly one-half of the Latin American states: only eleven voted for it, while three abstained and six opposed it. The only votes cast against the resolution were the six from Latin America.

Chief among the opponents of the Belgian resolution was Argentina, which played a major part in splitting the Latin American group wide open on this issue. Juan Perón, who had just consolidated his position by a decisive victory in a free election and was at the height of his prestige in Latin America, had a fellow feeling for Franco. His own regime was tainted with Nazi-Fascism, and Argentine's own admission to the United Nations had been strongly opposed outside Latin America, where a family feeling worked in her favor. As for the principle of non-intervention, Argentina had long taken the lead in asserting it. This gave greater validity to Perón's insistence that the same principle be applied to Franco Spain.

All in all, Franco had no more valuable friend than Perón in the first few years after World War II. His support was the more valuable because in that stage of its career the Perón regime seemed to belong to the category of "popular liberation" movements which in Latin America have typically been antagonistic to the Franco regime.

When the Spanish question next gave rise to a major controversy in the General Assembly, the Latin American governments completed the shift they had begun in 1946. This time the question was whether to repeal both the recall-of-ambassadors resolution of 1946 and a companion measure that had excluded Spain from the specialized organizations such as UNESCO. When the proposal first came to a vote in 1949, it was supported by twelve of the Latin American states, but failed to obtain a two-thirds majority. In 1950, however, after the outbreak of the Korean War, it was adopted by the General Assembly, by thirty-eight to ten, with sixteen of the affirmative votes being cast by Latin American states; Guatemala, Mexico, and Uruguay cast negative votes, and Cuba abstained. Latin America thus contributed decisively to repealing the ban that it had taken the initiative in imposing only five years earlier.

The change of attitude was due, no doubt, to many factors, which varied from country to country. Basically, however, the Nazi-Fascist issue had inevitably lost its overriding urgency, and many Latin Americans were no longer willing to support measures against the Franco regime that undermined their own treasured principle of non-intervention. Likewise, the sharpening of the cold war had convinced many doubters that this was no time to weaken the West by continuing the controversial and obviously ineffectual ban on Franco Spain. Finally, soon after the war the political atmosphere in Latin America had changed, to Spain's advantage. Public interest had become absorbed in domestic problems, especially economic development, so that the Spanish question was pushed far into the background. And in several countries, notably, Venezuela, Colombia, and Peru, liberals had lost ground to conservatives, or to dictators, whose predilections were in favor of Franco.[20]

Finis was written to this story when Spain was admitted to the United Nations under the "package deal" of 1955. All the Latin Americans voted for her admission except Mexico, always the most strongly anti-Franco member of the group.

OAS and United Nations: Jurisdiction

The issue of regionalism in relation to the United Nations has been raised in two cases of deep concern to both Latin America and the United States—those of Guatemala in 1954 and Cuba in 1960–61. Both involved the threat of Communist penetration in the Western Hemisphere, and neither could have arisen in the form it took but for the fact that, by the so-called Caracas Resolution of February, 1954, the OAS had declared that the control of any American government by international Communism would constitute a threat to the security of the Hemisphere. This laid the groundwork for invoking the Rio Defense Treaty and thereby, in the minds of American regionalists, strengthened the case for giving the OAS prior jurisdiction over security questions as well as disputes in the Western Hemisphere.

The first test of the respective roles of the OAS and the United Nations was provided by the international crisis over the Communist-infected government of President Jacobo Arbenz in Guatemala in May and June, 1954.[21] The crisis did not come as a surprise to any informed

[20] Arthur P. Whitaker, *Spain and the Defense of the West: Ally and Liability* (New York, Harper, 1961), 345–47. Quoted by permission of the Council on Foreign Relations.

person. President Arbenz took office in 1951, and by 1953, Communist influence in his government was notorious. Early in that year neighboring Honduras and Nicaragua were already charging it with fomenting subversive activities among their people. In April, Guatemala countered with a complaint to the Secretary-General and Security Council of the United Nations that intervention was being plotted against it, but it did not request action by the Security Council and none was taken.

By the end of the year high officials of the United States government were publicly referring to Guatemala as a Communist "beachhead" in America. Then in February, 1954, the Inter-American Conference at Caracas adopted the anti-Communist resolution mentioned above. Guatemala was not named in it, but the reference was clear. That the Rio Treaty was in fact never invoked in this case has been explained by the difficulty of proving Communist control of Guatemala, but this difficulty proceeded in part from the Latin Americans' widespread skepticism about the charge, sympathy for the Arbenz regime, dislike of intervention under any guise, and suspicion regarding the role of the United Fruit Company. On the other hand, the attitude of the United States continued to harden against Arbenz as he proceeded to expropriate extensive holdings of that company in Guatemala despite protests from Washington.

The crisis entered its last phase in mid-May, 1954, with the arrival in Guatemala of a large shipment of arms from behind the Iron Curtain —that is, from Czechoslovakia, by way of the Polish port of Stettin. The United States countered by shipping arms by air to Honduras and Nicaragua, with which it had just completed bilateral military pacts. In the next few weeks Guatemalan exiles, led by Colonel Carlos Castillo Armas, completed their preparations in Honduras for a "liberating revolution" against the Arbenz regime, and on June 10 the attack was launched from Honduran soil.

Eight days later, on June 27, Arbenz' own army forced him to resign. In this short interval his tergiversations complicated the controversy

[21] This account of the Guatemala case is reprinted, with a few alterations, from my article, "The Organization of American States," in London Institute of World Affairs, *The Year Book of World Affairs, 1959* (London, Stevens, 1959), 128–32. For a much more detailed account, see Philip B. Taylor, Jr., "The Guatemalan Affair: A Critique of United States Foreign Policy," *American Political Science Review*, Vol. L, No. 3 (September, 1956), 787–806.

that promptly arose over the question of jurisdiction in the case as between the OAS and the United Nations. Another complication arose
from the failure of the OAS Council to act with due diligence from the
beginning of the crisis in mid-May. Instead, it dragged its feet for the
next month until Guatemala took its case to the United Nations on
June 19.

Arbenz' tergiversations began with this action. On June 19 he also
appealed to the OAS and was immediately given a hearing by the Inter-American Peace Committee, but the next day he withdrew his request pending the outcome of his appeal to the Security Council. The
latter discussed it in two heated sessions (June 20 and 25) in which
the Soviet Union championed United Nations interposition on behalf
of Guatemala. In the end the United States, represented by Ambassador
Henry Cabot Lodge, obtained a decision which in effect left the case
in the hands of the OAS for the time being. In bringing this about, the
United States was greatly aided by the votes of the two Latin-American
members of the Security Council at that time, Colombia and Brazil.

Balked in the Security Council, Arbenz reverted to the Inter-American Peace Committee, which quickly set out to begin its own on-the-spot
investigation; but before it could reach Guatemala, Arbenz had been
ousted by his own army and the inquiry was called off. Similarly, an
emergency meeting of American Foreign Ministers was tardily called
on June 26 (the day after the Security Council's second session on this
question) for the consideration of the threat of international Communism in Guatemala, but was canceled when the threat disappeared
along with Arbenz' regime.

Both Ambassador Henry Cabot Lodge and Secretary of State John
Foster Dulles attached portentous significance to the Guatemalan case
for the development of relations between regional or other collective
associations and the United Nations. During the debate in the Security
Council, Lodge described it as a test case of Articles 51 and 52 of the
United Nations Charter. Those articles, he said, had solved "the most
critical single issue" at the San Francisco Conference of 1945, and he
warned that if these articles did not now stand the test, "then the
United Nations will have destroyed itself in 1954 as it would have
been destroyed stillborn in 1945." At the end of the test, Secretary
Dulles expressed particular satisfaction with the way in which it had

clarified the respective roles of regional organizations and the United Nations.

One may, as many persons do, have serious reservations on the latter point. The Security Council's final action in the case, on June 25, was inconclusive on the question of jurisdiction, and honest disagreement is still possible on the basic and highly technical issue of whether the Guatemalan situation constituted a "dispute," in which case the OAS would have jurisdiction,[22] or whether it constituted an "aggression" or an "invasion," in which case the Security Council would have primary responsibility for dealing with it.[23] As for the OAS, its dilatory and ineffectual course in this affair did nothing to strengthen the case for regionalism and contrasted sharply with its effective handling of several threats to the peace in the Caribbean area in 1949 and 1950. In fact, the situation in Guatemala and the neighboring countries unfolded in the traditional Central-American way, almost as if neither the OAS nor the United Nations had even come into existence.

Nevertheless, the United States made good use of that situation in forwarding its policies, and it found the OAS a useful instrument for doing so, both in getting rid of the Arbenz regime and in excluding the United Nations Security Council from any participation in the affair. The fact that the Soviet Union is of course a member of the Security Council with veto power suggests that the OAS was perhaps most useful of all as a curb on Soviet troublemaking in the Western Hemisphere. By providing such a curb it fulfilled one of the purposes that had inspired the strengthening of regionalism at the San Francisco Conference in 1945.

The case of Cuba came before the Security Council in three different forms between July, 1960 and January, 1961. On all three occasions the two Latin-American members, Argentina and Ecuador, voted with the United States and the majority of the Council, as was to be expected. The two members which Latin America has always had on the Council, under the gentlemen's agreement of 1945 concerning distri-

[22] According to Article 52, paragraph 3, of the United Nations Charter, "The Security Council shall encourage the development of pacific settlement of local *disputes* through ... regional arrangements or by ... regional agencies." (Italics added.)

[23] Article 39 of the Charter declares that "The Security Council shall determine the existence of ... act of aggression."

bution of the elected seats, have almost invariably voted with the United States, for the questions that come before the Council are generally of the kind on which there is maximum agreement between the two; and they have also nearly always voted with the majority.

In the first of these three cases, raised by Cuba's charge of economic aggression against it by the United States, the Council on July 18, 1960, adjourned its consideration of the matter pending a report on it from the OAS. The vote was nine to none, with the Soviet Union and Poland abstaining. The Ecuadorean member backed up his vote with a defense of the United States and a warning against intervention in Latin America by "any power . . . especially if it is a distant power"— referring to Premier Krushchev's recent declaration that the Soviet Union would "protect" Cuba against the United States, "with rockets" if need be.

The second case, which occurred early the following September, involved a Soviet motion that the Council "approve" a decision made by the OAS on August 20 recommending to its members that they impose diplomatic and economic sanctions on the Dominican Republic, whose dictatorial government had been implicated in an attempt to assassinate President Rómulo Betancourt of Venezuela. Since the power to approve clearly implies the power to disapprove, the adoption of the Soviet motion would have subjected decisions of the OAS and all other regional bodies to review by the Council. The Soviet delegate cited in support of his motion Article 53 of the Charter, which stipulates that "no enforcement action shall be taken under regional arrangements or by regional action without the authorization of the Security Council." The retort to this was that Article 53 is applicable only to enforcement actions and that the measures agreed upon in the OAS resolution did not involve the use of armed forces, hence, enforcement action which needed authorization by the Council. Moreover, the measures in question were only *recommended* by the OAS to its members for individual national action and were limited to matters of commercial and diplomatic relations which each state has full power to determine for itself. In the face of strong opposition, the Soviet delegate desisted but reserved his government's right to raise the issue again. The upshot was the adoption of a motion, jointly sponsored by the United States, Argentina, and Ecuador, according to which the Council merely "took note of" the OAS action in question.

Finally, early in January, 1961, Cuba again appealed to the Council against the United States, this time on the ground that the United States was planning military aggression against it. The supporting evidence was so flimsy that the Council took no action at all. No demand for further inquiry was made by even the Soviet and Polish delegates, not to mention the Latin-American members.[24] The incident indicated that Cuba was deliberately widening the gap between itself and the West but had not yet had any apparent success in taking other Latin Americans along with it in its secession and could not count on the unconditional support of its new friends in the Communist bloc.

The situation changed radically when, on April 17, a force of Cuban refugees invaded the island. In the complaint brought before the First Committee of the General Assembly, Cuba charged United States complicity in the invasion which came from Florida and Guatemala and that the mercenary force was organized, financed, and armed by the United States government. The only effect which Cuba's complaint had was a seven-power resolution from the Latin-American bloc urging the members of the OAS to take "such peaceful action as is open to them to remove existing tensions." Mexico was the only Latin-American country which opposed the resolution when it was voted in the plenary session, whereas the Dominican Republic and Ecuador abstained.[25]

In dealing with the great crisis of October, 1962, over Soviet missiles and other weapons in Cuba, the United States resorted to both the OAS and the United Nations, but for very different purposes. From the OAS Council it sought and at once obtained sanction for the quarantine or blockade of Cuba announced in President Kennedy's public address of October 22 as a first means of bringing about the removal of the offensive weapons. Simultaneously, it called on the United Nations Security Council to provide United Nations supervision of the withdrawal; such move was made only after Premier Krushchev backed down and ordered the weapons withdrawn.

The reason for seeking sanction of the quarantine from the OAS rather than the United Nations is obvious; in the appropriate United

[24] For a summary of the Security Council deliberations on the Cuban complaint, see *United Nations Review* (February, 1961), 26–31.

[25] See General Assembly Resolution 1616 (XV) (April 20, 1961), adopted by fifty-nine votes to thirteen, with twenty-four abstentions.

Nations body, the Security Council, it would certainly have been blocked by a Soviet veto. In the OAS Council, on the other hand, approval was obtained on the main and immediate issue by a unanimous vote (twenty to none), though on the question of authorizing further action there were three abstentions (Mexico, Brazil, and Bolivia). The legality of this essay in enforcement action by a regional organization was not clear; it was based on Articles 6 and 8 of the Rio Defense Treaty, but critics claimed that it did not accord with Articles 51 and 53 of the United Nations Charter. But whatever one may think about its legality, there can be no question that, politically and psychologically, this impressive show of Latin-American support was an important asset to the United States; and it is equally clear that only the existence of the OAS made it possible to obtain this demonstration.

Cold War Issues

This brings us to the third type of question to be considered here—the role of Latin America in the Cold War. As noted above, this is the question on which there has been maximum agreement between Latin America and the United States in the United Nations. This was particularly true during the first decade of the organization's life. Writing of that period, Houston concluded that in this type of issue "the United States for the most part has had no greater asset than the normally faithful support of the great majority of these [Latin-American] states."[26]

This conclusion is valid for the period in question, provided it is applied only to Cold War support in the narrowest sense, for no such support was forthcoming when the Cold War threatened to warm up for Latin America through its involvement in an armed conflict, whether a limited war or a more general one. The most striking illustration of this point is provided by the first stage of the Korean War. On June 27, 1950, the votes of the two Latin-American members of the Security Council made possible the passage of the resolution calling on the United Nations member states to aid the victim of aggression, South Korea, with armed force. On the following day all the Latin Americans joined in an endorsement of the call by the OAS. Yet no Latin-American state except Colombia responded to the call.

This is quite understandable, for the Latin Americans are not geared for war. Although they devote a large part of their budgets to their

[26] Houston, *Latin America in the United Nations*, 290.

armed forces, these are little if anything more than national police forces for home use. But there is more to it than that. Realizing that their voices would have no weight in the decision between peace and war, and convinced that a general war would be ruinous to them, they have thrown what weight they carry on the side of peace; and in the first decade of the United Nations history they believed that, on balance, the threat of war came mainly from the Soviet Union and that their best hope of preserving peace lay in co-operation with the United States for peaceful purposes. Moreover, this attitude is one that has been ingrained in them by their long experience with the United States in the OAS and its predecessor, the Inter-American System. To them, that has always been, and still is, an agency for international co-operation for peaceful purposes.

That spirit was carried over by the Latin Americans into the United Nations and characterized the attitude of many of them on most East-West issues, beginning with the case of Greece in December, 1946. When the United States denounced the incursion of guerrillas into Greece from neighboring Communist countries and urged that a commission be sent to Greece to restore "normal conditions along the frontiers," the Brazilian delegate supported it but the Colombian delegate opposed it as a punitive measure and called instead for a conciliation commission, to meet in a neutral city, such as Geneva. During the Berlin Blockade of 1948–49 both Latin-American Security Council delegates—this time a Colombian and an Argentine—made tolerance, comprehension, and compromise their unvarying theme. Simultaneously, in the Assembly the Mexican Peace Appeal won enthusiastic plaudits from the Latin-American group, whose members testified to "the yearning of the Latin American peoples for harmony and understanding" and cited America's achievement of peace by "conciliation and peaceful adjustment."[27]

Against this background there is a distinct element of novelty in the Latin-American group's strong and massive support of collective resistance to aggression in Korea, even though the support they gave was moral rather than material. They extended it from debates in the Assembly to the "Uniting for Peace Resolution" on the functions of the Assembly. Their support of the West remained firm through the middle phase of the Korean War. In the concluding phase it became hesitant

[27] *Ibid.*, 117.

and the pre-1950 pattern asserted itself again. The reasons are not entirely clear, but probably two of the most important were disillusionment over the stalemate in Korea and the encouragement that Stalin's death gave to the resumption of Latin America's role as peacemaker.

Subsequent events have strengthened this attitude. Recently there have been signs of disaffection toward the West in general and the United States in particular. The defection of Castro's Cuba to the Communist bloc is only one example, admittedly extreme. In the autumn of 1959 several Latin-American governments voted for the Communist-bloc candidate for the Security Council. Again, late in 1960 several of them voted with the Communist and Afro-Asian groups in favor of a resolution calling for a plebiscite in Algeria under United Nations auspices. On both occasions they were on the opposite side of the fence from the United States. The explanation seems to lie in the spread not so much of pro-Communism as of neutralism. The trend toward neutralism is strong even in Brazil, which has hitherto been one of the United States most constant and helpful friends, in the United Nations as well as in the OAS.

Arms Control and Regulation

The story of Latin America's role in the control and regulation of arms is soon told. The role of Latin America has been productive, but it has been so simple and constant that it can be summed up in a few lines: The Latin Americans have shown a high degree of solidarity on this question; they have always sided with the Free World on basic issues, but have put pressure on both sides to get together on a system of arms reduction and control; and they have made a considerable contribution by their insistence on the Great Powers' responsibility in this matter, on their obligation to reach an agreement on it, and on the proposition that "the privilege of disagreement [is] the privilege of suicide."[28]

The solidarity of the Latin-American states on this question has been due mainly to the fact that all of them are relatively weak and vulnerable and traditionally devoted to the peaceful settlement of disputes. That they supported the Western Great Powers group on this issue was to be expected since, as noted, they have usually voted with it on Cold War issues.

[28] *Ibid.*, 140–41.

The present tendency toward a weakening of the Latin Americans' general support has not yet affected their stand on the arms question. The development of hydrogen bombs, missiles, and a "balance of terror" has, however, led to fresh insistence by them on the urgent need for Great Powers agreement on a system of arms control.[29] Besides this, there has also been one new development in the Latin-American attitude on this subject in the past few years: in view of the lack of progress toward a general system of arms control, the Latin Americans have given increasing attention to the possibility of setting up a regional control system under OAS auspices. Costa Rica and Chile have produced some particularly interesting proposals for this purpose, but these lie outside the scope of the present chapter.

Economic and Social Questions

Latin America is an outstanding example of two of the most discussed world phenomena of the present era: the revolution of rising expectations (Castro's Cuba is only the most extreme example of an almost universal Latin-American ferment), and the population explosion.

In addition, Latin America as a whole is economically underdeveloped. It has several industrialized communities of large size, but the largest of these are relatively small islands in a sea of underdevelopment. Taking sea and island together, experts give the economies of five countries (Argentina, Chile, Cuba, Uruguay, and Venezuela) an "intermediate" rating. The remaining fifteen countries are underdeveloped, and among these are the two largest: Brazil, whose nearly seventy million inhabitants constitute one-third of the total population of Latin America, and Mexico, with a population of about thirty-five million persons. Finally, in their efforts to overcome these formidable obstacles to the realization of their aspiration to economic progress and a higher standard of living, the Latin Americans are prone to rely on government action rather than private enterprise.

As a result of this combination of circumstances, when economic and social questions arise in the United Nations, the Latin-American ma-

[29] As a result, the Latin Americans are becoming more active through participation as neutral states in disarmament talks being held at Geneva since March, 1962. The two countries so classified in a United Nations resolution convoking the Geneva Conference are Mexico and Brazil.

jority tends to side with the underdeveloped nations of Asia and Africa and is frequently at odds with the United States. The clashes between the two would have been even more frequent and severe but for the fact that the United Nations jurisdiction in such matters is so limited that most of the important issues are fought out in other areas—sometimes in the OAS, but more frequently through bilateral channels.

Nevertheless, the United Nations has been the scene of some important developments of this kind. Three of these will be noted briefly below, and a fourth will be discussed at greater length. They all relate directly to economic rather than social questions, but they also have important social implications. They point to the conclusion that, at least in the short run, the United Nations has been more useful to Latin America than to the United States in the economic field, but that, in the fourth and last case, the United States, too, stands to gain in the long run.

The first case involved a Latin-American effort to bring about the establishment of an international development fund under United Nations auspices. This was opposed by the United States, which argued that the need could be better met by private capital and existing lending institutions. Beginning in 1949, the debate on this subject continued sporadically for several years, and was often bitter. On a typical vote, in 1951, fourteen Latin-American countries voted against the United States and only one (Brazil) with it; the others abstained or were absent.[30]

In the second case, the Latin-American majority joined with other underdeveloped countries in the passage of a resolution affirming the right to nationalize natural resources. The United States, which opposed the resolution, offered an amendment that would have subordinated the right of nationalization to the rules of international law and the provisions of international agreements. None of the Latin Americans supported this United States amendment; eleven voted against it, four abstained, and the rest were absent.[31]

The third issue, which arose at the first meeting of the Economic and Social Council in 1946, related to the international commodity trade. The United States proposed an international conference for the lowering of trade barriers. Latin-American opposition was instantaneous and almost universal. It was based on the belief that the result would be

[30] Houston, *Latin America in the United Nations*, 240.   [31] *Ibid.*, 242–43.

to place the economically weak at the mercy of the strong and would, among other things, cripple or destroy infant industries. Such a conference was held at Havana in 1948, but the Latin Americans and other underdeveloped countries pierced the agreement adopted there with so many loopholes that the United States refused to ratify it. This was a victory for infant industry in Latin America, but it left unsolved the more important problem of stabilizing the prices of Latin-American agricultural and mineral products in the international market. The United States limited help in solving this extremely difficult problem has been channeled mainly through the OAS, and the problem remains still largely unsolved.

The fourth case, that of the Economic Commission for Latin America (ECLA), represents the Latin Americans' most successful use of the United Nations to free itself from the tutelage of the United States in regard to economic policy. When the Economic and Social Council established this commission in 1948, it had already created similar regional bodies for other areas, but in this case duplication would be involved because there was already in existence an Inter-American Economic and Social Council established in 1945 at Chapultepec. But the latter had its seat in Washington; the Latin Americans knew that it would be dominated by the United States; and they argued forcefully their need for a special United Nations body to consider the problems of their area in a world setting. They had their way, and the commission was set up, with headquarters at Santiago, Chile, five thousand air miles from Washington.

For some time after ECLA was first proposed in 1947 the United States objected to the duplication involved. For an even longer period after the new agency went to work, Washington was disturbed by the support which the Commission, under the leadership of the talented Argentine economist Raúl Prebisch, gave to unwelcome economic-political doctrines, such as the thesis that advanced nations are obligated to give extensive aid to underdeveloped nations, and to aid them through government loans and grants rather than private investment. Recently, however, both objections seem to have been met, at least in large part, by the adoption of co-operative arrangements at the staff level between ECLA and its OAS counterpart, and by policy concessions on both sides; indeed, ECLA leaders seem to regard the Alliance for Progress as their brain child.

The United States kept its own economic policies intact until 1958, when the mounting tide of anti-Americanism south of the border provided the most cogent argument in favor of a change. In 1959 the United States yielded one major point by joining the Latin Americans in the creation of the Inter-American Development Bank. The next year it made another concession by giving its blessing to a Latin-American Free Trade Association set up by a treaty adopted at Montevideo in February, 1960. More recently, the Alliance for Progress was ushered in as a co-operative venture for the development of the Latin-American countries on a broad front. Adopted at the Punta del Este Conference of Finance Ministers of the Hemisphere in August, 1961, the significance of the Alliance for Progress lies in the fact that it is a recognition on the part of the United States that the rising aspirations of the Latin-American peoples for a better life can only be brought about by a change in the economic and social structures of these countries. These policy changes were in effect concessions to Latin-American views most effectively presented through ECLA, and both promise to contribute to much-needed improvement in the United States relations with Latin America. In this sense the United States has ultimately gained by the use that Latin America has made of the United Nations to voice its discontent with its northern neighbor.

Conclusions

Because of their numbers and solidarity, the Latin Americans play an important role in the United Nations, and their role is particularly important to the United States because of its special relationship with them. Although the Latin Americans' relative numerical strength has been cut in half since 1945 by the admission of new members, their importance to the United States has increased rather than diminished, for the character of most of the newer members is such that the United States has had growing need of Latin-American support in order to maintain the majority position which it has held most of the time since 1945.

The solidarity of the Latin Americans normally stops short of unanimity. While theirs is one of the best organized blocs in the United Nations, group decisions are not binding and in the majority of cases one or more members of the bloc part company with the rest; occasionally the group has split wide open on important questions. Nevertheless, two-thirds or more of the Latin Americans vote together on most issues, and in the late 1950's their solidarity showed a slight but perceptible increase, probably as an offset to their declining relative strength.

Yet simultaneously signs of serious dissidence on Cold War issues began to appear for the first time. The culmination came in 1960 with the defection of Castro's Cuba to the Communist bloc. So far, there has been no indication that any other Latin-American government is likely to follow Castro's course. Yet several of them long opposed taking any action against him. Serious dissension over this issue developed at the Punta del Este Foreign Ministers' Conference of the Organization of American States, convened at the initiative of Colombia between January 22 and 31, 1962. There was unanimous support for some of the nine resolutions adopted at the conference such as the first resolution, which merely expressed a general concern of all the American states except Cuba about the dangers to the unity and democratic institutions of the Hemisphere arising from Communist efforts to establish totalitarian dictatorships at the service of extra-continental powers. But when it came to specifically condemning Cuba for having "identified itself with the principles of Marxist-Leninist ideology" and therefore to excluding the Castro regime from participation in the Inter-American system, the votes were divided. This resolution was adopted by a vote just reaching a two-thirds majority, with Argentina, Brazil, Mexico, Chile, Ecuador, and Bolivia abstaining.[32] Their abstentions were explained mainly on legalistic grounds, such as the Inter-American rule of nonintervention, but they also reflected some sympathy for the Cuban regime in the belief that it had successfully instituted internal reforms. Not until it was revealed in October, 1962, that Cuba had become a launching pad for Soviet missiles under Soviet control did the abstainers come around to supporting effective action.

The high degree of solidarity hitherto maintained by the Latin Americans, in the United Nations as in the OAS, has been due mainly to the fact that they are tied together by many common ideas, interests, problems, and aspirations. The nature of these has in turn largely determined their role with regard to the United States in the United Nations. Whether they have supported or opposed the United States

[32] See the *U.S. Dept. of State Bulletin*, Vol. XLVI, No. 1182 (February 19, 1962), 278–82, for the full text of the resolutions passed at the Punta del Este Conference.

has depended mainly on the type of issue in question. Until quite recently they have almost always given it strong support on Cold War issues, but have frequently opposed it in the economic field.

On these and all other questions the special relationship that has long existed between the United States and the Latin Americans, and which is now represented by the OAS, has on balance been an important asset to the United States in United Nations affairs. While there is no OAS bloc in the United Nations, the Western Hemisphere idea underlying this special relationship has constantly tended to strengthen the Latin Americans' support of the United States when they agree with it and to mitigate their opposition to it when they disagree. Moreover, the existence of the OAS has made it possible for the United States to achieve through that regional body international objectives that would have been unrealizable in the United Nations. The chief instances are the Caracas Resolution of 1954 providing for the use of enforcement measures to prevent Communist domination of any American government, and the quarantine of Cuba in October, 1962. It would obviously have been quite impossible to obtain such measures through the United Nations.

There have already been some changes in the respective roles of the United States and Latin America in United Nations affairs, and more may be on the way. It is no longer true that, as Houston wrote, the Latin Americans tend to "lay a degree of stress on the primacy of regional arrangements probably unacceptable to the United States."[33] At least in Western Hemisphere questions, no Latin American could lay stronger stress on the primacy of regional arrangements than the United States has done, from the Guatemala crisis of 1954 to the 1962 crisis over Cuba. Again, signs have recently appeared of a weakening of Latin-American co-operation with the United States on Cold War issues, whereas in the economic field a contrary trend toward better understanding has been encouraged by the concessions which Washington has recently made to the Latin Americans on important questions of economic policy. Closer co-operation will probably result on both types of issues, and on all other issues arising in the United Nations, if the Alliance for Progress achieves its objectives. For the attitude of the Latin Americans toward the United States in the United Nations de-

[33] Houston, *Latin America in the United Nations*, 292.

pends largely upon the state of their relations with each other, both bilaterally and in the OAS.

This brief sketch of the Latin Americans' role in the United Nations must not conclude without a reminder of the great diversity of the Latin-American countries and a caveat regarding the urgent need for further study of their role in international affairs. Almost all of them have for some time past been undergoing profound domestic changes that powerfully affect their behavior in the United Nations, as in the whole realm of their international relations. These basic but little-known transformations, added to the frequent changes of political regime for which Latin America has long been noted, make it dangerous to generalize about the roles of individual countries on the basis of their voting records in the United Nations.

The danger of such generalizations is illustrated by the statement of one commenator that, of all the Latin-American nations, Mexico, Guatemala, Argentina, Bolivia, and Costa Rica are, "on an over-all basis," the most likely to deviate from the group majority, particularly when that majority is supporting the United States and the Western powers.[34] This may be true of Mexico, but not of the rest. It was true, for example, of Guatemala only under the Communist-infected Arbenz regime and its immediate predecessor, and of Argentina only part of the time under the originally pro-Axis Perón regime (ousted in 1955). Subsequently, under regimes of a different kind, both Guatemala and Argentina have generally voted with the Latin-American majority and have been in the forefront in co-operating with the United States and the Western powers. In the shifting sands of Latin America a more instructive form of voting analysis would be one based not on countries but on types of regime.

In any case, we must know what lies behind voting records before we can understand what they mean. Closer study might, for example, show that some of the governments that have consistent voting records are—as in the case of Mexico—authentic spokesmen for their people, while others are highly responsive to Washington or some other outside influence, so that their voting records represent Latin-American attitudes in only a restricted sense, and so are of little value for either diagnosis or prognosis.

[34] Hovet, *Bloc Politics in the United Nations*, 69.

We need to examine more closely not only the individual nations but also the international groupings and rivalries within the Latin-American group. However small the scale may seem from the point of view of a world power, Latin America has its own internecine power politics; as Clarence Haring pointed out long ago, the larger and better developed countries of the area take a typical great-power attitude toward their weaker neighbors; and such rivalries and attitudes are not infrequently projected over the world scene.

Only when problems of this kind have been studied much more thoroughly shall we be able to arrive at a clear understanding of the Latin Americans' role in the United Nations and their attitude in it toward the United States.[35]

[35] Four books published since this chapter was written throw further light on some of the topics discussed in it: Adolph A. Berle, Jr., *Latin America: Diplomacy and Reality* (New York, Harper & Row, for the Council on Foreign Relations, 1962); John C. Dreier, *The Organization of American States* (New York, Harper & Row, for the Council on Foreign Relations, 1962); John C. Dreier, ed., *The Alliance for Progress* (Baltimore, Johns Hopkins Press, 1962); and J. Lloyd Mecham, *The United States and Inter-American Security, 1889–1960* (Austin, University of Texas Press, 1961).

CHAPTER VIII

Western Europe and the United Nations

BY FRANZ B. GROSS

THE POSITION OF THE EUROPEAN STATES in the United Nations is disquieting to them. Although they are the precursors of international organization, as the membership of non-European nations in the United Nations increases, the Europeans constitute a minority which exercises decreasing influence in that body. Two important European states, Germany and Switzerland, are not United Nations members; consequently of the 113 United Nations votes, Europe commands only 26, or less than 23 per cent of the total, and of these, 9 are Communist-controlled states and the tenth is Yugoslavia.

In many respects the United Nations has become the major platform of the new and developing nations. There is danger that the past experiences of the emerging nations with Europeans may prejudice their attitudes toward all issues brought before the United Nations and that latent resentment and hostility will motivate their activities in the world organization.

Essentially, the Concert of Europe, the League of Nations, and the United Nations were products of European wars. It was the great devastation, particularly in Europe, after two world wars which gave impetus to the determination to organize a new system which would safeguard world peace. The League experiment and the United Nations system were designed on the principle that peace among European powers would constitute the basis for world peace and security.

European nations had two basic motives in fostering international organization. Primarily they believed that anarchy among nations could be avoided only by a resort to co-operation in a type of international organization. Secondly, they felt that their national interest and security were best safeguarded by a universal institution such as the League of

Nations or the United Nations capable of acting in case of aggression. These ideas remain but are less convincing.

The United Nations was founded during a period of relative European weakness. This has constantly rankled their pride. On occasion, the United Nations has taken actions which have gone against the vital interests of the European powers. At times solutions were pushed through the United Nations which were unfavorable to the Europeans. These problems might have been solved without United Nations involvement along lines more propitious to Europe.

While they maintain a basic attachment to international organization, European governments suffer a growing sense of disillusionment with the United Nations as the evidence indicates that their particular interests are not sufficiently taken into account in United Nations decisions or resolutions.

Due to the self-imposed absence of the United States, Great Britain and France assumed leadership of the League of Nations. Despite its inability to prevent war, the League paved the way toward a common approach to world peace through collective security. Because of their hegemony in the League, a certain nostalgic pride persists among the Europeans. The United Nations is consequently evaluated in terms of their past participation in the League.

Furthermore, the United Nations has fostered the creation of new states. The western European considers the United Nations to have been a major contributing factor in the rapid dissolution of European power in Asia and Africa. Not only has western Europe been deprived of its power and prestige by the loss of influence and connections overseas, but within the United Nations, it has also lost the influence it once wielded in the League. Such conditions constitute the major causes of western European cynicism toward the United Nations. These apprehensions have multiplied with the Soviet domination of eastern Europe and the emergence of the new nations of Asia and Africa.

Any study of western European attitudes toward the United Nations must be placed within the context of the disillusionments and frustrations of the last fifteen years. The dilemma posed by the advocacy of co-operative federal direction of international order on the one hand, and the protection of sovereign interests on the other, has yet to be resolved in the minds of most European statesmen.

Western Europe and the United Nations

Western European Membership
and Groupings in the United Nations

For the sake of clarity it is useful to define the terms "Europe" and "western Europe" as they are employed in this chapter. Geographically, "Europe" is the western land mass of the Eurasian continent stretching from the Mediterranean and the Atlantic coast lines to the Ural Mountains. Politically, Europe may then be divided into two regions—western Europe and eastern Europe. Western Europe is defined as the non-Communist region of Continental Europe and is almost identical with the European membership of the North Atlantic Treaty Organization. The latter includes the bulk of Benelux, western Europe, and Scandinavian caucusing groups.[1] On the other hand, eastern Europe consists of the Iron Curtain countries which have lost practically all their political independence to the Soviet Union.[2] However, Yugoslavia and, lately, Albania, have developed a special position within the eastern European group.

The European countries which constitute western Europe have not organized themselves formally as a bloc in the United Nations, nor do they caucus regularly to formulate strategy and policies. There is little or no consciously contrived unity among them. The identity of the group is derived from the fact that it "has succeeded in uniting other groups in the Assembly against its position without developing sufficient real internal identity to offset any united opposition."[3] But, as pointed out above, there are three western European caucusing groups who do meet quite regularly to formulate common policies within the United Nations. Moreover, most of the western European countries are bound together in groupings such as NATO and the Council of Europe. Consequently, on a wide variety of issues their co-operation in the United Nations is the product of high- and intermediate-level consultations outside the framework of the United Nations, especially upon matters which provide a common basis for *ad hoc* alliances.

[1] Hovet, *Bloc Politics in the United Nations*, 99.

[2] For our purposes, Albania would, for the sake of convenience, be grouped among the Iron Curtain countries. Yugoslavia nearly always has taken an identical position to that of the Soviet Union. It is not considered part of the bloc since it has kept in close political touch with NATO, OEC, and the Balkan Alliance.

[3] Hovet, *Bloc Politics in the United Nations*, 99.

The oldest caucusing group, the Scandinavian, evolved during the League of Nations era. The group consists of Denmark, Iceland, Norway, and Sweden. They meet regularly during the Assembly sessions to discuss procedural and substantive questions and to formulate a common strategy and policy on almost all questions which come before the Assembly. Finland is not formally a member of the Scandinavian caucusing group. Despite pressure from the Soviet Union, however, it joined the Nordic Council in October, 1956. Thus, it has "a window" toward Western Europe through formal and informal consultations with the other Scandinavian countries. Scandinavian co-operation is primarily based upon geographical proximity, cultural bonds, similar political institutions, language, and strategic interests. When members of the Scandinavian group do not concur on an issue they tend to abstain from voting rather than express opposition to each other.[4]

The Benelux caucusing group was organized at the close of World War II. It consists of Belgium, Luxembourg and the Netherlands. On many occasions the collective view has been presented to the General Assembly by a single representative of the group. Since 1956 the Benelux group has functioned within a slightly larger caucus of west European nations which includes France and Italy.[5] The co-operative efforts of this larger group reflect their common historical development, similar political organizations, and regional organizational ties such as the ECSC, the EURATOM, and the EEC.[6]

Apart from the three caucusing groups in which western European countries participate, there are certain intra-continental regional groupings in which some European countries caucus with non-European states. The United Kingdom's senior membership in the British Commonwealth and France's relationship with the French Community of new African states are examples of such regional groupings. Similarly, the United Kingdom and the United States maintain close contacts in all matters of mutual interest, including those which come before the United Nations. Turkey, although considered a European country, is also a member of the Afro-Asian caucusing group.

Finally, certain west European countries do not formally belong to any caucusing group in the United Nations. These are countries such as Portugal, Spain, neutral Austria, and Ireland. All are countries which, for varying reasons, are more or less isolated.

[4] *Ibid.*, 73–76.   [5] *Ibid.*, 76–78.   [6] *Ibid.*, 91–93.

Responses to the United Nations organization have been varied, ranging all the way from blanket approval to open hostility. European attitudes toward the United Nations have been colored by their reduction to the role of secondary powers, as European statesmen still feel that they merit an important place in the councils of the world. Their forced adjustment to the decline in European power during the 1950's has had its unfortunate consequences; in particular, they lost confidence in the efficacy of international organization.

The general orientation of European thinking in regard to the United Nations was perhaps best illustrated by a French diplomat in 1948:

> For a European the United Nations is principally considered in relation to the idea of security, which constitutes his primary concern. . . . The European believes that a large part of the activities of the United Nations must be concerned with European problems not only in the interest of Europe, but in the interest of world peace.[7]

In 1963, General Lauris Norstad, speaking before the Atlantic Council, outlined the new European position:

> For more than a decade after the war, the weakness of Europe was a major factor influencing the policy of our country. In the decade ahead, the strength of Europe will play a major role in shaping our plans, our programs, and our objectives as a nation. We are no longer dealing with war-shattered peoples. We are dealing with countries which on the basis of their improved staus, their achievements in recent years, will demand increasing recognition as true partners.[8]

General Norstad, as former NATO commander, stressed Europe's demand for full partnership in NATO. There is, however, little doubt that Europe will make similar demands for full restoration of status in the United Nations.

In addition to concern over their relative power position and security, three more factors appear to influence the thinking of European statesmen and public alike. They are: 1) that the United Nations is essentially an American contrivance and Europe had little to do with the founding of that organization; 2) that Europe was poorly and inap-

[7] Jacques Fouques-Dupare, "A European Point of View on the U.N.," *International Conciliation*, No. 443 (September, 1948), 453–54.

[8] Address delivered at Atlantic Council dinner, Washington, D.C., January 14, 1963.

propriately represented at the time the United Nations was established
—of the fifteen European states which took part in the deliberations
at San Francisco, three were under pressure from the Soviet Union,
three others actually composed part of the Soviet Union, and seven
more were represented by governments in exile; 3) that the Charter
was essentially a document of American conception, modified to accommodate Soviet but not European demands.[9]

Europeans now feel that too many concessions were made involving
the political sovereignty of medium and small powers without com-
pensatory guarantees of security. There lingers a general consensus
among Europeans that the Covenant of the defunct League of Nations
was a superior document since it was built upon the idea of equality
of sovereign states, big or small, and on a fundamental belief in the
readiness of nation-states to shoulder responsibility. There was no provision for a decision-making body with coercive powers such as the Security Council. This attitude becomes significant in view of the reduced
status of European nations, other than Great Britain and France, to
that of small powers. The two giants, the United States and the Soviet
Union, form the nucleus of opposite ideological positions, and the smaller nations in Europe or outside have generally had to align themselves
behind one or the other. Thus the leadership of Great Britain and
France has been less than conspicuous.

The Division of Europe and the United Nations

One of the first concerns of the newly founded United Nations was
to assist in the rehabilitation of Europe. It was agreed among the Allied
Powers that the United Nations would not be involved with the responsibility for negotiating and concluding peace settlements with Germany, Japan, Italy, and the former German-occupied states. The United
Nations was designed to concentrate on the creation of a system for
the maintenance of international peace and security. The peace treaties
were thus to be kept apart from proceedings at the United Nations.
President Roosevelt desired to avoid any association of the Charter with

[9] The fifteen European states invited to the San Francisco Conference were Belgium,
Byelorussian Soviet Socialist Republic, Czechoslovakia, Denmark, France, Greece,
Luxembourg, Netherlands, Norway, Poland, the Soviet Union, Turkey, Ukrainian
Soviet Socialist Republic, the United Kingdom, and Yugoslavia. Poland, however, sent
no delegation.

the peace treaties, as had been the case with the League of Nations Covenant and the peace settlements of Versailles.

It was assumed that agreement on the peace treaties would constitute the first step toward continued postwar Great Power co-operation. At the conclusion of the peace settlements, postwar security measures were to have been planned according to Chapter VII of the Charter. Military arrangements were to follow which would co-ordinate the activities of troops earmarked for the purpose of maintaining security in case of any breach of the peace. However, it was over the question of the peace settlements that the first signs of the protracted conflict became visible.

At Yalta and at Potsdam the Soviet Union had agreed to free elections and the establishment of democratic regimes in eastern Europe. Democratic Czechoslovakia was therefore invited to be a founder-member of the United Nations. Poland was unable to take part in the San Francisco deliberations since the composition of its new government was announced too late. As events transpired, Poland was nevertheless admitted as an original member. However, Poland subsequently failed to establish a regime independent of the Soviet Union.

The Soviet Union had thus already achieved two advantages. Through the admission of Byelorussia and the Ukraine it was assured of three votes, and Communist control of Poland was never challenged by the United Nations even though no free and secret elections had been held.

In 1948 a *coup d'état* in Czechoslovakia resulted in a Communist take-over. The Czechoslovak delegate to the United Nations, opposed to the new government, protested and vainly attempted to present his case before the Security Council. He went unheeded, however, and the international community accepted Czechoslovakia's new regime under Communist control. Similar Communist take-overs were precipitated in Bulgaria, Romania, and Hungary, despite the fact that human rights were guaranteed in these defeated countries by the peace treaties.

Europe was subsequently divided into a Soviet-dominated eastern bloc and a group of western independent states which were both militarily and economically weak. This cleavage in Europe had considerable influence on the future development of the United Nations.

Thereafter, in a European bloc consisting of fifteen votes, Europe was divided six to nine. Western Europe could contribute a balance of only three votes to any issue where the voting split along East-West lines. It is no wonder that Europe's influence in the United Nations General Assembly was insignificant when compared to its world position.

A number of proposals have been presented to the United Nations which would bolster European influence by restoring some degree of independence to Communist-dominated European states. These efforts have proved all but futile. Only in the case of Austria were the Soviets induced to withdraw the Red Army, but this was accomplished outside of the United Nations.[10]

[In 1950 a last attempt to enforce human rights in Bulgaria, Hungary, and Romania according to the treaty obligations, and under the United Nations Charter, failed when the ruling of the International Court of Justice held that the Secretary-General could not appoint a member to an investigating commission before the two parties to the "dispute" nominated their respective representatives.[11] The west European delegates to the General Assembly were extremely frustrated over this failure of the United Nations even to investigate the alleged violations of human rights by the Communist regimes in Bulgaria, Hungary, and Romania.

During the period 1946–49, when the Communists were consolidating their position in eastern Europe, the United States government took military and economic initiatives in western Europe and thereby helped to create an effective deterrent against Communist subversive efforts in Greece and Turkey. The first move came on March 12, 1947, when President Truman proclaimed the Truman Doctrine in which he told the United States Congress that "it must be the foreign policy of the United States to support free peoples who are resisting attempted subjugation by armed minorities or by outside pressures."[12] This doctrine launched United States maneuvers to bring the civil war in Greece to a halt. This object was eventually accomplished with United Nations assistance.

The second decisive step was the promotion of the United States plan for a North Atlantic Treaty Organization. In 1949 it became obvi-

[10] An Austrian State Treaty restoring Austria's independence was signed in Vienna on May 15, 1955, by the Allied Powers—France, the United Kingdom, the United States, and the Soviet Union and Austria.

[11] For the conflicting views on the advisory opinions of the World Court, see *United Nations Bulletin*, Vol. IX, No. 9 (November 1, 1950), 479–82.

[12] *New York Times* (March 13, 1947).

ous that the Soviet bloc posed a distinctive threat to the security of western Europe and that European efforts to meet the Soviet threat were inadequate. The formation of NATO constituted a clear recognition by the western nations that the collective-security system envisaged under the Charter was stillborn. The concept of an international peace force which would guarantee the political integrity and territorial independence of all nations failed to materialize in practice. The Soviet Union repeatedly refused to accept and support any arrangement concerning "the number of types of forces, their degree of readiness and general location," which came under the jurisdiction of the United Nations Military Staff Committee. Thus, the failure of the United Nations to implement the Charter triggered the formation of NATO, which has become the main bulwark for the defense of western Europe. Its effectiveness is largely dependent upon American military power, and its organization serves to unite European power outside the framework of the United Nations.

On May 14, 1955, the east European countries, supposedly motivated by similar security considerations, formed a separate military arrangement—the Warsaw Pact. The cleavage of Europe was thus intensified. East-West tensions were not confined to Europe, but due to Soviet efforts, tensions flared in the United Nations, especially over the question of the future of Berlin.

The precarious balance of terror achieved by the two protagonists has resulted in a deadlock and a shift in Communist strategy from the Berlin question to the Middle East and the subject of colonialism. Since 1950 the United Nations has paid a great deal of attention to the problems of the non-self-governing territories and to European decolonization in Asia and Africa.

The United Nations Role in
the Termination of Colonies

Even before World War II, European statesmen clearly perceived that the colonial era was coming to an end. With the outbreak of the war, however, nationalist movements in the colonies gained unexpected momentum. The European colonial administrators obligingly pledged that self-government would be granted once the war was concluded. The European colonial powers, with the exception of Portugal, were all willing to liquidate their special position in the colonies, but differed with national leaders over the timing and methods to be used during the transition from colony to independent nation. This is well illustrated by the general support given to Chapter XI in the Charter relating to non-self-governing territories.

The movement toward self-determination for the colonies gained its initial impetus from Wilson's famous Fourteen Points and the subsequent establishment of the League's mandate system. Under Article 22, paragraph 1, of the Covenant, the administration of all colonies was to be based upon the principle that "the well-being and development of such peoples form[ed] a sacred trust of civilization."

When World War II spread to southeast Asia, nearly all of Europe's Asian possessions were overrun by Japan. It was a matter of Japanese policy to encourage nationalist movements in those countries, and consequently, after the defeat of Japan, the struggle for independence was intensified on an unparalleled scale. India's struggle for independence proved successful by 1947, when Great Britain proclaimed it a new dominion. Simultaneously, Pakistan gained its independence and was followed by Ceylon and Burma in 1948. These new nations were created with the consent of Great Britain and without United Nations intervention.

In the case of Indonesia, however, the United Nations contributed to its struggle for independence. The United Nations, generally with the full support of the United States, advocated complete independence for Indonesia. The United Nations efforts resulted in the release of the Indonesian government captured by the Dutch and the full restoration of Indonesian authority. This was the first case in which the vital interests of an important European nation—the Netherlands—were challenged by the United Nations. Subsequently, Indonesia abruptly cut its ties with the Netherlands, paying little, if any, regard to the well-being of the Dutch settlers and the many other nationality groups outside of Java. Between 1945 and 1950, when Indonesia finally became a member of the United Nations, the European nations held conflicting views on the matter. The Scandinavian countries supported Indonesian claims to independence. Great Britain took a neutral position, and France and Belgium opposed United Nations involvement in the issue.

Following the settlement of the Indonesian dispute, the question of determining the future disposition of the Italian colonies was brought

up. Due to a disagreement in the Council of Foreign Ministers between the Allies and the Soviet Union, the question was referred to
the General Assembly, in conformity with the Italian peace treaty, on
September 27, 1948. After much deliberation, the General Assembly,
in its Fifth Session, voted for "full and effective . . . realization of the
unity of Libya and the transfer of power to an independent Libyan
government." Independence was to be at the earliest opportune moment, not later than January 1, 1952, and Eritrea was to be constituted an "autonomous unit federated with Ethiopia under the sovereignty of the Ethiopian crown."[13] In an earlier resolution the
Assembly had placed Somaliland under the United Nations trusteeship
system, with Italy as the administering authority for a period of ten
years, after which time the territory would become independent.[14]
Throughout the debate, France's position was conditioned by her evaluation of the possible repercussions of such United Nations actions with
regard to her North African territories. The French abstained from
voting on the question of granting independence to Libya on the
grounds that, according to the four-power Commission of Investigation appointed by the United Nations, none of Italy's colonial territories were ready for independence. Thus, according to an observer, the
United Nations treatment of the matter was perhaps "the most significant of the U. N.'s actions in this field."[15] This decision clearly
showed that European influence in the United Nations was on the decline. For now the more numerous non-Europeans in the United Nations were able to force the west European powers to take actions which
did not coincide with their own best interests.

Korea, the United Nations, and Europe

The main source of European strength in the United Nations is its
representation on the Security Council. Three European nations hold
permanent seats, and normally one eastern European state and one
western European state are elected to the Council. The United Nations
Charter in Article 24, Paragraph 1, confers upon the Security Council

[13] General Assembly Resolutions 387 (V) (November 17, 1950) and 390 (V)
(December 2, 1950).

[14] General Assembly Resolution 289 (IV) (November 21, 1949).

[15] Harold K. Jacobson, "The United Nations and Colonialism: A Tentative Appraisal," *International Organization*, Vol. XVI, No. 1 (Winter, 1962), 50.

the primary responsibility for maintaining international peace and security in behalf of the members. Ever since the defeat of Soviet intentions toward Iran in 1946, the Security Council has come to a virtual deadlock on almost all issues which involve the interests of the United States, the United Kingdom, and France on the one hand and the Soviet Union on the other. This situation has made it necessary to refer issues back to the General Assembly, which has a proportionately small European membership. Such questions as recognition of Franco's Spain, British support for Greece, disarmament negotiations, and the establishment of a United Nations military force were vetoed in the Council and consequently sent down for consideration by the General Assembly.

Fully grasping the portent of the situation, the western European nations felt compelled to abandon their quest for a universal security system. Instead, they chose to enter into a defensive alliance with the United States and Canada, who wanted to safeguard security of the north Atlantic area. This alliance corresponded very closely to Sir Winston Churchill's wartime suggestion that the postwar world organize itself on the basis of regional grouping which would have collective armed forces at the disposal of their regional councils. Churchill would have had the world regulated by a supreme world council consisting of the Big Three—the United Kingdom, the United States, and the Soviet Union—and "certain other powers" which would be in control of the proposed three regional councils—one each for the Western Hemisphere, Europe, and the Pacific.[16]

Within the United Nations certain measures have been undertaken to strengthen the United Nations peace-keeping operations which would function in lieu of the veto-stricken Security Council. An Interim Committee of the General Assembly was established in 1947, and in November, 1949, the General Assembly adopted a plan to raise a field service staff and a panel of observers who would submit reports on trouble spots to the United Nations. Finally, in November, 1950, the General Assembly approved Dean Acheson's comprehensive plan, the "Uniting for Peace Resolution."

Before this proposal, however, on June 25, 1950, North Korea launched a full-scale military offensive against the Republic of South Korea. Europe was quick to react in view of the lesson which the League members had learned from the Japanese aggression against Manchuria

[16] See Russell and Muther, *A History of the United Nations Charter*, 102–108.

in 1931. With the Chinese intervention in early November, 1950, how-ever, certain European powers had misgivings about the United Na-tions police action. This was especially true in respect to the British Labour government headed by Clement Attlee. They felt that "the massive Chinese intervention on 24 November altered the whole character of war." In response to this new development, the major concern of the British government became "an endeavour to promote a peaceful settlement."[17]

Britain preferred a conditional approach, even though she did sup-ply combat forces for the United Nations police action. At that time the French were fully absorbed in their campaign in Indochina but they, nevertheless, took a stand which was sympathetic to the Ameri-can position. Perhaps they hoped to secure American support in the Indochina conflict. Belgium, Denmark, and the Netherlands also sup-ported the American position and pressed for a concerted action in the face of open aggression by North Korea and Communist China.[18] These small European nations almost always support action to stop aggression because of past experience as helpless pawns in wars of great European powers. Sweden was the only nation to abstain from voting on the American-sponsored resolution which labeled Communist China an aggressor and sought to continue the United Nations effort to meet the aggression.[19] Sweden doubted whether United Nations–sponsored collective action was consistent with the desire of the members to bring about a peaceful solution of the Korean crisis through negotiations.

The halfhearted support which the Arab-Asian bloc gave during the Korean police action, and the weariness and frustration which resulted from such a remote and indecisive war, gave rise to doubts of many European statesmen concerning the effectiveness of the United Nations peace-keeping functions. It suddenly became apparent to many Euro-peans that their hopes for the United Nations collective-security mech-anism as a cornerstone of their own security were perhaps too optimistic. Such attitudes only reinforced the growing skepticism which the Euro-peans felt toward the United Nations and which had led to the forma-

[17] Geoffrey L. Goodwin, *Britain and the United Nations* (Carnegie Endowment series on the United Kingdom) (New York, Manhattan Publishing Company, 1957), 137.

[18] See "United States Presses for Naming Aggressor," *United Nations Bulletin*, Vol. X, No. 4 (February 15, 1951), 157, 184–85.

[19] See General Assembly Resolution 498 (V) (February 1, 1951).

tion of NATO in 1949. These suspicions also had the effect of kindling dormant memories of the League and the loss of faith and confidence which that entailed. These misgivings were only further sharpened by the United Nations handling of the Suez, Hungary, and Congo crises.

The Suez-Hungary Phase

The conduct of the United States in the Guatemalan crisis of 1954 was closely watched by the European powers. It was clearly a case involving the vital interests of a major Western power. The west Europeans did not object when the Latin-American members of the Security Council supported the United States in its insistence that the Council was under an obligation to encourage the pacific settlement of local disputes by regional agencies. The American Ambassador, Henry Cabot Lodge, reminded the Council that without an arrangement allowing some balance between universalism and regionalism, qualified though it might be by the veto power, "there would never have been a United Nations."[20] The only west European initiative taken in the Guatemalan dispute was the French sponsorship of a mild resolution calling for immediate termination of any action likely to cause bloodshed and requesting that all members abstain from rendering assistance to such action.[21]

The 1956 Suez crisis and the Hungarian crisis of the same year involved crucial interests of major powers—those of Great Britain and France in the first case and those of the Soviet Union in the second.

The United Nations handling of those two situations clearly showed the west Europeans that different standards were being applied by the United Nations, depending upon which powers were in a particular dispute. This opinion was stated by Selwyn Lloyd, the British foreign secretary, in a speech delivered on May 31, 1957, to a meeting of the United Nations Association in London. After discussing the Suez and Hungary crises, Mr. Lloyd asked:

> Does it mean that the United Nations has one law for the reasonably fair-minded, and another for the unjust and the bully? Does it mean that the organization is powerless when its authority is flouted and can [only] make its views effective with those States which are prepared to be in-

[20] Security Council Official Records (SCOR), Ninth Year, 676th Meeting (June, 1954), paragraph 167.

[21] Security Council Resolution 3247 (645th meeting) (June 20, 1954).

fluenced by it? If this is to be accepted as the basis for United Nations' action, I think few of us here would maintain our faith in its useful continuance.[22]

Like Mr. Lloyd, other responsible European statesmen were angered by the inability of France and Great Britain to protect their economic and political interest in the Middle East. For the Europeans, the Suez crisis brought the usefulness of the United Nations into serious question. Because of ineffective action by the organization, the United Nations role of preserving security had already been nullified. By 1956 the United Nations was becoming an embarrassment for many European powers through its actions in areas in which the organization had originally been expected to play only a limited part.

The use of the veto, for example, was envisaged solely as a measure of last resort. It was designed to prevent action taken on the authority of a majority vote in the Security Council, which would be contrary to the vital interests of a great power. The "Uniting for Peace Resolution" amounted to a *de facto* revision of the Charter by providing for transfer of the security functions of the organization from the Security Council to the General Assembly. Certainly such a transfer of power was not foreseen at San Francisco in 1945. Although the British government did not then oppose American efforts to make the United Nations a more effective instrument for the maintenance of international security, there was widespread apprehension in Great Britain that "any attempt against the determined opposition of a major power to transform the United Nations into an enforcement agency can only result in its disruption."[23]

This was clearly demonstrated in the Hungarian crisis, when it proved impossible for the United Nations to take any viable action—it only managed to pass some well-meaning but ineffective resolutions, which fell on deaf ears. The United Nations felt itself constrained, in the Hungarian case, because any enforcement measures against the Soviet Union could have, in the opinion of some members, and particularly the United States, brought about a third world war. Some neutral states believed that any strong action against the Soviet Union would have caused the complete breakdown of the organization itself.

[22] *The (London) Times* (June 1, 1957).

[23] Henry L. Roberts and Paul A. Wilson, *Britain and the United States* (New York, Harper and Brothers, 1953), 61.

During the Suez episode, more decisive action was possible, as Mr. Lloyd pointed out, because the two major powers involved—Great Britain and France—were willing to be influenced by United Nations majority opinion.

The Suez and Hungary episodes caused the Europeans to reconsider the place of the United Nations in the maintenance of international peace and justice. Most will grant that the United Nations has had considerable success in assuring the localization of conflicts, but in other matters of equal weight the organization has not been as successful. All of the major international crises since World War II have shown the United Nations to be incapable of warding off acts of aggression against its members. Once an aggressive act has been committed, the United Nations "presence" may prevent expansion of the conflict, as was the case in Suez, Lebanon, Jordan, and the Congo; but the aggressor nonetheless goes unpunished for committing the original hostile act.

The United Nations possesses no effective machinery to enforce law and justice within the international community. Confiscation and nationalization are not the subjects of sanctions, and reprisals as used by states in the past are specifically prohibited by the Charter in Article 2, paragraph 4, which enjoins all members to refrain from the threat or use of force against the territorial integrity or political independence of any state. In these circumstances there are few safeguards available to members who wish to protect the lives or property of nationals abroad or to enforce compliance with treaties and other international obligations. Whether the United Nations was created to maintain peace or to remedy injustice, as some have argued, it is, nevertheless, difficult to condone the application of two different standards of behavior to the idea of justice. Mr. Van Langenhove, the Belgian delegate, pointed out these two standards in the course of his statement to the Second Emergency Special Session of the General Assembly on December 3, 1956:

> In the Soviet Union, public opinion is powerless, uninformed or badly informed; it cannot express itself freely and, even to the very slight degree that it is informed, it is virtually impotent—Are there many, in the circumstances, who have any illusions regarding the possibility of inducing the Soviet Union and the Budapest authorities to comply with the resolutions we have adopted? ... Little by little a double standard is being estab-

lished: on the one hand, the standard applicable to the democratic Powers, from which we require strict observance of our principles, our rules and our recommendations; on the other hand, the standard applicable to totalitarian communism, according to which we are resigned to the violation of our principles and our rules and the disregard of our resolutions whenever they run contrary to its interests.

Arguing in the same vein, Mr. Vitetti of Italy concluded his speech by saying that "We have to know . . . whether the United Nations has been established to enforce justice or to justify force. This is the real issue which confronts us . . . and to this question we must give an answer."[24]

Behind these and other statements of west European nations (with the exception of some states such as Greece, Finland, and Austria) there was vivid awareness of Soviet intransigence to and Franco-British compliance with the demands of "humanity." The Greeks, while maintaining a common stand with the other west Europeans on the Hungarian issue, expressed outright opposition to Anglo-French action in the Suez crisis—they were embittered by the Cyprus dispute which had severely strained Greek relations with Great Britain and Turkey. Similarly, the Danish delegate condemned the British, French, and Israeli actions in Suez, which were judged to be equally as reprehensible as those of the Soviet Union in Hungary. The stands taken by Finland and Austria on Hungary were obviously determined by their geographical contiguity to the Soviet Union and its satellites. Finland and Austria voted with the Free World on all nonpolitical resolutions but abstained on others.

Thus, a feeling of utter frustration developed in Europe. It was based on the cases of Suez and Hungary which, although possessing similar features, were subjected to different standards of justice, one for the democratic nations and the other for the totalitarian regimes. In the aftermath of the two episodes Sir Winston Churchill gave vent to the feeling of most responsible statesmen in western Europe when he proclaimed that "justice cannot be a hit-or-miss system."[25] Such was precisely what the world had witnessed in the United Nations during the debates on the Suez and Hungarian crises.

[24] General Assembly Official Records, Second Emergency Special Session (A/PV 604), (December 3, 1956), 465, 481.

[25] *The (London) Times* (August 1, 1957).

The Congo Phase

We have seen that the west European countries, with a few exceptions, took a common stand against Soviet action in Hungary. On the Suez question, on the other hand, the Scandinavian countries, Greece and Italy, opposed the military intervention of Great Britain and France, and the invasion by Israel, and underscored the need for a peaceful settlement of the Suez dispute.

Following the Suez-Hungary episode, the next issue to require major United Nations involvement was the Congo. Prior to the Congo crisis, however, in 1958, the United Nations successfully resolved tensions in the Middle East which were aggravated by foreign interference with and plots to overthrow the legitimate governments in Lebanon and Jordan. The success of the United Nations operations there owed much to the "preventive diplomacy" of the Secretary-General, Dag Hammarskjold. Thus, when the Congo difficulties began, Mr. Hammarskjold had the experiences of the UNEF "presence" in the Gaza Strip near Suez and the United Nations "presence" in Lebanon and Jordan to draw upon. However, the Congo incident was to present an altogether different set of problems than those of other postwar international crises. These complications made the United Nations mission in the Congo a highly complex and difficult undertaking. As a result, the United Nations, much against its wishes, has become so drawn into the domestic issues and conflicts of the Congo that it has since found it difficult to release itself from the many unwanted responsibilities entailed in the stabilization of the internal affairs of that nation.

The crisis in the Congo was precipitated by Belgium's granting it independence on June 30, 1960. Less than a week after independence, on July 6, units of the Congolese army, the Force Publique, mutinied at Thysville. Belgian citizens, residents of the Congo, fled in the ensuing chaos, and the Belgian government decided to take action. The Belgians dropped paratroopers in various parts of the Congo to protect Belgian lives and property in accordance with their treaty rights. On July 10, Premier Patrice Lumumba protested against Belgian intervention. On July 12 he and President Joseph Kasavubu appealed to the United States and the United Nations for help. The members of the Security Council voted unanimously to authorize the Secretary-General to supply military assistance against the Belgian "act of aggression."

Meanwhile, on July 11, Mr. Tshombe proclaimed the independence of Katanga, without, however, receiving recognition by other states.

The Security Council met on July 13 and the following day approved a Tunisian draft resolution which called upon Belgium to withdraw her troops from the Congo and authorized "the Secretary-General to take the necessary steps, on consultation with the Government of the Republic of Congo, to provide the Government with such military assistance as may be necessary, until . . . the national security forces may be able, in the opinion of the Government, to meet fully their tasks."[26] In another meeting on July 21 the Security Council adopted a second resolution whereby all states were requested "to refrain from any action which might tend to impede the restoration of law and order and the exercise by the Government of the Congo of its authority and also to refrain from any action which might undermine the territorial integrity and the political independence of the Republic of Congo."[27]

In their statements, the three west European members of the Council —France, Great Britain, and Italy—expressed the necessity of bringing about a speedy restoration of law and order in the Congo. Each declared its wish to support the United Nations in its Congo operation in order to end the chaos and destruction. The Belgians, as a party to the dispute, were invited to take part in the Council's deliberations. The Belgian delegate explained his country's actions by declaring that because the Congo had become a virtual power vacuum, the United Nations had intervened "to save the peace of the world" and Belgium had taken action to save its nationals still residing there. "Everyone does the job of which he is capable; but either you (the United Nations) are right or we are right, or we are both wrong."[28]

During the debate it became clear that the United Nations was more concerned over the intervention of Belgian troops than with the breakdown of law and order. Under the July 14 resolution the primary responsibility for the maintenance of law and order rested with the Congolese government, to which the United Nations, when asked, would render whatever assistance was necessary. The west Europeans, on the other hand, naturally felt that the question of law and order, upon

[26] United Nations Document S/4387 (July 14, 1960).

[27] United Nations Document S/4405 (July 22, 1960).

[28] Security Council Official Records, Fifteenth Year, 886th Meeting (August 8–9, 1960), paragraph 239.

which the life and safety of their nationals depended, should be given first priority. Speaking before the Security Council on August 8, 1960, the Italian delegate maintained that in Katanga the withdrawal of Belgian troops should coincide with the entry of the United Nations forces in order to prevent widespread disorder:

> The entrance of the United Nations Force should [take] place in such a way as to ensure that a) there is no break in internal security; b) the life of Europeans is adequately protected—and again at this point I (the Italian delegate) would like to emphasize once more that our Government is deeply concerned with the life of the Italian community there— and c) alarm should be avoided so that the Belgian and European communities there, which can still perform a precious and extremely important task for the economic welfare of the Province, are not so overcome by panic so as to flee the country.[29]

It was because his government believed that the resolution of August 9 did not provide adequately for the maintenance of law and order in Katanga, and, by implication, for the safety of the Italian community, that the delegate from Italy abstained.[30] The French did likewise but, in the official records at least, expressed no reason for abstaining. The failure of the United Nations to come to grips with the question of law and order and to look after the west European interests in the Congo brought back memories of the United Nations management of the Suez affair. Once again, the United Nations action disappointed some European countries whose interests the United Nations had often disregarded. Among them were the British, French, Belgians, Dutch, Italians, Portuguese, and Spanish.

[29] *Ibid.*, paragraph 117.

[30] The August 9 resolution confirmed the authority given to Mr. Hammarskjold by virtue of July 14 and July 22 resolutions and requested him to carry out his responsibility with the specific stipulation that "the United Nations . . . will not be a party to or in any way intervene or be used to influence the outcome of any internal conflict, constitutional or otherwise." See United Nations Document A/4426 (August 9, 1960). This principle of nonintervention by the United Nations has been questioned by Professor A. A. J. Bilsen, who raises the question "whether the non-intervention principle can be invoked by the United Nations against a state which has solicited this intervention and asked for their presence and when the United Nations have acquiesced by sending an army of 20,000 soldiers and a considerable body of technicians." See his article, "Some Aspects of the Congo Problem," *International Affairs* (January, 1962), 49.

Thus, the initial western European reaction to the United Nations Congo operations was that of either active support or complete indifference. With the death of Patrice Lumumba on February 12, 1961, however, the situation changed radically. The United Nations membership, including western European nations, was now divided into two factions, those who favored United Nations action in solving the problems still pending, such as the Katangan secession, and those who opposed the United Nations use of force to settle the Congo's domestic problems.[31] Their objections to intervening in domestic affairs were especially strong in a situation in which the United Nations could become the instrument of a government which was seeking to impose its solution against the "will" of the government and the people of an autonomous region of the Congo. According to the latter groups of nations, United Nations action could not be reconciled with the purposes and the principles of the Charter which specifically recognized the principle of domestic jurisdiction and self-determination as factors in relations between states.

Thus the protracted United Nations operations in the Congo caused much heart-searching among a number of west European countries. The French government opposed all the measures the United Nations undertook which could possibly influence the United Nations position on the Algerian situation. The Portuguese acted like the French in view of their African interests. Most Belgians supported the rights of the Katangans to seek autonomy from the Congolese government, which showed little prospect of effectively maintaining law and order. The Belgian government, which favored a central Congo government, finally gave full support to a unified Congo in which Katanga would be centrally controlled like the other Congo provinces. The British, on the other hand, were somewhat ambivalent in their approach, at one time supporting the United Nations action thesis and then opposing the use of force by the United Nations. Among the western European countries who favored the United Nations action were the Scandinavian countries, the Netherlands, Italy, Greece, Turkey, and Austria.

The United Nations Congo operation took a major step with the intervention in Katanga after January 21, 1963, followed by entry of the United Nations personnel into Kolwezi. The United Nations thus

---

[31] See Stanley Hoffman, "In Search of a Thread, the U.N. in the Congo Labyrinth," *International Organization* (Spring, 1962), 344.

secured "freedom of movement" of its personnel throughout the Republic of the Congo.[32]

The United Nations intervention in the Congo shaped European attitudes toward the organization in many ways. A number of new factors have influenced the European appraisal of the United Nations. In western European opinion:

1) The United Nations has almost consistently overlooked the interests of western European countries. The Suez crisis and then the Congo crisis confirm the United Nations preoccupation with Cold War problems arising out of the East-West rivalry. Consequently, European interests are generously sacrificed to the "beneficiaries" of the Cold War—the Afro-Asian countries.

2) There is clearly a double standard which the United Nations applies to the western powers vis-à-vis the Communist powers. The European countries happen to have world-wide interests whose legitimacy the United Nations appears constantly to challenge. The Congo crisis would appear to prove that the United Nations, instead of working hand in hand with European powers for the political and economic development of the less developed countries, seeks to replace them on account of "colonial bias," with no thought of the disruptive forces unleashed.

3) The United Nations has increasingly become dominated by the Afro-Asian countries, most of which were still colonies at the time the Charter was adopted. There is little realization among these countries that the Charter envisaged a limited role for the United Nations and that it was unthinkable that the United Nations should use coercive powers to settle domestic strifes and factionalism except when the Security Council considered such situations to be a threat to world peace. Clearly, there was no precedent for the United Nations use of force in support of the central government against a secessionist province in the Congo. Moreover, the United Nations, today a potent force encouraging self-determination of the non-self-governing territories, must not itself become an instrument of force to subdue groups within a state seeking self-determination after independence.

4) Finally, the United Nations ought not to commit itself to operations beyond its very means. The United Nations Congo operation

[32] See "Events in Katanga," *United Nations Review* (January, 1963).

was clearly an over-commitment which had a very doubtful constitutional basis in the Charter.

Growing Disillusionment among Western European Leaders

While public interest and concern over the relationship of the United Nations with United States foreign policy and national interest continued unabated in the United States, with statements of official support alternating with criticisms such as that of Senator Henry M. Jackson, the debate was even more vehement among western European nations. For Europe, already sensitive to its relative declining position of strength in the United Nations vis-à-vis the rest of the growing membership, most of the important issues before the United Nations were of direct and immediate concern and touched the very core of European sensibilities. Berlin, Suez, Hungary, Algeria, the Congo, and colonialism were all matters of vital interest to European states. Concern or disillusionment were expressed by European leaders over the apparent lack of impartial consideration which those virtually "domestic" matters received at the hands of the international body. In the aftermath of the Suez venture Sir Winston Churchill, a "founding father" of the organization whom none would deem a man of narrow vision, declared that "it is certain that if the General Assembly continues to take its decisions on grounds of enmity, opportunism or merely jealousy and petulance, the whole structure may be brought to nothing." Churchill's friend and colleague, Viscount Cherwell, spoke with greater vehemence: "The General Assembly gives every nation or pseudo-nation an equal vote . . . and this, of course, is perfectly ludicrous. . . . The most civilized nations are equated with tiny states, many of whose inhabitants are fetishists who cannot even read or write."

The discrepancy between Anglo-French compliance with United Nations resolutions calling for withdrawal of their troops from Egypt and the Soviet Union's refusal to comply with the resolution calling for the removal of their armies from Hungary confirmed Europe's contention that there was indeed a double standard of behavior in the United Nations. The French representative in the Security Council remarked that the question was "to find out whether the United Nations will once again provide two rules: one valid for the nations which by tradition and by principle, comply with its decisions or even its recommendations; the other for countries which can with impunity, consider these as null and void without any sanction of any sort whatsoever being applied to them."[33]

This conviction was not lessened by later events in Goa. In a speech in which he stated that "the British Government unswervingly supports the Charter of the United Nations and the United Nations Organization," the British Secretary of State for Foreign Affairs, the Earl of Home, attributed the United Nations difficulties to the forces of racialism and nationalism which were both contrary to the Charter, and which threatened to destroy the organization.[34] In unusually strong language which doubtless reflected Cabinet opinion, he described the United Nations inaction over Goa:

> It was one of those situations in which the United Nations not only failed to condemn an act of aggression but went some way to condone it. . . . The matter should have been taken to the General Assembly. I fear the best informed opinion was that peace would have taken a bigger beating in the Assembly than in the Security Council. But I am not concerned here with the special pleading. Goa may or may not have been a hard case. But hard cases make bad law at home; and they make bad international law too.
>
> For the fact is that if the United Nations Assembly compromises on essential principles and if it allows the use of force for expansionist national ends by certain nations in certain circumstances, it is finished. Do let the members understand that.[35]

In France the newly established Fifth Republic under General de Gaulle's leadership became even more critical of the United Nations, and the new government refused to pay the assessment for the Congo operation. President de Gaulle declared at a press conference on April 11, 1961:

> The United Nations no longer resembles the organization founded in 1945. The General Assembly wields additional powers and now includes representatives of more than one hundred states—soon they will number one hundred and twenty—most of which, at least many of which—are

[33] France disclaims its share of the financial burden that the United Nations has incurred in the Middle East and the Congo crises.

[34] United Nations Document S/PV 778 (May 20, 1957), 12.

[35] Annual Meeting of the General Council of the United Nations Association, London, July 13, 1962, British Information Service T-25.

improvised states and believe it is their duty to stress grievances or demands with regard to the older nations, rather than elements of reason and progress.

General de Gaulle went on to describe the meetings of the United Nations as "riotous and scandalous sessions" in which debates were "filled with invective and insults proffered especially by the Communists and by those who are allied with them against the Western nations." He declared that in these circumstances France could only adopt an attitude of the greatest reserve toward the "United, or Disunited, Nations."

Even a former president of the United Nations General Assembly, and an avowed internationalist, Paul-Henri Spaak, could not suppress his anxieties and declared, after his resignation in 1961 as secretary-general of NATO:

> The path which the United Nations is taking disturbs me. The organization is in danger; if it continues on the same course it will come to constitute a danger. The General Assembly has become a temple of hypocrisy —think of some of those who have set themselves up as judges to condemn that political crime, the assassination of Patrice Lumumba.[36]

But it was above all the issue of colonialism and the influence of the new, nonexperienced members in the General Assembly which fostered the growing disillusion and discontent among western European leadership. Again Lord Home, after stressing that the United Nations and its Charter were "man's best prospect for world peace" which must be supported in an interdependent world, felt constrained to describe resolutions passed by the General Assembly on colonialism as:

> . . . reckless and careless of peace and security. Everyone has seen the chaos in the Congo and everyone knows that it derives from a premature grant of independence to a country whose people were totally unprepared for their new responsibilities. Yet many delegates were instructed by their governments to sponsor and vote for resolutions which could only multiply and magnify that chaos in other places. When . . . we have reached a stage when a large part of the organization which is dedicated to peace openly condones aggression: when an organization which was founded to sustain law and order encourages policies which must endanger it, or when a refusal by many to carry their share of the

[36] Address to the Foreign Press Association, Washington, D.C., 1961.

cost brings a prospect of power without responsibility, it is an under-statement to say that there is cause for anxiety.[37]

These sentiments were echoed by Premier Salazar of Portugal in an address to the Portuguese National Assembly in which he described what he perceived to be a tendency in the General Assembly to engage in heated attacks against Portugal and her overseas territories, an issue used primarily by the new members in the United Nations for purposes of "propaganda" and "subversive action." He stated that the organization was drifting away from its original spirit and that there were created "through its tribunes and the resonance which they lend to the statements made there, waves of agitation, atmosphere of subversion, states of mind which function as means of pressure on those nations which are outside the great clans of the Assembly. The United Nations were instituted for peace but there we hear too many voices which do not presage it."[38]

However little sympathy there may have existed in Europe for Salazar's African colonial policy, there was certainly accord in viewing as completely irresponsible the constant insistence of the new nations on the subject of colonialism, with the support of the Soviet-bloc countries. To the Europeans, who felt that they had contributed much to the growth of the new nations and assisted in the demise of their own empires with a certain noblesse, the conflicts produced over colonialism were spurious, designed to embarrass, and merely afforded opportunity for constant Soviet troublemaking. Particularly frustrating too was the apparent Afro-Asian blind spot toward the Soviet brand of colonialism. The United Nations, created by Europeans, born of European concepts and ideals, was proving to be a particularly troublesome adolescent. These sentiments were well expressed by Lord Home in July, 1962, when he described how the new nations had been transformed into modern societies by European energies:

> I will never apologize for British colonialism or for the structure and shape and aim of the British Commonwealth. I think it has served the world very well. There is no place in which we have exerted our influence in the colonial field which has not been, on our departure, healthier

[37] Address to the United Nations Association, Berwick-on-Tweed, December 28, 1961.

[38] *Portugal and the Anti-Colonialist Campaign* (Portuguese Government Publication, 1961), 16.

and wealthier and better able to play its part in the world as a result of our activities in those territories.

But the Soviet representative at the U. N. conducts his activities with the sole purpose of promoting disorder and bad blood between Africans, Asians and Europeans, and the older nations and the new. Every spark of racialism or nationalism is deliberately fanned into flame.[39]

The hypocrisy of the Soviet posturing as the champion of oppressed people incensed western Europeans, mindful of the division of their own continent, and drew angry words, singularly devoid of British reserve, from Sir Patrick Dean in the General Assembly:

> The Soviet representative has often denounced the alleged non-co-operation of what he chooses to call "the colonial powers." The time has now come for his Government to give an example of cooperation in respect of their own dependent territories. For this reason, we urge the Soviet Government to examine its own record before it criticizes ours. In 1815, the whole of Ceylon came under British rule, at the same time as Azerbaidjan was being occupied by Russia. Ceylon achieved its independence in 1947: "When," may we ask, "can we hope to see Azerbaidjan independent?"

Sir Patrick continued in the same cynical vein, quoting a long list of British conquests and Russian conquests in the nineteenth century:

> Nigeria and Ghana came under British influence in the middle of the 19th century. Lagos was proclaimed a colony in 1862; a protectorate was declared for the Gold Coast in 1874. The same period saw the Russian conquest of the independent states of Central Asia with their ancient civilization; the last independent Kazakh State submitted in 1854, the conquest of the three Uzbek of Turkestan was completed by 1876, and the whole of Turkestan was finally subjugated and annexed in the early 1880's. After nearly a century of British rule Ghana became independent in 1957 and Nigeria in 1960; what is the target date for the independence of the Soviet Central Asian territories? After some years of British occupation, Cyprus was formally annexed to Great Britain in 1914; some three years previously, in 1911, Tannu Tuva was occupied by the Russians and declared a protectorate. Cyprus became independent in 1960; we trust that Soviet plans for the independence of Tannu Tuva will soon be made known.

[39] Speech in debate in House of Lords, July 25, 1962, British Information Service T-27, 9.

Finally Sir Patrick stressed the British record since World War I:

> Territories occupied by the British Government in the course of the 1914/18 war were placed under League of Nations mandate after that war, and after the Second World War those that had not achieved independence were placed under United Nations Trusteeship. Tanganyika, the last of these, became independent last year. What of the territories acquired by the Soviet Union during and since World War II, notably Estonia, Latvia, Lithuania, South Sakhalin and the Kuriles? Were these placed under trusteeship? Has the Colonial Declaration been implemented in respect of these territories? These are the questions which my delegation look forward to hearing the Soviet representative answer when the Committee of Seventeen turns its attention to this problem.[40]

Although it must be said that not all western European countries were directly involved in the question of colonialism (the Scandinavian countries, for instance, usually followed the United Nations majority on the colonial issues), such forthright expressions of dissatisfaction and concern coming from leaders of western European society give some indication of the disruptive influence of certain tendencies developing in the United Nations.

Conclusions

From the above discussion it is evident that western European attitudes toward the United Nations are far from unanimous. Perhaps one reason why the western Europeans never saw their problem as one of joint and common European interests was the presence among them of colonial powers. With the New Guinea issue peacefully settled, the Netherlands can now look to greater freedom and maneuverability in actively participating and using the United Nations for her national purposes. This applies also to Belgium and to a large extent to France and Great Britain as well. Any inhibitions which might exist by reason of being small powers, especially in the case of the Lowland countries, are counteracted by the common approach taken by them all under the aegis of the Rome Treaty group in the United Nations. Moreover, the European Economic Community caucusing group, which at times is subordinated to the western European caucusing group, may generate enough influence and strength to face the Afro-Asian majority in the

[40] Statement to the General Assembly, November 26, 1962, British Information Service T-44, 7-8.

United Nations. So long as the Afro-Asians do not adopt a common approach, but act along the traditions of the United Nations, they represent opportunities that parliamentary ethics permit in terms of give-and-take in support of European interests.

As for the relative importance that the western European governments attach to the United Nations in the formulation or direction of their foreign policies, one is safe in saying that throughout western Europe, "the U. N. seems distant, even remote, from the average person."[41] This is quite a contrast to the League of Nations, which was a European "child." Yet, despite growing cynicism toward the United Nations, there exists the realization that the organization has played a significant role in maintaining international peace. In European minds this is attributable to the skill and diplomacy of a great European of the mid-twentieth century, Dag Hammarskjold. His passing from the scene has not affected the attitudes that the Europeans developed for United Nations peace efforts, even though he has been replaced by a non-European. The feeling that persists is that there is an essential task for the United Nations to do; and peace is, assuredly, the concern of all. Moreover, there is the realization that if ever disarmament talks were to bear fruit, there would be a need for an international body, and the United Nations would then be entrusted with still another peace-keeping function and mission.

[41] Lincoln P. Bloomfield, "Western Europe and the U.N.: Trends and Prospects," (Cambridge, Massachusetts Institute of Technology, 1959), vi (Unpublished manuscript).

CHAPTER IX

Economic and Social Matters

BY HAROLD KARAN JACOBSON

IN THE ARENA of economic and social activities, the United Nations has been a scene of continuous and shifting conflict between the United States and many Western nations on one hand and the Soviet Union on the other. The confrontation in this area began even before the drafting of the Charter, with the fundamental question of whether the United Nations mandate should include economic and social functions at all. When an affirmative decision had been reached, the broad and vaguely defined nature of these functions gave ample opportunities for both sides to make ideological sounding boards of the institutions involved and to attempt to mold these functions according to their national objectives. The tactical importance of the United Nations economic and social activities has increased with the growing emphasis, over the last decade, on the underdeveloped nations as a battle front of the Cold War.

It was to be foreseen that the United States and the Soviet Union would clash in the economic and social arena. Both countries implicitly accepted the influence of economic and social problems on political events, including the threat of war. Marxist dogma was based on the concept of inevitable class struggle, while in the United States many leaders of the New Deal had identified a stable society with economic and social well-being. Communist ideology declared that the ills of men and nations, economic and social in origin, could be cured only by class struggle leading to the eventual collapse of the present system and culminating in the evolution of a classless and prosperous society. The American concept, spelled out principally in the various domestic measures taken in the 1930's, was not revolution but reform through cooperative welfare legislation and other means. This idea of eliminating the class struggle, of course, did not suit the theories or aims of the

226

Soviet Union. Here was a fundamental conflict, in which neither side could afford to yield in any essential. As such, it has pervaded almost every aspect of the economic and social activities of the United Nations. In turn, the course of the protracted conflict between East and West can—in part, at least—be measured by the gains achieved and losses suffered in this broad arena.

In the Dumbarton Oaks conversations, the positions of both states were affected by their perceptions of the League of Nations experience. The United States, although not a member of the League, had participated in some of its economic and social activities, and had favored their expansion, among other reasons because of the belief that international co-operation in these matters might facilitate political accord. The United States could point to the International Labor Organization as a League agency which had weathered the general debacle of the peace and security efforts of the mid-thirties, and to the increasing emphasis on economic and social functions among League members just prior to World War II.

The Soviet attitude was quite different. Although the Soviet Union had been a member of the League of Nations, its participation in the League's economic and social activities had been minimal and sporadic. Most of the League's efforts in this area had aimed at buttressing the Western order, a task which the Soviet Union could hardly be expected to share with enthusiasm. These programs also had greatest applicability for Western economic and social systems. The Soviet Union had seen the League as a possible device for gaining security against the Fascist powers. As a result of these factors, it strongly opposed the movement in the late thirties to give increasing emphasis to the League's economic and social functions and to downgrade its political and security functions. The Soviet Union's attitude toward the nascent United Nations followed a similar pattern. At Dumbarton Oaks, and in earlier correspondence, the Soviet Union argued that the United Nations should deal with political and security matters only, that it should avoid the confusion of purpose and overburdening with nonessential tasks which in its view had plagued the League of Nations. The Soviet Union claimed that it was not opposed to international co-operation concerning economic and social problems, but that it felt that such co-operation should occur in separate specialized organizations. The Soviet Union did not yield until the Dumbarton Oaks conversations had reached an advanced stage, and it did so then only reluctantly, and probably with the expectation of obtaining equivalent concessions in other issues then in contention, such as voting procedures in the Security Council and voting privileges for the Soviet Union's constituent republics. Moreover, it probably did not expect that the inclusion of economic and social functions would have any substantial effect on its relationship with the new organization.

Thus the Soviet Union came to San Francisco in 1945 with little real interest in the development of economic and social programs as part of the general purpose of the United Nations, since these programs presumably would be a continuation and expansion of those conducted by the League. In addition, such programs conceivably could constitute a challenge to the Soviet Union's closed system, proving a channel for the penetration of Western concepts and practices. Also, in political and security matters the Soviet Union would have the protection of its veto in the Security Council; in economic and social affairs it had only one voice among many. Faced with this situation, the Soviet Union chose at San Francisco to give little emphasis to the work of Committee II/3, which dealt with economic and social co-operation.

The United States, on the other hand, played a prominent role in Committee II/3, whose product—Chapters IX and X of the United Nations Charter—bore an American imprint. These chapters, well suited to American purposes, elaborated and expanded the concepts drafted at Dumbarton Oaks under the guidance of the United States. Thus the United States took the first initiative, under favorable circumstances, in the economic and social aspect of its confrontation with the Soviet Union.

It is highly doubtful that either state saw the situation in this light at the time. They were still allies in war. Soviet policy toward the future concentrated on political agencies and boundaries; and the United States, least ravaged among the Great Powers by the war, was concerned with rebuilding a peaceful and stable world rather than increasing its own strength vis-à-vis its Soviet ally. American initiative in developing the United Nations mandate with respect to economic and social activities was the result of a generous hope, which has since been tempered by experience and the East-West conflict. For the Soviet Union, too, has learned from experience the importance of the economic and social sphere toward the achievement of its own ends. Developments in the United Nations economic and social activities from 1945 until today reflect a varying pattern of conflict and compromise, impressed always with the basic differences between the United States and the Soviet Union as applied to the multiple activities which have been involved.

Any chronological division distorts reality; but, broadly speaking, the Soviet-American confrontation in the years since 1945 can be divided into three phases.

The first phase covers the year 1946. During that brief and chaotic period, problems connected with refugees and displaced persons, and relief and reconstruction, dominated the United Nations economic and social work. Both the United States and the Soviet Union had their interests in these problems. The Soviet Union, its nationals, and its territory, as well as its eastern European satellites, were involved; the United States, on the other hand, would have to bear the largest share of the financial burden. Both nations, from choice or necessity, used the United Nations and its agencies in attempting to achieve their disparate goals with respect to these problems. By the year's end, United Nations actions mainly favored the United States; Soviet national objectives had not been significantly advanced, nor had its obstructionist tactics succeeded to any great extent.

The second phase began in the winter of 1946–47 and continued until the winter of 1952–53. This six-year period, during which the United Nations settled into its long-range activities, witnessed an almost complete isolation of the Soviet Union in the economic and social matters, and in contrast, a dynamic United States leadership in these affairs.

During the United Nations first year the Soviet Union had, despite its obvious reluctance, gone so far as to negotiate within the organization's framework on those problems with which it was vitally concerned. Its policy on other matters had remained obscure. This obscurity vanished in 1947. From then until 1953, Soviet policy regarding the United Nations economic and social work can be characterized by two words—abstention and attack. The Soviet Union held membership in only four specialized agencies: the Universal Postal Union (UPU); the International Telecommunication Union (ITU); the World Meteorological Organization (WMO); and the World Health Organization (WHO). Shortly after the last agency began to function in 1949, the Soviet Union withdrew from it; participation in the other three (all of them highly technical agencies) was continued as a necessity for a major power. The Soviet Union refused to join in many other subsidiary agencies of the United Nations, including most significantly the majority of committees of the Economic Commission for Europe (ECE), which might have served as important channels for intra-European co-operation.

However, the Soviet Union continued to be elected to membership in the Economic and Social Council (ECOSOC), and participated actively in the debates of that broad supervisory organ, as well as in those of its regional and functional commissions. The Soviet Union used these discussions, and those in Committees Two and Three and the relevant plenary sessions of the Assembly, principally as forums from which to attack the institutions and policies of the West and even of the United Nations when these were seen as closely identified with Western aims. This use of ECOSOC and its agencies as fronts in a "cold war" against the West became less and less effective as it became more and more open and obvious in its aim. At first some of the Soviet proposals were adopted; but gradually the Soviet Union's unwillingness to share in the developing concrete work, such as the Expanded Program of Technical Assistance (EPTA), blunted the effectiveness of its attack. By 1950, and for the next two years, most votes in the United Nations on resolutions dealing with economic and social matters found the Soviet bloc alone in opposition or abstention.

This isolation, largely the result of Soviet policies, was also partly the product of an extremely active and creative American policy during these years. From 1947 through 1952 the United States played a leading role in the United Nations economic and social work. There were, of course, times when majority sentiment ran counter to American policy, and occasions when other nations would have preferred more rapid or stronger action than the United States was willing to pursue. For the most part, however, the important actions during these years were developed from American initiative; the United States had played a prominent role in all the specialized agencies, and had been responsible for the creation of several. The Expanded Program of Technical Assistance, perhaps the United Nations most significant program in the economic and social field, originated as an American proposal. It was an outgrowth of the famous Point Four program.

This American leadership reflected a generous endeavor to help solve the world's problems, and was generally seen in this light within the halls of the United Nations. That this policy ran counter to the aims of the Soviet Union, and frequently served to check its influence, could also be readily seen. It would not be accurate to say either that the United States sought to isolate the Soviet Union in the United Nations economic and social work or that it did not seek to do so. The fact remained that American policy contributed to this result. The comparative participation of the two nations was clear and devastating; and when they clashed in the arena of debate, the constructive nature of American policy spoke on its behalf before the world forum.

Then, beginning in the winter of 1952–53, the picture on both sides began to change. The Soviet Union, faced with the failure of its policy, became a willing participant in more and more of the United Nations economic and social activities. It joined or rejoined several of the specialized agencies: the World Health Organization; the International Labor Organization (ILO); the United Nations Educational, Scientific, and Cultural Organization (UNESCO); and the Intergovernmental Maritime Consultative Organization (IMCO). It also joined the International Atomic Energy Agency (IAEA) and began to participate in the technical committees of ECE which it had earlier boycotted. (As of 1963, though, there were still several agencies in which the Soviet Union did not participate: the Food and Agricultural Organization, the International Civil Aviation Organization, the International Monetary Fund, the International Bank for Reconstruction and Development, the International Finance Corporation, the International Development Association, and all of the United Nations agencies which deal with refugee problems.) The Soviet Union also began contributing to EPTA and to the United Nations Children's Fund (UNICEF). Its attacks on the West became less strident, and various agencies saw a series of new and far-reaching proposals put forward by Soviet delegates in an effort to seize the initiative.

The new policy of co-operation came to light in debate after debate. Now, when Soviet proposals were defeated, the representatives of the Soviet Union frequently did not force the issue or abstain from agreement with the majority, but voted for counterresolutions "in the interest of unanimity." The recognition in the United Nations that there were important and practical limits to the new Soviet policy of co-operation emerged only after some years and then in piecemeal form which diminished the effect of this recognition.

Meanwhile, the policies of the United States with regard to the United Nations economic and social work had also been altered. American participation in this work was not significantly reduced; but for a number of reasons, United States policy from 1953 through 1956 was less positive and dynamic than it had been since the United Nations inception. The United States found itself in disagreement with the majority on a number of basic issues; and it showed itself less willing than formerly to sponsor or support new activities, or to follow up on some which had already been initiated. Starting in 1957, American policy became more positive, but it has not regained for the United States the position of popular leadership that it had enjoyed before 1952.

Thus the comparative balance of initiative and support that had so strongly favored the United States, in its confrontation of the Soviet Union in the economic and social arena of the United Nations, now tipped somewhat toward the Soviet side. In factual analysis, the United States has still been contributing far more than the Soviet Union to the United Nations social and economic work. Nevertheless, the Soviet Union has seized some of the initiative and, with the growing importance of the underdeveloped countries in the world's political picture, has been using this initiative in psychological forays well in advance of the strength of its actual participation.

This brief introduction may now serve as an outline for a more detailed study of Soviet-American policies and relationships in the formidably complex patterns of the United Nations economic and social programs and agencies, from the organization's inception to the present, with emphasis upon the confrontation of the two powers during the three periods noted above.

The economic and social problems facing the United Nations in 1945–46 were the staggering aftermath of global war. As early as 1943 the Allies had formed an organization to begin coping with these problems, the United Nations Relief and Rehabilitation Administration (UNRRA). When the United Nations was formed, UNRRA was not formally associated with it, but there were important symbolic and intellectual links between the two, as well as a sharing of key purposes. If the emergent United Nations were to gain political stability through social and economic betterment—part of the American dream at San Francisco—it must obviously concern itself with the relief of the war-devastated nations and with the rehabilitation of displaced persons numbering in the millions. These were the functions for which UNRRA had been created.

Both the United States and the Soviet Union were active participants in the work of UNRRA. Because of their divergent aims and philosophies, however, their views of the organization's functions conflicted considerably. For the United States, UNRRA offered a means toward postwar stability, a symbol of hope and strength to the Axis-occupied countries whose populations had been exploited by the Axis powers, and a way of disposing of surplus commodities and regulating the market in scarce goods. To the Soviet Union, UNRRA represented a source of assistance to itself (through the Byelorussian Soviet Socialist Republic and the Ukrainian Soviet Socialist Republic) and the countries of eastern Europe soon to become satellites, rather than an obligation to serve in working toward a new peace. Almost half the commodities distributed by UNRRA were given to eastern European states which came to be under Communist control or strongly dominated by their Soviet neighbor.[1]

UNRRA had always been viewed as a temporary institution, and as early as August, 1945, the United States proposed that the agency's operations should be brought to a close in 1947. Later the United States insisted that this terminal date be kept, and since it was the principal donor, it was in a position to enforce its view. The growing Soviet-American split was one of several factors responsible for the American obduracy.[2] The United Nations would have considered the problems which UNRRA handled even had the agency continued, for its functions were relatively restricted. But the scheduled liquidation of UNRRA gave added cause for taking up these issues.

One major problem was that over one million individuals, most of whom were nationals of eastern European countries, would still be outside their countries of origin after UNRRA completed its operations. It was evident that an overwhelming majority did not desire repatriation. Negotiations on the question began during the meetings of the

---

[1] George Woodbridge, *UNRRA: The History of the United Nations Relief and Rehabilitation Administration* (3 vols., New York, Columbia University Press, 1950), III, 248.

[2] See John C. Campbell, *The United States in World Affairs, 1945–1947* (New York, Harper and Brothers, 1947), 329–38.

Preparatory Commission in the fall of 1945, and final decisions were not taken until December, 1946.

The Soviet Union originally argued that the United Nations should not be concerned; that the problem should be solved by bilateral agreements between the states which were directly concerned. Later the Soviet Union conceded that the United Nations might take action, but only if certain conditions were met which were spelled out in a statement of principles submitted in early 1946.[3] According to this statement the United Nations "main task" should be to facilitate the "early return" of displaced persons to their native countries. Some displaced persons, provided that they were not "quisling, traitors or war criminals," could be resettled if their country of origin agreed.

The United States also submitted a statement of principles at about the same time.[4] This statement emphasized that no individual should be compelled to return to his country of origin against his wishes.

It was decided, fairly early in the negotiations, that the United Nations should create a temporary specialized agency, the International Refugee Organization (IRO), to conduct operational activities. The Soviet Union's proposals all implied that IRO's principal (and probably only) function would be repatriation; those of the United States and the West, that it would be resettlement. The Soviet Union apparently was willing to condone the creation of a specialized agency that would do about the same things that UNRRA had; the West wanted a considerably broader mandate, and this view prevailed. As a consequence, the Soviet Union voted against the establishment of IRO, and in the following years it used every possible opportunity to attack the agency.

In concrete terms, if IRO were to engage in extensive resettlement operations, a large share of its activities would be devoted to aiding dissidents who were seeking to escape from Communist regimes. At various points in the negotiations, the Soviet Union made it clear that it could not support any agency which performed such a function.[5] Probably few if any states would have taken a different position.

[3] United Nations Document A/c.3/19.   [4] United Nations Document A/c.3/20.

[5] See ECOSOC Official Records, Second Session, Special Supplement No. 1, "Report of the Special Committee on Refugees and Displaced Persons," 16; and E. F. Penrose, "Negotiating on Refugees and Displaced Persons," in Raymond Bennett and Joseph E.

The United States position appears to have been more the product of the general American commitment to the principle of freedom of choice than the result of a desire to have the United Nations take anti-Soviet action. Indeed, the United States government was not originally committed to handling the problem through a United Nations agency.[6] It was willing to use other solutions, such as the Inter-Governmental Committee for Refugees (IGCR), which had been established in 1938. Apparently the United States decided to support the creation of IRO because of urging from other Western states and on the assumption that broader financial support would thus be secured. Whether or not the outcome justified the tedious and acrimonious negotiations that were required for the creation of IRO and the introduction of a controversy which spilled over into other aspects of the United Nations economic and social activities is debatable. The principal contributors to IRO were also those which had provided the greatest financial support for UNRRA and IGCR. On IRO's side of the balance sheet, though, must be placed the weight of moral sanction by the United Nations in the support of its work of social and individual justice.

Beyond the work of aiding individuals displaced by the war, the United Nations devoted a great deal of attention in 1946 to problems of relief, rehabilitation, and reconstruction. Food and other supplies were needed in devastated areas, and it was imperative that institutions be created to facilitate international co-operation. Negotiations on these issues also began in the meetings of the Preparatory Commission and continued throughout 1946. Unlike the negotiations leading to the establishment of IRO, at first both the Soviet Union and the United States seemed eager to have the United Nations consider these problems. However, as relief and reconstruction activities began to take form, both nations indicated strong reservations in their support. The Soviet Union saw in the proposed regional and international agencies a

Johnson (eds.), *Negotiating with the Russians* (Boston, World Peace Foundation, 1951), 139–68, 174.

[6] See U.S. Dept. of State, *Report of the United States Delegation to the First Part of the First Session of the General Assembly of the United Nations, London, England: January 10–February 14, 1946* (Dept. of State Publication 2484; Washington, D.C., Government Printing Office, 1946), 22; and Louis K. Hyde, Jr., *The United States and the United Nations: Promoting the Public Welfare* (New York, Manhattan Publishing Company, 1960), 58.

danger to its closed political system and to the establishment and consolidation of the Soviet bloc, and the United States drew back from full financial commitments to agencies over which it could not exercise direct control.

The acute problem of food shortage was transferred early from the United Nations to a specialized agency, the Food and Agricultural Organization (FAO). Organized during World War II as an American concept, FAO convened in 1946 a Special Meeting on Urgent Food Problems, and established an International Emergency Food Council (IEFC) to effect a system of voluntary allocations for agricultural commodities in short supply.

Even though the Soviet Union was a co-sponsor of the General Assembly resolution from which these activities stemmed, it boycotted FAO and declined special invitations to attend the Special Meeting or join IEFC. The Soviet spokesmen severely criticized the work of FAO and IEFC during the discussion of food shortages at the second part of the first session of the General Assembly, a lead that was gradually followed by the eastern European satellites. In 1946, Czechoslovakia, Hungary, Yugoslavia, and Poland were active participants in FAO; but eventually they also boycotted it. (Poland resumed participation in 1957.) The Communist view was that Western agricultural policies kept the food market out of balance and contributed to shortages. The United States, on the other hand, took a leading part in the activities of FAO and IEFC, but drew the line at suggestions for establishing international machinery to control the agricultural market. Once again the fundamental differences between the two opposing systems were shown in clear light.

On the more general question of assistance to devastated countries, the year 1946 witnessed several resolutions adopted in both the General Assembly and the Economic and Social Council. Here again, the example of UNRRA supplied argument for opposing points of view. The Soviet Union wanted assistance for its devastated areas and those of its satellites, but on its own terms and without great financial liability. In short, it favored resolutions that reflected the limitations which characterized the earlier agency. The Soviet Union withheld necessary information from United Nations bodies and refused to permit them to investigate devastated areas in Soviet territory. By these actions and its pronouncements it clearly indicated that it did not want any international body to have more power than UNRRA had had.[7]

American policy during the early discussions was not clear-cut. However, the United States was determined that UNRRA, soon to be disbanded, should not be replaced by another agency with similar characteristics. This was the situation when debate was taken up, late in 1946, in the General Assembly as to whether aid to devastated countries should be channeled through an international organization. The majority of the Assembly, including the smaller states of eastern Europe, strongly favored such a step; and Fiorello H. La Guardia, in his capacity as director-general of UNRRA, fervently argued for international action. Here was an opportunity for the United States to assume leadership even among the satellites of the Soviet Union, a chance to penetrate the Iron Curtain within the United Nations framework. The American government, however, decided against support of an international agency for aid, probably through fear of losing control of its own financial and political policies in the international arena. Because of its opposition, the Assembly did not recommend the establishment of an agency to replace UNRRA in this field. Instead, future assistance to devastated countries was left to bilateral arrangements; and in the following year, the United States carried its viewpoint into action with development of the Truman Doctrine and the Marshall Plan, neither of which involved the United Nations.

Regardless of how assistance was distributed, there was need for international co-operation among the devastated countries. To facilitate this, the General Assembly recommended that ECOSOC create two regional commissions, an Economic Commission for Europe (ECE) and an Economic Commission for Asia and the Far East (ECAFE). The dream behind ECE was that of a more closely united Europe, whose reconstruction following the war offered a real opportunity for

---

[7] The Soviet Union also made this evident in its reaction to General George Marshall's offer of assistance to Europe. See France, Ministère des Affaires étrangères, *Documents de la Conférence des Ministres des Affaires étrangères de la France, du Royaume-Uni, de l'U.R.S.S. tenue à Paris du 27 juin au 3 juillet 1947, et pièces relatives aux négociations diplomatiques engagées à la suite du discours prononcé par le Général Marshall, ministre d'État d'États-Unis, le 5 juin 1947* (Paris, Imprimerie Nationale, 1947). The United Nations was given an insignificant role in the proposal which the Soviet Union presented to the Paris Conference: "Le Comité de Coopération établit avec la Commission économique européenne de l'O.N.U. des relations correspondant aux attributions qui lui sont données."(*Ibid.*, 41.)

co-operative planning. Once more the hope was tempered by lack of support from the Soviet Union, and by caution on the part of the United States—the one from unwillingness to permit any activity that would interfere with consolidation of Communist control in eastern Europe, the other from refusal to delegate financial authority to the international body.

The Soviet Union, beginning in late 1946, bitterly criticized the United Nations for not providing more aid to eastern Europe. It is true that this region fared less well under new allocations than it had under UNRRA. However, this could in part at least be laid at the door of the Soviet Union itself, for its refusal to co-operate with the endeavor, and for its alarm at the prospect of its satellites being wooed by the Western bloc. Some in eastern Europe were ready to use the United Nations economic agencies as a means of escape from Soviet domination.[8] Whether stronger United States support of these agencies would have brought this about it is impossible to know. Certainly the odds were against the non-Communist forces there. But the United States, by insisting on gaining unilateral control over the assistance which it granted, probably did not do all it could to exploit the opportunities offered it to impede Soviet domination in eastern Europe. If nothing else, American support for the United Nations in this area would have dramatized the Soviet Union's unwillingness to co-operate in international affairs. As it turned out, when the Soviet Union later criticized the United States for bypassing the United Nations in the Truman Doctrine and the Marshall Plan, the counter-arguments were not as easy to document as they might have been.

Out of the tentative beginnings in the social and economic fields that characterized the United Nations first year, long-range issues emerged that were to widen further and clarify the split between American and Soviet purposes. These included, in general, five categories: social welfare, economic welfare, human rights, international trade, and economic development. By the winter of 1952–53, programs were well under way in each of these fields; and in every case the balance of decision and of world opinion clearly favored the United States.

[8] David Wightman, *Economic Co-operation in Europe: A Study of the United Nations Economic Commission for Europe* (London, Stevens and Sons, 1956), 16. See also Trygve Lie's account of Jan Masaryk's remarks on this point—*In the Cause of Peace*, 233.

In the area of social welfare, the United Nations inherited programs and functions both from the League of Nations and from UNRRA. It accepted the responsibilities formerly the League's in regard to population, the control of narcotics, and the prevention of traffic in persons and obscene publications. The United Nations' most important operational programs in social welfare were a legacy from UNRRA. These were its program of advisory social welfare services, a venture in technical assistance, and the United Nations Children's Fund. Additional areas of work were those relating to crime prevention and the treatment of offenders, and the general field of social betterment in matters of housing, family maintenance, and community development. Two specialized agencies were created, the World Health Organization and the United Nations Educational, Scientific, and Cultural Organization.

The Soviet record in the area of social welfare from 1946 to 1953 was one of abstention and propagandistic attack and—in general—of isolation and failure. The Soviet Union refused to join UNESCO and, except for a brief period, WHO. It would not contribute to the UNICEF budget and argued that recipient countries should bear the costs of the advisory social welfare program. It claimed absolute domestic jurisdiction over such areas as crime prevention and internal migration, and gave little useful data to the United Nations on social welfare matters. On the other hand, it suggested programs for United Nations consideration in areas traditionally accepted as domestic matters, and which would have required submission of extensive information from participating nations. Among other things, the Soviet Union proposed investigation and recommendations concerning unemployment compensation, free compulsory education, and free medical care.[9] These proposals had great popular appeal in many countries, and the Soviet Union was able to score some propaganda victories when non-Communist countries voted against them on the grounds that they were not within jurisdiction of an international organization. The Soviet Union made further propaganda use of discussions concerning such social problems as drug addiction, prostitution, traffic in women and children and in obscene publications. The Soviet delegates declared that these social evils were the corrupt fruit of capitalism, and boasted that they did not exist in Communist countries.

[9] United Nations Document E/CN 5/L.139.

The effectiveness of Soviet propaganda in the field of social welfare was increased by the difficulty encountered by the United States and the United Kingdom in explaining their constitutional commitments. Many of the United Nations activities in this field were based on conventions which bound signatory states and established systems of enforcement. In this situation the United Kingdom had to ensure inclusion of a "colonial application" clause, whereby the ratification of the metropolitan state would not bind all its dependencies, since England's constitutional relationship with many of its dependencies allowed them to determine their own obligations. In like manner, inclusion of "federal state" clauses in agreements was vital to the United States because of the constitutional division of powers between the United States federal government and the constituent states. The Soviet delegates concentrated propaganda fire on these clauses as mere subterfuges to escape responsibility and allow continued social evils. More frequently than not, this emotional appeal won out in debate over constitutional logic. On the other hand, the Soviet Union was unable to prevent inclusion of clauses in conventions that provided for referral of disputes to the International Court of Justice (ICJ)—a provision especially irritating to the Soviet policy of avoiding binding adjudication.

In short, the Soviet Union's consistent pattern with regard to social welfare programs developed in the United Nations from 1947 to 1953 was one of limiting its own commitment as much as possible while seizing every opportunity to criticize the West.

Against such tactics, and despite some propaganda success on the Soviet side, the United States, during these years, established a just reputation for positive leadership and co-operation in the interests of social welfare. Its early reservations about UNESCO's orientation gave way to active participation in the refocusing of that agency's activities. American contributions amounted to 70 per cent of government funds given to UNICEF. The United States proposed the launching of the advisory social welfare services and defended this program even against the United Kingdom. It led the movement to revise and renew the conventions concerning social evils which the United Nations had inherited from the League. While Soviet spokesmen were contributing principally propaganda, United States representatives tended to concentrate on the technical aspects of several problems and their solutions. Thus, during these six years the United States clearly outdistanced the

Soviet Union in the actual work of this aspect of United Nations activity.

In the area of economic welfare, the International Labor Organization had been active since 1919, and at the San Francisco Conference most states assumed that ILO would continue to have responsibility in this field. Both the United States and the Soviet Union had joined ILO in 1934. But while the United States became one of the agency's strong supporters, the Soviet Union's membership terminated in 1939 when it was expelled from the League of Nations. The potential conflict thus germinated over jurisdiction in economic welfare activities was realized with the formation, in 1945, of a new trade union international, the World Federation of Trade Unions (WFTU). The WFTU clamored for, and received, consultative privileges in the United Nations as a nongovernmental organization. Organized when the camaraderie of war was still high, it quickly became Communist-controlled. From 1946 to 1953, the United Nations activities in the field of economic welfare were a compound of Soviet efforts to advance the WFTU and Western endeavors to protect non-Communist trade union organizations and the prominent position of ILO. It may be added, on the basis of the evidence, that the Soviet purpose was single-mindedly to attack and undermine the West in the eyes of the world's laborers, while the Western incentive was not merely to counter this attack but to get on with some useful programs.[10]

This was one of the clearest conflicts in the United Nations arena. Its results were an explosive debate, an unmistakable propaganda victory for the West, and several significant accomplishments. True, the Soviet Union introduced some of the issues leading to these accomplishments, as, for example, trade union rights and equal pay for equal work for men and women. The Soviet delegates emphasized the problem of unemployment and sought to have the United Nations investigate the effects of the arms race on standards of living. In these matters they assumed vigorous leadership on behalf of causes already obviously in need of study and often already receiving it, but as the champion of which the Soviet Union was entirely willing to pose. As a counter-attack, the American Federation of Labor (AF of L), with the full support of the United States government, raised the issue of forced labor. Further, the West turned the issue of trade union rights against

[10] See Harold Karan Jacobson, "Labor, the UN and the Cold War," *International Organization*, Vol. XI, No. 1 (Winter, 1957), 55–67.

the Soviet bloc by pointing to the controlled and subservient status of the trade unions in Communist countries. In these debates, some of the central differences between the Communist and Western ways of life were aired, even if the air was more frequently heated than not.

By the end of 1952 the United States and the West had ample reason for satisfaction. Most of the Soviet proposals had been defeated, even though voting against them had caused occasional embarrassment for Western delegates, since they were phrased in popular terms.[11] The major non-Communist trade unions had left the WFTU in 1949 in protest against its obvious use as an instrument of Soviet foreign policy. Moreover, its consultative privileges in the United Nations had been reduced. ILO had been reaffirmed as having principal responsibility for most activities in the field of economic welfare. Those concrete steps proposed by the Soviet Union—matters of trade union rights and equal pay for women—had been developed by ILO as technical conventions regarding freedom of association and equal remuneration, stated in terms far removed from the propaganda slogans under which they had been first presented by Soviet delegates. Without membership in ILO, the Soviet Union had been excluded from the detailed consideration of these matters. On other labor fronts, the Soviet Union found the issue of trade union rights backfiring upon it, and it was clear that the United Nations investigation of forced labor would result in a resounding condemnation of the Soviet Union and its satellites.[12] Over the six years, the West had won substantive gains as well as a propaganda victory.

The work of the United Nations in the field of human rights was closely related to its activities concerning social and economic welfare.

---

[11] Illustrative of this difficulty was a vote in the Ninth Session of ECOSOC in 1949, on a Soviet-backed proposal concerning unemployment. (United Nations Document E/1332/Add.2.) On a vote by paragraphs, all the specific provisions were adopted, the Soviet bloc voting for them all, Lebanon for the first three (after which the Lebanese delegate left), and the other member states abstaining. Then the proposal as a whole was defeated (three ayes—Soviet bloc; thirteen nays; one abstaining—India). This embarrassing sequence was repeated later that year at the Fourth Session of the General Assembly. As a consequence the rules of the procedure of both bodies were changed so that this could not happen again.

[12] See ECOSOC Official Records, Sixteenth Session, Supplement No. 13, "Report of the *Ad Hoc* Committee on Forced Labor" (Geneva, 1953); also reproduced as United Nations Document E/2431.

Unlike the situation in those fields, however, this work was conducted almost entirely within the United Nations, and it had virtually no precedents. While previous international organizations had sought to protect the rights of special groups, such as ethnic minorities, they had never attempted to promote the rights of all individuals.

During the early years of the United Nations, the United States figured prominently in the work regarding human rights. Mrs. Franklin Delano Roosevelt was the first chairman of ECOSOC's Commission on Human Rights, and American initiative sparked the activities of this body. The United States position was not always accepted, of course; but the United Nations principal accomplishments in this area during the years under consideration—the Universal Declaration of Human Rights, the Convention on the Prevention and Punishment of the Crime of Genocide, and the Convention on the International Transmission of News and the Right of Correction—were compatible with American concepts and traditions.

Soviet delegates vociferously proclaimed the need for measures to protect and promote human rights. However, their proposals were tinged with the Communist emphasis on the state and its privileges rather than the rights of the individual; and again and again the Soviet proposals were rejected. In the end, the Soviet Union voted against the Convention on the International Transmission of News and the Right of Correction, abstained from voting on the Universal Declaration of Human Rights, and only reluctantly voted for the Convention on the Prevention and Punishment of the Crime of Genocide.

In the last years of the period, however, trends developed in the United Nations work concerning human rights which created difficulty for the West. These trends became evident in discussions over the drafting of covenants on human rights and conventions on freedom of information. The General Assembly's growing anti-colonial spirit was injected into these discussions, and some underdeveloped nations came to see in the formal conventions a means of validating their aspirations for higher social and economic standards. The Soviet Union encouraged these trends, and, to some extent, was successful in exploiting them to the detriment of the West. Consequently, and despite rebuffs, the Soviet position in 1952 was probably better in the area of human rights than in any other field of the United Nations economic and social work.

In the field of international trade, the United Nations launched an ambitious and diffuse program involving the General Assembly, the Economic and Social Council, a number of ECOSOC's subordinate bodies, and several specialized agencies. Originally there was apparent consensus that the purpose of this program should be to facilitate expansion of international trade on as free and multilateral a basis as possible. Certainly this was the goal of the United States administration, even though it was to encounter strong domestic opposition in its attempts to enact policy on the matter.

A field as technical in its complexities as international trade would require specialized agencies to conduct most of the activities. The American plan envisaged the United Nations as co-ordinator of these activities rather than as their prime mover. Two specialized agencies had already been created during World War II: the International Monetary Fund (IMF, or Fund) and the International Bank for Reconstruction and Development (or Bank). These groups were concerned with currency and investment problems associated with international trade; their mandates, on the whole, reflected American views. In 1946 the United States proposed an agency more directly concerned with commercial issues—an International Trade Organization (ITO), to be developed under the aegis of ECOSOC. Negotiations concerning ITO continued through 1948. The background of its proposed Charter, as finally drawn up, was described by the United States Department of State in these words: "The final charter naturally reflects the problems and aspirations of other countries, although it retains the essential provisions of the original United States draft."[13] This somewhat defensive statement, although accurate, reflected opposition within the United States;[14] and eventually it became apparent that the United States Congress would not ratify the Charter of this key agency for promoting international trade.

Despite this setback to American policy within the United Nations,

[13] U.S. Dept. of State, *United States Participation in the United Nations: Report by the President to the Congress for the Year 1949* (Dept. of State Publication 3765; Washington, D.C., Government Printing Office, 1950), 113. For a comprehensive analysis of the ITO Charter, see Clair Wilcox, *A Charter for World Trade* (New York, Macmillan, 1949).

[14] For an excellent account of the extent to which this opposition was vocal even during the negotiations on the Havana Charter, see Holbert N. Carroll, *The House of Representatives and Foreign Affairs* (Pittsburgh, University of Pittsburgh Press, 1958), 40–48.

activities in the field of international trade developed between 1946 and 1953 largely according to the American plan. The Fund and Bank were functioning soundly, if somewhat ponderously, under American guidance. Under a system of weighted voting, the United States held about one-third of the voting strength in each agency, and Americans held several high administrative posts. And while ITO died on the vine, another agency was able to carry forward some of the work which it had been designed to accomplish. This was the General Agreement on Tariffs and Trade (GATT), created during the negotiations on ITO. It represented, in American eyes, a step toward internationalizing the policy embodied in the United States Reciprocal Trade Agreements Acts. Under GATT's influence, tariffs and other barriers to trade were substantially reduced. The United Nations itself took a direct hand in promoting freer trade by activities regarding restrictive business practices and the movement of samples and advertising materials across national frontiers. "Free trade," in the full sense of the words, was still a long way off; but the steps taken in that direction prior to 1953 were generally in accord with American hopes and viewpoints.

By comparison, Soviet participation in the United Nations work to promote international trade was narrow and critical. Soviet doctrine stressed the goal of self-sufficiency for Communist states rather than the benefits of expanding multilateral trade. For the Soviet Union, international trade was a means of obtaining imports essential to its economic plans, and also a device for promoting its political aims.

Thus the Soviet Union refused, for the most part, to join or support the agencies created to further the Western concept of open trade. Although it had sent delegates to the Bretton Woods Conference where the Fund and Bank were established, it did not become a member of either agency. It did not even attend the conferences where the ITO Charter was drafted, nor those subsequently held under GATT. Most of the activities undertaken by the United Nations itself, the Soviet Union refused to support on the grounds that they were matters purely domestic. The economic data which it supplied for United Nations analysis was pitifully weak. Instead, it spent its time in bitter attacks against the West, even against the United Nations and its agencies. The Fund and Bank were alleged to be "tools of imperialism," and ITO and GATT, devices to ensure American domination of world markets. The principal target of Soviet attacks, however, was the Western system of controls on export of strategic goods to the Soviet bloc. The Soviet Union assailed these controls on every possible occasion, and sought to have the United Nations condemn them. On the whole, these efforts failed, both in altering the functioning of the bodies attacked and in establishing the Soviet viewpoint as a propaganda victory.

The one Soviet success in the field of international trade during these years was the establishment of an ECE Committee on the Development of Trade. This committee resulted from Soviet initiation, but even here the Soviet Union's success was qualified. While the Committee's mandate was revival and promotion of trade between eastern and western Europe, it never accepted the Soviet view that its function was to take a stand against the Western controls on the export of strategic goods. Nor did any other United Nations body ever condemn these controls.

The first activities of the United Nations in the field of economic development were groping and tentative. Other needs were pressing; the process of development was little understood; and the pressure, both economic and political, which was to come increasingly from underdeveloped nations was not felt as strongly during the United Nations first years.

Nevertheless, in 1947 a number of United Nations bodies began to study the problems involved in economic development, and to outline possible steps to facilitate the process in underdeveloped areas.

In its confrontation with the West, the Soviet Union had here a golden opportunity to further its own designs and interests in various parts of the world. It appeared at the outset ready to seize the occasion. At several points the Soviet delegates were able to insinuate in United Nations reports the idea that Western colonialism was responsible for economic backwardness, and that the Soviet Union provided a model for rapid industrialization and true economic policies.[15]

The underdeveloped countries, however, soon wanted more than rhetoric; they wanted concrete assistance. This pressure came to a head

[15] See, for example, ECOSOC Official Records, Ninth Session, Supplement No. 11A, "Report of the Second Session of the Sub-Commission on Economic Development." The best general analysis of Soviet policy in the United Nations with regard to economic development is Alvin Z. Rubinstein, "Soviet Policy toward Under-Developed States in the Economic and Social Council," *International Organization*, Vol. IX, No. 2 (May, 1955), 232–43.

at the Third Session of the General Assembly, which opened in September, 1948. As a result of the insistence of underdeveloped states three resolutions were passed. One established the United Nations program of technical assistance; a second provided for a training program in public administration; and the third set in motion a series of studies centering on the problem of financing economic development.

Shortly thereafter, the United States seized the initiative through a dramatic step which capped these developments. In accord with the well-publicized Point Four program proclaimed by President Truman in his inaugural address of January, 1949, the United States proposed, in the spring of that year at ECOSOC's Ninth Session, an Expanded Program of Technical Assistance, to be financed by voluntary contributions. This was to be the United Nations largest operational program, involving both the United Nations and several specialized agencies. EPTA got under way in 1950, and for the next two years the United States supported it with contributions amounting to about 60 per cent of the total. Despite the hope of the underdeveloped countries for capital grants and loans as a result of the President's declaration, EPTA was appreciated and the United States role in establishing and maintaining it was acclaimed.

The American action had caught the Soviet Union in a dilemma. The Soviet Union had not supported the regular technical assistance program established in 1948 because its position had not been accepted that costs should be borne by the recipient. It could not now object to EPTA's arrangement of voluntary contributions, nor could it take a stand of direct opposition to what was clearly a popular program with the underdeveloped states. On the other hand, it was hardly willing to concede American leadership with these nations. After taking little part in the discussion leading to EPTA's establishment, the Soviet Union finally voted in favor of it. However, as American delegates were delighted to point out, during the first three years of EPTA's operations, the Soviet Union did not contribute "one red ruble." In 1951, Soviet acquiescence changed to verbal nonsupport, and finally to open attack on EPTA.

This proved a major tactical defeat for the Soviets. From 1948 the increasing emphasis in all aspects of the United Nations economic and social work was toward problems of economic development. The Soviet failure to respond effectively to these problems created a barrier between it and those nations which were emerging not only with a strong voice in world affairs but also as a major battleground in the Cold War between East and West. The Soviet delegates' repeatedly expressed concern for the welfare of the underdeveloped countries came to have a hollow ring, and their charges about the imperialistic ambitions of the West and the pernicious effects of colonialism came to appear less and less relevant to the moment's needs.

Of course, not all currents were running against the Soviet Union. In the latter years of the period, trends appeared in the United Nations activities for economic development that were to cause uneasiness among influential businessmen in the West and create some rifts in the fabric of good will knitted by EPTA's program. The underdeveloped nations began to press more urgently for a United Nations agency to provide capital grants and loans on easy terms, a demand supported by the United Nations studies on problems of financing economic development. More critically, at the General Assembly's Seventh Session in 1952 these same states pushed through Resolution 626 (VII) which proclaimed the inherent right "of peoples freely to use and exploit their natural wealth and resources." The American financial community interpreted this as a repudiation of foreign investors' rights.[16]

Although this trend foreshadowed American retrenchment in the years to come, the Soviet Union was unable to capitalize on it at the moment. By 1952 it was almost universally recognized that Soviet participation in the United Nations economic and social work consisted essentially of using it as a forum in which to attack the West and thus to promote its own private ends. It was equally clear, probably even to the Soviet leaders, that this effort had failed. The period closed with the East in isolation and the West in an extremely strong position.

The winter of 1952–53 witnessed the beginning of changes, almost simultaneously, in both Soviet and American policy with respect to the

[16] After the Resolution was adopted in the Second Committee, Keith Funston, president of the New York Stock Exchange, sent Isador Lubin, United States representative on the Committee, a public letter which stated: "The Resolution serves notice on investors everywhere that rights of long standing will no longer be respected. Investors are told, in effect, that their investments will be subject to nationalization without compensation" (New York Stock Exchange Press Release, December 16, 1952). Although the resolution was modified before passage in Plenary Session, the attitude of American financial circles did not change.

United Nations economic and social activities. It cannot be said that either shift caused the other; both were the results of complex mixtures of external and internal forces and, among other things, changes in government leadership. The changes in Soviet policy were undoubtedly influenced also by its clear failure to achieve its aims prior to 1953 within the framework of the United Nations economic and social agencies. Whatever the causes, the effect was to increase the voice of the Soviet Union in these agencies, and to strengthen its position in comparison to that of the United States, whose policy (or practice) was in many ways one of reduced participation. Where the United States had ⟨ ⟩, it now began to restrain; and where the Soviet Union had rejected, ⟨ ⟩ow began to affirm with something more than words.

The reasons for policy shift in a closed society must always be conjectural to some extent. However, there are several likely explanations for the new developments in Soviet participation in the economic and social work of the United Nations and its affiliates in this field. No doubt the death of Stalin was important in betokening a general shift in strategy. But Soviet policy in the United Nations social and economic affairs began to shift before Stalin's death, and new viewpoints were at least foreshadowed in his last major work, *Economic Problems of Socialism in the USSR,* published in October, 1952.

By this time postwar economic reconstruction had been completed in the Soviet Union, and the nation had consolidated its power in the Soviet bloc. These accomplishments gave the Soviet Union greater maneuverability in its confrontation of the West. At the same time, the Soviet leaders had become increasingly aware of centrifugal forces in the West, and also of the divergent viewpoints of the West and the underdeveloped nations. Earlier Soviet policies, in striving to exploit these, had rather minimized them. Now the Soviet Union was prepared to learn from the experience. It was faced with the alternatives of complete withdrawal—abandoning the field—or changing its strategy. In many ways the costs of remaining in the arena were seen to be slight in comparison to withdrawal. The United Nations had not become the strong supranational organization in economic and social affairs that many had envisioned it would be, and against which Soviet policy had been directed. Increased participation now would not radically change the *status quo* in this respect, but would serve rather to give the Soviet Union new stature, especially in the eyes of the underdeveloped nations. And, given its earlier abstention, small contributions from the Soviet Union would now receive disproportionate attention and acclaim. Nor, in the light of developments in the economic and social field, would such participation endanger the Soviet Union's closed system or require surrender of important aspects of Soviet sovereignty. Moreover, even then the increasing role and importance of underdeveloped countries in the United Nations economic and social activities were becoming more and more apparent. Simultaneously, broader Soviet strategy was increasingly becoming focused on these countries. The two trends coincided. Thus may the Soviet leaders have reasoned; certain it is that they acted accordingly.

A new administration also took office in the United States in 1953. Whatever its broad policies, they had the effect of retrenchment in international commitments. One reason was the great emphasis on internal economic stability, viewed as a unilateral problem. Coupled with this was a lessening of American enthusiasm for the United Nations in the wake of the Korean War. And Congress' initial reaction to the increased Soviet participation was to cut back and limit American participation.[17] Finally, the new conservative temper in the United States saw in the growing activities of the United Nations in the field of social and economic relations a danger to traditional American patterns and beliefs, as well as a growing centralization of domestic power. One consequence of this temper, the Bricker Amendment concerning treaties and executive agreements, was defeated, but only at the cost of reversal of American policy in the United Nations, and subsequent loss of influence there.[18] Another policy change, taken in 1954, the decision to integrate all Department of State personnel into the foreign service, resulted in the loss of several key individuals in the Office of International Economic and Social Affairs, the agency responsible for preparing, and in some cases executing, American policy in this field. Their replacements, competent though they may have been, lacked experience and detailed knowledge of the United Nations and its procedures and prob-

[17] See Holbert N. Carroll, *The House of Representatives and Foreign Affairs*, 160.

[18] See U.S., 83 Cong., 1 sess., Senate Committee on the Judiciary, *Treaties and Executive Agreements: Hearings before a Subcommittee of the Committee on the Judiciary* (Washington, D.C., Government Printing Office, 1953), 825. Secretary of State John Foster Dulles told the Senate Committee that under the Eisenhower administration the United States would not become a party to any covenant dealing with human rights, and would not submit any such covenant to the Senate for ratification.

lems. Moreover, some of the individuals appointed by the the administration to posts in the United Nations economic and social agencies were of less stature than their predecessors. In sum, the United States effort in this work was less wholehearted at the very moment when the Soviet policy was gaining new effectiveness. American policy showed renewed vigor in 1957; but the opportunities afforded by the relative positions of the United States and the Soviet Union in 1952 had been largely lost.

The Soviet-American confrontation within the United Nations in the fields of social and economic welfare and human rights during the period since 1953 can be treated as a unit. Speaking generally, the work in these areas followed patterns already established, but the nature and extent of the two nations' participation became altered.

The new Soviet approach in these specific areas was one of joining agencies it had previously shunned and modifying its viewpoint on some issues, at least on the surface. In 1954 the Soviet Union rejoined the ILO and joined UNESCO. The following year it began to contribute to UNICEF, and in 1957 it resumed participation in WHO. The quantity and quality of its data furnished to United Nations agencies gradually improved. Without really altering essential policies, the Soviet delegates softened the tone of their debates with the West and were apparently ready to conciliate. An example of this was the altering of the earlier boast that under Communism drug addiction had been eliminated; now it was stated that the problem had been reduced to insignificant proportions.[19] Again, after rejoining ILO, the Soviet Union ratified several of the agency's conventions, including some which it had previously attacked.[20] It now claimed that it supported ILO's work concerning freedom of association, but argued that the concept needed expanding to take into account the different role of trade unions in Communist societies.

Concerning the issue of human rights, the great influx of African

[19] See United Nations Document E/NR. 1956/Summary, Commission on Narcotic Drugs, "Summary of Annual Reports Relating to Opium and Other Narcotic Drugs," 54.

[20] For analyses of Soviet policy in ILO, see Alfred P. Fernbach, *Soviet Coexistence Strategy: A Case Study of Experience in the International Labor Organization* (Washington, D.C., Public Affairs Press, 1960); and Harold Karan Jacobson, "The U.S.S.R. and ILO," *International Organization*, Vol. XIV, No. 3 (Summer, 1960), 402–28.

and Asian states into the United Nations, starting in 1955, placed the Soviet Union in a better position. Many of these states were violently anti-colonial and doubtful of the applicability of Western democratic institutions to their situations. In the Assembly it became more and more difficult to muster a two-thirds majority for Western positions on human rights, and the Soviet spokesmen skillfully exploited these difficulties.

Meanwhile, the United States had been cutting back the extent of its involvement in the fields of social and economic welfare, as well as losing ground in the debate over human rights. Both UNESCO and ILO were more openly criticized in the United States, and this was reflected for a time in official United States policy. In line with its new economic viewpoint, the United States contributed relatively smaller proportions of the budgets of the United Nations, of its programs such as UNICEF and EPTA, and of the specialized agencies. Although the United States proposed a new program in the field of human rights, its voice in this area was weakened by its announced rejection of covenants. Evidence of United States negativeness was added by its refusal to ratify the Convention on Genocide, or the Supplementary Convention on Slavery, the Slave Trade, and Institutions and Practices Similar to Slavery. For a while the American government would not even vote for the new ILO Convention on the Abolition of Forced Labor, although the convention was the result of an investigation instigated by the AF of L with government blessing.

Such evidence obscured for a time the fact that the United States was still affirmatively active in the United Nations economic and social work to a far greater degree than the Soviet Union. Starting in 1957, United States policy became more flexible respecting treaties, and American delegates again took leadership in proposing new programs for ILO, WHO, and other agencies. Still, the Soviet Union was in considerably better position in these fields in 1962 than it had been a decade earlier.

In the fields of international trade and economic development, changes in the Soviet–United States confrontation were still more pronounced. An economic offensive was one of the salient points of the new Soviet strategy, and its first signs appeared in the work of the United Nations.[21] There the Soviet Union actively sought to seize the

[21] For analyses of this, see Robert Loring Allen, *Soviet Economic Warfare* (Wash-

initiative in proposing programs of international trade, and in aligning its policies concerning economic development with the views of the underdeveloped countries. In contrast, American policy became rigid and even defensive.

The Soviet trade offensive in the United Nations began in the Economic Commission for Europe. Its earlier view of this agency had been one of suspicion regarding Western motives and resentment against any effort to pierce the Iron Curtain. At the same time, it had repeatedly expressed its desire to trade with the West and to break down the restrictions against export of strategic goods into its bloc. These irreconcilable approaches were altered in the economic offensive which began in January, 1953. Thereafter the Soviet Union successfully urged ECE to expand its activities with respect to East–West trade.[22] The most far-reaching Soviet proposals were offered at the Commission's Eleventh Session in 1956. These entailed formulation of an all-European economic agreement, creation of a subsidiary body to consider peaceful uses of atomic energy, and facilitation of increased contacts between countries of eastern and western Europe.[23] After modification, the last proposal was adopted; the others were tabled in effect, although they were returned to discussion in various forms at later sessions of ECE.

Increased contacts between East and West had now become a basic Soviet theme throughout the activities and agencies of the United Nations. As if to show its good faith, the Soviet Union made expansive gestures concerning world trade in general. In 1955, at the Twentieth Session of ECOSOC, it suddenly announced its support of the International Trade Organization, which it had previously attacked as a device for continued Western domination of world trade. Now the Soviet Union proposed that the Council appeal to member states to ratify ITO's Charter drawn at Havana.[24] Following defeat of this pro-

ington, D.C., Public Affairs Press, 1960); and Joseph S. Beriner, *Soviet Economic Aid: The New Aid and Trade Policy in Underdeveloped Countries* (New York, Harper and Brothers, 1958).

[22] See United Nations Document E/ECE/166; Michael L. Hoffman, "Problems of East-West Trade," *International Conciliation*, No. 511 (January, 1957), 259–308; and Harold Karan Jacobson, "The Soviet Union, the UN and World Trade," *The Western Political Quarterly*, Vol. XI, No. 3 (September, 1958), 673–88.

[23] United Nations Document E/ECE/243.

[24] ECOSOC Official Records, Twentieth Session, 77; and United Nations Document E/L. 677.

posal, the Soviet Union kept affirming its willingness to co-operate by suggesting at subsequent United Nations meetings the creation of a new world trade organization, the convocation of a world economic conference, and the convocation of a conference of experts. None of these were realized immediately, but they served to remind member nations of "the new Soviet look." And as time passed, the United Nations took actions which embodied at least some of the features of the Soviet proposals. For example: ECE convened meetings of senior economic advisers in March, 1961, and November, 1962; decisions were taken to convene a United Nations Conference on Trade and Development in early 1964, and progress was made on drafting a Declaration on International Economic Co-operation. All three issues involved long-sought Soviet objectives.

This new approach somewhat camouflaged the fact that the real purpose of Soviet policy had not been changed. Soviet affirmations were still accompanied by attacks, more subtle than before, on alleged discrimination in Western trade policies, and especially on the West's continuing controls against export of strategic goods to the Soviet bloc. The Soviet Union's attempts to establish new agreements under ECE respecting intra-European trade and uses of atomic energy were obviously designed as alternatives to the increasingly successful extra–United Nations developments of the European Economic Community (EEC) and the European Atomic Energy Community. And later the promise of co-operation in ECE was counterposed against the concept of the Organization for Economic Co-operation and Development (OECD). Nor did the Soviet intentions include any real embracing of world-wide multilateral trade.[25] The Soviet Union's attacks on the Fund, the Bank, and GATT were softened during this period; but it made no gesture toward these agencies. In short, the new Soviet trade policies implied that the United Nations should provide an umbrella for bilateral contacts which were designed to favor increased Soviet trade, rather than that the United Nations should serve as an instrument to further free multilateral trade.

Despite their restricted nature, the Soviet proposals created difficulties for the United States. They sounded better than their realization in action would show them to be; and in many ways they ran counter both to United States interests and the true development of world

[25] See ECE, *Economic Bulletin for Europe*, Vol. XI, No. 1 (June, 1959), 54–55.

trade. Thus the United States was obliged to vote against these proposals at times, although to do so appeared negative and selfish. At the same time, American delegates found it necessary to defend those agencies and policies which the Soviet Union was attacking in its broad economic offensive. Among these were the controls on exports of strategic goods, which the United States felt were vital to its security; the continued integration of western Europe's economy, the Organization for European Economic Co-operation (OEEC), and later, the Organization for Economic Co-operation and Development; and the activities of GATT in promoting the objective of free multilateral trade.

In taking a stand against the Soviet proposals concerning international trade, the United States sought to regain the initiative by introducing or supporting counterproposals, especially in ECOSOC and the General Assembly. However, its ability to do this was limited by its past failure to ratify ITO's Charter. And the internal disunity which had led to that impasse was evidenced once more when the United States Congress clearly indicated that it would also refuse to ratify a new agreement for a similar agency, the Organization for Trade Co-operation (OTC)—this despite the fact that the United States had taken the lead in proposing OTC. The United States even had reservations about the expansion of GATT to include nations from the Communist bloc. Yugoslavia and Poland were brought into association with GATT, but only with difficulty; and the divergent concepts of state-controlled and other economies created exceedingly complex problems within the agency. This, of course, was not the fault of the United States; but once again American caution was made to appear negative to the interests of world trade as a means of international co-operation.

The growing ferment among the underdeveloped countries also proved a source of trouble for the United States in this field. In 1954 these countries succeeded in having ECOSOC establish a Commission on International Commodity Trade (CICT). The "main task" of this Commission was, in the Resolution's terms, "to avoid excessive fluctuations in the prices of and the volume of trade in primary commodities, including measures aiming at the maintenance of a just and equitable relationship between the prices of primary commodities and the prices of manufactured goods in international trade."[26] The United States feared that under these terms of reference the Commission would

[26] ECOSOC Resolution 512A (VII).

inevitably recommend a world-wide system of price supports for commodities. This the United States was unwilling to countenance; consequently it voted against establishment of the Commission and refused to participate in its sessions. The Soviet Union, on the other hand, supported every proposal of the underdeveloped countries, publicly bewailed their plight, and suggested that their problems would be solved by long-term trade agreements with Communist countries. In 1958 the mandate of CICT was modified in such a way that the United States felt that it could participate in the Commission's work. However, this did not mask the fact that the United States was unwilling to endorse the steps favored by the underdeveloped countries. That the Soviet Union did not really favor them either was not so readily recognized.

With regard to the United Nations work in economic development the Soviet Union also did an about-face beginning in 1953. In this area, too, it gained improved position vis-à-vis the United States—not so much by its own initiative as by its obvious support of moves favored by the underdeveloped nations. The economic development programs were designed to benefit these countries; and they also became the center of the new, more subtle strategy on the part of the Soviet Union in its "coexistence" approach to world conflict.

The Soviet Union's announcement at ECOSOC's Sixteenth Session in July, 1953, that it would contribute four million rubles (one million dollars at the rate of exchange then in effect) to the Expanded Program of Technical Assistance removed a major barrier between the Soviet Union and the underdeveloped states.[27] Other actions followed in swift succession. The Soviet Union used various organs of the United Nations to publicize its new willingness to trade with and aid the underdeveloped countries.[28] In debate after debate, Soviet delegates offered industrial equipment and technical assistance to these countries, as well as attractive credit arrangements such as the possibility of repayment in local currencies. These offers were supported by concrete action outside the United Nations.

One of the chief contentions of the underdeveloped nations was the need for an agency which would provide capital grants and loans for

[27] ECOSOC Official Records, Sixteenth Session, 142.

[28] For a study of this in one organ, see Alvin Z. Rubinstein, "Soviet Policy in ECAFE: A Case Study of Soviet Behavior in International Economic Organizations," *International Organization*, Vol. XII, No. 4 (Autumn, 1958), 459–72.

economic development. This was expressed in a drive to create a Special United Nations Fund for Economic Development (SUNFED). The changing attitude toward this proposal was revealing. At first, the Soviet Union was as opposed to SUNFED as were the Western powers. Indeed, the speech in which Professor Arutiunian announced that the Soviet Union would contribute to the Expanded Program of Technical Assistance was primarily an attack on SUNFED. By the fall of 1953, however, the Soviet Union was willing to support a resolution concerning SUNFED at the General Assembly's Eighth Session, on the grounds that this was strongly desired by the underdeveloped nations. By 1956 acquiescence with reservations had yielded to active support for the establishment of SUNFED, and Soviet delegates announced that the Soviet Union would make a contribution to the agency.

Against the Soviets' tactical offensive in this area of growing political importance, the United States response was, until 1957, comparatively ineffectual. The United States was strongly opposed to the creation of SUNFED or any similar agency. Since the United States would inevitably be the principal contributor of funds, its viewpoint determined United Nations action; but it was a formal victory at the cost of prestige and leadership with the underdeveloped nations. To the American argument that it could not afford this financial commitment as long as the burden of armament remained a necessity, these nations turned an indifferent ear. They were engrossed in their own problems, and—in view of the new Soviet theme of co-existence—could not see the great need stressed by the United States. The establishment in 1956 of the International Finance Corporation to encourage "productive private enterprise in developing areas" fell far short of the aspirations of these countries; and even though the United States played a major part in establishing IFC, this was overshadowed by its rejection of SUNFED.

Thus, while the balance of economic power in United Nations affairs remained with the United States, the balance of political opinion swung for a time toward the interests of the Soviet Union. After a few years, however, the glitter of Soviet promises wore off, and at the same time American proposals became more positive in the eyes of other nations.

The Soviet contribution to EPTA proved over the long haul to be something less than its beginnings in 1953 had promised. Until 1960 the Soviet Union declined to increase its contribution to the program. Further, the original contribution was made in nonconvertible rubles, creating complications as to its use.[29] It could only be used for Soviet goods or the services of Soviet nationals; related administrative expenses such as travel costs had to be financed from other funds—i.e., with contributions from other nations. Since many underdeveloped countries seemed reluctant to accept the services of Soviet experts, the Soviet contribution stood largely idle for a time. Eventually ways were found to use the whole amount, but the solutions were not wholly satisfactory either to the Soviet Union or to the West. On the one hand, the Soviet Union agreed to make 25 per cent of its contributions available in convertible currencies for administrative expenses connected with its use. At the same time, urged by the United Nations Secretariat, more countries began to accept Soviet equipment; but they still showed little eagerness for Soviet experts. For example, of 3,739 United Nations experts in the field in 1961 under the Regular and Expanded Programs of Technical Assistance, only 71 were Soviet nationals, while 458 were Americans. Even Chile supplied 69.[30] And during that same year, out of 7,951 United Nations–sponsored fellowships, only 247 persons chose to study in the Soviet Union, 113 chose Chile, and 437 chose the United States.[31] While the West resented the fact that the United Nations Secretariat was "pushing" Soviet equipment, the Soviet Union was more embittered by the lack of response to its offers of experts and to opportunities for study within its borders. The underdeveloped countries hailed the new Soviet participation; but for the most part they sent their students to, and invited experts from, the Western nations.

Beginning in 1957 the American position in the broader work of economic development was also strengthened. The United States in that year countered the pressure for SUNFED by proposing creation of a different agency with a deceptively similar name—the Special Fund. Its functions were to be quite different from those envisaged for SUNFED. It would not make capital loans, but would rather supplement EPTA by financing longer-range and larger projects and thus making more funds available for underdeveloped countries. The Special Fund was

---

[29] See Robert Loring Allen, "United Nations Technical Assistance: Soviet and East European Participation," *International Organization*, Vol. XI, No. 4 (Autumn, 1957), 615–34.

[30] ECOSOC Official Records, Thirty-fourth Session, Supplement No. 5, "Annual Report of the Technical Assistance Board for 1961," 27–28.

[31] *Ibid.*, 37–39.

established in 1958. That same year, and in 1959, the United States proposed the expansion of the capital of the Fund and the Bank, the creation of an Inter-American Development Bank, and the establishment under the Bank of the International Development Association. Although these moves did not meet all of the objectives involved in the pressure for the creation of SUNFED, they did mean that there would be more money available for purposes of economic development, and the last two especially meant that some of it would be available on easier terms. The transformation of the Organization for European Economic Co-operation, in 1960 and 1961, into the Organization for Economic Co-operation and Development marked another step in the direction of increasing the flow of assistance from the "have" to the "have-not" nations. With the change in administration, the United States went even further by proclaiming the Alliance for Progress and suggesting that the 1960's be designated as the "United Nations Development Decade."

Even with these moves, however, the pressure for creation of SUNFED continued, although that title was dropped. The underdeveloped countries continued to seek the creation within the United Nations itself of a capital development fund, and in 1962 a special committee appointed by the Assembly over the opposition of the United States prepared a draft statute for such an agency. The interesting point is that at the Seventeenth Session of the General Assembly, despite their clear voting strength, the underdeveloped countries refrained from taking the next step and creating a capital development fund. Their restraint was at least partly a consequence of the positive steps which had been taken by the United States.

Along with the positive initiatives on the part of the United States, there came a growing realization that Soviet support of SUNFED or a capital development fund did not carry endorsement of the type of institution that the underdeveloped nations were seeking.[32] Among other things, it became clear that a Soviet contribution to such an agency

---

[32] A comprehensive exposition of the Soviet position with regard to SUNFED may be found in United Nations Document A/AC.83/L.1/Add.19. The differences between the Soviet position and that of the underdeveloped countries were made quite clear in 1962 discussions of the *ad hoc* committee—United Nations Documents (with reference to a Capital Development Fund) A/AC.102/SR.16, 4–5, 8; A/AC.102/SR.18, 8–9; A/AC.102/SR.23, 11.

would involve some of the same problems encountered in its participation in EPTA.

For all of these reasons, the relative status of the United States improved steadily after 1956 in the field of the United Nations work for economic development. This has also been true in the general activities of the United Nations economic and social programs. Nevertheless, the Soviet Union has greatly improved its position in these areas over the last decade. Most significantly, it succeeded in breaking out of its isolated position; and while its performance in the last years did not live up to the hopes created by its new policies inaugurated in 1953, its stance in the confrontation of East and West has been immeasurably strengthened during the period as a whole.

From the foregoing review of the Soviet-American confrontation in the United Nations economic and social activities and agencies, one fact must clearly emerge. At no time was there real opportunity for genuine and lasting co-operation between the two powers. Viewed from the standpoint of early hopes for economic and social harmony as the *point d'appui* toward political peace, this situation must be regarded as disappointing, if not as a downright failure.[33] Indeed, ECOSOC and the other institutions designed to further mutual aims in the realm of economic and social activity have been turned frequently, at least in the public meetings, into arenas for political and ideological warfare. Given the widespread divergencies of the modern world, this was probably inevitable, even though it has been decried by a number of statesmen and scholars. But in a world where international considerations have been dominated by the Cold War between East and West, it is futile to look back for what might have been. The United States–Soviet conflict in the United Nations is an actuality; and economic and social policies, as weapons of the Cold War, must recognize this.

Although the Soviet Union's tactics have changed, there is no real indication that its basic aims and attitudes regarding international co-operation have altered. It may be argued that the Soviet stance is a reactive one, since most of the United Nations economic and social work has been dominated by Western patterns and assumptions. However,

---

[33] From the Soviet point of view, of course, this failure was to be expected. As Alexander Dallin has pointed out, 'the Soviet Union has not indulged in any optimism with regard to 'functionalism' of 'welfare internationalism' through the U.N." *The Soviet Union at the United Nations* (New York, Praeger, 1962), 190.

it is the Soviets who have opposed these patterns; and the burden of proof that their revolution looks to generous ends has yet to be shown, in the face of a closed society ruled by totalitarian and repressive measures.

Faced with this condition and with uncertain prospects concerning its cessation, the United States must continue to view the economic and social activities of the United Nations in two ways: as a means to stronger co-operation and prosperity among the world's nations, and as a front along which to strengthen its own security. The two needs are necessarily related. Our continuing strength in the protracted conflict will depend in some measure upon the success of our mutual endeavors with other nations of the West and with the underdeveloped countries throughout the world. Concurrently, economic prosperity and social stability among the nations requires the free interplay of many forces in an open society. This could not be preserved in a world dominated by the Soviet system and ideology. It is also possible that the United Nations economic and social activities—especially those of ECE—can have some usefulness within the framework of a policy designed to encourage evolution within the Soviet bloc.

The openness of democratic society sometimes places the Western nations at a disadvantage in comparisons with the Soviet bloc, particuuarly in the view of the newly emergent countries which stand between the two. In the world forum, the faults of an open society are more easily seen. Moreover, the pluralistic nature of Western society leaves it more susceptible to pressures, natural or artificially stimulated, that tend to split it apart. Yet these are conditions that should not be otherwise; and in the spotlight of the United Nations as a forum, they can be turned to advantage. Indeed they have been, in some of the most promising economic and social developments of the postwar period. The need, in face of the Soviet threat, to find common modes of action has led to real co-operation among the non-Communist countries, especially in Europe. Many of the specialized agencies have seen similar co-operation within the framework of the United Nations. And real work in aiding the underdeveloped countries has been done in the face of opposing pressure.

Despite Soviet tactics, the United Nations offers many opportunities for constructive work toward solving economic and social problems. The challenge facing the United States is to assume positive leadership in this work. This it has done in the past. In the period immediately following 1947 the Marshall Plan and the Point Four program were inaugurated; and within the United Nations the regional economic commissions were created, and the Expanded Program of Technical Assistance begun. Since 1957 there have been hopeful signs of similar steps. But regardless of past successes or failures, American efforts cannot afford to flag. When the United States has assumed leadership in advancing positive, forward-looking programs, it has gained ground on the economic and social front. By definition, the protracted conflict is a condition of indefinite duration. The United States can do much to reduce its effects and, indeed, to ensure the triumph of democratic values by using the opportunities provided by the economic and social work of the United Nations.

CHAPTER X

Conclusion

BY FRANZ B. GROSS

THE PRECEDING PAGES have presented a critical analysis of the United Nations based on its performance. All of the authors have reached the conclusion that the United Nations has become an intrinsic part of United States foreign policy. The question, therefore, is no longer whether to support the organization or to leave it, but how to advance the aims of United States foreign policy in and through the United Nations.

To establish an effective United States foreign policy in the United Nations it is necessary to clarify the objectives which we seek to attain within it and to set some standards by which the performance of the United States can be measured.

The first and foremost aim of the United States is the achievement of a just and honorable peace. Since the United States is not interested in the acquisition of new territories, a just peace depends on peaceful settlements of disputes which, in turn, hinge on the observance of international law.

Before any community abides by enforceable law, it must agree upon what the law is. In the international world of the mid-twentieth century the problem is *what* law, or *whose* law.

International law as it is known today is a combination of Judaic, Greek, Roman, British, French, and other Western concepts; most members of the United Nations did not even exist while that body of law was being evolved, had no part in its making, and have neither approved nor disapproved it. Even if these new states were ready to approve some body of enforceable law, they would have little chance of imposing it upon the world at large until the Great Powers dropped those cautious reservations which, thus far, have hedged their commitment to a law enforceable against any and all states. Both the United

States and the Soviet Union made it quite clear in San Francisco in 1945 that their interest in endowing the United Nations with the power to make enforceable law was, to say the least, limited. The two biggest powers rejected any procedure for amendment of the Charter that did not include their individual approval; nor was the International Court of Justice automatically to have jurisdiction over disputes in which the United States was involved. In the United States, the strength of the opposition to binding undertakings manifested itself in the Connally Amendment to the Senate's acceptance of compulsory jurisdiction of the Court in August, 1946. In refusing to vest in the Court jurisdiction over any legal dispute which the United States considered to be a domestic matter, the United States was saying in effect: "The International Court of Justice shall not decide any dispute except in those areas where we want international jurisdiction."

Although the Connally reservation was a blow to those who hoped that the United Nations would speed the codification and development of international law, the United States was spared the trouble of refuting its critics. The Soviet Union refused to accept any compulsory jurisdiction of the Court whatsoever and agreed only to accept the mediation by the international organization.

Different as may be their motivations, the Soviet Union and the United States are not alone in their refusal to establish common rules of international law. The simple fact is that the members of the United Nations are not yet ready to accept the rule of international law, except in special cases, and are even less inclined to furnish the means for enforcing it.

Under such circumstances, what should be the role of the United States in questions bearing upon the development of international law? The American system of freedom is based on the principle of due process of law, and the only kind of world community in which Americans would want to live would be a community regulated by due process of law. But that kind of a world community does not yet exist. What does exist is a United Nations in which many governments, though not all, are striving to create the same kind of universal community, regulated by law, to which the United States aspires. Here the United States should be able to provide the leadership which it has thus far rejected. In the protracted conflict the United States has shown itself far more observant of law than has the Soviet Union. But this is not enough, for in matters of ethics a double standard prevails: the rest of the world expects more from the United States and the Western powers than it does from the Soviet Union. This double standard troubles many people, but it is probably as great a compliment to Western civilization as Asia and Africa can possibly pay. However, it does create very real policy and strategy problems.

As first steps to assure the world of its good faith and support for the high ethical principles of law that it espouses, the United States should undertake some practical moves. Nothing would give better support to the American concept of due process of law, or show more clearly the difference between the United States and the Soviet Union's ideas of the relationship between ethics and law, than the repeal of the Connally Amendment. As long as the United States refuses to permit the Court to adjudicate any international legal dispute in which the United States is involved, there will remain in the minds of many grave doubts concerning the sincerity of American pretensions. As a second step, the genocide convention should be removed from its pigeonhole and placed before the Senate for its ratification. When the Senate of the United States refuses to approve as innocuous a convention as this, it is not difficult to understand why some members of the United Nations wonder if there is a difference between what Americans say they believe and what they are willing to do. In an organization still seeking agreement upon basic legal principles, the most important step for the United States is to see that its deeds conform to its words.

In surveying the difficulty of establishing a common rule of law and developing a set of rules acceptable to all, we may consider for a moment the importance of the Charter.

The United Nations Charter, which is essentially based on Western—and in particular on American—concepts, is considered by some as a constitution and by others as a multilateral treaty. The designation is really not important. In fact, the Charter is a binding legal document, signed and ratified by all states of the world except Switzerland, three divided states (Germany, Korea, and Vietnam), and Communist China. While it is not to be expected that all states will fully comply with all its provisions, it has become the accepted standard for international behavior and as such implements the main aspiration of American foreign policy.

In essence, the Charter guarantees stability and the *status quo*, with enough flexibility to permit, outside of the Communist bloc, self-determination to take its proper course.

As we read in Chapter VI above, the United Nations has succeeded in playing a leading part in the settlement of nearly all disputes and in the establishment of self-determination and independence for a substantial part of the globe.

While the latter function—assisting new nations in gaining independence—is in the process of self-liquidation, the function of peace-keeping still finds the United Nations groping for effective procedures.

One example of how the United Nations seeks to keep peace and thus serves American interest is the Congo incident. Deputy Assistant Secretary of State Richard N. Gardner in a recent article described how the first appeal of the newly independent Congo for United States troops was refused in order to avoid giving the Soviet Union an excuse and occasion for a competitive intervention in Africa.

> Kasavubu and Lumumba then sent a second appeal—this time to the United Nations. . . . The alternatives open to the United States, therefore, were clear:
>
> We could do nothing—in which case the Congo would wallow in chaos and bloodshed and the Soviet bloc would be free to move in to pick up the remains.
>
> We could intervene directly—and trigger a confrontation which could lead to another "Spanish Civil War" and be the prelude to a wider conflict.
>
> Or we could do what we in fact did—propose that assistance to the Congo be given through the United Nations.
>
> No one pretends that the United Nations operation in the Congo has been an unqualified success. How could it have been, when 20,000 troops from 21 different countries, speaking different languages and following different military traditions, sought to keep order in a country one-third the size of the United States with no effective public administration or basic services?
>
> The test of the Congo operation is not whether it achieved some imaginary standard of peace-keeping excellence. It is whether the operation resulted in a situation better than would have occurred through the use of any available alternative.[1]

[1] Speech at a meeting of Lowell House Visitors Series, *Harvard Today* (Spring, 1963).

The emphasis which Mr. Gardner placed on the value of the peace-keeping operation reflected a previous statement by President Kennedy:

> In the world we seek, the United Nations Emergency Forces which have been hastily assembled, uncertainly supplied and inadequately financed will never be enough.
>
> Therefore, the United States recommends that all member nations earmark special peace-keeping units in their armed forces—to be on call of the United Nations—to be specially trained and quickly available—and with advance provision for financial and logistic support.
>
> In addition, the American delegation will suggest a series of steps to improve the United Nations' machinery for the peaceful settlement of disputes—for on-the-spot fact-finding, mediation and adjudication—for extending the rule of international law. For peace is not solely a matter of military or technical problems—it is primarily a problem of politics and people.[2]

From the above statements it seems clear that the Kennedy administration considered one of the functions of the United Nations to be that of offering an alternative to direct United States military involvement in international affairs. Obviously, it was not the policy of the administration to solve all problems through the United Nations or to restrict military action, in defense of American interests, to the United Nations.

The important question confronting us can be put as follows: "What role do we actually expect the United Nations to play in the future?" Senator Henry M. Jackson answers:

> The United Nations is not, and was never intended to be, a substitute for our own leaders as makers and movers of American policy. The shoulders of the Secretary-General were never expected to carry the burdens of the President or the Secretary of State.[3]

Operating from this assumption the Senator declared:

> The truth is, though we have not often spoken it in recent years, that the best hope for peace with justice does not lie in the United Nations. Indeed, the truth is almost exactly the reverse. The best hope for the United Nations lies in the maintenance of peace. In our deeply divided

[2] An address to the United Nations, September 25, 1961. (See Appendix I in this volume.)

[3] "The U.S. in the U.N.: An Independent Audit," an address before the National Press Club, March 20, 1962. (See Appendix II in this volume.)

world, peace depends on the power and unity of the Atlantic Community and on the skill of our direct diplomacy.[4]

There is no question that the United Nations can take the place of the alliance system that the United States has built up over the years. The interests of our allies all over the world, but especially in western Europe, must be given at least the same priority as our stakes in the United Nations.

Perhaps the dichotomy of our allegiance to the Charter and of our alliance policies need not weigh quite as heavily upon our conscience as Senator Jackson tells us they should. Undersecretary of State George H. Ball took a more sanguine view:

> In view of the need for different instruments to serve the diverse purposes of our foreign policy, I find the suggestion quite curious that, by seeking to use NATO or the OECD as a means of cooperation with our European friends, we are somehow turning our back on the U.N. I find equally curious that belief that in seeking to work within the United Nations we are betraying our friendship with our Atlantic partners.[5]

Indeed, the United States need not make a categorical choice between its NATO allies and the United Nations. Loyalty to our allies does not rule out an active and loyal participation in the United Nations. Both are instruments and objectives of United States foreign policy, and to support one does not automatically rule out support of the other.

As a matter of fact, a good case can be made on grounds of morality as well as expediency that the United States, while leading the Atlantic Alliance, should seek to identify with the United Nations as closely as possible. NATO and the United Nations exist for different purposes. It is for its inherent purpose that each merits our support.

The value of our partnership with western Europe needs no defense; it constitutes the backbone of the Free World, the main obstacle to the Communist bid for global domination, and the principal defender and champion of the ideals of free men everywhere. It should be obvious that the United Nations, since it includes Communist and neutralist members, cannot fill the same purpose as the Atlantic Alliance. The United Nations, by its very composition, imposes limits on the range

[4] *Ibid.*

[5] "The United Nations and the Real World," an address to a foreign-policy briefing conference, March 26, 1962. (See Appendix III in this volume.)

of United States decision-making. We need not "turn our back" on the United Nations; it fills specific and important needs of the United States. Mr. Ball, with commendable realism, drew this distinction:

> It is true that the United Nations cannot, by itself, maintain the peace between the major powers. It is equally true that NATO was not qualified to supervise the peaceful change from colonialism to independence. Their roles are quite different and distinct. Each is essential, and therefore we support each for different reasons.[6]

The advantages of our alliance system around the globe and the emphasis which we must continue to place on it should be apparent to our people, to our allies, and to all free nations. Let us examine briefly the advantages of the United Nations to United States foreign policy.

First, the United Nations provides a channel for continuous diplomatic communications with all the other 112 members of the organization, including the Soviet Union. Thus, it provides both formal and informal contacts between all members of the world community on such important problems as arms control and economic assistance. Especially worth while are the day-by-day contacts with the Soviet Union, the only other nation, besides ourselves, with enough nuclear power to destroy a large portion of the globe.

Second, to quote Secretary of State Dean Rusk, the United Nations is "a school for understanding—the understanding which reaches beyond a sense of passing amiability, and establishes its roots in a more accurate knowledge of nations who are otherwise strangers to each other."[7] In this sense the United Nations serves a highly relevant purpose in our policy vis-à-vis the underdeveloped areas; it identifies our interests with their interests and demonstrates the sincerity of our friendship toward them. Through the United Nations we can extend various types of assistance to the newly independent states, thus contributing to their social betterment and economic development.

Third, the United Nations provides respite in moments of international crises. When both sides harden their stands on issues highly charged with emotion, the United Nations affords the balm of reflection and second sober thought. At the same time, the "presence" of the United Nations in certain areas of tension and danger provides an

[6] *Ibid.*

[7] An address before the Ninth Annual Conference on International Affairs, February 22, 1963. (See Appendix IV in this volume.)

international "shock absorber," thus dampening local violence which might easily escalate into all-out war.

Finally, again quoting Secretary Rusk:

> It [the United Nations] fosters the steady growth of law—the law which enlarges our area of freedom by reducing, through predictable conduct, the chances of harsh collisions as sovereign states pursue their eccentric orbits. . . . It keeps before us the constant reminders of the unfinished business of the human race: peace, safety, human dignity, prosperity—and the freedom which is our own most basic commitment.[8]

The United Nations does have a vital part to play in the future conduct of United States foreign policy.

To many sincere individuals the United Nations is the closest step toward the ultimate goal of world government. James Henderson of the University of London writes:

> During the last two thousand years quite a few civilizations have risen and fallen, and today, for the first time in human history it is a question of world civilization or no civilization, world government or no government, which means international chaos, global war and race suicide.[9]

The vision of a universal world state where all member nations would unite in peace is a noble ideal. It is precisely the schism over values which impedes its realization. The absence so far of a world government is not so much a *cause* of world tension as it is a *symptom* of prevailing conditions. Until these conditions change for the better, any scheme for the establishment of world government remains utopian. The Iron Curtain—as long as it bars international co-operation and the free movement of peoples and ideas, not to speak of vital agencies of the United Nations itself—obstructs the coming of the true universal government.

The world federalists and other groups seem to receive some support from the Encyclical *Pacem in Terris*. Pope John XXIII asserted that the political problems facing the human race are of such dimensions that they cannot be tackled or solved except on a world-wide basis. It was his earnest wish that the United Nations both in structure and means become transfigured into a genuine world political community. Yet the encyclical seemed to pass over the rending spiritual and philosophical cleavage separating the Communist-controlled nations from the rest

[8] *Ibid.*

[9] As quoted in Chesly Manly, *The U.N. Record* (Chicago, Regnery, 1955), 179.

of the world community. Until this wide gap is closed, the United Nations is not likely to develop into a world state.

Perhaps the best that we can hope for during the next few decades is the promotion within the framework of the United Nations of the continued growth of regional and functional organizations. Statesmen all over the world have seemed to recognize the need for wider associations, and the difficulties of universal organization have induced them to form regional organizations. The nations of the Western Hemisphere were the first to organize regionally in 1948 with the foundation of the Organization of American States. In 1949, when western Europe and the United States realized the need for unity to prevent further Communist penetrations, the North Atlantic Treaty Organization was formed. Then followed the OECD, the Council of Europe, and finally, the Common Market. An Atlantic partnership would become the most powerful and the widest of regional arrangemnts. In 1963 the African states formed their own organization, the Organization of African Unity.

While some distinguished Americans plead for more support of the United Nations, other Americans, no less distinguished than Herbert Hoover, are calling for greater reliance on our allies than on the United Nations:

> If the free nations are to survive they must have a new and stronger world-wide organization to meet this [Communist] menace. . . . it may be called the Council of Free Nations. It should include all those nations who are willing to stand up and fight for their freedom and independence.[10]

This type of a council would not, in the former President's eyes, replace the United Nations, but would step in only "when the U.N. is prevented from taking action, or if it fails to act to preserve the peace."[11]

The United Nations may be the "transitional phase" to a world community. But regionalism, not internationalism, is the "wave of the immediate future." It seems clear, however, that we are not faced with the question of choosing either the United Nations or regional groupings. We should continue to support the United Nations as much as we can in a "disunited" world; but, for the time being, our very security depends on our partnership with western Europe, Latin America, SEATO, and our other allies the world over.

[10] Herbert Hoover, Dedication Speech, August 11, 1962.   [11] *Ibid.*

The development of regional groupings throughout the world does not run counter to the United Nations. The need for such groupings is acknowledged by the United Nations Charter. If the groupings abide by the general principles of the United Nations they can provide the world body with that strengthened foundation which will sustain it in its passage through the present, the transitional stage.

The advanced industrial nations of the Free World, whose ethical-legal traditions are enshrined in the Charter of the United Nations, have a special responsibility to concert their power and thus reassert their political influence upon the course of world history. Given the actual world division, the time is not ripe for one political framework which encompasses all of *civitas humana*. The United Nations cannot give more than it has been given by its makers: The United Nations, a common forum, provides a platform and a quasi-parliamentary organization to discuss, debate, and, if possible, adjust the interests of many nations with the common denominator of universal society.

One common denominator already transcends all borders and all "curtains"—namely, the determination to achieve an improved economic and social lot for mankind. Both East, West, and uncommitted sincerely avow their devotion to this cause. The conflict is one of system, not of aim. The role of the United Nations and its agencies in technical and economic assistance has been considerable. Under its aegis, it is the United States which has proved to be foremost in the ranks of those ready to assist the poorer nations.

Indeed, so successful was the United States in winning this phase of the protracted conflict that the Soviet Union had to reverse its policy of noncontribution to voluntary economic and social programs, such as the Expanded Program of Technical Assistance.

Anything that the United Nations does to improve the living standards in a country tends to strengthen an uncommitted government and make it less susceptible to Communist infiltration. The Soviet Union has complained that the United Nations found it difficult to spend its contribution in rubles. Few members cared to accept, together with the rubles, Soviet technicians and experts. Even when they did not have to choose between rubles and hard currencies, members have been shy of accepting Soviet or other Communist technicians. The Soviet Union has complained, too, of the large number of American technicians used by United Nations agencies. Unwittingly, the Soviets conceded to the

United States an important victory in the protracted conflict in the United Nations—a victory that, though it was neither planned nor foreseen, justified the United States contribution to the various technical assistance programs.

It has been argued that this victory has cost dearly: that the United States has paid about half the entire bill, as compared to the Soviet Union's contribution of about 5 percent.[12] Be that as it may; compared with other types of United States foreign spending, the United States financial stake in United Nations technical assistance programs is a mere pittance.

The leadership supplied by the United States in the economic and social fields declined when the Soviet Union began, in 1953, to move into the business of supplying economic assistance to uncommitted nations. One aspect of the problem is what has been termed the "revolution of rising expectations." Great numbers of people in the underdeveloped lands have been led to believe that it is possible to bring about rapidly very substantial improvement in their living conditions. They have learned a little of what has been accomplished in the United States and even in the Soviet Union, and can see no reason why they should not only expect but secure improved standards of living. They either discount or are not aware of the fact that the living standards in the United States developed over a long period of time and, in the Soviet Union, were achieved only at very heavy sacrifice and suffering. Rightly or wrongly, the underdeveloped half of the world expects the developed half to provide substantial assistance in equalizing their standards of living.

Before 1953 members of the United Nations had reason to believe that the United States, and not the Soviet Union, was interested in helping them realize their respective "revolutions of rising expectations." Since 1953, however, the United States has argued against the creation of the Special United Nations Fund for Economic Development and has tried to reduce the scope of other economic aid measures.

Soviet tactics suggest that the United States strategy in debates on economic and social matters in the United Nations should be to initiate proposals, or support at least some of those made by the underdeveloped

---

[12] This figure includes both contributions to voluntary programs and assessments for the regular budget of the United Nations, but excludes the budgets of the specialized agencies.

countries. When it comes to raising funds, the United States, instead of claiming that it cannot afford further contributions, thus playing into the Soviets' hands, should propose specific sums for different categories of members—the United States and the Soviet Union always to subscribe the largest contribution. This initiative would place the Soviet Union in the position of having to "put up or shut up." If it paid, which is not likely, the money so contributed would be used to strengthen uncommitted nations against Communist influence. If it refused to pay, the onus of failure of a projected program would fall on the Soviet Union and not on the United States.

The new dimension of the United Nations is not only the development of international law, the peace-keeping machinery, and the settlement of disputes but also the implementation of a world-wide policy of economic and social development. In this area the United Nations family—that is, the Economic and Social Council and the regional commissions as well as the specialized agencies—have been an effective alternative for direct United States technical assistance.

The United Nations has broadened its parliamentary process. Previously, the diplomatic approach was essentially bilateral, although the international-conference method had its origins in the nineteenth century. Through the development of the United Nations and the creation of a permanent General Assembly in New York, voting behavior has assumed a new importance.

The 113 members of the United Nations have become organized into groups, caucuses, and blocs. The United States is one of four countries still not formally integrated into any one group. Voting behaviors vary from group to group—the Soviet bloc always votes as a unit, while the Afro-Asian group rarely casts a solid vote on any issue except colonialism. In the opinion of some, the United States has gained advantage by staying outside the groups. Yet it would seem that now the point has been reached when the United States should assert itself as chief spokesman for a large group of nations, based not necessarily on geographical limits. Once aserted, such leadership would lessen the danger of irresponsible voting, a mischievous practice which, more than any other failings of the membership, weakens and might undermine altogether United States adherence to the United Nations.

To this end, the United States should strongly advocate changes or modification of the rules of procedure so that more weight would be given to the views of responsible states. The president of the Seventeenth Session of the General Assembly, Muhammad Zafrulla Khan, assisted by his training as a lawyer and his experience as a judge of the International Court of Justice, was able to raise the level of conduct of the Assembly as a whole merely by enforcing many of the existing rules of procedure.

All in all, there is ample justification for contending that, in today's world, the United Nations fulfills a useful and, indeed, vital function and that it is likely to be a key instrument of American policy in the future. In the first place, were the United States to leave the United Nations, it would but abandon the organization to the machinations of the Soviet Union. Secondly, the United Nations has grown into its role—that of a trustee of the security of all nations. The members have become accustomed to the club, no matter how little they may like some of its rules and formalities. Not one of the least compelling of the reasons which prompt most states to stay, for better or for worse, with the United Nations is the instability of the sovereign state in a shrunken and unquiet world.

Technological developments in weapons and communications have created a situation in which, with the questionable exception of the two nuclear giants, no independent state can any longer give a reasonable assurance of security to its citizens. Yet, at the same time, national loyalties still furnish the common basis of our state system. The continued belief of peoples in the superiority of "their" state over all other legal entities is still the keystone of international politics.

To this dilemma—the insufficiency of the state along with continued, even growing, nationalism—institutional internationalism seems to supply the only saving solutions. The dilemma, since it is embedded in the conflict of system over power and values, is likely to baffle the world for a long time. In the interim, the only, though narrow, bridge to amelioration and adjustment short of war is the United Nations system. The United Nations provides at least the opportunity for discussion of issues, for resolutions for settlement, and for maintaining a peace-keeping force to be sent to marginal areas of trouble.

The United Nations, being the least evil in most conflicts, is likely to survive despite refusals by one state or another to support it over individual issues. Its dynamic is likely to gain momentum since, for practical purposes, it has responded to the national interest of the United

States and of the West, without driving the Soviets into a position in which they would have chosen to leave the United Nations to the exclusive care of the United States and the West.

The United Nations has passed from crisis to crisis. The financial and ideological strains upon its structures have been magnified by the influx of newly independent nations. Yet it is likely that the new nations will adjust themselves to international realities, adopting a position akin to that of India in the 1960's, rather than succumbing to the siren song of the Soviets. President Kennedy, speaking to the United Nations on September 21, 1963, voiced his deep concern with the travails of "emergent nationhood." He said:

> I hope that not only our Nation but all other multi-racial societies will meet these standards of fairness and justice. We are unalterably opposed to apartheid and all forms of human oppression. We do not advocate the rights of black Africans in order to drive out white Africans. Our concern is the right of all men to equal protection and opportunity; and since human rights are indivisible, this body cannot stand aside when those rights are abused or neglected by any member state.

The wisdom and forcefulness of United States leadership are, therefore, the strongest guarantees for the continuity of a trend which aligns the United Nations with the United States broad interest. Only continual critical analysis, adroit diplomacy, and devotion to freedom and social progress under law will enable the United States to retain its place as the most purposeful and exemplary, hence the most influential, member of the United Nations.

An *Address* to the United Nations

BY PRESIDENT JOHN F. KENNEDY[1]

MR. PRESIDENT, *honored delegates, ladies and gentlemen:*

We meet in an hour of grief and challenge. Dag Hammarskjold is dead. But the United Nations lives. His tragedy is deep in our hearts, but the task for which he died is at the top of our agenda. A noble servant of peace is gone. But the quest for peace lies before us.

The problem is not the death of one man—the problem is the life of this organization. It will either grow to meet the challenge of our age—or it will be gone with the wind, without influence, without force, without respect. Were we to let it die—to enfeeble its vigor—to cripple its powers—we would condemn the future.

For in the development of this organization rests the only true alternative to war—and war appeals no longer as a rational alternative. Unconditional war can no longer lead to unconditional victory. It can no longer serve to settle disputes. It can no longer concern the great powers alone. For a nuclear disaster, spread by winds and waters and fear, could well engulf the great and the small, the rich and the poor, the committed and the uncommitted alike. Mankind must put an end to war—or war will put an end to mankind.

So let us here resolve that Dag Hammarskjold did not live—or die—in vain. Let us call a truce to terror. Let us invoke the blessings of peace. And, as we build an international capacity to keep peace, let us join in dismantling the national capacity to wage war.

II.

This will require new strength and new roles for the United Nations. For disarmament without checks is but a shadow—and a community without law is but a shell. Already the United Nations has become both

---

[1] An address delivered in New York City on September 25, 1961.

the measure and the vehicle of man's most generous impulses. Already it has provided—in the Middle East, in Asia, in Africa this year in the Congo—a means of holding violence within bounds.

But the great question which confronted this body in 1945 is still before us—whether man's cherished hopes for progress and peace are to be destroyed by terror and disruption—whether the "foul winds of war" can be tamed in time to free the cooling winds of reason—and whether the pledges of our Charter are to be fulfilled or defied: pledges to secure peace, progress, human rights and world law.

In this Hall, there are not three forces, but two. One is composed of those who are trying to build the kind of world described in Articles I and II of the Charter. The other, seeking a far different world, would undermine this organization in the process.

Today of all days our dedication to the Charter must be maintained. It must be strengthened, first of all, by the selection of an outstanding civil servant to carry forward the responsibilities of the Secretary General—a man endowed with both the wisdom and the power to make meaningful the moral force of the world community. The late Secretary General nurtured and sharpened the United Nations obligation to act. But he did not invent it. It was there in the Charter. It is still there in the Charter.

However difficult it may be to fill Mr. Hammarskjold's place, it can better be filled by one man rather than by three. Even the three horses of the Troika did not have three drivers, all going in different directions. They had only one—and so must the United Nations executive. To install a triumvirate, or any rotating authority, in the United Nations administrative offices would replace order with anarchy, action with paralysis, and confidence with confusion.

The Secretary General, in a very real sense, is the servant of the General Assembly. Diminish his authority and you diminish the authority of the only body where all nations, regardless of power, are equal and sovereign. Until all the powerful are just, the weak will be secure only in the strength of this Assembly.

Effective and independent executive action is not the same question as balanced representation. In view of the enormous change in membership in this body since its founding, the American delegation will join in any effort for the prompt review and revision of the composition of United Nations bodies.

But to give this organization three drivers—to permit each great power to decide its own case—would entrench the Cold War in the headquarters of peace. Whatever advantages such a plan may hold out to my own country, as one of the great powers, we reject it. For we far prefer world law, in the age of self-determination, to world war, in the age of mass extermination.

III.

Today, every inhabitant of this planet must contemplate the day when this planet may no longer be habitable. Every man, woman and child lives under a nuclear sword of Damocles, hanging by the slenderest of threads, capable of being cut at any moment by accident or miscalculation or by madness. The weapons of war must be abolished before they abolish us.

Men no longer debate whether armaments are a symptom or a cause of tension. The mere existence of modern weapons—ten million times more powerful than anything the world has ever seen, and only minutes away from any target on Earth—is a source of horror, and discord and distrust. Men no longer maintain that disarmament must await the settlement of all disputes—for disarmament must be a part of any permanent settlement. And men may no longer pretend that the quest for disarmament is a sign of weakness—for in a spiraling arms race, a nation's security may well be shrinking even as its arms increase.

For 15 years this organization has sought the reduction and destruction of arms. Now that goal is no longer a dream—it is a practical matter of life or death. The risks inherent in disarmament pale in comparison to the risks inherent in an unlimited arms race.

It is in this spirit that the recent Belgrade Conference—recognizing that this is no longer a Soviet problem or an American problem, but a human problem—endorsed a program of "general, complete and strictly an internationally controlled disarmament." It is in this same spirit that we in the United States have labored this year, with a new urgency, and with a new, now-statutory agency fully endorsed by the Congress, to find an approach to disarmament which would be so far-reaching yet realistic, so mutually balanced and beneficial, that it could be accepted by every nation. And it is in this spirit that we have presented with the agreement of the Soviet Union—under the label both nations now accept of "general and complete disarmament"—a new statement of newly-agreed principles for negotiation.

But we are well aware that all issues of principle are not settled—and that principles alone are not enough. It is therefore our intention to challenge the Soviet Union, not to an arms race, but to a peace race—to advance together step by step, stage by stage, until general and complete disarmament has been achieved. We invite them now to go beyond agreement in principle to reach agreement on actual plans.

The program to be presented to this assembly—for general and complete disarmament under effective international control—moves to bridge the gap between those who insist on a gradual approach and those who talk only of the final and total achievement. It would create machinery to keep the peace as it destroys the machines of war. It would proceed through balanced and safeguarded stages designed to give no state a military advantage over another. It would place the final responsibility for verification and control where it belongs—not with the big powers alone, not with one's adversary or one's self—but in an international organization within the framework of the United Nations. It would assure that indispensable condition of disarmament—true inspection—and apply it in stages proportionate to the stage of disarmament. It would cover delivery systems as well as weapons. It would ultimately halt their production as well as their testing, their transfer as well as their possession. It would achieve, under the eye of an international disarmament organization, a steady reduction in forces, both nuclear and conventional, until it has abolished all armies and all weapons except those needed for internal order and a new United Nations Peace Force. And it starts that process now, today, even as the talks begin.

In short, general and complete disarmament must no longer be a slogan, used to resist the first steps. It is no longer to be a goal without means of achieving it, without means of verifying its progress, without means of keeping the peace. It is now a realistic plan, and a test—a test of those only willing to talk and a test of those willing to act.

Such a plan would not bring a world free from conflict or greed—but it would bring a world free from the terrors of mass destruction. It would not usher in the era of the super state—but it would usher in an era in which no state could annihilate or be annihilated by another.

In 1945, this Nation proposed the Baruch Plan to internationalize the atom before other nations even possessed the bomb or demilitarized their troops. We proposed with our allies the Disarmament Plan of 1951 while still at war in Korea. And we make our proposals today, while building up our defense over Berlin, not because we are inconsistent or insincere or intimidated, but because we know the rights of free men will prevail—because while we are compelled against our will to rearm, we look confidently beyond Berlin to the kind of disarmed world we all prefer.

I therefore propose, on the basis of this Plan, that disarmament negotiations resume promptly, and continue without interruption until an entire program for general and complete disarmament has not only been agreed but has been actually achieved.

IV.

The logical place to begin is a treaty assuring the end of nuclear tests of all kinds, in every environment, under workable controls. The United States and the United Kingdom have proposed such a treaty that is both reasonable, effective and ready for signature. We are still prepared to sign that treaty today.

We also proposed a mutual ban on atmospheric testing, without inspection or controls, in order to save the human race from the poison of radioactive fall out. We regret that that offer was not accepted.

For 15 years we have sought to make the atom an instrument of peaceful growth rather than of war. But for 15 years our concessions have been matched by obstruction, our patience by intransigence. And the pleas of mankind for peace have met with disregard.

Finally, as the explosions of others beclouded the skies, my country was left with no alternative but to act in the interests of its own and the Free World's security. We cannot endanger that security by refraining from testing while others improve their arsenals. Nor can we endanger it by another long, uninspected ban on testing. For three years we accepted those risks in our open society while seeking agreement on inspection. But this year, while we were negotiating in good faith in Geneva, others were secretly preparing new experiments in destruction.

Our tests are not polluting the atmosphere. Our deterrent weapons are guarded against accidental explosion or use. Our doctors and scientists stand ready to help any Nation measure and meet the hazards to health which inevitably result from the tests in the atmosphere.

But to halt the spread of these terrible weapons, to halt the contamina-

281

tion of the air, to halt the spiraling nuclear arms race, we remain ready to seek new avenues of agreement. Our new Disarmament Program thus includes the following proposals:

—First, signing the Test-Ban Treaty by all Nations. This can be done now. Test-ban negotiations need not and should not await general disarmament.

—Second, stopping the production of fissionable materials for use in weapons, and preventing their transfer to any nation now lacking in nuclear weapons.

—Third, prohibiting the transfer of control over nuclear weapons to states that do not own them.

—Fourth, keeping nuclear weapons from seeding new battlegrounds in outer space.

—Fifth, gradually destroying existing nuclear weapons and converting their materials to peaceful uses; and

—Finally, halting the unlimited testing and production of strategic nuclear vehicles, and gradually destroying them as well.

v.

To destroy arms, however, is not enough. We must create even as we destroy—creating world-wide law and law enforcement as we outlaw world-wide war and weapons. In the world we seek, the United Nations Emergency Forces which have been hastily assembled, uncertainly supplied and inadequately financed will never be enough.

Therefore, the United States recommends that all member nations earmark special peace-keeping units in their armed forces—to be on call of the United Nations—to be specially trained and quickly available—and with advance provision for financial and logistic support.

In addition, the American delegation will suggest a series of steps to improve the United Nations' machinery for the peaceful settlement of disputes—for on-the-spot fact-finding, mediation and adjudication—for extending the rule of international law. For peace is not solely a matter of military or technical problems—it is primarily a problem of politics and people. And unless man can match his strides in weaponry and technology with equal strides in social and political development, our great strength, like that of the dinosaur, will become incapable of proper control—and like the dinosaur vanish from the earth.

VI.

As we extend the rule of law on earth, so must we also extend it to man's new domain: outer space.

All of us salute the brave cosmonauts of the Soviet Union. The new horizons of outer space must not be riven by the old bitter concepts of imperialism and sovereign claims. The cold reaches of the universe must not become the new arena of an even colder war.

To this end, we shall urge proposals extending the United Nations Charter to the limits of man's exploration in the Universe, reserving outer space for peaceful use, prohibiting weapons of mass destruction in space or on celestial bodies, and opening the mysteries and benefits of space to every nation. We shall further propose cooperative efforts between all nations in weather prediction and eventually in weather control. We shall propose, finally, a global system of communications satellites linking the whole world in telegraph and telephone and radio and television. The day need not be far away when such a system will televise the proceedings of this body to every corner of the world for the benefit of peace.

VII.

But the mysteries of outer space must not divert our eyes or our energies from the harsh realities that face our fellow men. Political sovereignty is but a mockery without the means of meeting poverty and illiteracy and disease. Self-determination is but a slogan if the future holds no hope.

That is why my Nation—which has freely shared its capital and its technology to help others help themselves—now proposes officially designating this decade of the 1960's as the United Nations Decade of Development. Under the framework of that Resolution, the United Nations existing efforts in promoting economic growth can be expanded and coordinated. Regional surveys and training institutes can now pool the talents of many. New research, technical assistance and pilot projects can unlock the wealth of less developed lands and untapped waters. And development can become a cooperative and not a competitive enterprise—to enable all nations, however diverse in their systems and beliefs, to become in fact as well as in law free and equal nations.

VIII.

My Country favors a world of free and equal states. We agree with those who say that colonialism is a key issue in this Assembly. But let the full facts of that issue be discussed in full.

On the one hand is the fact that, since the close of World War II, a world-wide declaration of independence has transformed nearly 1 billion people and 9 million square miles into 42 free and independent states. Less than 2 percent of the world's population now lives in "dependent" territories.

I do not ignore the remaining problems of traditional colonialism which still confront this body. Those problems will be solved, with patience, good will and determination. Within the limits of our responsibility in such matters, my Country intends to be a participant and not merely an observer, in the peaceful, expeditious movement of nations from the status of colonies to the partnership of equals. That continuing tide of self-determination, which runs so strong, has our sympathy and our support.

But colonialism in its harshest forms is not only the exploitation of new nations by old, of dark skins by light—or the subjugation of the poor by the rich. My Nation was once a colony—and we know what colonialism means: the exploitation and subjugation of the weak by the powerful, of the many by the few, of the governed who have given no consent to be governed, whatever their continent, their class or their color.

And that is why there is no ignoring the fact that the tide of self-determination has not reached the communist empire where a population far larger than that officially termed "dependent" lives under governments installed by foreign troops instead of free institutions—under a system which knows only one party and one belief—which suppresses free debate, and free elections, and free newspapers, and free books and free trade unions—and which builds a wall to keep truth a stranger and its own citizens prisoners. Let us debate colonialism in full—and apply the principle of free choice and the practice of free plebiscites in every corner of the globe.

IX.

Finally, as President of the United States, I consider it my duty to report to this Assembly on two threats to the peace which are not on your crowded agenda, but which cause us, and most of you, the deepest concern.

The first threat on which I wish to report is widely misunderstood: the smoldering coals of war in Southeast Asia. South Vietnam is already under attack—sometimes by a single assassin, sometimes by a band of guerrillas, recently by full battalions. The peaceful borders of Burma, Cambodia and India have been repeatedly violated. And the peaceful people of Laos are in danger of losing the independence they gained not so long ago.

No one can call these "wars of liberation." For these are free countries living under governments. Nor are these aggressions any less real because men are knifed in their homes and not shot on the fields of battle.

The very simple question confronting the world community is whether measures can be devised to protect the small and weak from such tactics. For if they are successful in Laos and South Vietnam, the gates will be opened wide.

The United States seeks for itself no base, no territory, no special position in this area of any kind. We support a truly neutral and independent Laos, its people free from outside interference, living at peace with themselves and with their neighbors, assured that their territory will not be used for attacks on others, and under a government comparable (as Mr. Khrushchev and I agreed at Vienna) to Cambodia and Burma.

But now the negotiations over Laos are reaching a crucial stage. The cease-fire is at best precarious. The rainy season is coming to an end. Laotian territory is being used to infiltrate South Vietnam. The world community must recognize—all those who are involved—that this potent threat to Laotian peace and freedom is indivisible from all other threats to their own.

Secondly, I wish to report to you on the crisis over Germany and Berlin. This is not the time or the place for immoderate tones, but the world community is entitled to know the very simple issues as we see them. If there is a crisis it is because an existing peace is under threat—because an existing island of free people is under pressure—because solemn agreements are being treated with indifference. Established international rights are being threatened with unilateral usurpation. Peaceful circulation has been interrupted by barbed wire and concrete blocks.

One recalls the order of the Czar in Pushkin's Boris Godunov: "Take steps at this very hour that our frontiers be fenced in by barriers. . . .

That not a single soul pass o'er the border, that not a hare be able to run or a crow to fly."

It is absurd to allege that we are threatening a war merely to prevent the Soviet Union and East Germany from signing a so-called "treaty" of peace. The Western Allies are not concerned with any paper arrangement the Soviets may wish to make with a regime of their own creation, on territory occupied by their own troops and governed by their own agents. No such action can affect either our rights or our responsibilities.

If there is a dangerous crisis in Berlin—and there is—it is because of threats against the vital interests and the deep commitments of the Western Powers, and the freedom of West Berlin. We cannot yield these interests. We cannot fail these commitments. We cannot surrender the freedom of these people for whom we are responsible. A "peace treaty" which carried with it the provisions which destroy the peace would be a fraud. A "free city" which was not genuinely free would suffocate freedom and would be an infamy.

For a city or a people to be truly free, they must have the secure right, without economic, political or police pressure, to make their own choice and to live their own lives. And as I have said before, if anyone doubts the extent to which our presence is desired by the people of West Berlin, we are ready to have that question submitted to a free vote in all Berlin and, if possible, among all the German people.

The elementary fact about this crisis is that it is unnecessary. The elementary tools for a peaceful settlement are to be found in the Charter. Under its law, agreements are to be kept, unless changed by all those who made them. Established rights are to be respected. The political disposition of peoples should rest upon their own wishes, freely expressed in plebiscites or free elections. If there are legal problems, they can be solved by legal means. If there is a threat of force, it must be rejected. If there is desire for change, it must be a subject for negotiation and if there is negotiation, it must be rooted in mutual respect and concern for the rights of others.

The Western Powers have calmly resolved to defend, by whatever means are forced upon them, their obligations and their access to the free citizens of West Berlin and the self-determination of those citizens. This generation learned from bitter experience that either brandishing or yielding to threats can only lead to war. But firmness and reason can lead to the kind of peaceful solution in which my Country profoundly believes.

We are committed to no rigid formula. We see no perfect solution. We recognize that troops and tanks can, for a time, keep a nation divided against its will, however unwise that policy may seem to us. But we believe a peaceful agreement is possible which protects the freedom of West Berlin and Allied presence and access, while recognizing the historic and legitimate interests of others in assuring European security.

The possibilities of negotiation are now being explored; it is too early to report what the prospects may be. For our part, we would be glad to report at the appropriate time that a solution has been found. For there is no need for a crisis over Berlin, threatening the peace—and if those who created this crisis desire peace, there will be peace and freedom in Berlin.

x.

The events and decisions of the next ten months may well decide the fate of man for the next ten thousand years. There will be no avoiding those events. There will be no appeal from these decisions. And we in this hall shall be remembered either as part of the generation that turned this planet into a flaming funeral pyre or the generation that met its vow "to save succeeding generations from the scourge of war."

In the endeavor to meet that vow, I pledge you every effort this Nation possesses. I pledge you that we shall neither commit nor provoke aggression—that we shall neither flee nor invoke the threat of force—that we shall never negotiate out of fear, we shall never fear to negotiate.

Terror is not a new weapon. Throughout history it has been used by those who could not prevail, either by persuasion or example. But inevitably they fail—either because men are not afraid to die for a life worth living—or because the terrorists themselves came to realize that free men cannot be frightened by threats, and that aggression would meet its own response. And it is in the light of that history that every nation today should know, be he friend or foe, that the United States has both the will and the weapons to join free men in standing up to their responsibilities.

But I come here today to look across this world of threats to the world of peace. In that search we cannot expect any final triumph—for new problems will always arise. We cannot expect that all nations will

287

adopt like systems—for conformity is the jailer of freedom, and the enemy of growth. Nor can we expect to reach our goal by contrivance, by fiat or even by the wishes of all.

But however close we sometimes seem to that dark and final abyss, let no man of peace and freedom despair. For he does not stand alone. If we all can persevere—if we can in every land and office look beyond our own shores and ambitions—then surely the age will dawn in which the strong are just and the weak secure and the peace preserved.

Ladies and gentlemen of this assembly—the decision is ours. Never have the nations of the world had so much to lose—or so much to gain. Together we shall save our planet—or together we shall perish in its flames. Save it we can—and save it we must—and then shall we earn the eternal thanks of mankind and, as peace makers, the eternal blessing of God.

"The U.S. in the U.N.: An Independent Audit"

AN ADDRESS BY SENATOR HENRY M. JACKSON[1]

MR. CHAIRMAN, *distinguished guests and members of the National Press Club:*

The place of the United Nations in American foreign policy is now receiving a good deal of attention. Unfortunately, the debate seems to be polarized around extreme positions. On the one hand, there are those who say—"the UN is the only source of hope," "let's leave everything to the UN." On the other hand, there are those who say—"the UN is the source of catastrophe," "let's get out of the UN." Each view is like the distorted reflection in a carnival mirror—one too broad, the other too narrow. Neither view is really helpful.

No doubt the quiet, steadying majority of the American people have a more balanced view of the United Nations, and see it for what it is: an aspiration and a hope, the closest approximation we have to a code of international good conduct, and a useful forum of diplomacy for some purposes.

The United Nations is, and should continue to be, an important avenue of American foreign policy. Yet practices have developed which, I believe, lead to an undue influence of UN considerations in our national decision-making. Indeed it is necessary to ask whether the involvement of the UN in our policy-making has not at times hampered the wise definition of our national interests and the development of sound policies for their advancement?

The test of the national security policy process is this: Does it identify our vital interests and does it develop foreign and defense policies which will defend and promote these interests? In our system, two men must bear the heaviest responsibility for giving our national security policy

---

[1] An address before the National Press Club on March 20, 1962.

focus and structure. One is, of course, the President. The other is his first adviser, the Secretary of State.

The United Nations is not, and was never intended to be, a substitute for our own leaders as makers and movers of American policy. The shoulders of the Secretary-General were never expected to carry the burdens of the President or the Secretary of State. But do we sometimes act as though we could somehow subcontract to the UN the responsibility for national decision-making?

At the founding of the United Nations there was the hope that all its members shared a common purpose—the search for a lasting peace. This hope was dashed.

The Soviet Union was not and is not a "peace-loving" nation. Khrushchev has announced his support for "wars of liberation." He has threatened to "bury" us. In their more agreeable moments the Russians promise to bury us nicely, but whatever their mood, the earth would still be six feet deep above us.

We must realize that the Soviet Union sees the UN not as a forum of cooperation, but as one more arena of struggle.

The maintenance of peace depends not on the United Nations as an organization but on the strength and will of its members to uphold the Charter.

The truth is, though we have not often spoken it in recent years, that the best hope for peace with justice does not lie in the United Nations. Indeed, the truth is almost exactly the reverse. The best hope for the United Nations lies in the maintenance of peace. In our deeply divided world, peace depends on the power and unity of the Atlantic Community and on the skill of our direct diplomacy.

In this light, some basic questions need to be asked:

First: Are we taking an exaggerated view of the UN's role?

In one way and another the conduct of UN affairs absorbs a disproportionate amount of the energy of our highest officials. The President and the Secretary of State must ration their worry time—and the hours spent on the UN cannot be spent on other matters. All too often, furthermore, the energies devoted to the UN must be spent on defensive actions—trying to defeat this or that ill-advised resolution—rather than on more constructive programs.

The Secretary of State has called the United Nations "a forum in which almost every aspect of our foreign policy comes up." The fact is correctly stated, but does it reflect a desirable state of affairs? Should we take a more restricted view of the organization's capacity for helpfulness?

I think we should. The cold war may destroy the United Nations, if that organization becomes one of its main battlegrounds, but the United Nations cannot put an end to the cold war.

As a general rule, might it be more prudent, though less dramatic, not to push the UN into the fireman's suit unless we are sure the alternatives are worse and, above all, that we are not seeking to evade our own responsibilities.

I believe the United Nations can best gain stature and respect by undertaking tasks which are within its capabilities, and that its usefulness will be diminished if it is impelled into one cold war crisis after another and asked to shoulder responsibilities it cannot meet.

With these thoughts in mind, I read with some concern proposals to increase the "executive responsibilities" of the organization. Also, I have serious doubts about current suggestions to provide "more pervasive and efficient 'UN presences'" to help "halt infiltration of guerrillas across frontiers; and to help halt internal subversion instigated by a foreign power. . . ."

Dag Hammarskjold, who was a brilliant and devoted servant of the United Nations, clearly saw the dangers in overrating the peacekeeping power of the organization. In a letter to a private citizen, he once decried the tendency to force the Secretary General into a key role in great power disputes "through sheer escapism from those who should carry the responsibility."

Second: May not the most useful function of the United Nations lie in serving as a link between the West and the newly independent states?

Most international business is best handled through normal bilateral contacts or through regional arrangements among the states concerned.

However, the United Nations provides a useful meeting ground for many new governments with other governments. These relationships may be of mutual benefit.

The UN affords good opportunities to explain Western policies, to correct misrepresentations of the Western position, and to expose the weaknesses in the Soviet line. In fact, the Soviet singing commercials themselves offend the most hardened ear. They inspire a healthy skepticism about Russian three-way cold war pills—guaranteed to end the arms race, relieve colonial oppression, and ease poverty, if taken regularly, as directed.

The UN and its specialized agencies may be of great usefulness in supplying technical assistance for economic development, in providing financial aid, and in preparing international development programs.

The organization may sometimes be helpful in reaching peaceful settlements of certain issues and disputes of concern to the newly independent states—especially if it is used to seek out areas of agreement rather than to dramatize conflicts of interest.

In this connection there has been too great a tendency to bring every issue to a vote. Indeed, there are too many votes on too many issues in the UN—and too much of the time and energy of every delegation is spent in lobbying for votes.

A vote requires a division of the house, a sharpening and even an exaggeration of points at issue, and it emphasizes the division of opinion rather than the area of agreement. Not every discussion needs to end in a vote. The purposes of the members might be better served if the UN forum becomes more often a place where diplomatic representatives quietly search for acceptable settlements of issues between their countries.

Voting has a way of raising the temperature of any body, and I think that we should be doing what we can to keep the temperature of the United Nations near normal.

Third: In our approach to the UN, do we make too much of the talk and too little of the deed?

New York City is the foremost communications center of the United States, if not the world. Once the decision was made to locate the headquarters of the United Nations in New York, it was inevitable that what went on there would receive attention disproportionate to its significance. Newsmen and photographers have to produce news stories and pictures, and politicians from any land rival the celebrities of stage and screen in their hunger for free publicity.

The United States is of course host to the United Nations. Day in and day out we are conscious of the presence of the organization in our midst. And the role of host entails special obligations. Consequently, it is often difficult to keep one's sense of proportion. There is, for example, a tendency, to which the press itself is not immune, to believe the UN makes more history than it really does.

A Secretary of State—responsible for policy—must weigh his words carefully. For that reason he seldom makes good copy. One of the reasons for the extensive coverage of the United Nations is that the right to the floor of the General Assembly is not subject to the sobering influence of responsibility for action.

I have been struck, for example, by the serious disproportion in the press, radio, and television coverage of our UN delegation and the coverage of the Department of State. The space and time devoted to the former does not correctly reflect the relative importance of what is said in New York against what is said in Washington.

If the UN were used less for drumbeating on every nerve-tingling issue, and if its energies were quietly devoted to manageable problems, there might be fewer headlines from the UN but more contributions to the building of a peaceful world.

Everyone talks too much. It is a worldwide disease. Sometimes it seems that the appropriate legend to place above the portals of the UN might be: "Through these doors pass the most articulate men and women in the world."

Fourth: Should our delegation to the United Nations play a larger role in the policymaking process than our representatives to NATO or to major world capitals?

I think the answer is no, and the burden of proof should lie with those who advocate a unique role for our embassy in New York.

Our delegation to the United Nations is, of course, frequently and necessarily involved in promoting or opposing particular actions by the United Nations which may have an important bearing on our national security policies. If it is not to commit the United States to positions inconsistent with our national security requirements, the delegation must be kept in closest touch with, and have a thorough understanding of, these requirements. Furthermore, the President and Secretary of State require information and advice from our UN delegation.

This is not to say, however, that the requirements of sound national policy can be more clearly seen in New York than elsewhere, or that our embassy in New York should play a different role in policymaking from that played by other important embassies.

The precedent set by President Eisenhower in this matter, and continued by this Administration, seems unfortunate. The Ambassador to the United Nations is not a second Secretary of State, but the present arrangement suggests a certain imbalance in the role assigned to the UN delegation in the policymaking process.

The problem is not to give the UN delegation a larger voice in policymaking but to give it the tools to help carry out the policy.

Rational, effective negotiation on complex and critical matters, like the reduction and control of armaments, requires unified guidance and instruction to those conducting the negotiations. This is a basic principle of sound administration and avoids the dangers of freewheeling. The unified source of instructions should be the Secretary of State, acting for the President, or the President himself—not others in the White House or the Executive Office, not lower levels in State, certainly not the UN delegation itself.

The UN delegation in New York should not operate as a second foreign office. Such confusion of responsibility reinforces a tendency to give undue weight in national policy formulation to considerations that seem more important in New York than they ought to seem in Washington, D. C. The effect of decisions on something called "our relations in the UN" may receive more weight than their effect on, say, the strength and unity of the Atlantic Community. The result may be a weakening or dilution of policy positions in deference to what is represented in New York as world opinion.

The concept of world opinion has been, I fear, much abused. Whatever it is and whatever the importance that should be attached to it, I doubt that it can be measured by taking the temperature of the General Assembly or successfully cultivated primarily by currying favor in New York. To hide behind something called "world opinion" is all too often the device of the timid, or the last resort of someone who has run out of arguments.

Fifth: Is our UN delegation properly manned for the diplomatic and technical tasks we require of it?

We have established the tradition of choosing for top UN posts Americans of considerable prestige—prestige acquired, furthermore, not in the practice of diplomacy but in national politics, business, the arts and sciences and other fields of endeavor. For the most part, these people have served us well, in effective advocacy of America's concerns, and in persuasive championship of progress toward a world of good neighbors.

A start has been made in staffing the UN mission more as other embassies, with experienced diplomats and experts in technical fields in which the United Nations may be able to make quiet but useful contributions. Further progress in this direction should be encouraged.

The sum of the matter is this:

We need to take another look at our role in the United Nations, remembering that the UN is not a substitute for national policies wisely conceived to uphold our vital interests. We need to rethink the organization and staffing of our government for United Nations affairs.

For this purpose, we should have a top-level review conducted under the authority of the President and the Secretary of State. The review should, of course, be handled in a nonpartisan manner.

Debate over the United Nations is now centered on the UN bond issue. This debate reveals some of the symptoms of the basic disturbance. Congress has been requested to approve the purchase of UN bonds up to a total of 100 million dollars to help cover the cost of two controversial peace-keeping operations. The money in question has been spent and it would be a serious mistake to prolong the financial crisis. I trust the Congress can help find a wise way to help cover the deficit.

But the fundamental questions will still remain, and will plague us until they are answered:

Do our present relations with the United Nations assist the wise definition of our vital interests and the establishment of sound policies? Are we sometimes deferring to the United Nations in the hope that we may somehow escape the inescapable dilemmas of leadership? Are we failing to make the most of the United Nations by encouraging it to attempt too much?

Mr. Chairman, I close as I began: The United Nations is, and should continue to be, an important avenue of American foreign policy. But we need to revise our attitudes in the direction of a more realistic appreciation of its limitations, more modest hopes for its accomplishments, and a more mature sense of the burdens of responsible leadership.

"The United Nations and the Real World"

AN ADDRESS BY UNDERSECRETARY OF STATE GEORGE H. BALL[1]

~~~☆~~~☆~~~☆~~~☆~~~☆~~~☆~~~

STATESMEN, journalists, pundits, and politicians are fond of reminding us that these are times of rapid change and vast transformation in human affairs. It is well that they do, for the pace and pervasiveness of scientific, political, and social change have given a special character to the postwar world.

Yet it is not enough to recognize, as a general proposition, that change is taking place. We must define the direction of that change if we are to adjust our attitudes and policies to the shifting requirements of the times. For as the world changes, our conventional wisdom is called into question, inherited doctrine becomes obsolete, and human institutions perforce take on new forms and new functions. It requires all the perception and imagination we can muster—and then some—if we are to know even imprecisely what we are doing or where we are going.

This morning I want to talk with you about what we are doing and where we are going with one of the most ambitious and misunderstood of our postwar institutions—the United Nations.

I refer to the United Nations as misunderstood because the current discussion of the effectiveness and utility of that institution displays a wide area of difference as to its purposes and objectives. If one would look back to San Francisco in 1945 when the Charter was being drafted and then look at the world today, the reason for this misunderstanding becomes apparent. The assumption—or at least the hope—that inspired the drafters of that noble document was that the great powers, allied in World War II, would be able to live in relative harmony and together

---

[1] An address made at a foreign-policy briefing conference for the press and broadcasting industry at the Department of State on March 26, 1962. Reprinted from the *U.S. Dept. of State Bulletin* (April 16, 1962).

police the postwar world. They could settle whatever differences arose among them within the forum of the Security Council.

As we know all too well, the effort to fashion one world with one treaty hardly lasted through the first General Assembly. The Soviet Union joined the United Nations in name only. Over the next 4 years the Iron Curtain slammed down to form a cage around one-third of the world's population, living on a great landmass that stretches from the Brandenburg Gate to the Yellow Sea.

The United Nations was thus frustrated in its original objective of serving as a forum for reconciling differences among the great powers. This has not, however, destroyed its usefulness—indeed its indispensability.

Instead the United Nations has found its postwar destiny in quite different and enormously effective endeavors.

That is why I thought it might be useful, in the few moments we have together this morning, to describe the major role that the United Nations has in fact played in this turbulent postwar decade and a half and to suggest how the United Nations fits into the whole of American diplomacy.

Transformation in World Power Relationships

The brief moment of time—less than a generation—since the end of World War II has seen the world transformed. If one-third of the world population has been encircled by the Iron Curtain, in this brief period another one-third has made the eventful passage from colonial status to some form of national independence. Almost 50 new states have come into being; a dozen more are actively in the making.

Such a revolutionary movement on a worldwide scale has no precedent. The great changes of the past have taken place only over centuries; the sudden denouement of the 20th-century anticolonial revolution has been compressed in a mere 15 years.

The breakup of the European empires meant the collapse of a long-standing system of world order. It meant the sudden rupture of old ties, the sudden emergence of new states, the sudden liberation of a billion people from colonial dependence. The world has never known a comparable political convulsion—so abruptly begun, so quickly concluded.

Even under the best of circumstances one could well have expected this to be a period of violent conflict, chaos, and vast bloodletting. But the collapse of the European empires did not take place in the best of circumstances—almost in the worst. For it took place in a world polarized between the great powers of East and West, where the Sino-Soviet bloc had everything to gain by the vigorous promotion of chaos.

The Communists tried hard to exploit the turmoil implicit in rapid change. They sought to capture and divert the nationalist revolutions into Communist channels. They did their best to turn political instability into political collapse, to rub salt into the wounds of racial antagonisms, to fan jealousies between the poor and the rich, to exploit the inexperience of the new governments, to capitalize on economic misery, and to heighten tensions between new states and their neighbors wherever they existed.

In retrospect, of course, it seems extraordinary that, since the Red Chinese takeover in 1949, the Iron Curtain countries have failed in almost all their efforts to convert nationalist revolutions into Communist revolutions. In spite of the extension of the Communist conspiracy through highly organized local party organizations, in spite of the disruptive force of violent change, in spite of the political inexperience of the leaders of the new countries and the natural antagonisms between the new countries and their former colonial overlords, the greatest political upheaval of all time has still taken place—within a fantastically short timespan—with amazing smoothness and good will and with a surprising lack of bloodshed.

In this great process of change the interests of the great powers were at all times deeply involved. Lurking in the background of political changes all over the world was the disturbing question of relative big-power advantage. Because of this the world has lived in constant danger that a jungle war in Southeast Asia or a tribal conflict in the heart of Africa could become the occasion for a great-power confrontation—and that what began as a brush fire could be fanned into a nuclear holocaust. Yet this has not happened. Except in Korea, the direct confrontation of great-power troops has been averted.

This, it seems to me, suggests quite clearly one of the major roles of the United Nations. Unable to bring the great powers together, it has played a decisive role in keeping them apart. And all the while it has served as overseer of the vast and for the most part nationalist transformations which have been taking place all over the world.

In appraising the success of the United Nations, in appraising its usefulness to the United States, I think it is this standard of judgment that we should employ: How effectively has it facilitated the peaceful revision of the relations between the billion colonial peoples largely in the Southern Hemisphere and the billion economically advanced peoples in the Northern Hemisphere—in the face of constant efforts of subversion and interference from the Communist powers that control the billion people behind the Iron Curtain?

End of the Colonial Era

One of the most frequently heard complaints against the United Nations is that it has precipitated change at too rapid a pace. By providing each emergent new state a voice equal to that of a great power, it is said, the United Nations has given an excessive impetus to the breakup of colonialism. As the new nations have gained in numbers and thus in votes in the General Assembly of the U.N., they have mounted pressures that have forced the colonial powers to move beyond the speed limits set by prudence. As a result, independence has been conferred upon peoples unprepared for the complex tasks of nation-building.

Evidence can be marshaled to support this thesis. Examples can be cited of nations born prematurely, nations lacking the educated elite to operate the difficult business of government, nations illogically conceived, with national boundaries that have little rational meaning either in ethnic or economic terms.

But on the other side there are powerful arguments for maintaining the momentum of change. When the world is faced with a convulsion so profound as the ending of colonialism, it is well to get the process completed just as quickly as it can be done peacefully. A great political and social revolution of this kind cannot be achieved without major adjustments, and in a world where half of the dependent peoples have achieved independence the lot of the other half must become increasingly irksome. Under such circumstances a long deferment of their own independence is likely to produce frustrations and bitterness that will impede and complicate their ultimate accommodation to the environment of free nations.

It must be recognized, of course, that the colonial era is not yet finally completed; there is still substantial unfinished business to be done. In the areas of Africa where many Europeans have made their homes, there remains the task of reconciling the rights of white minorities with the rights and aspirations of African majorities. The troublesome problem remains, moreover, of how to deal with the bits and pieces of former colonial systems—fragments that are themselves so small as not to fit neatly into the pattern of new nation states. There are altogether about 50 fragments of this kind. We ourselves are the administering power for several groups of Pacific islands under a United Nations trusteeship. We are seeking to devise appropriate long-term arrangements for these areas that will permit the maximum of opportunity for the peoples involved.

Yet if the colonial era is not concluded it is well on the way toward being so. The vast bulk of the population formerly under colonial rule has now achieved self-government. Certainly for the major powers of the West, colonialism is largely a matter of history.

By and large the major European powers, which are our natural partners in most of our activities, have either seen the transformation of their former colonial possessions into sovereign states or are in the process of doing so.

This has created difficult problems for them, but, for the most part, these problems have been met and solved more easily than had been anticipated. In spite of fears that the loss of colonies might enfeeble the colonial powers, this has not proved to be true. In fact one can say without being fanciful that, just as the shattering of their colonial systems—like the fission of the atom—has unleashed fierce energies, the former colonial powers—the great powers of Western Europe—are themselves generating vast forces, not through fissions but through the fusion of their economies in the European Common Market. In ceasing to think of themselves as the centers of individual colonial systems they have found a common destiny as Europeans. In undertaking the business of building a united Europe they have already developed a new prosperity, a new purpose, and the beginning of a new relationship with the new nations carved out of their old empires.

We ourselves have a direct interest in the completion of the decolonization process for, as colonialism becomes a dead issue between the peoples of the less developed countries and the major powers of Western Europe, the free world as a whole should become increasingly cohesive. President Kennedy has described the 1960's as a "decade of development." Certainly the major powers of the West must devote themselves intensively over the next few years to assisting the newly emerging countries toward a level of political and economic independence that will enable them to play a constructive role in the family of nations.

In this endeavor it is essential that the major Western Powers be able to work closely together, just as they work closely together in resisting threatened aggression from the Communist bloc. In the past, however, the existence of colonialism has often proved an impediment to common actions or policies among the Western Powers. With its passing we should be able to look forward to a further and freer development of the Atlantic partnership, which is, after all, the hard core of free-world strength.

Converting Nationalism Into Nationhood

For most of the colonial peoples the end of the colonial ordeal marks the start of a new process, the conversion of nationalism into nationhood. Sovereignty is sometimes a heady wine. It encourages exuberant voices and sometimes irrelevant argument. But perhaps this is a function of growing up—a normal aspect of the transformation from dependent status to independence. Let us remember that we were ourselves a young, brash, and rather cocky nation at the end of the 18th century.

We should not, therefore, be put off by the fact that representatives of the new nations are sometimes given to irrelevant talk. Neither we nor they should permit it to obscure the relevant business that every new state has to tackle as it enters the age of engineering and economics.

In fact, instead of being irked by the occasional exuberance of some of the representatives of newer nations in the General Assembly, we should be eternally grateful to the U.N. that the complex business of transforming almost 50 new states from dependence to sovereignty has, for the most part, been accompanied by speeches rather than by shooting. This is, I think, one of the striking achievements of our time.

In trying to understand the actions of the new nations we should realize that in their eyes the U.N. has a very special meaning. The immediate and natural ambition of every new nation is to establish its national identity. Membership in the United Nations has served this purpose; it has become the badge of independence, the credentials of sovereignty, the symbol of nationhood, and the passport to the 20th century. When the delegation of a new nation takes its place in the grand hall of the General Assembly, that nation has arrived; it can look the world in the eye and speak its piece. And even if that piece may be discordant to our ears, the fact that it can be spoken has helped to stabilize the postwar world.

Yet the U.N. is more than a place for letting off steam; it is also a school of political responsibility. While some of its members may represent closed societies, it is itself an open society. The General Assembly is staged for all the world to see, and performing upon that stage sometimes—though not always—helps turn demagogues into statesmen. How else can one explain the fact that at the last General Assembly the most "anticolonial" members of the United Nations decisively rejected a Soviet resolution calling for independence of all remaining dependent areas by 1962? They sponsored instead moderate and sensible resolutions for which we and most of our European friends could vote without reservation.

The growing sense of responsibility in the new nations is only partly the result of finding themselves on stage before a critical world. It is also the result of a growing conviction that the business of economic and social development in their own countries is tough and demanding. They find the problems of food and health, education and technology, enterprise and administration will not yield to repetitive slogans carried over from the fight for independence. And they discover, too, the need to develop a new relationship with the Europeans and with the North Americans.

The framework of the United Nations provides a basis for such a new relationship—a political system in which the less developed nations can have a full sense of participation, which makes possible a family of technical organizations whose international staffs can help conceive and carry out the development plans every people now expects its government to pursue with vigor.

Two Aspects of U.N.'s Peacekeeping Role

In one aspect, then, the United Nations is an instrument through which the industrial societies and the less developed nations can be brought together. In another aspect, as I have earlier suggested, one of the principal achievements of the United Nations has been to keep the great powers apart. It has accomplished this by bringing about the settlement of conflicts through conciliation and debate and by interposing itself as the agency to keep the peace in areas where chaos might otherwise attract great-power intervention.

The U.N. was scarcely organized before it was involved in the difficult and dangerous business of peacekeeping—in Iran, Greece, Indonesia, Kashmir. Since then it has played a part in stopping aggression, threatened aggression, or civil war in Palestine, Korea, at Suez, in the Lebanon and the Congo. In all of these conflicts the great powers had interests. In the absence of the U.N. they would in all likelihood have intervened to defend those interests. Intervention by both sides could have led to a dangerous confrontation.

The most recent, and perhaps most spectacular, of the trouble spots in which the U.N. has acted to prevent great-power confrontation is, of course, the Congo. Here the U.N., with full United States support, interposed itself in the heart of Africa in the nick of time. The Soviet Union was already moving in, and we could never have stood by while they set up shop in the heart of Africa. The intervention of the U.N., difficult though it may have seemed at the time, prevented the chaos that could well have turned the Congo into another Korea. Today, by patience and effort, it is helping to bring about the conditions under which an integrated Congo republic can work its way toward stability and peace.

I would suggest, therefore, that, in thinking about the Congo and about other areas where the United Nations is brought in to keep the peace, we should ask ourselves this question: From the point of view of our national security, would it have been better to send in the American Marines or to act with others to send in the United Nations in the name of the world community?

Obviously the U.N. cannot keep the peace without expense. Today it has over 20,000 men in the field, patrolling the truce lines in the Middle East and keeping the lid on in the Congo. Manifestly this is the work of something more than a League of Nations—more than a debating society grafted on a pious commitment to unattainable goals. It is the work of an executive agency of considerable capacity and skill, capable of performing pragmatic tasks—such as mobilizing, transporting, commanding, and supplying substantial forces in the field when an emergency arises.

U.N. an Instrument of U.S. Foreign Policy

Much of the discussion about the United Nations has not been concerned so much with what it does as how its activities fit in with the larger purposes of our own foreign policy. To those of us in the Department of State who have responsibility for the formulation and administration of that policy the relationship is clear enough. The United Nations is an instrument of United States foreign policy just as it is an instrument of the foreign policy of every other member state. In addition the U.N. provides us with a mechanism by which we can seek to persuade other member states not only that they should agree with us on our foreign policy but that they should express that agreement by actively supporting resolutions that accord with our own national objectives.

Because our policies have tended to be right and have thus appealed to the interests of other nations and because Ambassador Stevenson and his staff have displayed exceptional leadership, we have been remarkably successful in obtaining international approval of our own national policies.

This is illustrated clearly by the record of the 16th General Assembly. You will recall that this Assembly convened last September in an atmosphere of somber crisis—the secession of Katanga Province in the Congo, the death of Dag Hammarskjold on a mission of conciliation, the Soviet Union's revival of its infamous troika proposal for a three-headed Secretary-General, and the prospect of imminent bankruptcy.

Such was the state of affairs when President Kennedy addressed the General Assembly in September. He made a ringing affirmation of U.S. support and confidence in the future of the United Nations—and backed it up with three major initiatives.

The President laid before the membership a comprehensive U.S. plan for general and complete disarmament, made realistic by its insistence on a simultaneous improvement of international peacekeeping machinery. This put the U.N. in business again on this vital if frustrating subject—and seized the initiative for the United States on the issue of peace.

President Kennedy also called for an active program of U.N. activity on the peaceful uses of outer space. The General Assembly acted on this American proposal in a resolution that extended the Charter of the United Nations to outer space and set up the Committee on Peaceful

Uses of Outer Space, which began its work last week in an atmosphere unusual for the absence of cold-war policies.

Finally the President called for a U.N. Decade of Development to speed economic and social growth in the less developed world. This was approved unanimously; a general goal of a 50-percent expansion in national incomes was adopted for the next decade; and a wide range of specific programs and projects is in the course of preparation.

Thus did the U.N. General Assembly respond to American leadership and react to American initiatives that are both in our own interest and in the interest of a great majority of the members.

Meanwhile the Assembly resolutely preserved the integrity of the Secretariat against Soviet attack; rejected the Soviet effort to replace Nationalist China with Communist China; drew up an emergency plan to restore financial order to its affairs; and dealt in a generally responsible manner with the emotional subject of colonialism.

Functions of Regional Institutions

But if the United Nations is an instrument of United States policy it is only one of many instruments available to us. It is one of the tasks of the Secretary of State and his staff, when confronted with a particular problem, to select and utilize that instrument most appropriate for the purpose.

It is therefore important to be clear not only about what the United Nations does but what it does not do—what it is not, as well as what it is. Clarity on this score helps resolve the contradiction some people seem to find in American foreign policy, a contradiction between our reliance on the institutions of the Atlantic community and our participation in the United Nations.

No such contradiction in fact exists. The founders of the United Nations recognized the necessity for regional institutions and explicitly provided for them in the Charter. Indeed the Charter calls upon members to seek settlement of disputes within the framework of regional institutions before they are brought to the U.N. at all.

In practice we use the various institutions to which we belong for quite different purposes. The North Atlantic Treaty Organization (NATO) is, of course, the backbone of our military defense of the free world against the Communist bloc. Through our own massive forces and through NATO we maintain the armed strength that is the principal deterrent to Communist aggression. But just as the U.N.'s capabilities are limited, so are NATO's. Quite clearly NATO could not have intervened in the Congo to restore order when Belgium withdrew. Only a world organization could do so without arousing anticolonialist emotions.

It is true that the United Nations cannot, by itself, maintain the peace between the major powers. It is equally true that NATO was not qualified to supervise the peaceful change from colonialism to independence. Their roles are quite different and distinct. Each is essential, and therefore we support each for different reasons.

The same observation can be made with regard to the OECD—the Organization for Economic Cooperation and Development—which came into being in September, 1961. Through this organization we are developing means for close cooperation in economic matters with the major industrialized powers on either side of the Atlantic. This kind of cooperation cannot be achieved within the larger framework of the United Nations. But the building of workable international relationships with the smaller, poorer countries requires arrangements in which the weaker nations can participate, with dignity, as full-fledged members—which is the secret of success of the World Bank, the U.N. Special Fund, and other world wide institutions for technical aid and development lending.

I could, of course, go on to mention other regional arrangements in which we participate. The Organization of American States, for example, gives institutional form to the American system. And the Alliance for Progress provides for a massive cooperative effort between the United States and Latin America.

In view of the need for different instruments to serve the diverse purposes of our foreign policy, I find the suggestion quite curious that, by seeking to use NATO or the OECD as a means of cooperation with our European friends, we are somehow turning our back on the U.N. I find equally curious the belief that in seeking to work within the United Nations we are betraying our friendship with our Atlantic partners.

Nothing could be further from the truth. The fact of the matter is that, in 41 key votes in the last General Assembly, the United States and a majority of the NATO members voted together 41 times. Members of NATO do not, of course, vote as a bloc at the United Nations;

only Communist members vote consistently as a bloc. But if loyalty to a majority of our NATO allies within the United Nations is a test, the United States has proved the most loyal of all—and this record was made in an Assembly in which there were 14 major votes on so-called colonial issues.

I cannot understand the contention that the United States must make a choice between the U.N. and NATO, that we are compelled for some strange reason to put all our eggs in one basket. It seems to me a curious concept that in world affairs we can do only one thing at a time—that if we stand firm in one place we cannot move ahead in another, that if we are in favor of quiet diplomacy we must be against parliamentary diplomacy in the General Assembly, that if we are for a strong concert of free nations we must be against a strong world community, that if regional organizations are realistic world organizations are necessarily unrealistic.

It seems to me that the present maturity of our foreign policy lies precisely in our ability to stand firm against threats of aggression while simultaneously taking constructive initiatives to build a world free of the threat of aggression—building up the regional organizations of the Atlantic and Western Hemisphere communities while simultaneously supporting the world community represented by the United Nations— practicing at the same time bilateral diplomacy, regional diplomacy, and global diplomacy through the United Nations.

U.N. Serves National Interests

In this world of interlocking partnerships the quality of our country-by-country diplomacy has to be supplemented with a diplomacy of regional organizations, and both must be complemented by our effective participation in the parliamentary diplomacy of the United Nations.

The U.N.'s New York headquarters has become, for the newer and smaller nations, the diplomatic capital of the world. Some of the smaller nations can hardly afford to be represented in more than a few capitals, but they are always represented at the United Nations. Thus if an African nation has business with Japan or India or Brazil, it is more than likely these days to tell its mission in New York to talk to the Japanese or Indian or Brazilian delegation to the U.N. And in the U.N. building itself there were 2,217 meetings this past year in the ceaseless process of building relationships among 104 countries whose independence is declared but whose interdependence is essential.

This is why the United States Mission to the United Nations bears such a heavy burden and why its quality is so critical to the national interest. This is why there is a "U.N. angle" to so many different parts of American foreign policy. This is why President Kennedy reached out for a man of Cabinet stature and world renown to head the United States Mission at the United Nations.

The center of decision and the source of instructions is Washington— on U.N. affairs as on all other parts of our foreign policy. These instructions give considerable weight, as they should, to the facts and recommendations received from the U.S. Mission to the U.N. And the combination of American ideas and initiatives, backed by American power and carried into action by American diplomacy, enables the United States to carry more weight in the United Nations than any other member.

Because it does things we want to see done and makes possible some relations with other countries we want to see established—and because it operates, in the words of the Charter, as "a center for harmonizing the actions of nations"—the United Nations serves the national interests of the United States. It will, we believe, continue to do so as long as the United States is its leading member and exercises day by day, the year round, the function of leadership.

An *Address to the Ninth Annual Conference on International Affairs*

BY SECRETARY OF STATE DEAN RUSK[1]

I AM HAPPY to take part in this Conference on foreign affairs. It is a great pleasure to meet a number of old friends—many of them veterans of public service along the Potomac—and a special pleasure to be introduced by my one time colleague Karl Bendetsen.

I should like, first, to bring you a greeting from President Kennedy.

The Cincinnati Council on World Affairs, the University of Cincinnati, and Xavier University are to be commended for organizing this Ninth Annual Conference on International Affairs. The subject of your conference—"Victory in the Cold War—What Is It, and How Can We Gain It"?—is of central importance to us all. I heartily subscribe to the statement of your Conference Chairman, Mr. Bendetsen, that "we need public opinion which is intelligently informed and responsible—a citizenry committed to the sustained effort required for victory." I would add that we in government have no monopoly on wisdom. Conferences such as yours can help in developing sound national policies. My warmest greetings and thanks go to all of you who are participating in this effort.

I would underline two points. The first is that by victory in the cold war we do not mean the victory of one nation or one people over others, but a victory for freedom. We are not talking about an *imperium Americanum*. The second—closely related to the first—is that by "we" we mean not just 185,000,000 American citizens of the United States but all men and women throughout the world who share our basic aspirations.

On Washington's Birthday we can talk about the meaning of a worldwide victory for freedom—and the means for its achievement. For enlarging the area of freedom has been the business of this country since

[1] An address made at Cincinnati, Ohio, on February 22, 1963.

the First Continental Congress chose Washington as Commander-in-Chief. It was Washington who said, in his first inaugural, that "the preservation of the sacred fire of liberty and the destiny of the republican model of government are justly considered as *deeply*, perhaps as *finally*, staked on the experiment intrusted to the hands of the American people."

Washington and his contemporaries clearly regarded free choice as good not just for some three million persons, chiefly of British descent, living on the eastern fringes of North America. The ideas underlying the American experiment in freedom were not to be just for Americans, but for "all men"—the very words used in the Declaration of Independence.

We Americans do many things about this conviction of ours that freedom must prevail. Tonight I should like to talk about what we do in and through the United Nations.

Now I am aware of the fact that some of you have already slumped back a bit to be bored. But take care, for you have chosen "Victory in the Cold War" as your central theme for discussion. Among other things, the Cold War is a sustained and cynical effort by the Communist world to destroy the world of the United Nations Charter, and to substitute their own world revolution in its place. We tend to forget so much—and so fast. Nowadays there are those who seem to think that Cold War talk is "realistic" talk, having little to do with the United Nations—that the United Nations is a fanciful exercise for those who wish to talk somewhat idly about a world which has not and cannot come into existence. In truth, a central issue of the Cold War is the United Nations itself—its Charter, its concept of a decent world order, its commitment to the peaceful settlement of disputes, its concern for human rights, the expansion of trade, economic and social progress, our deepest aspirations toward a disarmed and peaceful world.

Have you forgotten that in July 1945 our Senate consented to the ratification of the United Nations Charter by a vote of 89 to 2. It was a serious and solemn act, and was recognized as such at the time, particularly by those of us who were wearing the uniform at that time. It represented long and sober thought about our national purposes in our relations with other peoples, about our abstention from full responsibility between the two World Wars, about the tens of millions lost in World

War II. The Charter opens—have you read it?—with a short statement of what can accurately be called the long range foreign policy of the American people—and of most other ordinary people in other countries. The action of the Senate at that time reflected the words of Theodore Roosevelt decades before—"The question is not whether America shall play a great part in the affairs of the world, but whether she shall play it well or ill."

Our commitment to the United Nations was not empty phrasing. We threw ourselves into its beginnings with all our energy and resources. We set about the binding up of the wounds of war. We demobilized our armed forces and reduced our defense budget to less than $10 billion. A strenuous effort was made to put atomic energy under international control and to abolish nuclear weapons. The alliances formed to fight World War II were expected to vanish. New alliances aimed at anyone else were not at that time contemplated.

What went wrong? The Cold War was born. Joseph Stalin, even before the guns were silent, set about to prevent the United Nations system from succeeding; one nation returned to its dogma of unlimited appetite and ambition. War-time agreements about the countries of Eastern Europe were brushed aside. Pressures were applied against Iran, Greece, and Turkey. Occupation arrangements in Germany were ignored and Berlin was soon subjected to blockade. Czechoslovakia was seized by a coup engineered from the outside. The shadow of the Red Army lent support to Communist parties and agents throughout Western Europe. Participation in the Marshall Plan was rejected. Aggression was unleashed in Korea. The walkout and the veto underlined an attitude of contempt for the United Nations itself. The Cold War is not a bilateral controversy between Washington and Moscow but an offensive by the Communist bloc against all the rest.

In his address to the United Nations General Assembly in September, 1961, President Kennedy said, "In this hall there are not three forces, but two. One is composed of those who are trying to build the kind of world described in Articles 1 and 2 of the Charter. The other, seeking a far different world, would undermine this Organization in the process."

I am profoundly convinced that this is the essential issue in this period of world history through which we are living. Man is in the process of deciding whether we shall build a decent world order, resting upon the consent of peoples and governments, or become subjected to forces of coercion and tyranny. I am equally convinced that the overwhelming majority of peoples and governments are committed to the promise of the Charter. This is made manifest at moments of crisis, such as the one which arose in Korea in June 1950 and the one in Cuba in October 1962. It was discovered anew when "troika" was proposed to cripple the United Nations itself, a proposal rejected almost unanimously except for those who made it. As one who spent five years in uniform in World War II, as one who has some comprehension of the almost unimaginable differences between World War II and any third World War, I am deeply committed to the realistic necessity of making the United Nations system work.

I suspect that most of us Americans know both too much and too little about the United Nations: too much to give it the continuing attention it deserves, too little to understand deeply its vital importance in the conduct of our foreign relations. Time does not permit more than the briefest allusions to the more important aspects of its function.

The United Nations provides the elementary structure for international arrangements which are simple practical necessities in the daily work of the modern world. Were it to disappear today, it would have to be rebuilt tomorrow.

It provides a busy, if informal, diplomatic center where governments can be in regular touch with each other about a wide range of bilateral problems, an opportunity especially important for those who do not have world-wide diplomatic representation in capitals.

It is a school for understanding—the understanding which reaches beyond a sense of passing amiability, and establishes its roots in a more accurate knowledge of nations who are otherwise strangers to each other.

It affords the smaller countries, the bulk of its membership, their primary chance to influence the course of events as well as the principal protection of their security in a somewhat turbulent world.

It can extend types of assistance to newly independent and developing countries too sensitive to be handled on a bilateral basis. Through such agencies as the World Bank, it can organize and coordinate aid provided to individual countries by combinations of national effort.

It serves as the custodian of prestige at moments of crisis, providing a pause for reflection and sober thought and machinery for the peaceful settlement of disputes before the fire becomes universal.

It provides a "United Nations presence" in certain areas of tension and danger, an international safeguard against the violence which might escalate rapidly into war.

It fosters the steady growth of law—the law which enlarges our area of freedom by reducing, through predictable conduct, the chances of harsh collisions as sovereign states pursue their eccentric orbits.

It keeps before us the constant reminders of the unfinished business of the human race: peace, safety, human dignity, prosperity—and the freedom which is our own most basic commitment.

Of course, the United Nations has problems which need attention. It is a political institution, within which 110 members are pursuing their national interests as they see them. We do—we in the United States— and so do 109 others. It is impressive to see the extent to which common interests evolve, but this is not always the result. Looking ahead, it seems to me that there are at least two problems which need further attention.

The first is the role of debate in the peaceful settlement of disputes. The drafters of the Charter wisely looked upon debate as a drastic remedy. Article 33 states:

> 1. The parties to any dispute, the continuance of which is likely to en-
> danger the maintenance of international peace and security, shall, first of
> all, seek a solution by negotiation, enquiry, meditation, conciliation, arbi-
> tration, judicial settlement, resort to regional agencies or arrangements, or
> other peaceful means of their own choice.

We have made certain suggestions on this point: for example, with respect to the more liberal use of a rapporteur, in an effort to explore quietly the possibilities of settlement without the inflammatory effect of acrimonious debate. We are pleased to know that other members are thinking about the same problem and an improvement in procedures to increase the chances for constructive results.

A second problem which is getting intensive attention is that of financial responsibility within the United Nations system. The United Nations is called upon to bear very heavy responsibilities; this costs money and there is no other source for it than its members. We believe that when decisions are taken the matter of costs should be a part of the decision, that votes should be cast with this responsibility in mind, and that costs should be shared equitably among all the membership. A large step was taken during 1962 toward financial responsibility; the World Court held that assessments by the General Assembly for peace-keeping activities in the Near East and the Congo were obligatory upon members, a judgment subsequently approved by a large majority of the Assembly itself.

I suppose that no United Nations responsibility has raised more searching questions or has been more difficult for the United Nations itself, than those activities in the Congo since July 1960. The severity of the test has made the present prospects of a successful conclusion all the more gratifying. One difficulty is our short memory, forgetfulness about the origins of the problem and the issues involved in it. The Congo problem in its present form started in the years 1957–60 with rapidly increasing insistence by the Congolese themselves upon their own independence. The Congo, an area more than one-third as large as the United States and with more than 13,000,000 people, pressed for independence before it had developed a structure of indigenous administration, before it had any significant experience in elections or in managing a constitutional system. However, a round table conference was convened in Brussels in early 1960 at which more than twenty Congolese political groups were represented, and which included all of the leaders whose names have become familiar to us: Kasavubu, Lumumba, Gizenga, Tshombe, Kalonji and others. They agreed on a basis for independence, more particularly on the idea of a unified Congo. Elections were held on that basis throughout the country for both the Central and Provincial Governments. Independence came on July 1, 1960 under a basic law passed by the Belgian Parliament but subject of course to amendment by the new state itself.

Immediately upon independence, the fragile nation descended into chaos. Its troops rebelled and law and order disappeared. Belgium sent certain of its own forces back to the Congo to offer some measure of protection to the large number of its own nationals living there. The Central Congolese Government thereupon issued three requests for military assistance including troops—one to the United Nations, one to the United States and one to the Soviet Union. These were the alternatives with which President Eisenhower was confronted in July 1960.

He wisely decided to support the request to the United Nations and to give that organization our backing, to prevent the Congo from becoming a major threat to the peace of Africa and perhaps to the world through a direct confrontation there between the great powers. An emergency meeting of the United Nations Security Council told Dag Hammarskjold, the Secretary-General, to organize a peace-keeping mission. The first troops, a Tunisian force, arrived in less than twenty-four hours. Before long the United Nations with United States help had a force of twenty thousand, contributed by approximately twenty countries, backed up by one of the largest continuous airlifts in the recent decade.

This was not an intervention by the United Nations in the internal affairs of a single country; it was a response to the formal invitation of the government of the country itself to assist it to eliminate chaos and to prevent unwanted intrusion into its affairs from the outside.

Several months later, the Kennedy Administration took a careful look at Congo policy, and decided to give full and effective support to the earlier decision to back the United Nations. The road has been rocky, but the effort has been more than justified in the event.

In the thirty-one months since July 1960, three secessions have been set back—Communists in the north in Stanleyville, diamond smugglers in Kasai, the Katanga mining area in the south. No one of these secessions was based upon a mandate, either by law or by the expressed will of the peoples concerned. The United Nations has supported the arrangements agreed to by the Congolese themselves and has sought to create the conditions under which peaceful settlements could be reached without outside interference. A moderate anti-Communist government has been in business now for more than a year, and the United Nations Force has succeeded in its mission to preserve the "territorial integrity and political independence" of the Congo. The United Nations has brought in teachers, physicians, and half a hundred other technicans to get the Congolese economy working—which has a fabulous potential if it can be allowed to work—and a service which is marked with as much gallantry on the civilian side as it has been marked by gallantry and discretion on the political side. But let us before we concern ourselves about the details of these particular weeks, remember what the alternatives were, what the objectives have been, what the prospectives are, and realize that in this process the United Nations has been severely tested and has every chance to make good on its basic commitments.

315

We in the United States, on this matter of the cold war, will continue to try to build the strength, political, economic and social strength, as well as the military strength of the free world, and we will continue this struggle for freedom and defend our vital interests because they are indeed vital to the survival of freedom.

May I say with complete candor, in order that I may not be misunderstood, that if there is anyone here who wants victory in the cold war and wants to slash our defense budget, I don't know what you are talking about. If there is anyone here who wants victory in the cold war and is unwilling to spend less than one-tenth of our defense budget in foreign aid, I don't know what you are talking about. If there is anyone who wants victory in the cold war and is unwilling to back the rapid expansion of trade within the free world, surely you do not understand the sinews of strength among the nations of the free world.

And if there is anyone here who wants victory in the cold war and wants us to withdraw from the United Nations or fail to support it then let me say *don't quit*. There are many ways of quitting or abandoning the field to the enemy, and no surer way than to withdraw our support in pique or frustration because we find ourselves in great majorities in the United Nations only 98% of the time, instead of 100% of the time.

And if there is anyone—and one can sympathize with the frustrations of this turbulent world in which we live—if there is anyone who wishes to precipitate the issues to settle tomorrow every question in front of us through a great conflagration, if necessary, let me say that we cannot let our glands take over from our intelligence. For the underlying reason is this, freedom is rooted in human nature. Freedom is a result of a discourse which has been going on for two thousand years among men of many countries, many races, about the political consequences of the nature of man. These aspirations are a part of our own heritage. It is no accident that Articles 1 and 2 of the Charter of the United Nations are so congenial to the long-range foreign policy of the American people because they came out of a tradition of which we are a part.

We are strong with our arms, strong enough so that Mr. Marshal Malinovsky's speech today can be discounted for what it was worth. We are strong in our arms, we are strong in our economy. Where we are strongest of all is in these shared commitments we have with people in every country in every continent. At times of great testing, as I have indicated earlier, we know where the sympathies of the ordinary people of the world are, because they understand that we have no national purposes which we are trying to impose upon them, that the strength of this giant is a strength committed to decent objectives, and that the freedom of our people means to us the freedom of those other people, that the commitments of the Charter apply to us, [that they] are commitments we expect to apply to them, and that we and they continually spin the infinity of threads which bind peace together, and that these powerful common interests makes allies of us all in times of great testing.

I have no doubt about how this thing we call the cold war is going to come out, because we are talking about human beings, we are talking about people, and I think we know a good deal about their commitments, their commitments in decency, and those commitments we share, and on those commitments we have allies. Whether under alliances or not, we have allies with people right around this globe.

We *will* win this cold war because it is a war directed by tyranny against all the rest, and the great majority is struggling for freedom. That struggle will surely prevail.

Thank you very much.

APPENDIX V

"Applied Ethics: The United Nations and the United States"

AN ADDRESS BY WILLIAM Y. ELLIOTT[1]

THIS ARTICLE EXAMINES THE RELATION of ethics to community as it bears on our own values and as it relates to the idea of legitimacy, and considers the possibilities and limits of world law through the United Nations. It tests these conceptions as they bear realistically on suggested methods for maximizing the advantages of the United Nations to the United States and minimizing the dangers and disadvantages of the United Nations both to the United States and to the rest of the Free World. In that light, it suggests workable changes which could strengthen future American policy.

Some Assumptions Concerning the United Nations

Since all policies must be logically developed from assumptions about facts and moral objectives, a few assumptions should be stated at the outset. These are held in common by nearly all persons who believe rationally in personal responsibility, in moral individual development as the only true morality, and in freely shared values as the basis of a real *consensus juris*. They are the widely held and tested ethics of freedom. Yet they need succinct statement to provide orientation points and criteria for further application. Otherwise it is difficult to escape being led down deceptively easy, frequently accepted false roads which profess by signposts to take us "toward a peaceful world order," when in fact they lead the other way. While these signposts profess to lead to peace, security, and freedom under law—all good goals—they can easily result in mistakes that would force our surrender, and with it the loss of all con-

---

[1] This speech was originally delivered as the first of two John Findley Green Foundation lectures at Westminster College, Fulton, Missouri, in October, 1957. It was later revised for inclusion in this volume.

318

stitutional freedom, as well as the hopes of a just and lasting peace. Pleasantly deceptive to wishful thinkers who judge every effort to create a regime of law only by its self-professed objectives, such a projection of "world law" must be tested in terms of its claim to being a true moral community, one capable of supporting the sanctions of just law: "By their fruits shall ye know them."

Francis Bacon put it another way: "God forbid," said Lord Verulam, "that we should mistake a dream of the imagination for a true picture of the world."

The assumptions upon which catchwords about the United Nations are based—that the United Nations is man's "last, best hope for peace and justice" and variations on that theme used freely by both our political parties—represent ideals which are desirable goals of policies. But these ideals must not be treated as facts unless we can make them facts and change existing facts.

Stated in terms of ethics, the assumption that the United Nations is the only road to peace rests on something like the following progression:

1. The United Nations was accepted in good faith at the end of World War II by the non-Communist nations which possessed real power as states. It seemed to promise the best available protection for peace-loving peoples through joint action called "collective security." It was hoped that the Communist nations would follow this lead. In any case, the rest of the world—which came to be called the "Free World"—must pool enough armed strength, practically all of which is found in the West, to prevent the recurrence of an overbalance of power on the side of totalitarian states. Only thus could it counter the threat to all peace-loving peoples from regimes that could arm secretly and strike by surprise, with weapons of a type that by 1945 had already revolutionized warfare and made total destruction of a nation possible.

The outbreak of World War II was attributed to the failure of the democracies to give their full backing to the League of Nations. In the postwar period, however, Western proposals to "internationalize" control of atomic energy, pool weapons, and set up a United Nations Emergency Force to keep the peace, though arising from a real world need, foundered in the face of Communist determination to reject necessary measures of inspection and international controls or sanctions. The Communists never deviated from their plan to make satellites out of every country and race on the globe. This truth is still too unpleasant to be believed by many neutralists, neutrals, and even some allies, as well as certain Americans.

2. It was cheerfully and wishfully assumed that the Soviet Union and even Communist China could be cleansed of aggressive intentions by evidence of our good faith. We sought to alter their belief in the "necessary" conflict of all free "capitalism" with all state-capitalist ("Communist") systems. This would be done by assuring the latter of security against aggression and permitting coexistence through peaceful "competition of systems," which wartime professions as allies had led many to accept as genuine. This was apparently the world which Franklin D. Roosevelt sought to create by his wartime diplomacy.

Had it been an accurate assessment, the chasm between Communism and Western constitutionalism might have been bridged by a form of coexistence which allowed each to "live and let live." The United Nations might have represented both a League to Enforce Peace and a vehicle for peaceful change through genuine negotiations rather than changes dictated by the Communist world's credo of protracted conflict which ends in the surrender of one system to another as the sole basis for peace, the peace of either "the slave or the grave."

This creed, on the evidence so far available, the Communist systems have never given up. They have adjusted their tactics to take account of their own strength and, even more, the degree of determination shown by their opponents in the Free World. They have now completely replaced the West as colonial powers. They are much more ruthless exploiters and imperialists for their own state capitalism; the savagely destructive designs of their leaders, possessed of great power, make them history's most ruthless Khans. Who, today, believes that if Moscow possessed decisive military power, with a margin sufficient to ensure certain victory and tolerable survival, anything other than satellite status would be left for us and the rest of the Free World? The nature of our fate if Peking had its way, unchecked by Western will and ability to counter its aggression, is even more certain. Prime Minister Nehru found that negotiation without a will to fight did not protect his own boundaries from the Chinese Communist invaders.

If today we accept these assumptions about Communist conduct—driven home by megatonnage, Hungary, and shoe-pounding—the chasm remains unbridged. How shall we derive a "world rule of law" based on the ethics of mutual respect which we recognize as the only foundation of any true system of law if the Communists with their collective and deterministic ethics are committed to destroy that mutuality by a world crusade? Ours is not the ethics of an imposed design—a Procrustean way of stretching out or lopping off human beings to fit the giant's bed. We do not "condition" human beings to accept freedom— *à la* Pavlov. That is not an ethics on which can rest a rule of law consonant with what the West has now generally accepted as the truth of Cicero's *consensus juris.* It will not serve—either for a village or for the world.

A true "world rule of law" conforming to any concept of justice—to say nothing of moral obligation to obey—can emerge only when the world has become enough of a moral community to protect the rights of responsible choice and provide for the moral growth of its citizens. Any conditioned rule of law that professes to bridge this moral gulf is only an uneasy truce. As Kant said in *Toward a Perpetual Peace* (what Lincoln called a "just and lasting peace"), a world order under law is possible only if nations are themselves based on what he called "republican" principles (what we today call "constitutionalism"). These exist where governments protect both civil and political liberties for individuals and for all really free groups, i.e., those not controlled by an outside sovereignty or by the internal coercion of their members.

We should never forget that the stated aims of the United Nations, unlike those of the League of Nations, do not include the words "self-governing" or enshrine civil and political liberties for its members as qualifications for membership. The United Nations stretched its qualifications in an effort to achieve something called "universality." "Peace-loving" as a description of peoples has been stretched into an ambiguity that retains little power to limit admission. It does afford the United States a bar to hang a veto on, however, in the case of so blatant an exception as Red China, if her admission gains more ground in a future Assembly. And only by the most blatant "double-talk" can the Soviet Union pretend that its subjects enjoy either political liberty or the "rule of law." The severe sanctions of its laws maintain, at least, their external enforcement, if not their internal acceptance by a free conscience. But Dumbarton Oaks and the San Francisco Conference paid the price of accepting totalitarians and satellites for the United Nations' birth, under the mistaken idea that universality of inclusive coverage meant universality of moral acceptance of world law.

The salient fact to remember is that every Communist society and many of the new countries that have been promoted into statehood from little more than tribal status have an authoritarian character entirely different from our own political system. *The fact is that our ethics is acceptable only to advanced cultures and people.* The notions of rights and justice, responsible government, and limits on arbitrary behavior by rulers are not deeply ingrained in many of the new nations. Tribalism has councils, but it governs by authority of traditional rulers and customary law.

The United Nations was founded on a compromise designed, on both sides, to conceal by its wording this profound abyss, which nevertheless appears every time the realities come up—for instance, on the issue of effectively applying the Convention on Human Rights. The position of the Great Powers was protected by the veto in the United Nations, with France and China called "great powers" for the sake of history, or hope. The reality of the power cleavage (as well as the moral gulf) between the United States and the Soviet Union is complicated by the emergence of Great Britain and France as nuclear powers and the nuclear potential of Communist China and other nations.

The Communist rulers necessarily profess to have "law," and even to cherish it, since law is a universal myth of men and a uniform requirement of any system that maintains its monopoly of force for long in a given area. But it is not a law that rests either on tested consent or on any form of freely expressed *consensus*. One must hope that, as in any regime which continues in power for as long as forty-seven years, the forms of law will more and more protect the development of at least orderly procedures. Severity, even if untempered, is better than blinding terror. Apparently the continuous intervention of the secret police has been somewhat eased. But, like any system that depends on a single will or an unchecked party oligarchy, Soviet rule can only be one of *imposed* law—imposed, as it now is, by the party and the rulers in Moscow. The Communist world, whether it remains under Moscow or eventually falls under Peking, would have to find some new legitimacy to secure continuity in the succession for a predictable single world system of order or unified policy directives. The struggle to maintain a single dictatorship for the world would go on, but not under any semblance of Marquis of Queensbury rules. Nor would we have increased the chances of avoiding nuclear destruction by following Bertrand Russell's counsels to survive by surrender. We could be both Red and dead; slaves in our graves by any future falling out (and fall outs) between any combination of Red rulers.

If we could keep the United Nations under the influence of the great civilizations whose concepts of law and justice, like their ancient religions, stem from the same roots as ours, then the United Nations undoubtedly could be more central to all our policy. It should then be the prime objective of our policy to strengthen the United Nations as a true community. It always helps us when others share our burden.

But NATO and the more advanced Latin countries of South and Central America, the Western-oriented remnants of the disturbed Middle East, and those states in the Far East that wish to defend their own freedom are no longer numerous enough in voting strength to guarantee that the United Nations will retain any such character. The present trend would have to be reversed. The states included in the above list form a doubtful and sometimes divided majority of that body. It is a majority that is disappearing with every new session. Unless our missionaries and colonial tutelage have done a more miraculous job than at present seems apparent, the growing number of new African states can hardly be counted on to achieve this cultural maturity in the near future.

Thus if we are to continue to cherish the United Nations as a main forum for working out and announcing our own moral concepts and our policies, and if we are not to be pressed into negotiations and inevitable one-way concessions, the future membership and voting conditions and the political and moral as well as the ambiguous legal competence of the United Nations become crucial to our diplomacy. The stakes are no less than the preservation of our kind of world, which the balance of power in civilized hands has preserved for us. Freedom and justice are possible through accepted laws, backed by force when needed. The alternative is the disappearance of law into at least temporary anarchy as more and more "nations" are created by native governments stirred to action against "colonialism" and eager for the recognition implied by membership in the United Nations.

We may, on the present trends, be faced at some future time by a revolutionary take-over of the Portuguese overseas territories. Then Mozambique and Angola would claim membership in the United Nations. Other new members would probably include governments claiming statehood for former German Southwest, as well as Southeast Africa, and the Native Trust Territories (Basutoland, Bechuanaland, and Swaziland). British, French, and Dutch Guiana and, for that matter, British Honduras, Malta, the Rock of Gibraltar, and Guam would have as good a claim as these others.

A fantastic price would have to be paid for creating such "states," with all their costly apparatus of sovereignty and diplomacy. Even if they were not immediately added to the Assembly's swollen roster, the price must be paid both in misery and in somebody's capital savings. Capital for development simply cannot be ground or wrung, even by the most totalitarian methods, from the poverty-stricken peoples of these really underdeveloped lands. The United Nations, unless a halt is called to this reckless inflation of its membership, would, by a sort of Gresham's law in politics, be in danger of being "voted" into whatever is decided by those who properly should be its wards in trusteeship. It would also have to support them in a style to which they were neither accustomed nor entitled, because they would then have the votes, and votes count—at least when they go against the West. Yet today a considerable body of respectable American intellectuals can find some grounds in this pietistic estimate of the United Nations for urging an increase in the "legislative" powers of such a United Nations as is now in very clear prospect.[2]

To summarize: The United Nations has proved, up until the full flood of this membership inflation, a manageable vehicle for what some take comfort in as United States "propaganda victories," though all the while our "power" position, including secure access to the world's raw material resources, was being whittled away. The creation of new state "members" from colonies has often amounted to legalizing an apparatus capable of being turned against the West by Communist influence. There are strong inherent probabilities of take-over, with no remedy available from the United Nations or the Court, of lawful property and investments, either through measures of punitive taxation

[2] See the 13th Report of the Commission to Study the Organization of Peace, *Developing the United Nations, A Response to the Challenge of a Revolutionary Era*, prepared under the chairmanship of Arthur N. Holcombe (New York, 1961).

or through simple confiscation.[3] The jury is being "packed" and perhaps "stacked" by every new admission of an unprepared former colony to United Nations membership.

Of course, some of these results probably would have occurred without the United Nations, through the disintegration of Western rule and the revolt against colonialism. In states with a long cultural history and real leaders, the change was inevitable. We in the United States recognized this fact and welcomed the coming of age of the Philippines. But we have also paid a bitter price for pushing Cuba into complete independence before its own people were ready for self-rule and constitutional responsibility. And did not our competition with Moscow for votes and support by the new states in the Assembly of the United Nations permit the Congo and other states to proceed prematurely to full statehood and to United Nations membership? What was already a well-marked tendency in 1957 has now become a seemingly irreversible trend.[4]

Since this is a record of the uses to which the United Nations has been put, we need to emphasize only that President Eisenhower added to President Truman's record of resort to the United Nations three principal points: He proposed to Moscow a mutual agreement limiting the use of the veto, up to then used by the Soviet Union on many occasions but not by the United States.[5] He turned the threat of United Nations

[3] The 1952 Resolution of the United Nations Assembly which affirmed the rights of "sovereign" take-over of property developed by others without any effective method of preventing bold confiscation and without adequate legal restraints or remedies has been accepted by courts in several countries, though not our own. See "Permanent Sovereignty over Natural Wealth and Resources," *American Journal of International Law*, Vol. L, No. 856 (1956). See also Gilliam White, *Nationalization of Foreign Property* (London, 1961), for a view sympathetic to the forces behind confiscation; W. Y. Elliott's chapter on "Freedom and Responsibility" in *The Idea of Colonialism*, edited by Robert Strausz-Hupé and Harry W. Hazard (New York, 1958), for a philosophical defense of the rights of special private property versus national confiscation; and "The Act of State Doctrine and Rule of Law," *American Journal of International Law*, Vol. LIII, No. 635 (1959).

[4] See my article "A Time for Peace?" in *Virginia Quarterly Review* (Summer, 1946), reprinted as "Can We Organize a Free World, Under Law?" in *The Western Political Heritage* (1949), 965–74.

[5] Letter to Bulganin, January 12, 1958: "I propose that we should make it the policy of our two governments at least not to use the veto power to prevent the

collective security measures against Britain, France, and Israel—the first two are NATO allies—on what amounted to an assumption of aggression against Nasser, whose hands were surely not spotless. Finally, he nailed the flag of the United States to action through the United Nations in the case of the troubled Congo, with a presumptive bearing on what our reliance would be in similar future cases. Of course, all international commitments have a built-in and implied *rebus sic stantibus* clause. And Eisenhower did not propose to limit United States action *only* to United Nations channels; fortunately, neither did President Kennedy, in spite of his original proposal to let the United Nations inspect Soviet removal of offensive weapons from Cuba.

One ought to remember, too, the growing attachment of a large and influential body of opinion in the United States, dating back to the 1920's, to the principle of accepting any settlements by the International Court of Justice. This piety toward "court law" is reflected in an effort to have our government declare its willingness to accept the Court's decisions as binding. On the record, both of our major political parties, through authoritative spokesmen and by platform pronouncements, propose to repeal the Connally Amendment, although neither has moved strongly for such implementation when in office. The important issue that produced this Senate amendment to our adherence to the optional clause for obligatory court jurisdiction is, "What constitutes a question that is exclusively within the 'domestic' jurisdiction of a nation under Article 2, paragraph 7?" The record of the United States is one of general adherence to the optional clause, as written, to ensure the International Court's jurisdiction over facts. But the Connally Amendment on our adherence to that article of the statute (Article 36) dealing with acceptance of its compulsory jurisdiction (paragraph 2) makes our determination final concerning what is "domestic" in any cases directly affecting the United States. Of course, this reservation gives an equal opportunity to others, who can claim the same finality in disputes which we might like to settle with them through the Court.

The Ethical Issues That Limit the United Nations Claim to Make World Law

The following questions summarize the most important focal points

Security Council from proposing methods for the pacific settlement of disputes pursuant to Chapter II."

for analyzing the real ethical significance (not the "pious hope") of the United Nations. They comprise not only the applied ethics of this address but also the assumptions about the United Nations' role in promoting a basis for reciprocal justice, rather than mere "forms of law" limiting only the free nations in our divided world.

1. To what degree is the United Nations, as presently organized, staffed, and operated, capable of becoming a vehicle for creating and maintaining a community of law which rests upon principles of justice acceptable to the United States? Note that the question is one of finding "to what degree," rather than requiring a categorical "yes" or "no." Presumably it also requires a clarification and an assertion of what we ourselves will insist upon as the effective conditions that relate law to justice before accepting any "law" as binding on the United States.

2. Has the United Nations the capability of mustering adequate force to ensure that its sanctions will be maintained and that its "recommendations" and its committees of inquiry, if not its writ, can operate behind the Iron Curtain, as well as among those who accept its decisions as morally binding? The sample case of Hungary or the efforts to get truce teams into North Korea or Bulgaria serve as instructive examples of the limitations of the United Nations in this regard.

3. Can the United Nations—in an international community capable of assuming any of the functions of a superstate—become a true instrument of the ethical sense of right on which law, other than a dictum of unenforceable character, can be erected? What meaning can be attached to recommendations, on any other basis, for extending its "legislative" powers? *Whose* will be those powers? *Where* operative? Where *not*?

4. Even if the United Nations cannot be made an instrument for world law comparable to the law of a national state and fully recognized internationally, can it reflect a sufficient moral community to impose useful limits on the political and psychological offensives (ranging from peace propoganda and attitudes developed in the Pugwash Conferences to actual terror and brutal threats of aggression) which the Soviet Union is aiming not only at the undeveloped and uncommitted areas, but at its own satellites, at NATO and other United States allies, and at the people of the United States as well? Can it serve as a useful and effective counter to Soviet forms of protracted Cold War? Or does it tie our hands—and change our tune even where it does not stop our tongues?

5. On balance, does the United Nations afford to the United States

the right kind of vehicle for framing its basic diplomacy and taking measures for the protection of its national security? Is it our only guide and vehicle? Our main one? Or one to be used with care not to overplay our commitments and forget the probable future prospects?

6. Does the United Nations tend to preclude the full development of regional or other forms of international associations more real in their communities of moral purpose and in their capabilities for common defensive action than the United Nations itself has so far proved to be?

7. In the light of this analysis, what sort of changes may be suggested in policies of the United States toward the United Nations and its organs?

8. Can the existing mechanisms of the United Nations be more effectively used to promote the basic objectives of the United States and to strengthen the sense of justice and right as the only basis for a true moral world community?

Can Political Community
Overleap National Responsibility?

The conflict over establishing the ethical and legal basis for the true international community of the future is, in the last resort, a conflict of moral values, which must be fought out until one side or the other emerges victorious. Otherwise, it will be settled through stalemate and historical adjustment, by change to a different system. There is encouraging evidence that those who have seen, from within, the true nature of Communism accept this choice without hesitation: The Berlin Wall is the symbol of the whole Communist system as a prison. Those within wish to change it or escape it where they cannot change it. Communism must control revolution from within its own centers as well as in its satellites. It is, on the evidence to date, not possible to brainwash freedom out of the minds of men. It is, generally speaking, only in the neutralist areas that the danger of Communist deception lies. Thus, their leaders can speak of Hungary as an "episode" and pretend to believe Soviet Russia's intentions to be nonaggressive, probably because they are at a distance. Where the facts are close at hand, the lie is evident, and no true man loves it.

If this is a just analysis of the nature of the struggle in which the Free World is engaged with the Communists, we must have the hope and dedicated faith to act so that it will be the Communists' "myths," by their actions revealed to be brutally imposed delusions, that will give way in the protracted conflict of systems. That hope cannot father delusions concerning present facts without increasing our risks.

It is in the light of both faith and facts that the United Nations must be examined as an instrument of national policy for the Free World. Its structure and its powers deserve very careful consideration. It has the initial advantage, which was the realistic hope of its free founders, of being a forum where completely open debate can take place, so far as the nations wish it or dare to demand it. But free debate did not mean the right of international inquisitions into domestic issues, merely the right to criticize when the Assembly so voted. Above all, it did not mean the right to coerce internal political or social patterns. Moscow saw to that—and we concurred. Now Moscow is adamant within its own system, but turns the new United Nations on us.

Nevertheless, the United Nations still has precious uses. It serves a great educational purpose in showing free people the true behavior of those accustomed to rule without responsibility. To watch the Soviet spokesmen in action is to learn the manners of terror as we see them use the double-edged weapon of freedom that may in the end more wound the wielder. That is true, of course, only if Khrushchev proves to be wrong about the timidity and servility of men and women in the world which he regards as degenerate—fit only to be intimidated by shoe-pounding.

The New Balance of Voting Strength

In order to protect itself, the United States early learned to insist, in connection with agencies like the International Bank and the Monetary Fund, upon voting formulas that related any decision concerning the funds to the amount of fiscal support given to the organ under consideration by the voting participants. This is an application of the ethics of proportionate (Aristotelian) equality and justice which is the essence of constitutional freedom and protected human rights. Without such a formula, we should have been open to universal plunder through abuse of the power to spend our money, which would have meant the power to tax, which, John Marshall earlier reminded us, "involves the power to destroy." The Soviet Union, after helping at Bretton Woods to launch the Bank and the Fund, withdrew.

It is significant that UNESCO does not really function as a free

329

cultural activity in any country behind the Iron Curtain, although the Soviet Union and its satellites have made vigorous efforts to turn the covenants on human rights and other cultural media to their own propaganda uses. They have recently, for propaganda purposes, adhered to UNESCO and insisted on the distribution of Communist-authored propaganda picturing the Soviet relation to its satellites as non-imperialistic. Similarly, they have used UNRRA and UNICEF (the Children's Fund), but only under conditions (behind the Iron Curtain) that they could control for their party and national advantage. United Nations technical assistance afforded a useful distribution belt for Soviet agents—in its earlier stages, at least. Any steps toward allowing SUNFED, or its lineal descendants in the United Nations, to dictate distribution of our own food surpluses and spend the proceeds would follow the same well-beaten path of concessions to Soviet advantage by drawing down our strength—often from our own sources of supply.

These lessons should not be forgotten when we expect the United Nations, now packed with "states" that are not modern nations, to provide a happy or even a lasting solution to world problems, including disarmament and the use of sanctions. A careful look at the nature and the composition of the body the Assembly has now become, and will become with every increment of new countries, reveals that former colonies are not "equal" nations. They are certainly not capable of bearing true international responsibility and are frequently not capable of supporting or governing themselves. If the United Nations is ever to serve its true purpose, it must certainly apply different standards of membership from this time forth. Continuing the present trend, it will see the principles of representation and the international equality of states subjected to the grossest distortions in modern human history.

The United Nations cannot become a superstate, under such membership and organizing principles, without perverting justice and destroying our own real and responsible strength for freedom. We ought not to expect it to act like, nor should we treat it as, a true superstate in judicial, legislative, or executive functions. We should, on the contrary, treat it as no more than it is—namely, a means of lining up public support for our views in other countries. Even this limited use of the United Nations could backfire wherever the fetishes of anti-colonialism or anti-Westernism are worshiped and get majority voting strength. As a propaganda forum it has uses that, if we are firm against abuses, can discomfit the

Soviets more often than the United States, the NATO powers, and Japan.

A recognition of this fact has led the United States and many of the other free states to set up regional groupings in matters vital to the defense of freedom and to restraining Soviet or Chinese Communist aggression. This has been true not only in the case of NATO but of SEATO and of the aid plans which were intended to strengthen the communities participating in them and to help some neutrals and neutralists remain free. Regional defensive associations under such conditions do not hold forth the illusory and dangerous prospect of submerging in a universal sovereignty the basic protections of free peoples. Nor do they offer easy possibilities for exploitation to those who are bent on the destruction of freedom. If we operate internationally, as we must, it is useful not to be taken in by what used to be called "Globaloney."

But there were also regional and other groups of neutralists whose neutralism was so clearly one-sided that they found the United States to be "imperialist"—while the Soviet Union was not. Like Sweet Alice in "Ben Bolt," they "trembled with fear, at a (Soviet or Chinese) frown." They had not been absorbed by the Soviet Union; in their resentment of their own past they could not blame backward czarism. We in the West were, they held, responsible for their balked expectations. We proved it by catering to their grievances as if we were paying for past guilt. To assume guilt for the world's whole past is both wrong and inversely arrogant.

After the Bandung Conference dire prophecies were made concerning the use of the United Nations by the Afro-Asian bloc against the United States or NATO. So far these prophecies have not materialized in positive action. But additional chaos in Africa, north, middle, and south, might confirm them—with a United Nations paralyzed or even dominated by the new members. The African states of the former French Community have exhibited remarkable stability. But Algeria and Ghana tend, like Nasser's friends, to move in an orbit that brings them dangerously close to becoming Red satellites—by increasing their dependence on Moscow, in arms and economics, of which fact they seem blindly unconscious.

Fortunately, many of Nehru's collaborators and certain other leaders of the Bandung powers were not misled concerning the true nature of Soviet imperialism. They did *not* lend themselves to a unified attitude which would have swept into the United Nations a solid anti-Western bloc of newly liberated states. Even those countries which had achieved a somewhat precarious sovereignty through the liquidation of the British, Dutch, and French colonial rule in Asia did not all follow Ceylon and Indonesia. Nevertheless, the combination of some Eastern powers with some new African and Asian countries, aligned against Western policy and interest, generated dangerous tendencies for the United Nations to attempt both to legislate and to execute policies that would destroy free markets and investments.

The balance of voting strength in the Assembly came to depend in increasing measure upon the attitude of the Latin-American states and the reluctance of certain new states to pursue common policies with the rest of the so-called Afro-Asian bloc. On many issues, such as nationalization of basic resources, the Latin-American states have shown sharp divisions from the NATO powers in voting in the Assembly. With the addition of other Soviet satellites through the misguided policy of "swap" for increasing the membership of the United Nations, the prospects fade of maintaining a majority of any safe proportions in favor of NATO objectives in the General Assembly.

Prospects of reforming voting strength in the Assembly are now dim. We should oppose "troika" methods, whether in the Secretariat or in Assembly blocs, as Nigeria has valiantly done. But if we are confronted by the hard fact of growing neutral and neutralist alignment of the new states, we must certainly revise our trustful past policies of increasing the powers of the United Nations. It must begin to operate in a more realistic way, returning to its original Charter conception, and we must use the veto power to curb dangerous United Nations invasions of clearly "domestic" jurisdiction everywhere. This resistance would equally apply to the serious blow to our whole world status and prospects which would result from the admission of Red China to the United Nations. An India which, while fighting a Chinese invasion, still supports the admission of such a "peace-loving" country into the United Nations seems sometimes hardly worth saving. We ought to demand a changed attitude from Nehru's successors as the price of continued large-scale military aid.

What Present Working Methods Can Be Used?

Several methods of working carefully and constructively through the United Nations suggest themselves in the light of the foregoing evidence:

The first line of policy requires a more determined initiative and more coherent agreements among the Western powers, the Latin-American countries in particular, to utilize the moral sentiments of the members of the United Nations when occasions arise, such as the ruthless Soviet suppression of Polish rioting and the Hungarian rebellion, which reveal the true nature of Soviet imperialism. It is significant, however, that the British, French, and Israeli efforts to settle the Suez Canal issues and to topple Nasser were so timid and ill defended on their true moral grounds as to take a considerable part of the edge off the Kremlin's brutal suppression of Hungary—which might otherwise have offered a temporarily unifying moral front with a chance to isolate the Soviet bloc. The United States was left in the ambiguous position of crying, "A plague on both your houses," with more legality than honest morality in its own position.

Failure to recognize suppression of the Hungarian Nagy government as Soviet imperial control over people of European origins indicated a certain color prejudice on the part of Nehru regarding what constituted imperialism. This same color blindness no doubt affected many of those new states which abstained from voting for United Nations resolutions demanding the withdrawal of Soviet armed forces from Hungary and providing for a United Nations mission that might have given Nagy's government at least recognition and moral support.

The United States has assumed the difficult role of an anti-colonial power in principle, often with the result that it has supported the actions of former colonies, in fact, on the grounds that they "must always be right," in order to avoid being labeled a Western imperial and colonial power. Here, again, the Latin-American states are important in the United Nations, and their views are colored by a rather remote colonial past, even more than are our own. Do we really buy any useful support by complaisance toward irresponsibility? If United Nations support has to be bought by abandoning or failing our NATO allies, would it be either morally or politically wise for us to do so? By extension, are we truly prudent in withdrawing any missile bases before the Cuban matter has been settled on our original terms?

A second, alternative line of policy, which has been in part pursued, is to work out, through regional associations including the OAS, NATO, and SEATO, defense agreements and certain types of economic supplements which would maintain an effective moral unity among the free nations and counter the efforts of the Soviet bloc to exploit the divisions outlined above. But alliances do not automatically ensure the unity of a strong front; indeed, they sometimes endanger it by pressing either for too much common military commitment or for concessions to carry along the most timid allies. We must reserve freedom to act, when action means *salus populi*.

A third policy, not yet envisaged by the United States or, presumably, by other Western powers, would be an effort to reconsider and fundamentally revise the nature and the organization and membership of the United Nations. This would mean a frontal challenge to the equality of many present members which are not really states. To reorganize at this time would alienate many, if not all, of the small powers who can exploit their own weakness under the moral guise of liquidating the last remnants of European colonialism. Some of them, like Indonesia, have imposed their own colonialism on areas like West Irian, those portions of New Guinea which remained under Dutch control after the 1949 treaty with Indonesia and withdrawal of Dutch forces. West Irian was never, in any known period of history, under the control of any rulers of Indonesia, nor are its people related ethnically to those of Indonesia. It has no organic past connection by cultural, political, or any other ties. Yet it was surrendered to a paltry show of force, to avoid offending other former colonies.

If, in fact, Egypt could make a single federal union of Arab states, or of any other African states, the present large voting strength of these states ought, by the logic of international law and practice, to be reduced to a basis more commensurate with the voting strength of other powers. This was done when Syria was incorporated. However, when Syria withdrew from the Union, it regained its vote in the General Assembly, reestablishing the old imbalance. But if we have to wait for mergers of this type to reform the voting strength of the United Nations, we may wait long and get unexpected results.

Only if the United Nations proves to be a strong threat to responsible freedom will voting reform become a real issue, with the possible dangerous alternative of scrapping the organization. Under such circumstances, we might be forced to reconstitute what can be salvaged into an international community of a new order—not a world order perhaps, but an order bent on regrouping the forces of freedom and saving those who are prepared to seek a genuine moral basis for a law transcending nationalism. Some anticipatory thinking along these lines is surely indicated, although it must be discreetly done. What we cannot trumpet from housetops we should study deeply in order to find better remedies for real diseases of our body politic.

Conclusions

What should be the cardinal principles in shaping United States policy toward the United Nations for effective protection of our own ethical base? Note that moral objectives have been related at all stages of this inquiry to the realities of the world we confront. So they must be for any sound ethics or policy in defending our own and others' freedom. Utopias merely serve to encourage escapism and wishful thinking—moralizing, not morality.

1. We should be guided in all our attitudes toward the United Nations by a recognition of its true nature. The United Nations cannot be treated as a world legislative body whose writ can be expected to run behind the Iron Curtain. In the light of its composition, it is not a "legislature" for the world. It runs some danger of developing sanctions against parts of the Free World by moralizing resolutions that encourage boycotts and other punishments, as if resolutions created legal judgments and supported punitive actions. So long as this is true, the United Nations should not be permitted, either directly or indirectly, to "legislate" on any matters, especially those which might be turned to the disadvantage of the vital interests of the United States. This would suggest a generally strict interpretation on our part of what are truly domestic questions and what are issues affecting the peace of the world, on the general theory that a true international community for settling these issues legally, i.e., justly and legitimately, does not exist under present circumstances.

Matters should be referred to the United Nations for action under the "Uniting For Peace" resolutions, which Secretary Acheson pushed through the Assembly in the different world of 1950, only if the United Nations seems a better agent for securing the defense of the vital interests of the Free World, and particularly of the United States, than some of the alternative regional groupings like NATO and SEATO. We ought to retain the power to do more than block action on a two-thirds basis. If we are judiciously strict on future admissions, we might hope to command a majority for support against hostile blocs. If conditions deteriorate, we should not hesitate to use the veto for *our* protection.

To rely on the United Nations for the kind of judgments which one would expect from a superstate, based upon a shared moral community, or to give it real legislative powers would limit the freedom of the United States to secure its own defenses. Korea should have been an adequate lesson to us in this respect. To ask the United Nations to deal with as thorny a question as Cuba's propaganda attacks on the United States is to invite division of support, just as to ask United Nations intervention to prevent actual Castro offensives against neighbors would be of little benefit and would take the problem out of its proper legal channels of settlement by self-defense.[6]

2. It follows that the United States should oppose every effort to debase further the voting currency of the United Nations. We should block the introduction of additional states in the General Assembly with equal voting privileges unless they have valid claims to be the sort of states envisaged by the Charter of the United Nations itself, that is, peace-loving nations who do not aim at aggression; unless they possess enough power to assist in carrying out policies which they may vote in the General Assembly; or unless they are capable of acting under the concepts of moral responsibility envisaged in any genuine system of international law and morals. We might get a purge of members incapable of this responsibility by insisting on withholding our financial contributions until the expulsion of nonpaying members had been accomplished in accordance with the Charter.

3. We should offer to join some of the more responsible former colonies of Africa, such as Nigeria and Tunisia or other non-Communist-oriented African powers, and some noncolonial European powers like Norway or Sweden or Eire in setting up trusteeships under the United Nations for the remaining colonial areas whose dates for independence have been left open, keeping their present administrators in office during

---

[6] This proved subsequently to be the weak point in the otherwise admirable speech of President Kennedy, putting what amounted to an ultimatum to Khrushchev on the removal of missiles with United Nations inspection. Since United Nations inspection proved impossible and would have been fooling only ourselves, the practical alternative vanished, to our discomfiture and continued grave and growing danger.

the transition period. Any joint proposal of this kind should be positive, moving them toward independence with agreed-upon tests, with African powers associated in the United Nations trusteeships. Under no circumstances should we permit externally controlled "revolutions" to take them over, *à la* Cuba. This goes for Portuguese territories, also: no guided revolutions—no "volunteers."

4. Since we must, because of our past commitments and because of the facts which confront us, rely heavily upon the existing United Nations, we must attempt to work with other like-minded states to revive the organization as a moral community opposed to real (i.e., Communist) imperialism instead of chasing the shadows of departed colonial ghosts. Our defense seldom takes the sound form of a moral offensive, vigorously pressed. We seem plaintive, when we leave off being playful or placating. This impression stems in part from our choice of spokesmen.

5. We should be explicit in stating that the United States will never recognize mere "universality" as grounds for membership in the United Nations or population of a nation as the sole basis for voting power—i.e., one man, one vote, to be extended on a world scale to some future idea of representation.[7] For example, to count the alleged seven hundred million people of China, who *may* exist under Mao's regime, on proportionally equal terms with the free and mature populations of the United States or of Great Britain or France or Germany is a manifest absurdity on two counts:

First, as has been shown, the United Nations does not represent the peoples of the world but their governments. Moreover, even if the United Nations did represent peoples, the people of Red China are not the equals of United States citizens in terms of capability for self-government or exercising the privileges of human beings toward moral development or in their power to affect the destiny of the world in the foreseeable future.[8]

Second, there is really only one voice for Communist China, that of the dictator or his immediate associates under the party dictatorship.

[7] This was proposed as an ultimate ideal for the future world organization by Hugh Gaitskell in his Harvard Godkin Lectures. See his book, *The Challenge of Coexistence* (Harvard University Press, 1957).

[8] See Lord Lindsay of Birker, *Is Coexistence Possible?* (Michigan State University Press, 1961).

Such a state ought not to be admitted to the United Nations if peace and freedom are objectives, since its aim is to destroy peace and freedom for the free. We have a veto, and can use it to defend the character of the Charter we agreed to—to block any action that displeases us, as the Soviet system has done approximately a hundred times.

If it is possible to move in this direction, positive leadership by the United States in the United Nations might succeed in getting moral pronouncements which would outlaw the use of so-called volunteers and technicians or the furnishing of arms for subversion in situations where the United Nations has jurisdiction, as it had in Korea and might have in Laos. If it is impossible to get effective bans against supplying weapons in such a situation, defensive action by the United States alone is justified under regional pacts and the final right of self-defense. Moscow threatens missiles, but it withdraws them from Cuba when we meet the issue squarely. Every effort should be made to show the facts—Soviet aggressions by airlift, by use of outside organizers, technicians, and even satellite troops, or Castro's aggressions through volunteers trained in sabotage and assassination. These moves are aggressive, not defensive. We must and can show who creates tensions and, rather than concede what has been won by aggression, demand that the Communists remove these tensions. President Kennedy's Berlin speech and his Cuban speech offer models if one leaves out the United Nations as the proposed instrument of inspection. At times it may be more possible to be effective in our own use of force where force has already been invoked by aggressors.

7. If actions of this character cannot win the support of the so-called Afro-Asian bloc or others too timid to oppose Soviet and Peking intimidation, it is important to prevent the United Nations' being used as a forum for loaded censure. It is also important to prevent aggressive nations from utilizing the action of the United States in the United Nations *against* those who are attempting to resort to measures of self-defense; e.g., to coerce by aggression or sanctions the Republic of South Africa to accept United Nations judgments, or to coerce Angola to overturn Portuguese rule by outside intervention. Whom will we put in the place of those who built up these areas? Can we prevent others from putting in puppets any less native than the Portuguese?

We need and should champion a realistic appraisal of the true nature of the well-established pattern of Communist aggression by controlled agents, which does not always lend itself to the easy legal definitions of conventional international law and practice. Aggression may be systematically prepared and advertised by a series of border forays and probing actions or by the introduction of subversive and revolutionary forces, arms, and technicians—as was the case in the Egyptian-Syrian efforts to overthrow the government of Jordan while raising a Macedonian cry of the danger of being itself attacked by Turkey. The case of Cuba is even clearer.

8. On the positive side, the United Nations may lend itself to a great many uses through its agencies, including both UNESCO and the ILO. Related agencies like the International Bank of Reconstruction and Development and the Monetary Fund will continue to be more useful because of the nature of their proportionate voting arrangements and the character of their actions. We are engaged on all these fronts, and we should treat them more seriously to prevent their being staffed, or overstaffed, by incompetents, by enemies of a market economy or sound public financing, or, worst of all, by known fellow travelers. Our own delegations need strengthening. States that cannot pay are not entitled to share in the staffing of the United Nations agencies.

9. We can also strengthen the positive efforts of the United Nations which have helped to restrain direct Soviet intervention through controlled volunteers, airlift, technicians, and arms and munitions. In addition, we should work to strengthen the feeling of the new delegations that the United Nations is their protection against real imperialism only if the United States is not crippled. The United Nations can inculcate conceptions of orderly discussion and appeals to reason and right, which many African as well as Asian nations share to the degree that they have participated in the great traditional cultures of the world. The United States must help it to do so, without being apologetic, placating, or lacking in firmness and self-respect. Parliamentary manners at least are useful, particularly if bluster and threats are met not only by calm strength in words but by deeds—done in time.

10. Finally, in the protracted political warfare which the Soviet system has declared on all the Free World, the United Nations and its organs are necessarily a great and continuous battlefield. Engagements are being fought or broken off, avoided or forced, in every one of its organizations, but most dramatically in the General Assembly and the Security Council. Our strategy should carefully anticipate where we can mobilize support and when we can reasonably count on it. We do well

to avoid treating the United Nations as a superstate or as a legislature speaking with even the moral sanctions appropriate to a true community which can and will back up law by force. The Soviets—if Khrushchev can trap us onto this terrain with reservations concerning our commitments not only of forces and money but of moral support—may one fine day take us by surprise and have the United Nations direct us to "free" Guam or Puerto Rico or "reconstruct" Mississippi by force. Or we may be called on to use force against Free World allies, under others' controls and restraints, without real authority to act, as in Korea. Disarmament negotiations are always full of booby traps for the trustful and overeager.

But since we are engaged, and must be, in this arena, we should lose no opportunity to expose the shams of Soviet claims and to carry the moral offensive through every channel that the United Nations affords. And we should, after careful preparation, push the reforms which would assure that the United Nations is not turned into the most unrepresentative, misrepresentative, and therefore ethically illegitimate legislative body (beginning to claim executive powers) that even bad dreams could conjure up. At least by our efforts to create a true community of nations based on a *consensus juris* of the ethics of freedom with justice, we can keep alive the "last best hope" and not be led into a Serbonian bog along a slippery one-way path marked "Road to Peace."

Membership in the United Nations

(As of January, 1964)

Original Members

Argentina	Lebanon
Australia	Liberia
Belgium	Luxembourg
Bolivia	Mexico
Brazil	Netherlands
Byelorussian Soviet Socialist Republic	New Zealand
	Nicaragua
Canada	Norway
Chile	Panama
China	Paraguay
Colombia	Peru
Costa Rica	Philippines
Cuba	Poland
Czechoslovakia	Saudi Arabia
Denmark	Syria
Dominican Republic	Turkey
Ecuador	Ukrainian Soviet Socialist
Egypt (United Arab Republic)	Republic
El Salvador	Union of South Africa
Ethiopia	Union of Soviet Socialist
France	Republics
Greece	United Kingdom of Great
Guatemala	Britain and Northern Ireland
Haiti	United States of America
Honduras	Uruguay
India	Venezuela
Iran	Yugoslavia
Iraq	

Admitted in 1946

Afghanistan	Sweden
Iceland	Thailand

Admitted in 1947

Pakistan	Yemen

Admitted in 1948

Burma

Admitted in 1949

Israel

Admitted in 1950

Indonesia

Admitted in 1955

Albania	Italy
Austria	Jordan
Bulgaria	Laos
Cambodia	Libya
Ceylon	Nepal
Finland	Portugal
Hungary	Romania
Ireland	Spain

Admitted in 1956

Japan	Sudan
Morocco	Tunisia

Admitted in 1957

Ghana	Malaya (Malaysia)

Admitted in 1958

Guinea

Admitted in 1960

Cameroun	Madagascar
Central African Republic	Mali
Chad	Niger
Congo (Brazzaville)	Nigeria

Congo (Leopoldville)
Cyprus
Dahomey
Gabon
Ivory Coast

Senegal
Somalia
Togo
Upper Volta

Admitted in 1961

Mauritania
Mongolia

Sierra Leone
Tanganyika

Admitted in 1962

Algeria
Burundi
Jamaica

Rwanda
Trinidad and Tobago
Uganda

Admitted in 1963

Kenya
Kuwait

Zanzibar

Index

The United States and the United Nations has been printed on paper which is expected to last for three hundred years bearing the watermark of the University of Oklahoma Press. The text type used is machine-cast Caslon, a reconstruction of English foundry type widely used among English-speaking peoples for two centuries.

UNIVERSITY OF OKLAHOMA PRESS

NORMAN